SUPERMAN

THE BLACK RING

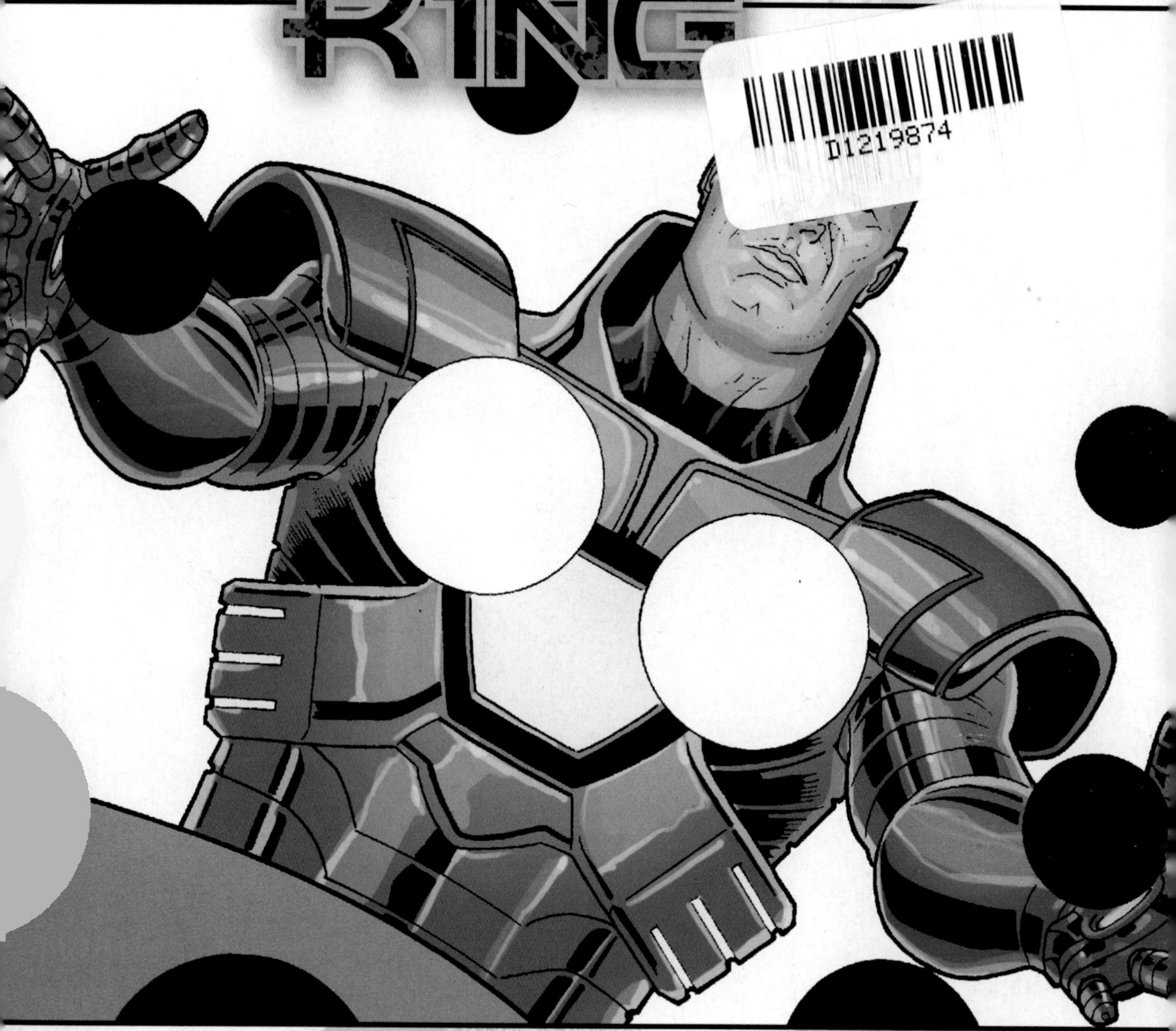

volume two

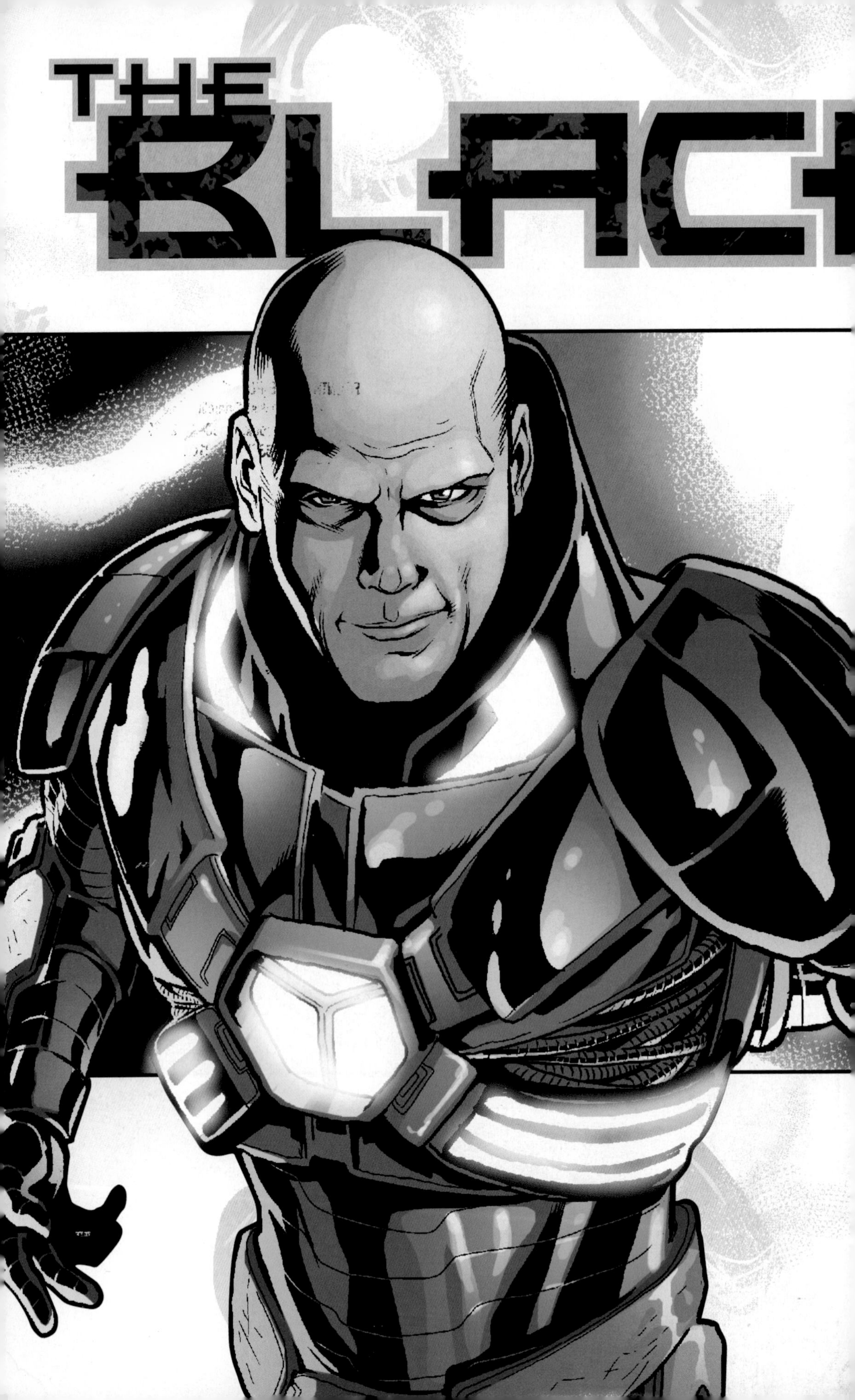
THE

SUPERMAN

K RING

volume two

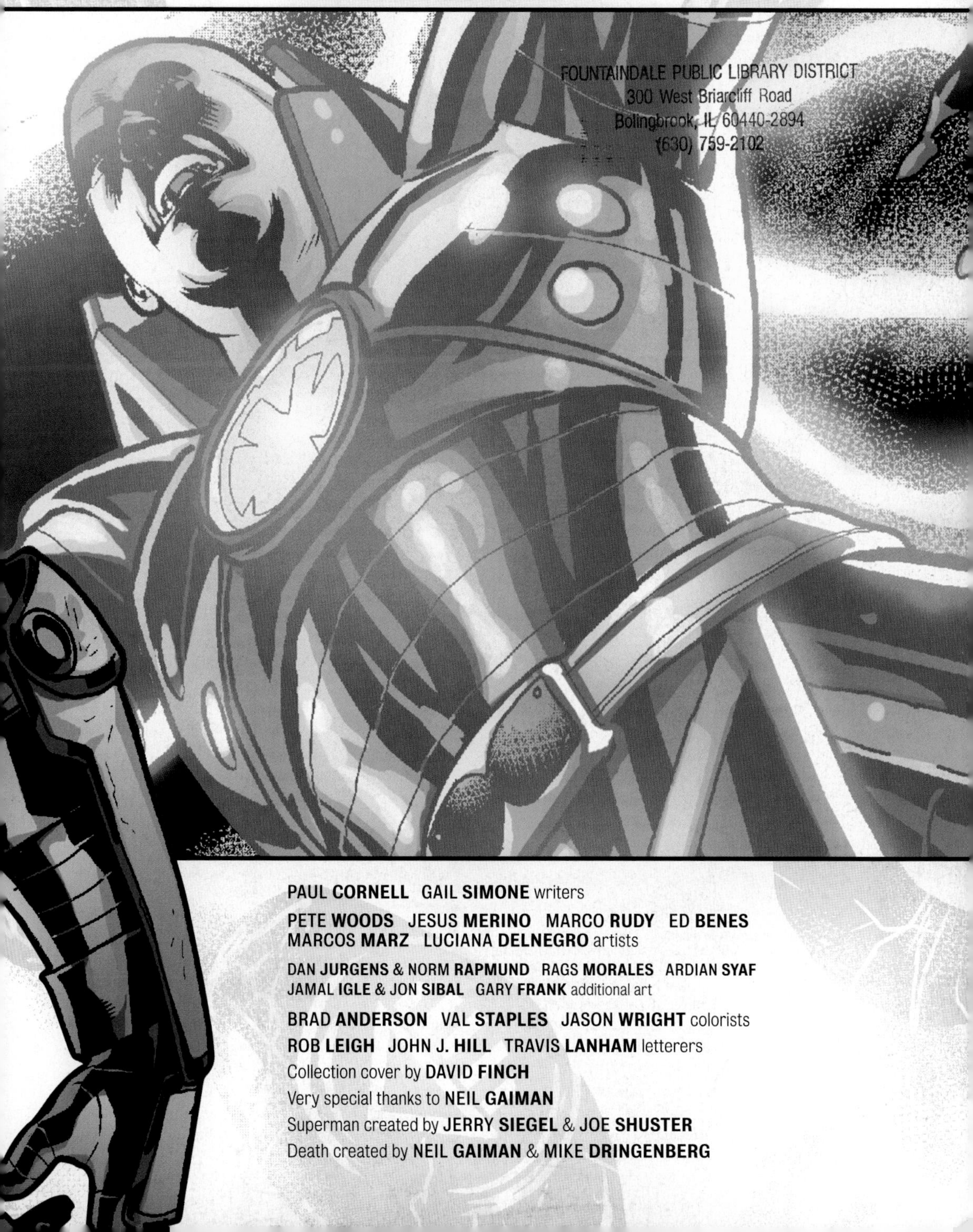

PAUL **CORNELL** GAIL **SIMONE** writers

PETE **WOODS** JESUS **MERINO** MARCO **RUDY** ED **BENES**
MARCOS **MARZ** LUCIANA **DELNEGRO** artists

DAN **JURGENS** & NORM **RAPMUND** RAGS **MORALES** ARDIAN **SYAF**
JAMAL **IGLE** & JON **SIBAL** GARY **FRANK** additional art

BRAD **ANDERSON** VAL **STAPLES** JASON **WRIGHT** colorists

ROB **LEIGH** JOHN J. **HILL** TRAVIS **LANHAM** letterers

Collection cover by DAVID **FINCH**

Very special thanks to NEIL **GAIMAN**

Superman created by JERRY **SIEGEL** & JOE **SHUSTER**

Death created by NEIL **GAIMAN** & MIKE **DRINGENBERG**

MATT IDELSON SEAN RYAN EDITORS – ORIGINAL SERIES **WIL MOSS** ASSOCIATE EDITOR – ORIGINAL SERIES
ROBBIN BROSTERMAN DESIGN DIRECTOR – BOOKS **ROBBIE BIEDERMAN** PUBLICATION DESIGN

BOB HARRAS VP – EDITOR-IN-CHIEF

DIANE NELSON PRESIDENT **DAN DIDIO** AND **JIM LEE** CO-PUBLISHERS **GEOFF JOHNS** CHIEF CREATIVE OFFICER
JOHN ROOD EXECUTIVE VP – SALES, MARKETING AND BUSINESS DEVELOPMENT **AMY GENKINS** SENIOR VP – BUSINESS AND LEGAL AFFAIRS
NAIRI GARDINER SENIOR VP – FINANCE **JEFF BOISON** VP – PUBLISHING OPERATIONS **MARK CHIARELLO** VP – ART DIRECTION AND DESIGN
JOHN CUNNINGHAM VP – MARKETING **TERRI CUNNINGHAM** VP – TALENT RELATIONS AND SERVICES
ALISON GILL SENIOR VP – MANUFACTURING AND OPERATIONS **HANK KANALZ** SENIOR VP – DIGITAL
JAY KOGAN VP – BUSINESS AND LEGAL AFFAIRS, PUBLISHING **JACK MAHAN** VP – BUSINESS AFFAIRS, TALENT
NICK NAPOLITANO VP – MANUFACTURING ADMINISTRATION **SUE POHJA** VP – BOOK SALES
COURTNEY SIMMONS SENIOR VP – PUBLICITY **BOB WAYNE** SENIOR VP – SALES

SUPERMAN: THE BLACK RING VOLUME TWO

Published by DC Comics. Cover and compilation Copyright © 2011 DC Comics. All Rights Reserved.

Originally published in single magazine form in ACTION COMICS 896-900, SECRET SIX 29 and ACTION COMICS ANNUAL 13 © 2011 DC Comics.
All Rights Reserved. All characters, their distinctive likenesses and related elements featured in this publication are trademarks of DC Comics.
The stories, characters and incidents featured in this publication are entirely fictional. DC Comics does not read or accept unsolicited
submissions of ideas, stories or artwork.

Library of Congress Cataloging-in-Publication Data

Cornell, Paul.
Superman : the black ring, Volume two / Paul Cornell, Pete
Woods.
p. cm.
"Originally published in single magazine form in Action Comics
896-900, Action Comics Annual 13."
ISBN 978-1-4012-3444-7
1. Graphic novels. I. Woods, Pete. II. Title. III. Title: Black ring.
PN6728.S9C683 2012
741.5'973—dc23
2012022177

DC Comics, 1700 Broadway, New York, NY 10019.
A Warner Bros. Entertainment Company.
Printed by RR Donnelley, Salem, VA, USA. 8/17/12.
First Printing. ISBN: 978-1-4012-3444-7

Certified Chain of Custody
At Least 25% Certified Forest Content
www.sfiprogram.org
SFI-01042
APPLIES TO TEXT STOCK ONLY

S T O R Y   S O   F A R

Lex Luthor has tasted unlimited power. To help defeat the Blackest Night that nearly extinguished all life in the universe, Superman's brilliant archnemesis was briefly granted an Orange Power Ring, an unstoppable weapon fueled by his own insatiable avarice. The ring is gone, but now this criminal mastermind's hunger for power has reached a new level.

And he thinks he knows how to satisfy it. The incredible power of the Black Rings he battled against is still out there, concentrated in ten black spheres of energy scattered across the globe and throughout the universe. With the help of his assistant, "Lois Lane" – a robotic construct built with technology stolen from Superman's home planet Krypton and his alien enemy Brainiac – Luthor sets out to track down the spheres and claim their power for himself.

His quest is perilous from the start. First he is assaulted by a team of mercenaries manipulated by the psychic insect Mister Mind, whom Luthor discovers (while being dangled upside-down, no less) is himself being manipulated by an even more powerful force. Then, with the help of the deadly mercenary Deathstroke, Luthor finds the first of the ten black spheres in the Antarctic and makes two shocking discoveries: The sphere is attuned to negative emotions, and the very act of analyzing it changes it, unlocking a new and unknown power.

Luthor finds the next sphere in the hands of the psychic gorilla warlord Grodd and nearly dies in the attempt to change it – but when Luthor encounters Death of the Endless, he finds that she's more interested in joking about magic singing ponies and simply "checking on" him than in actually claiming his life.

Now more convinced than ever that his quest is leading to something huge, Luthor sets his sights on the next two spheres, both of them in the possession of the immortal crime lord Vandal Savage. Savage believes Luthor and the spheres are the key to a millennia-old prophecy that will lead him to happiness, so he will stop at nothing – including planting explosives that will destroy Luthor's entire business empire – to keep all three under his control.

But Savage doesn't count on Luthor's escape plan: The Secret Six, a fiercely independent team of villains Luthor once secretly led – and who count Scandal, Savage's own estranged daughter, as one of their number...

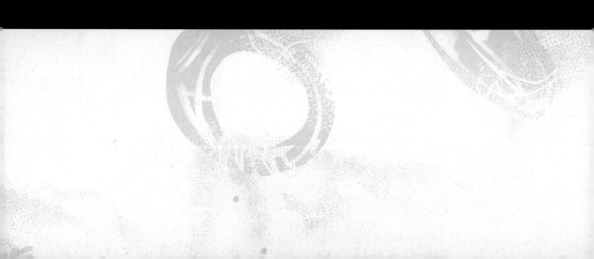

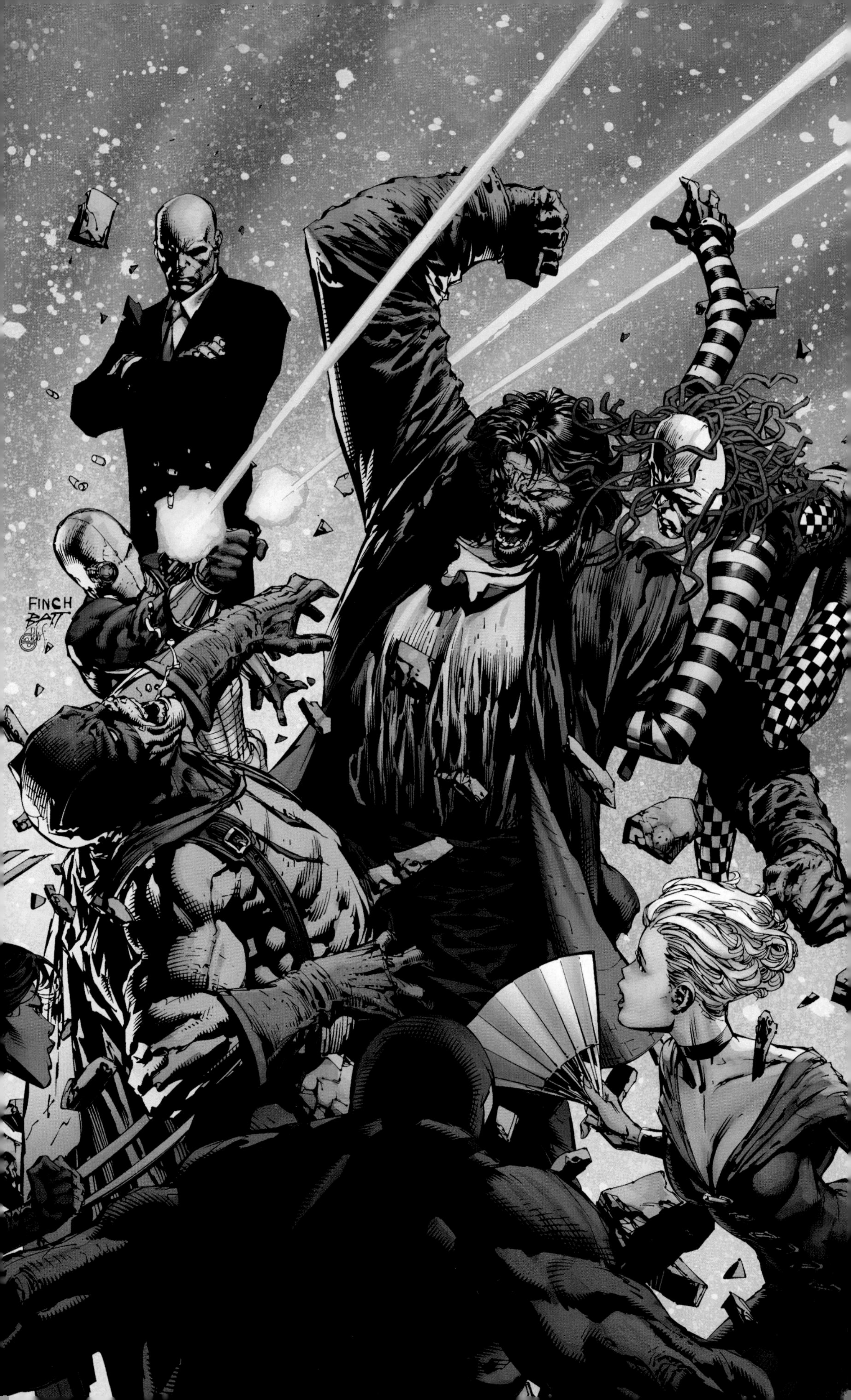
FINCH
BATT

THE BLACK RING

part seven

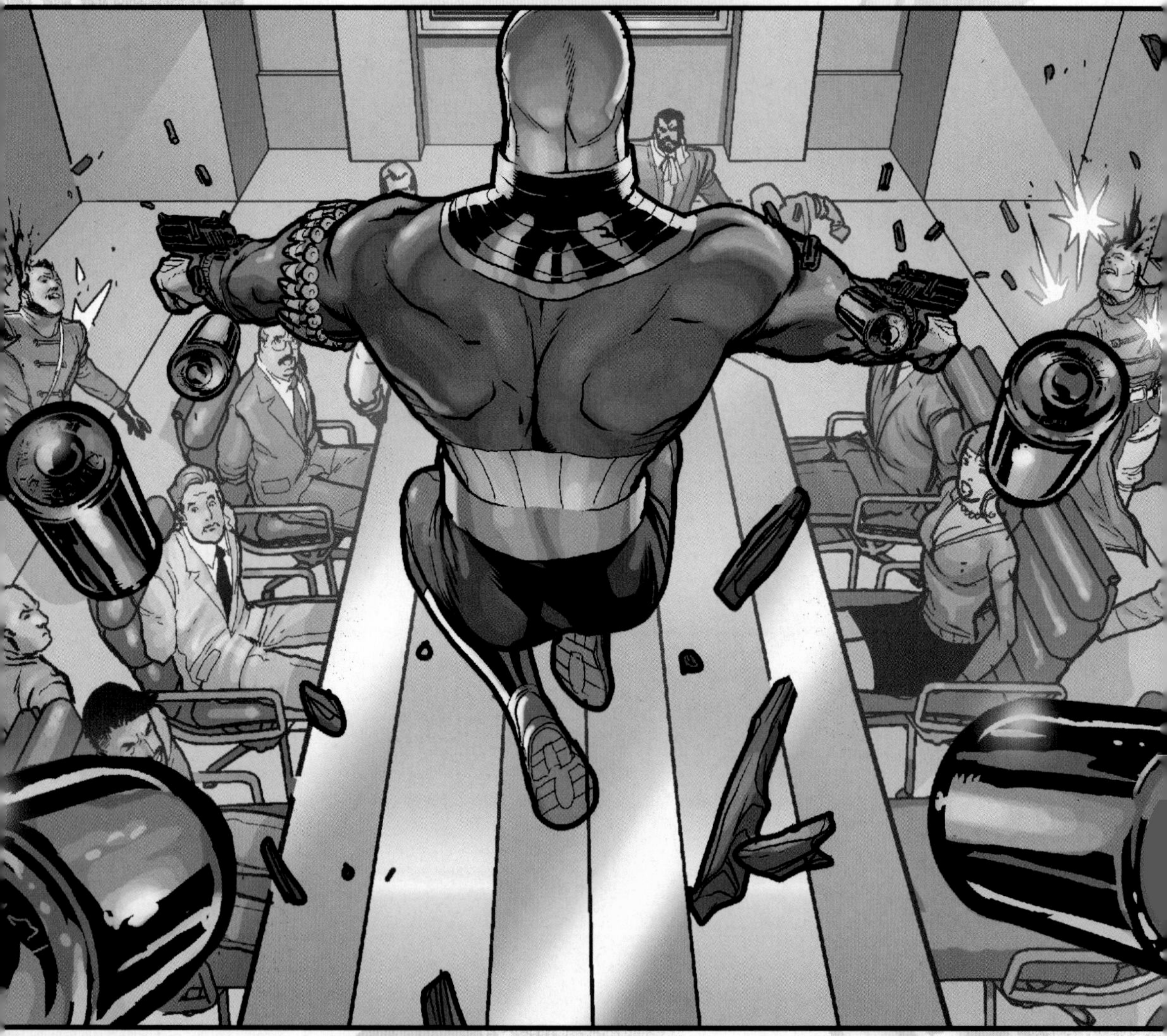

PAUL **CORNELL** writer
PETE **WOODS** artist

cover by
DAVID **FINCH, BATT** & PETER **STEIGERWALD**

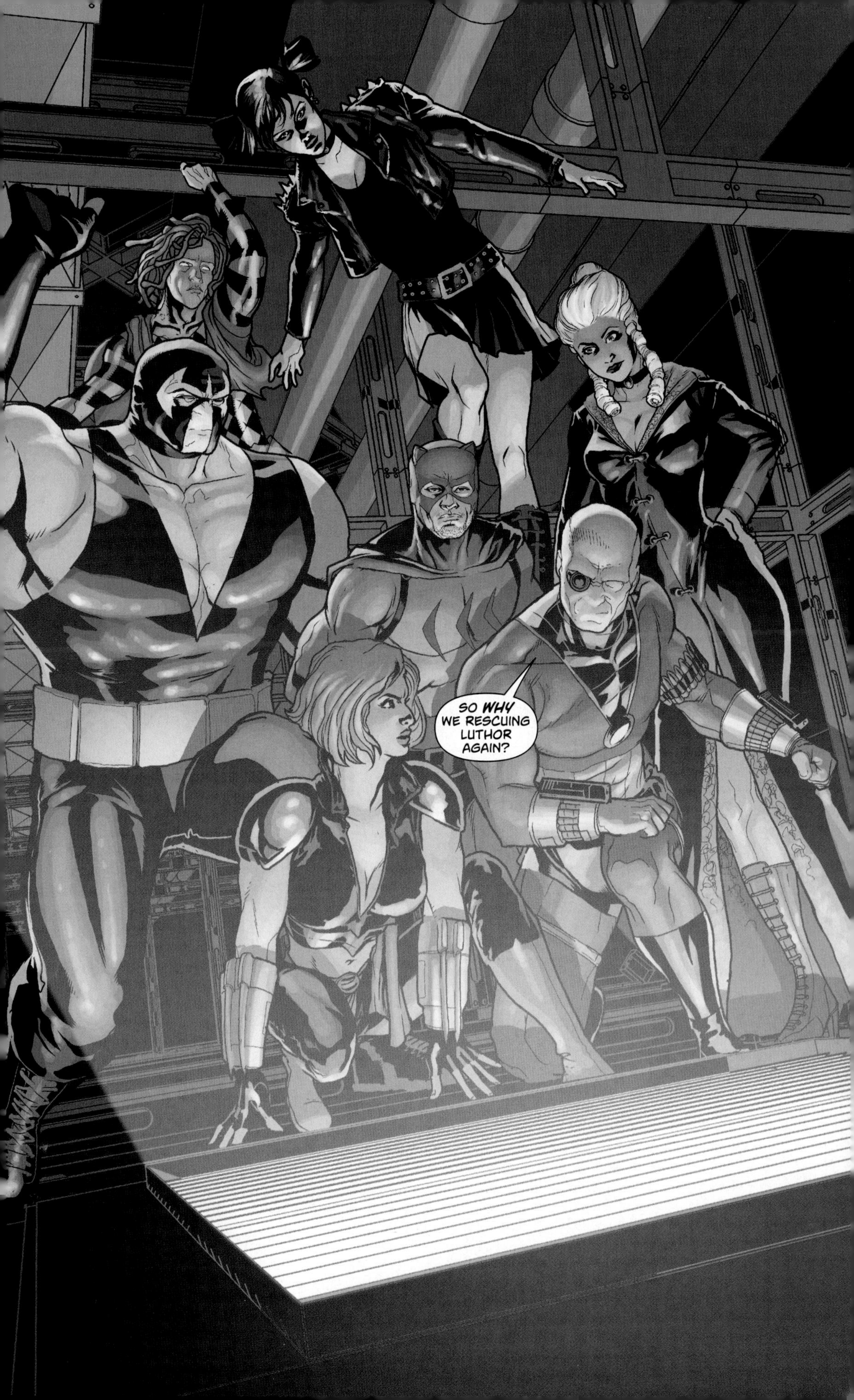
SO WHY WE RESCUING LUTHOR AGAIN?

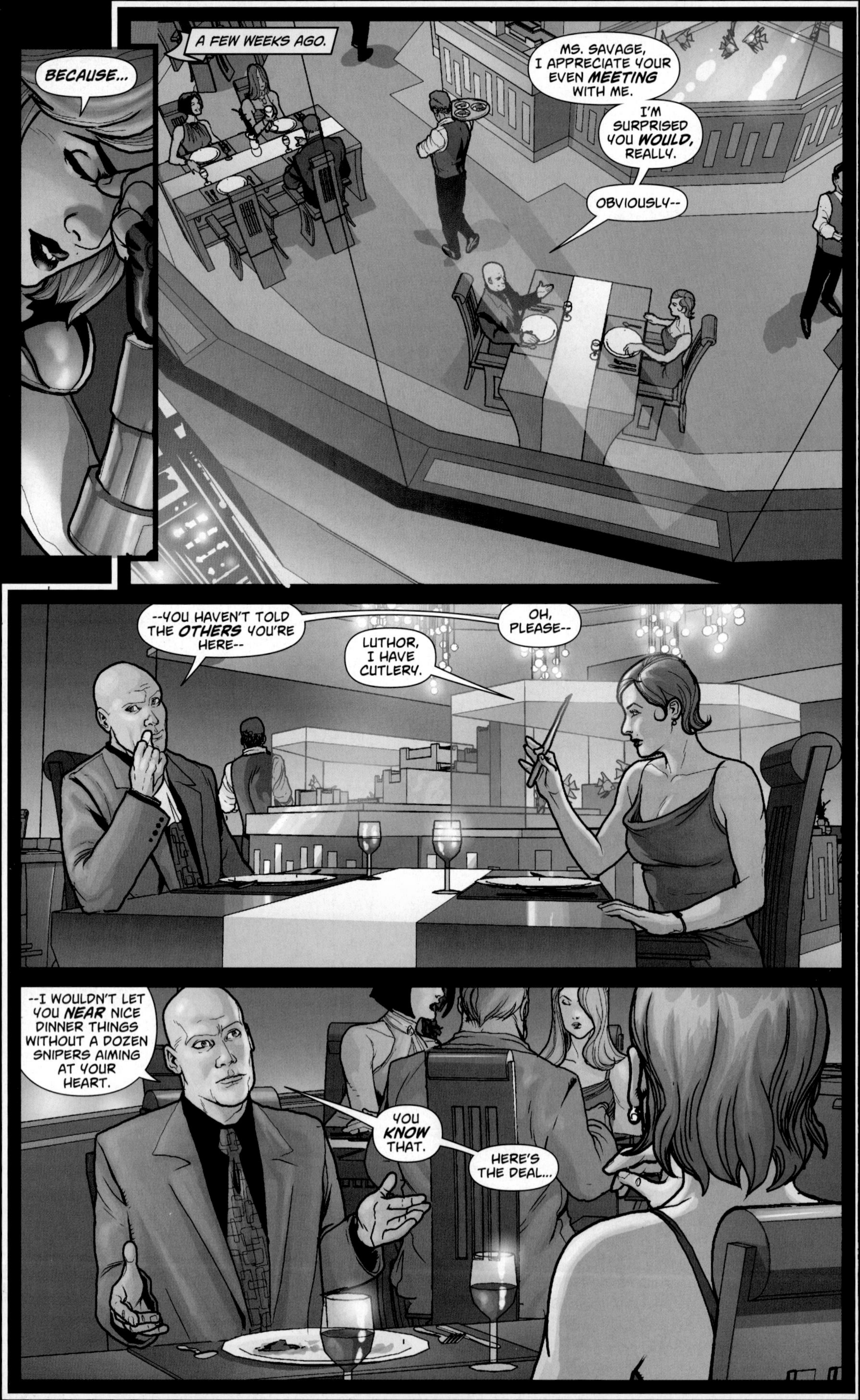
BECAUSE...
A FEW WEEKS AGO.
MS. SAVAGE, I APPRECIATE YOUR EVEN MEETING WITH ME.
I'M SURPRISED YOU WOULD, REALLY.
OBVIOUSLY--
--YOU HAVEN'T TOLD THE OTHERS YOU'RE HERE--
OH, PLEASE--
LUTHOR, I HAVE CUTLERY.
--I WOULDN'T LET YOU NEAR NICE DINNER THINGS WITHOUT A DOZEN SNIPERS AIMING AT YOUR HEART.
YOU KNOW THAT.
HERE'S THE DEAL...

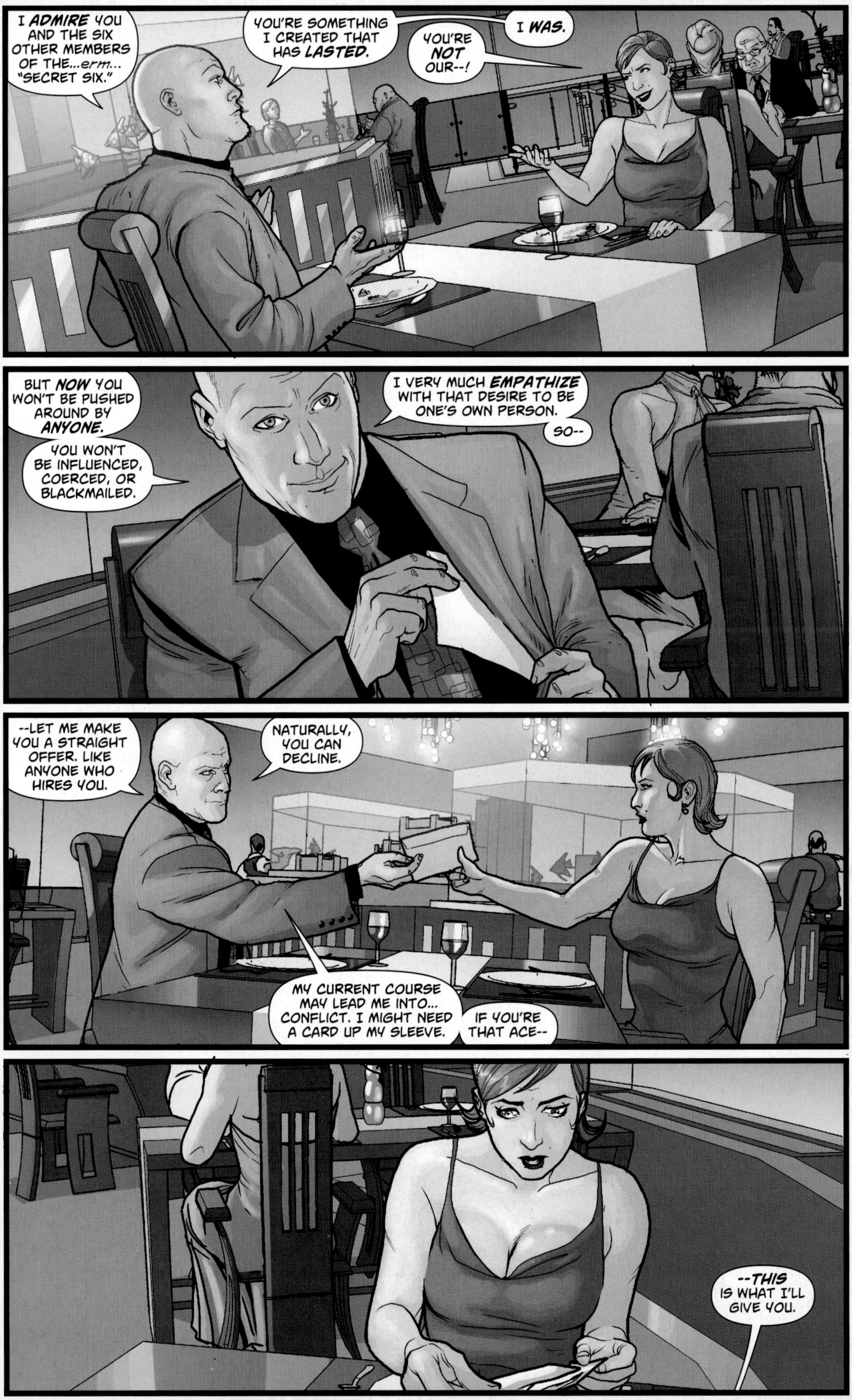
I ADMIRE YOU AND THE SIX OTHER MEMBERS OF THE...erm... "SECRET SIX."
YOU'RE SOMETHING I CREATED THAT HAS LASTED.
I WAS.
YOU'RE NOT OUR--!
BUT NOW YOU WON'T BE PUSHED AROUND BY ANYONE.
YOU WON'T BE INFLUENCED, COERCED, OR BLACKMAILED.
I VERY MUCH EMPATHIZE WITH THAT DESIRE TO BE ONE'S OWN PERSON.
SO--
--LET ME MAKE YOU A STRAIGHT OFFER. LIKE ANYONE WHO HIRES YOU.
NATURALLY, YOU CAN DECLINE.
MY CURRENT COURSE MAY LEAD ME INTO... CONFLICT. I MIGHT NEED A CARD UP MY SLEEVE.
IF YOU'RE THAT ACE--
--THIS IS WHAT I'LL GIVE YOU.

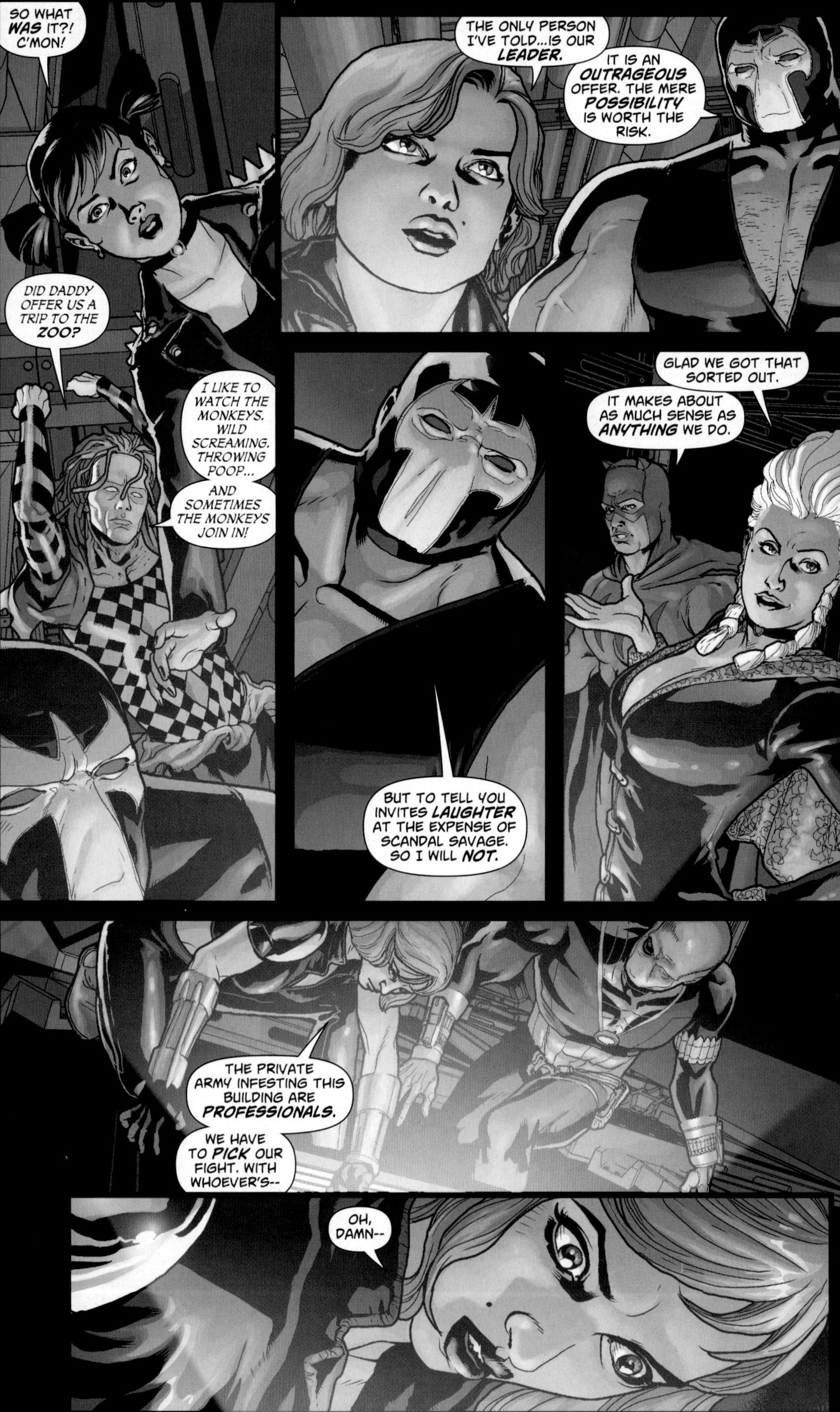
SO WHAT WAS IT?! C'MON!
THE ONLY PERSON I'VE TOLD...IS OUR LEADER.
IT IS AN OUTRAGEOUS OFFER. THE MERE POSSIBILITY IS WORTH THE RISK.
DID DADDY OFFER US A TRIP TO THE ZOO?
I LIKE TO WATCH THE MONKEYS. WILD SCREAMING. THROWING POOP...
AND SOMETIMES THE MONKEYS JOIN IN!
BUT TO TELL YOU INVITES LAUGHTER AT THE EXPENSE OF SCANDAL SAVAGE. SO I WILL NOT.
GLAD WE GOT THAT SORTED OUT.
IT MAKES ABOUT AS MUCH SENSE AS ANYTHING WE DO.
THE PRIVATE ARMY INFESTING THIS BUILDING ARE PROFESSIONALS.
WE HAVE TO PICK OUR FIGHT. WITH WHOEVER'S--
OH, DAMN--

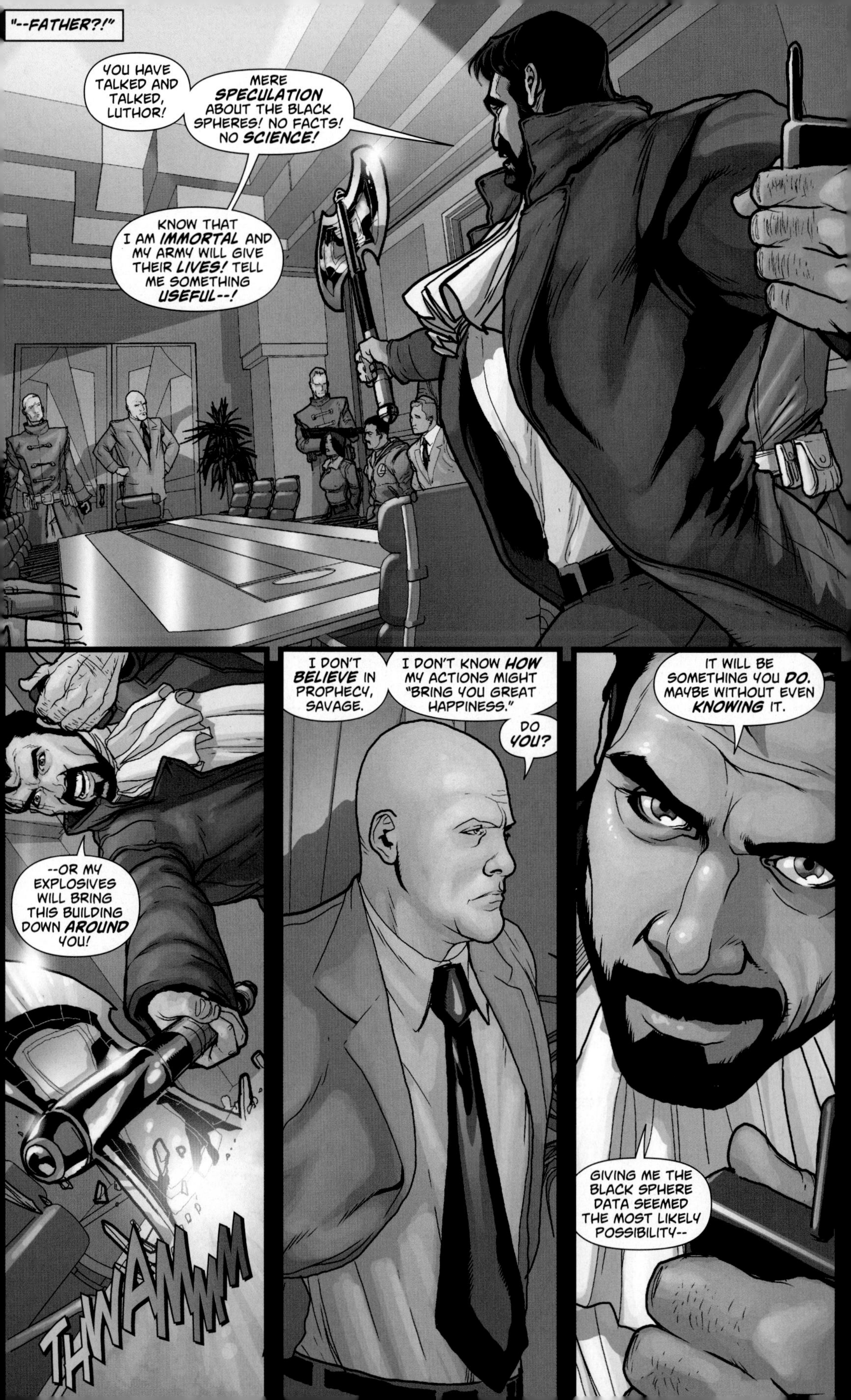
"--FATHER?!"
YOU HAVE TALKED AND TALKED, LUTHOR!
MERE SPECULATION ABOUT THE BLACK SPHERES! NO FACTS! NO SCIENCE!
KNOW THAT I AM IMMORTAL AND MY ARMY WILL GIVE THEIR LIVES! TELL ME SOMETHING USEFUL--!
--OR MY EXPLOSIVES WILL BRING THIS BUILDING DOWN AROUND YOU!
THWAMMM
I DON'T BELIEVE IN PROPHECY, SAVAGE.
I DON'T KNOW HOW MY ACTIONS MIGHT "BRING YOU GREAT HAPPINESS."
DO YOU?
IT WILL BE SOMETHING YOU DO. MAYBE WITHOUT EVEN KNOWING IT.
GIVING ME THE BLACK SPHERE DATA SEEMED THE MOST LIKELY POSSIBILITY--

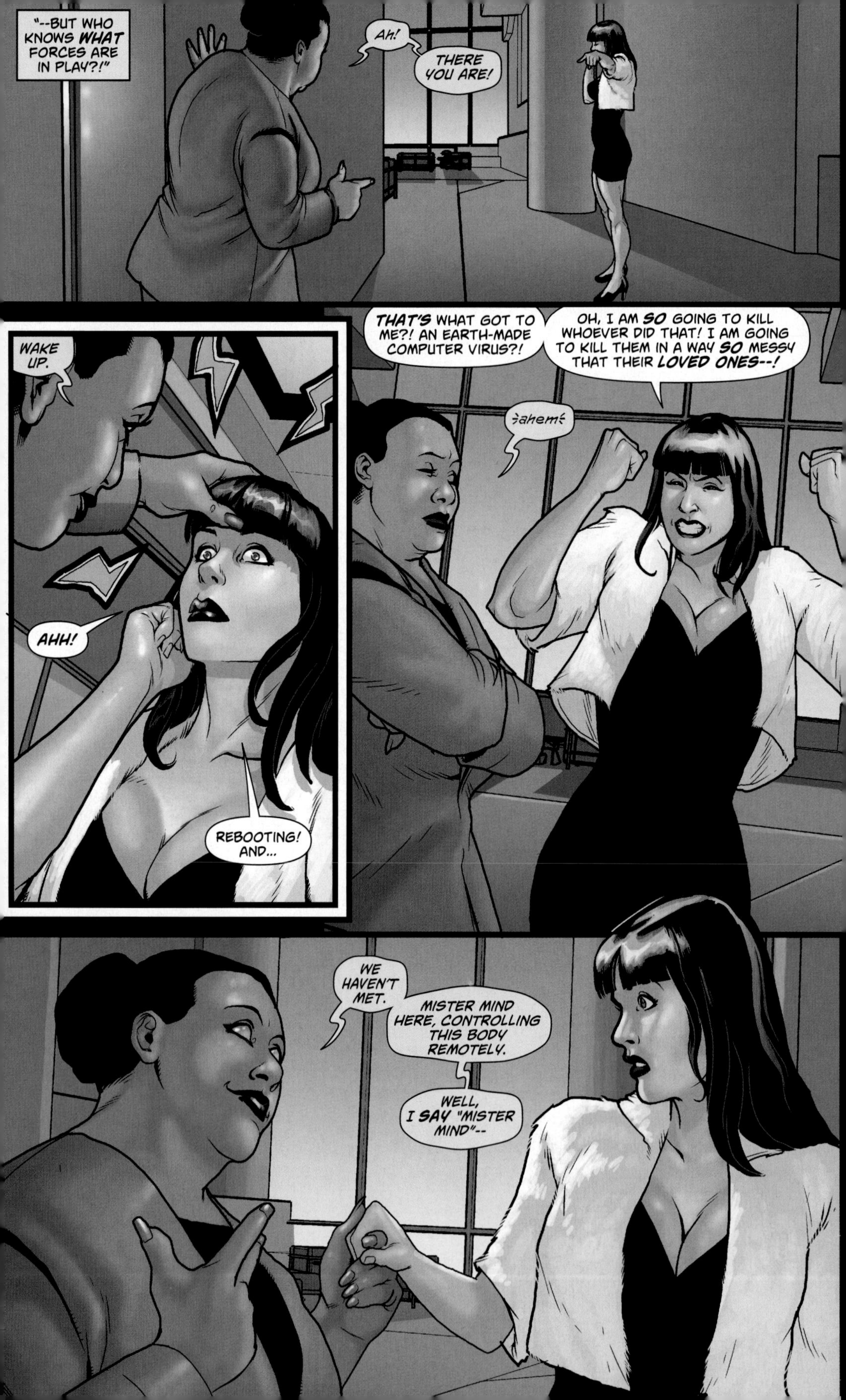
"--BUT WHO KNOWS WHAT FORCES ARE IN PLAY?!"
Ah!
THERE YOU ARE!
WAKE UP.
AHH!
REBOOTING! AND...
THAT'S WHAT GOT TO ME?! AN EARTH-MADE COMPUTER VIRUS?!
OH, I AM SO GOING TO KILL WHOEVER DID THAT! I AM GOING TO KILL THEM IN A WAY SO MESSY THAT THEIR LOVED ONES--!
ahem
WE HAVEN'T MET.
MISTER MIND HERE, CONTROLLING THIS BODY REMOTELY.
WELL, I SAY "MISTER MIND"--

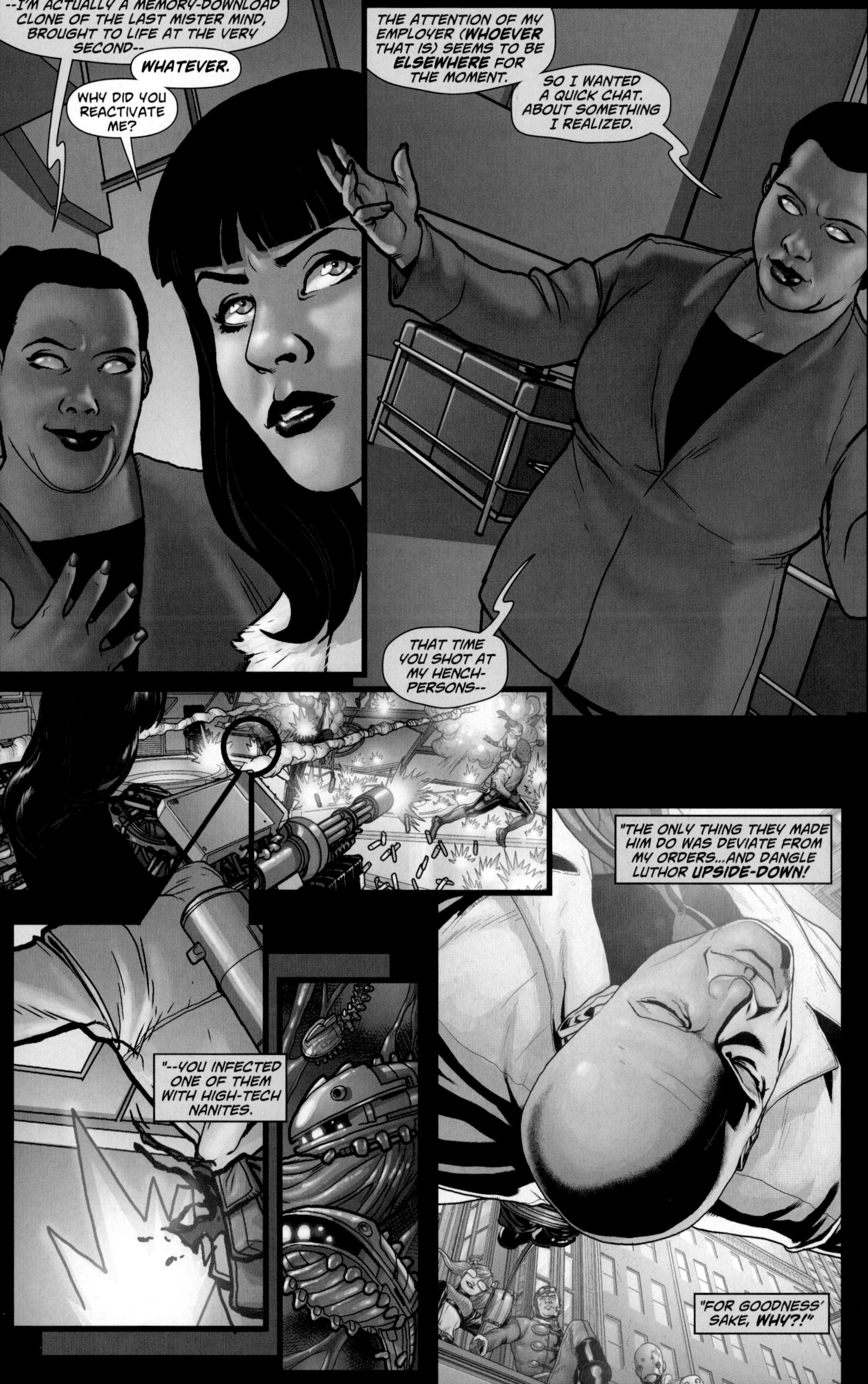
--I'M ACTUALLY A MEMORY-DOWNLOAD CLONE OF THE LAST MISTER MIND, BROUGHT TO LIFE AT THE VERY SECOND--
WHATEVER.
WHY DID YOU REACTIVATE ME?
THE ATTENTION OF MY EMPLOYER (WHOEVER THAT IS) SEEMS TO BE ELSEWHERE FOR THE MOMENT.
SO I WANTED A QUICK CHAT. ABOUT SOMETHING I REALIZED.
THAT TIME YOU SHOT AT MY HENCH-PERSONS--
"--YOU INFECTED ONE OF THEM WITH HIGH-TECH NANITES.
"THE ONLY THING THEY MADE HIM DO WAS DEVIATE FROM MY ORDERS...AND DANGLE LUTHOR UPSIDE-DOWN!
"FOR GOODNESS' SAKE, WHY?!"

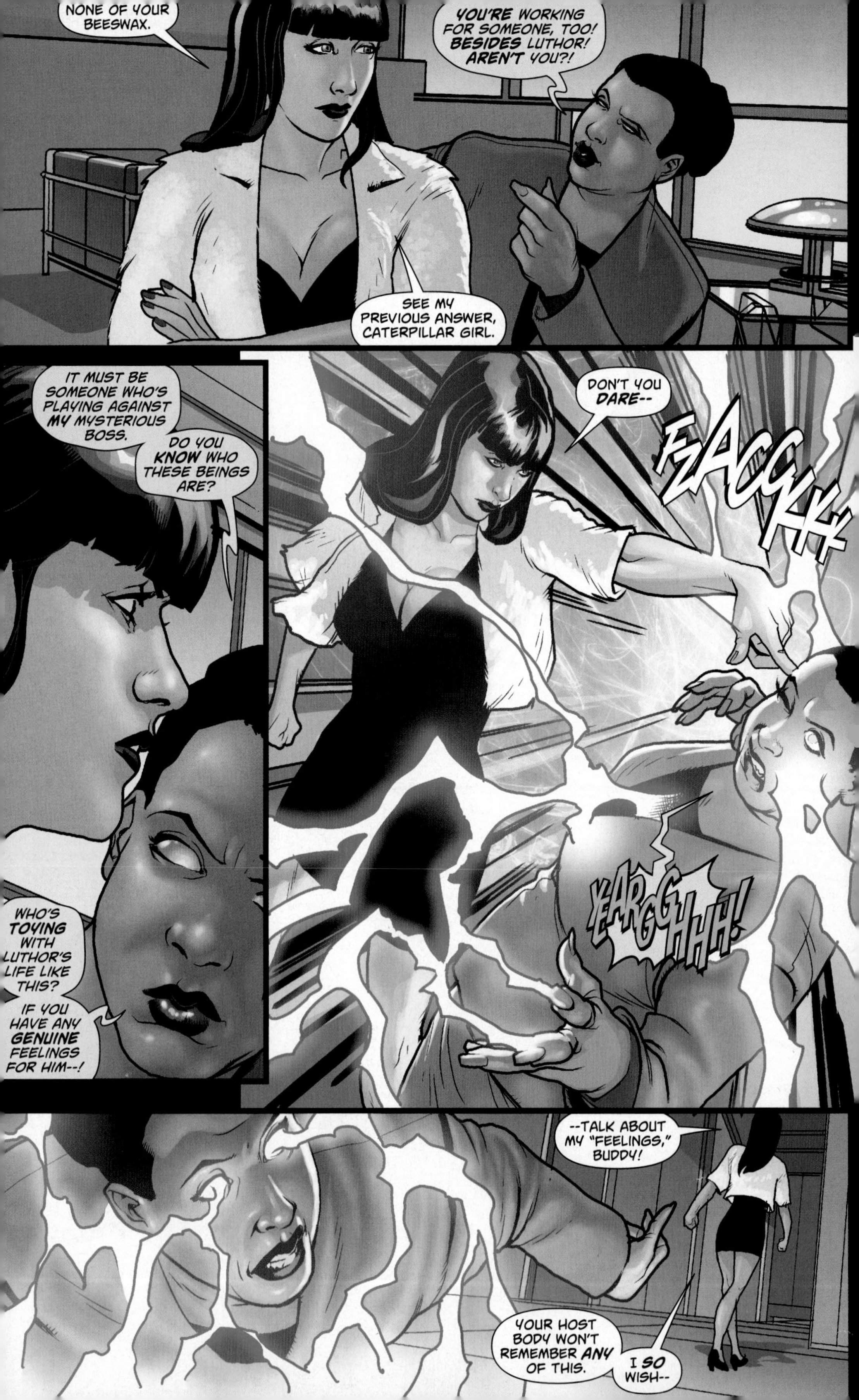
NONE OF YOUR BEESWAX.
YOU'RE WORKING FOR SOMEONE, TOO! BESIDES LUTHOR! AREN'T YOU?!
SEE MY PREVIOUS ANSWER, CATERPILLAR GIRL.
IT MUST BE SOMEONE WHO'S PLAYING AGAINST MY MYSTERIOUS BOSS.
DO YOU KNOW WHO THESE BEINGS ARE?
WHO'S TOYING WITH LUTHOR'S LIFE LIKE THIS?
IF YOU HAVE ANY GENUINE FEELINGS FOR HIM--!
DON'T YOU DARE--
FZACGKK
YEARGGHHH!
--TALK ABOUT MY "FEELINGS," BUDDY!
YOUR HOST BODY WON'T REMEMBER ANY OF THIS.
I SO WISH--

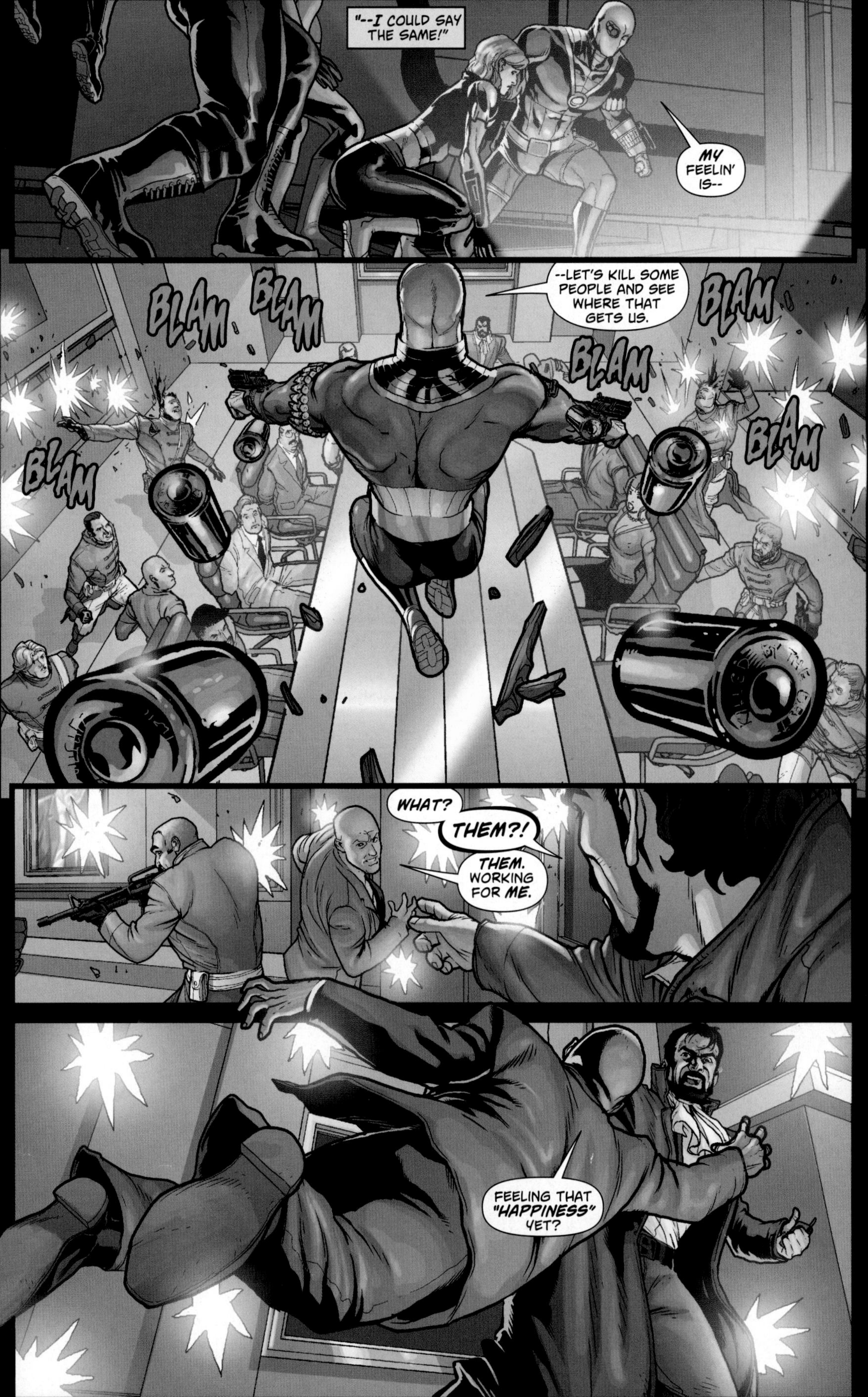
"--I COULD SAY THE SAME!"
MY FEELIN' IS--
BLAM
BLAM
--LET'S KILL SOME PEOPLE AND SEE WHERE THAT GETS US.
BLAM
BLAM
BLAM
BLAM
WHAT?
THEM?!
THEM. WORKING FOR ME.
FEELING THAT "HAPPINESS" YET?

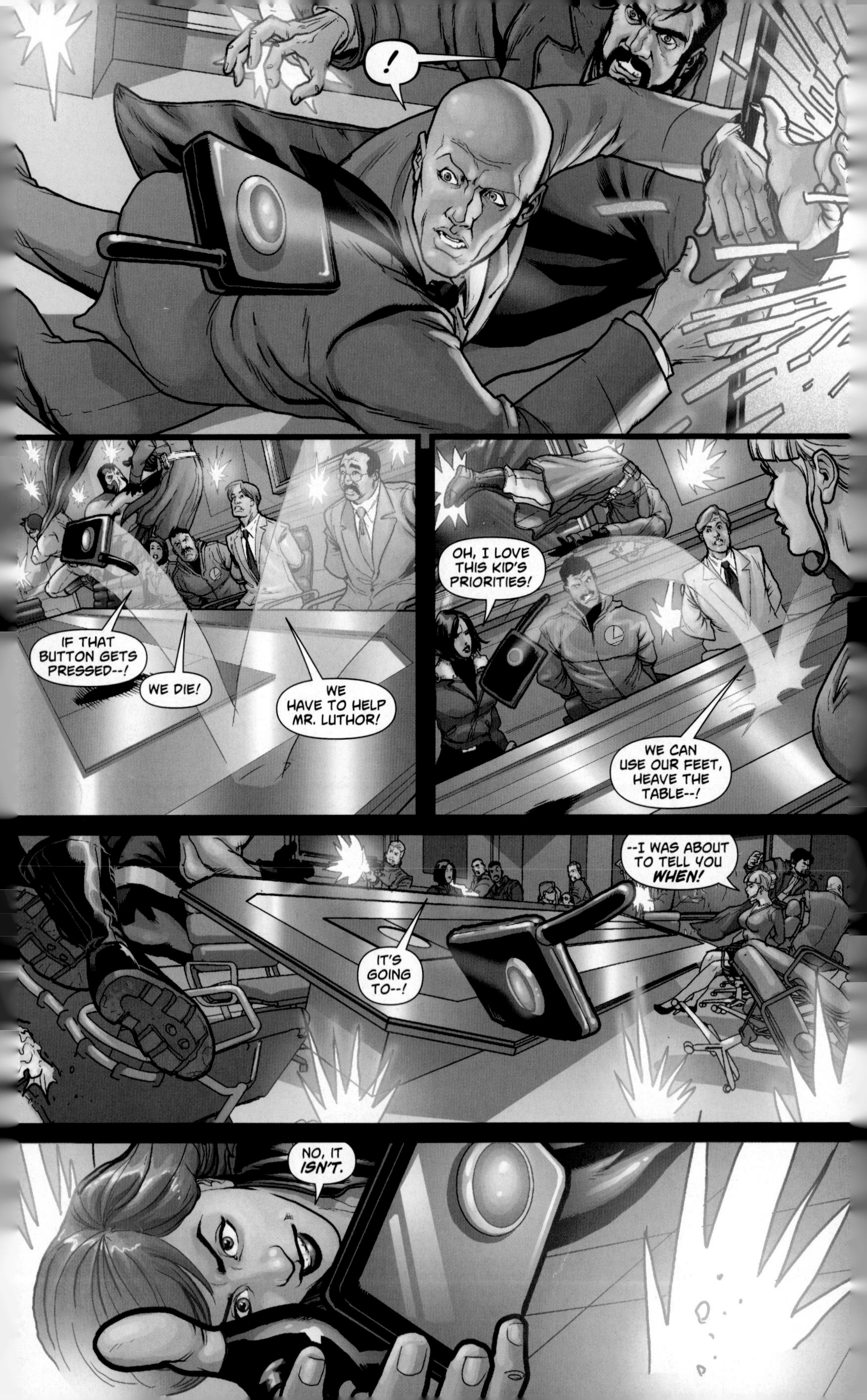
!
IF THAT BUTTON GETS PRESSED--!
WE DIE!
WE HAVE TO HELP MR. LUTHOR!
OH, I LOVE THIS KID'S PRIORITIES!
WE CAN USE OUR FEET, HEAVE THE TABLE--!
--I WAS ABOUT TO TELL YOU WHEN!
IT'S GOING TO--!
NO, IT ISN'T.

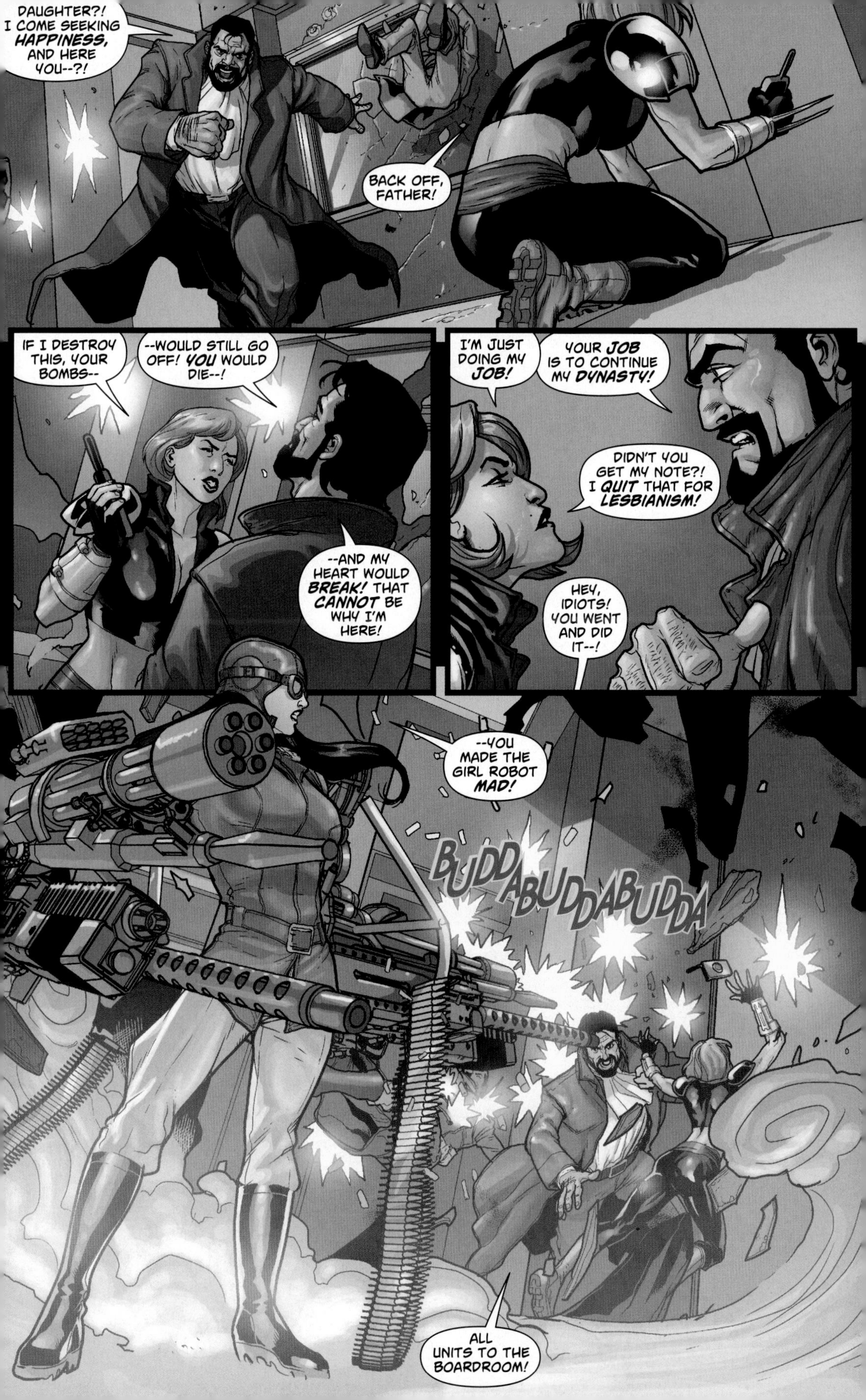
DAUGHTER?! I COME SEEKING HAPPINESS, AND HERE YOU--?!
BACK OFF, FATHER!
IF I DESTROY THIS, YOUR BOMBS--
--WOULD STILL GO OFF! YOU WOULD DIE--!
--AND MY HEART WOULD BREAK! THAT CANNOT BE WHY I'M HERE!
I'M JUST DOING MY JOB!
YOUR JOB IS TO CONTINUE MY DYNASTY!
DIDN'T YOU GET MY NOTE?! I QUIT THAT FOR LESBIANISM!
HEY, IDIOTS! YOU WENT AND DID IT--!
--YOU MADE THE GIRL ROBOT MAD!
BUDDABUDDABUDDA
ALL UNITS TO THE BOARDROOM!

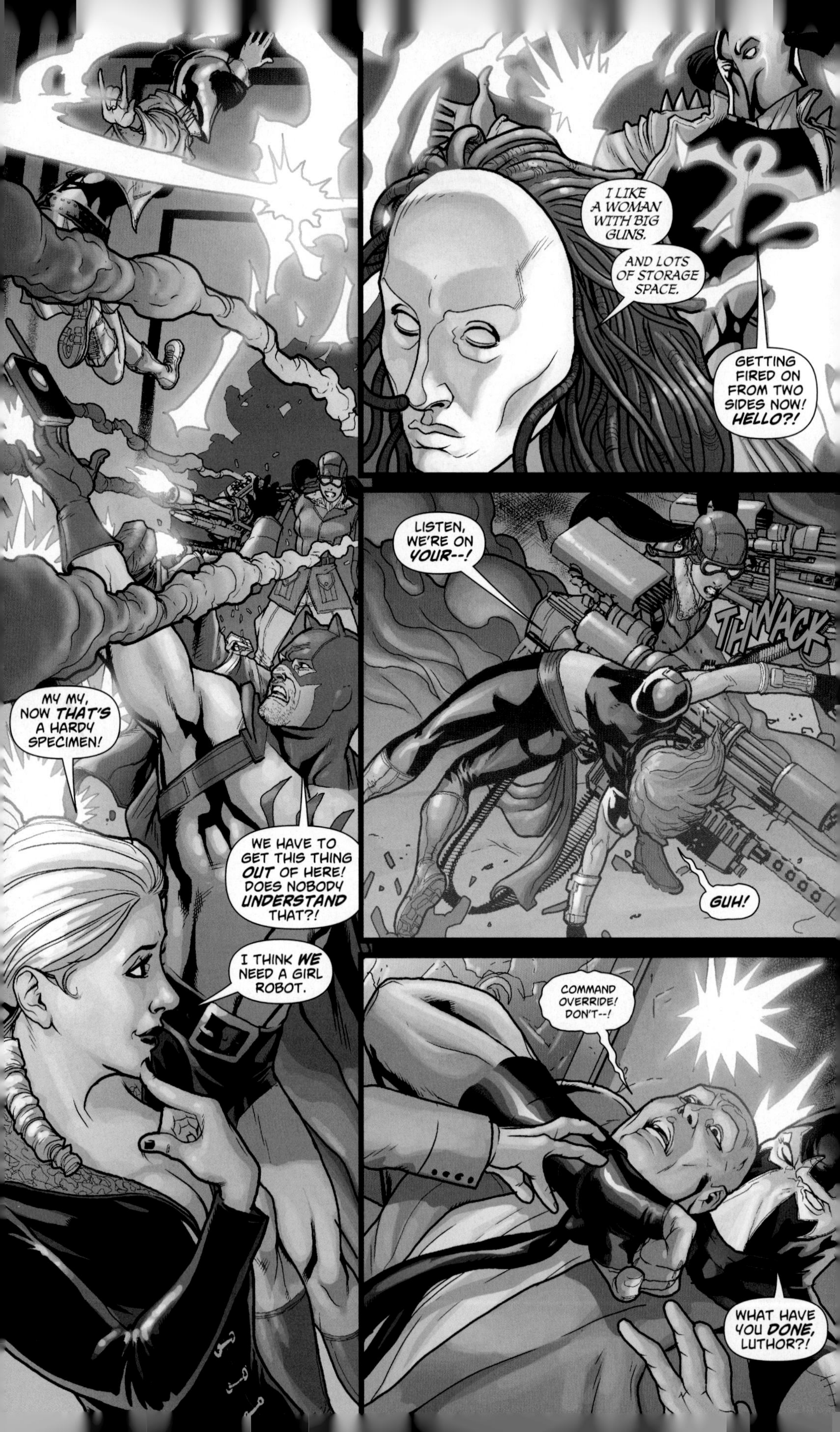

I LIKE A WOMAN WITH BIG GUNS.
AND LOTS OF STORAGE SPACE.
GETTING FIRED ON FROM TWO SIDES NOW! HELLO?!
LISTEN, WE'RE ON YOUR--!
THWACK
GUH!
MY MY, NOW THAT'S A HARDY SPECIMEN!
WE HAVE TO GET THIS THING OUT OF HERE! DOES NOBODY UNDERSTAND THAT?!
I THINK WE NEED A GIRL ROBOT.
COMMAND OVERRIDE! DON'T--!
WHAT HAVE YOU DONE, LUTHOR?!

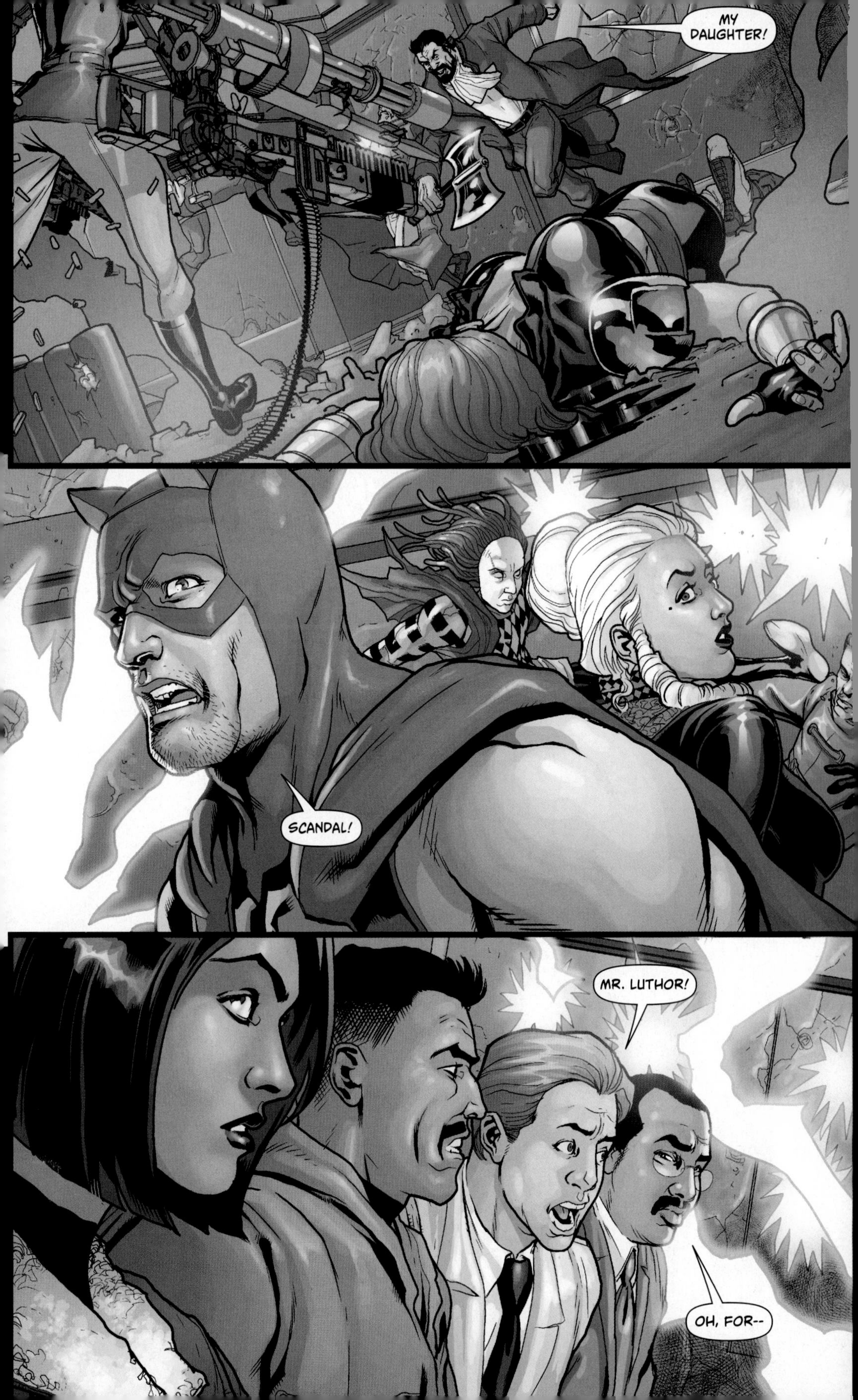
MY DAUGHTER!
SCANDAL!
MR. LUTHOR!
OH, FOR--

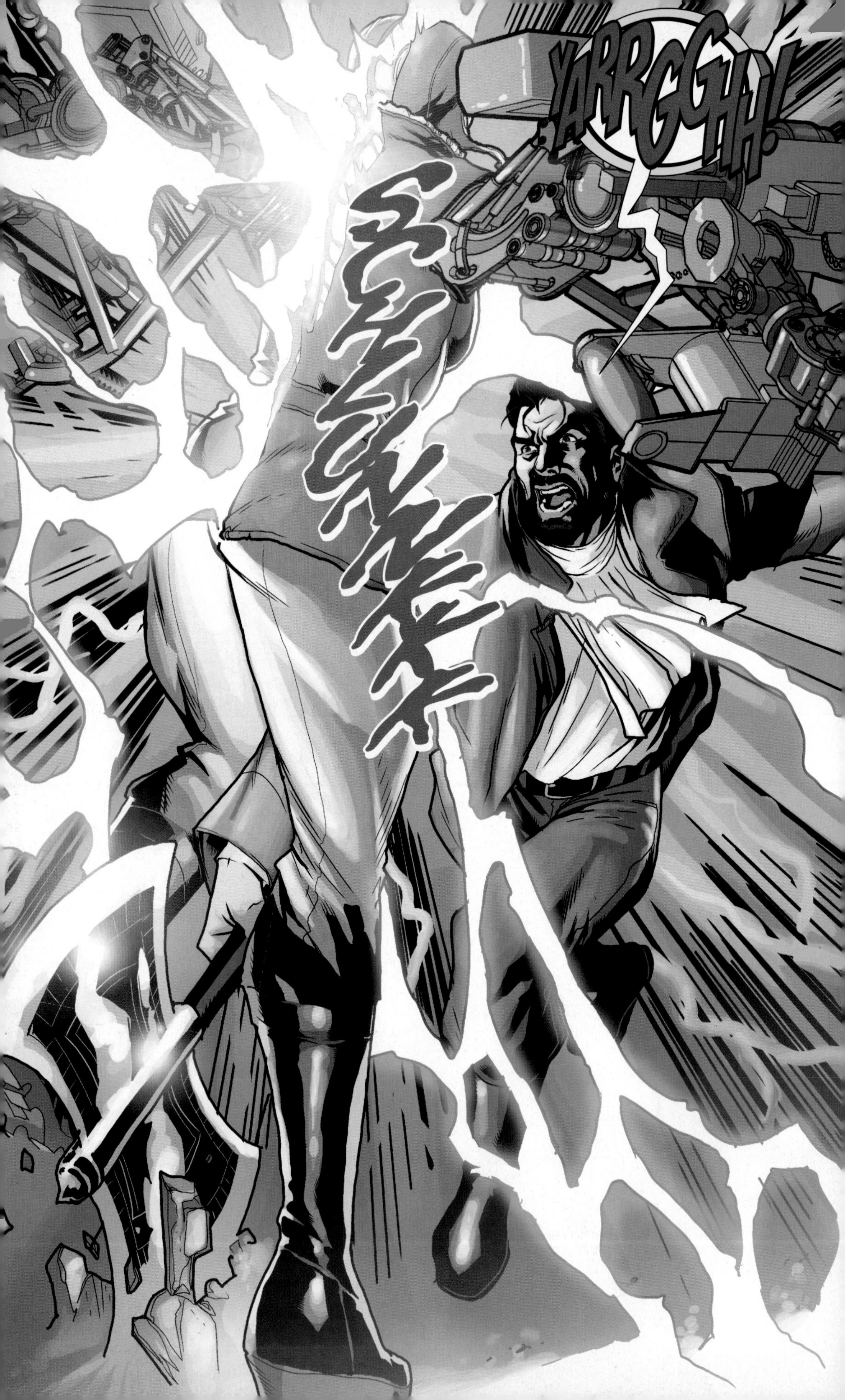
YARRGGHH!

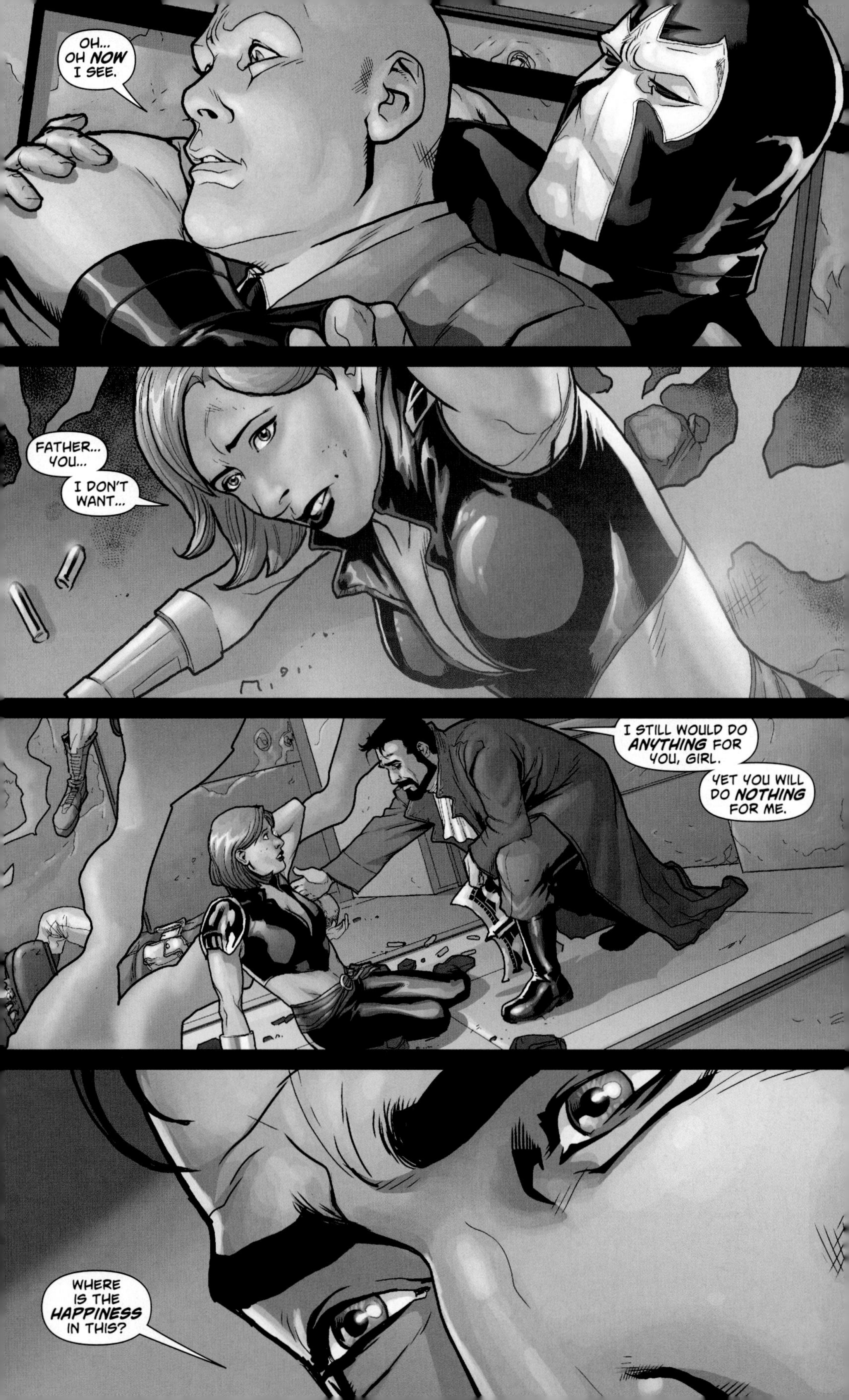
OH... OH NOW I SEE.
FATHER... YOU...
I DON'T WANT...
I STILL WOULD DO ANYTHING FOR YOU, GIRL.
YET YOU WILL DO NOTHING FOR ME.
WHERE IS THE HAPPINESS IN THIS?

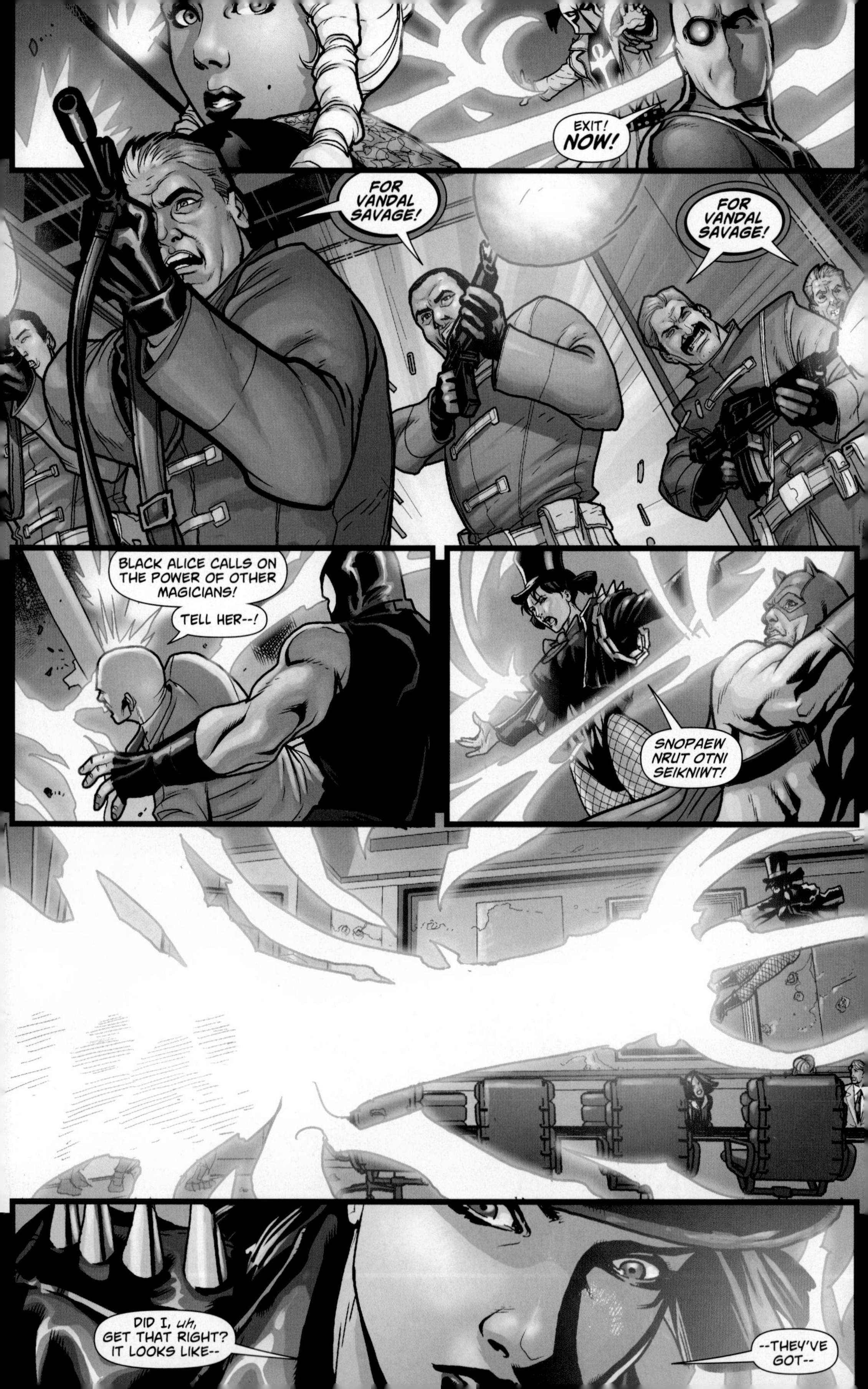
EXIT! NOW!
FOR VANDAL SAVAGE!
FOR VANDAL SAVAGE!
BLACK ALICE CALLS ON THE POWER OF OTHER MAGICIANS!
TELL HER--!
SNOPAEW NRUT OTNI SEIKNIWT!
DID I, uh, GET THAT RIGHT? IT LOOKS LIKE--
--THEY'VE GOT--

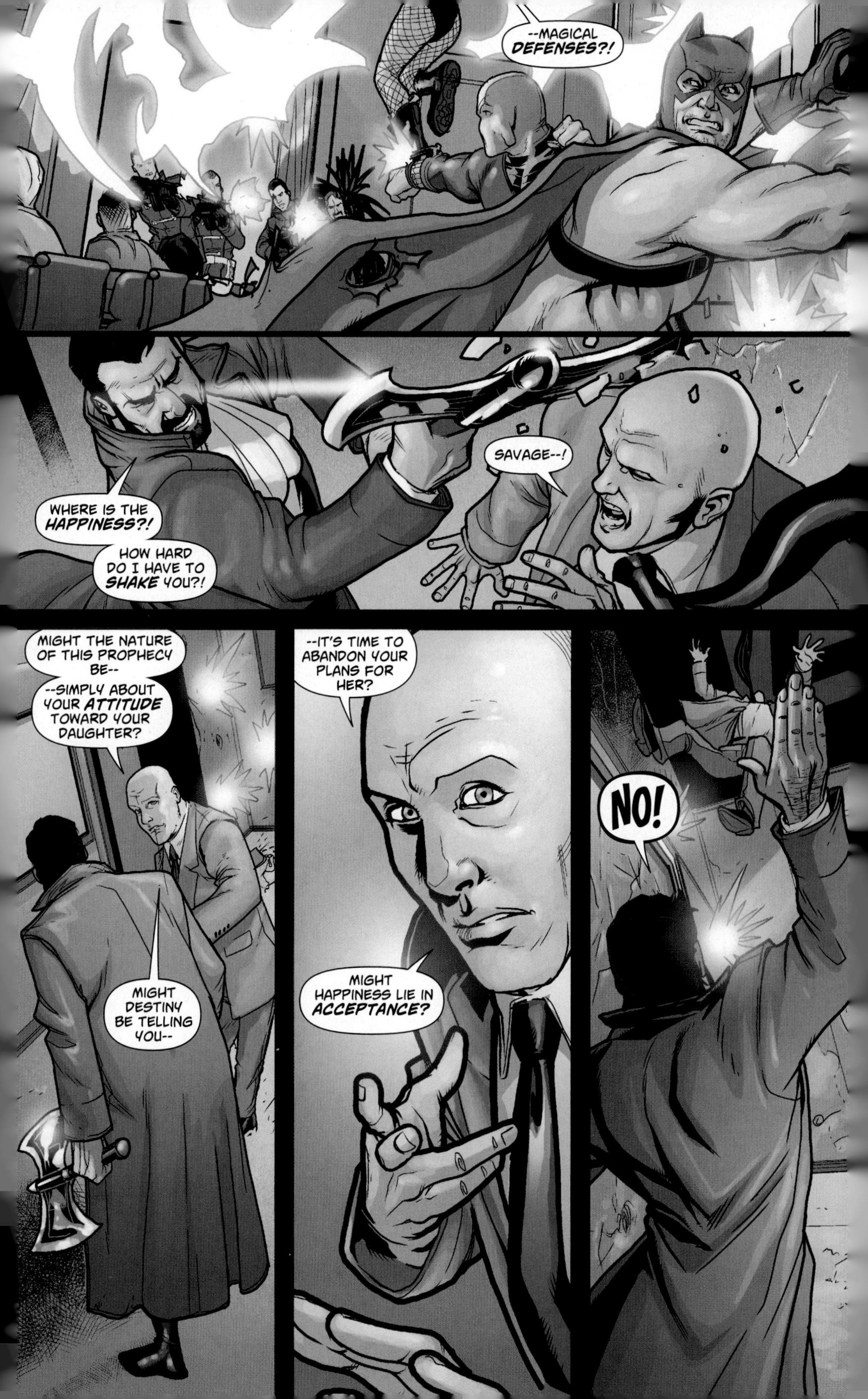
--MAGICAL DEFENSES?!
SAVAGE--!
WHERE IS THE HAPPINESS?!
HOW HARD DO I HAVE TO SHAKE YOU?!
MIGHT THE NATURE OF THIS PROPHECY BE--
--SIMPLY ABOUT YOUR ATTITUDE TOWARD YOUR DAUGHTER?
MIGHT DESTINY BE TELLING YOU--
--IT'S TIME TO ABANDON YOUR PLANS FOR HER?
MIGHT HAPPINESS LIE IN ACCEPTANCE?
NO!

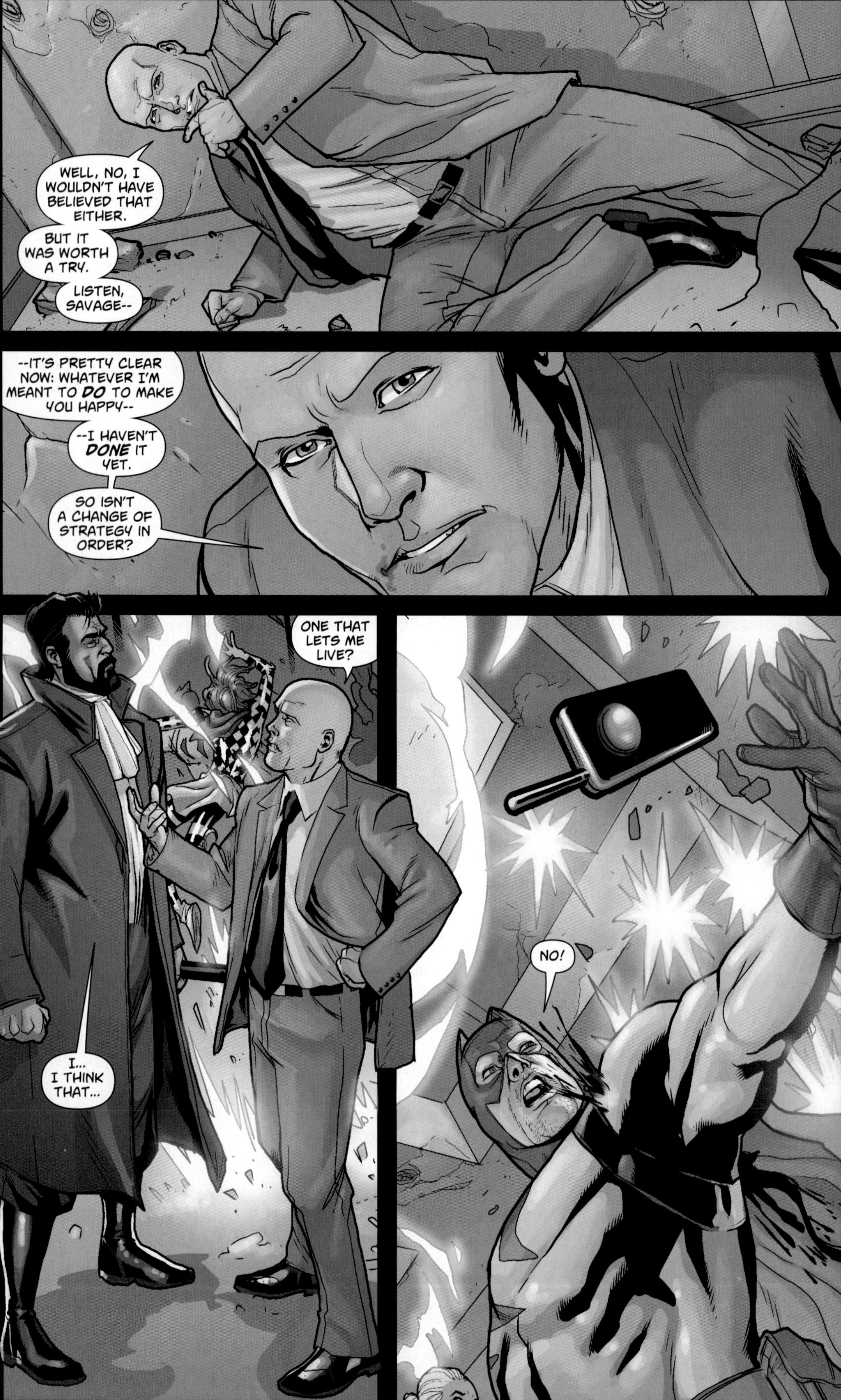
WELL, NO, I WOULDN'T HAVE BELIEVED THAT EITHER.
BUT IT WAS WORTH A TRY.
LISTEN, SAVAGE--
--IT'S PRETTY CLEAR NOW: WHATEVER I'M MEANT TO **DO** TO MAKE YOU HAPPY--
--I HAVEN'T **DONE** IT YET.
SO ISN'T A CHANGE OF STRATEGY IN ORDER?
ONE THAT LETS ME LIVE?
I... I THINK THAT...
NO!

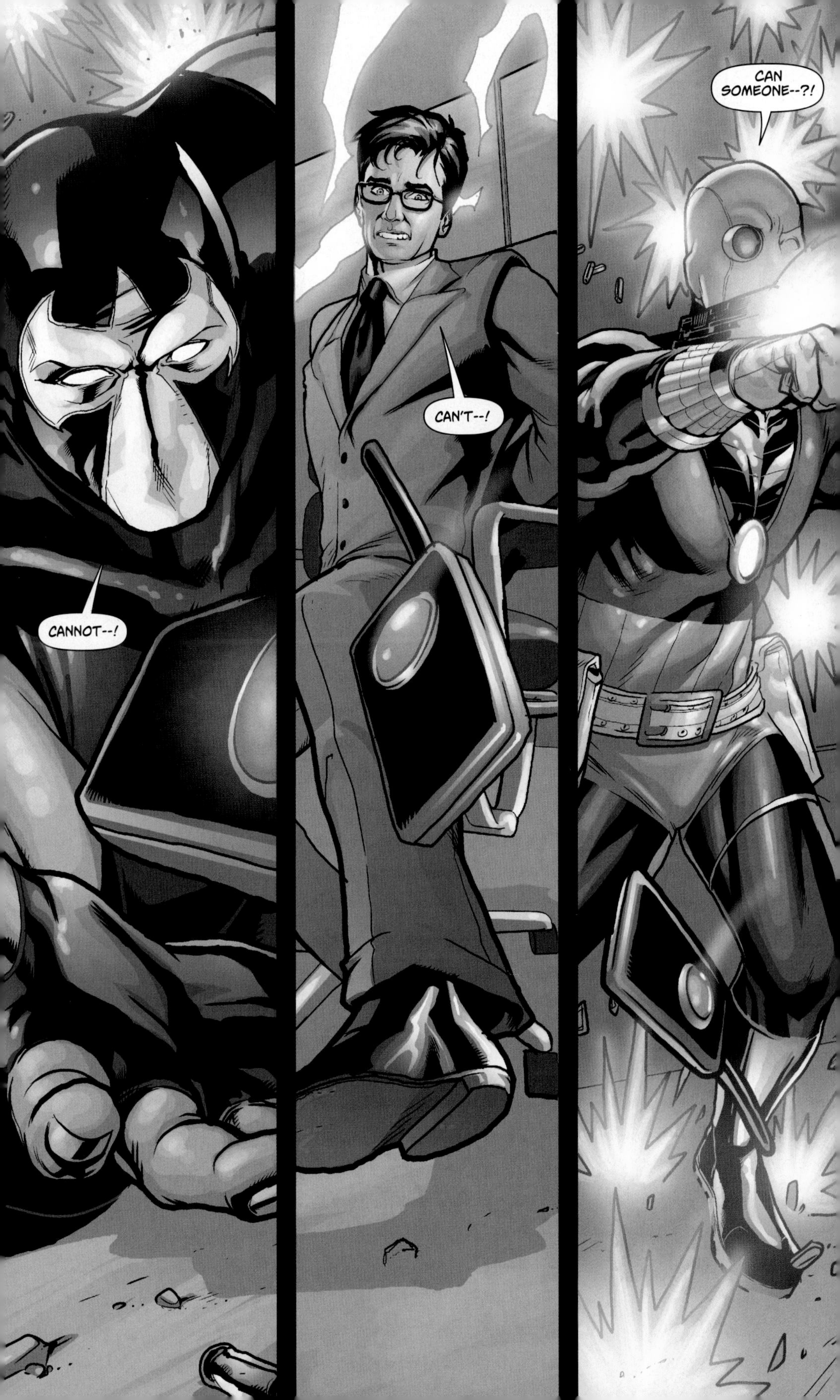
CANNOT--!
CAN'T--!
CAN
SOMEONE--?!

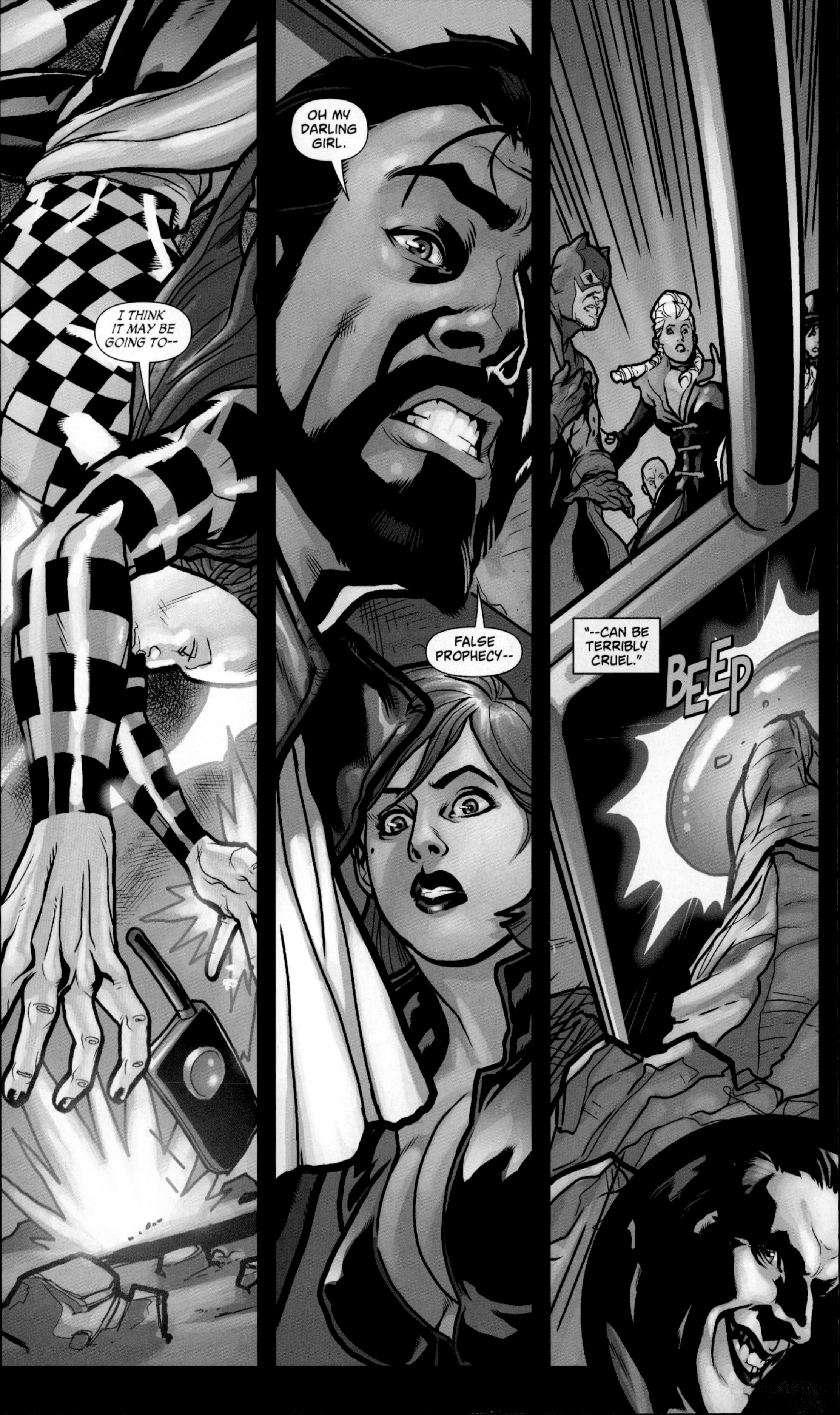
I THINK IT MAY BE GOING TO--
OH MY DARLING GIRL.
FALSE PROPHECY--
"--CAN BE TERRIBLY CRUEL."
BEEP

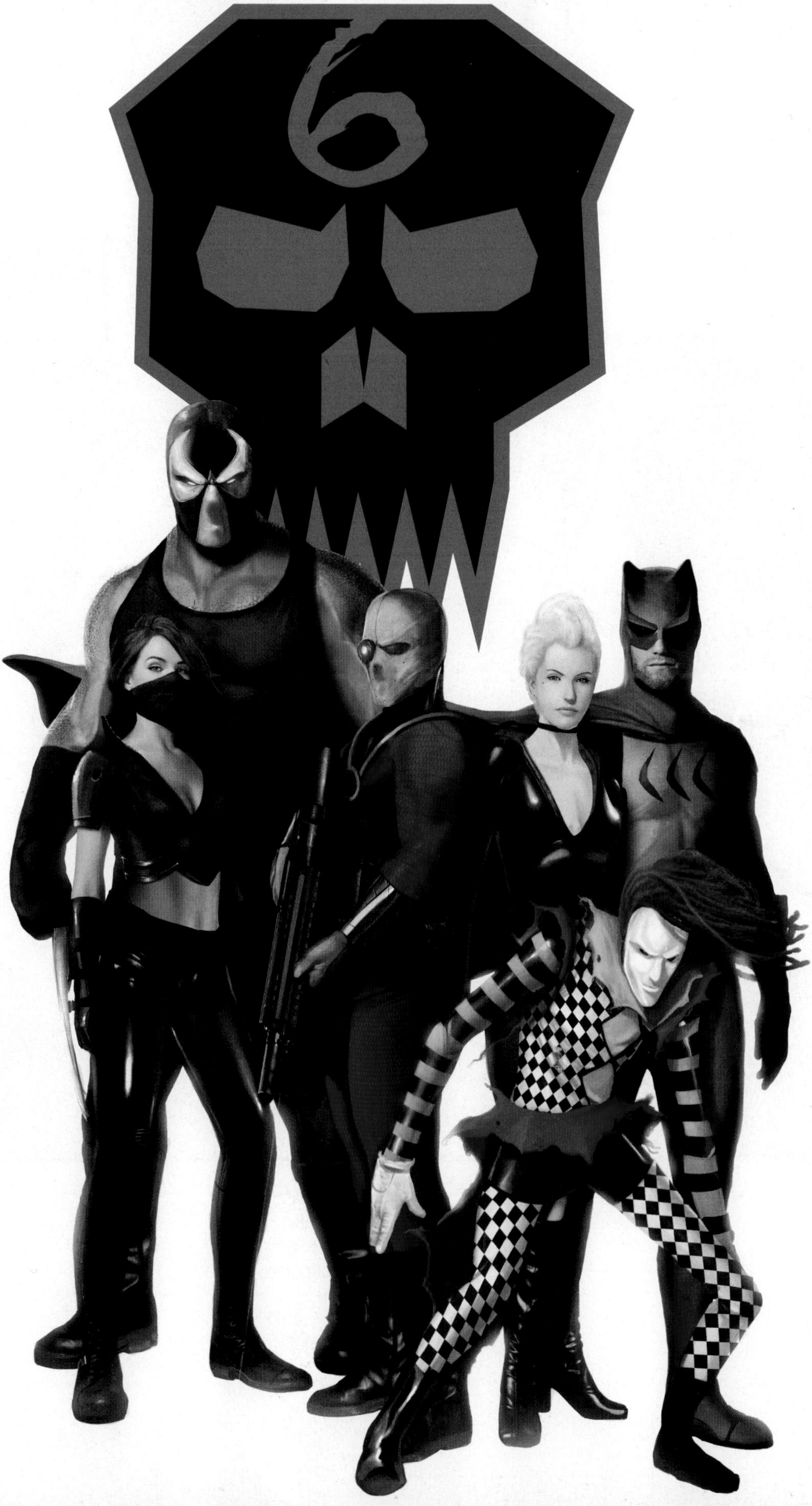

WHAT LUTHOR HAS WROUGHT

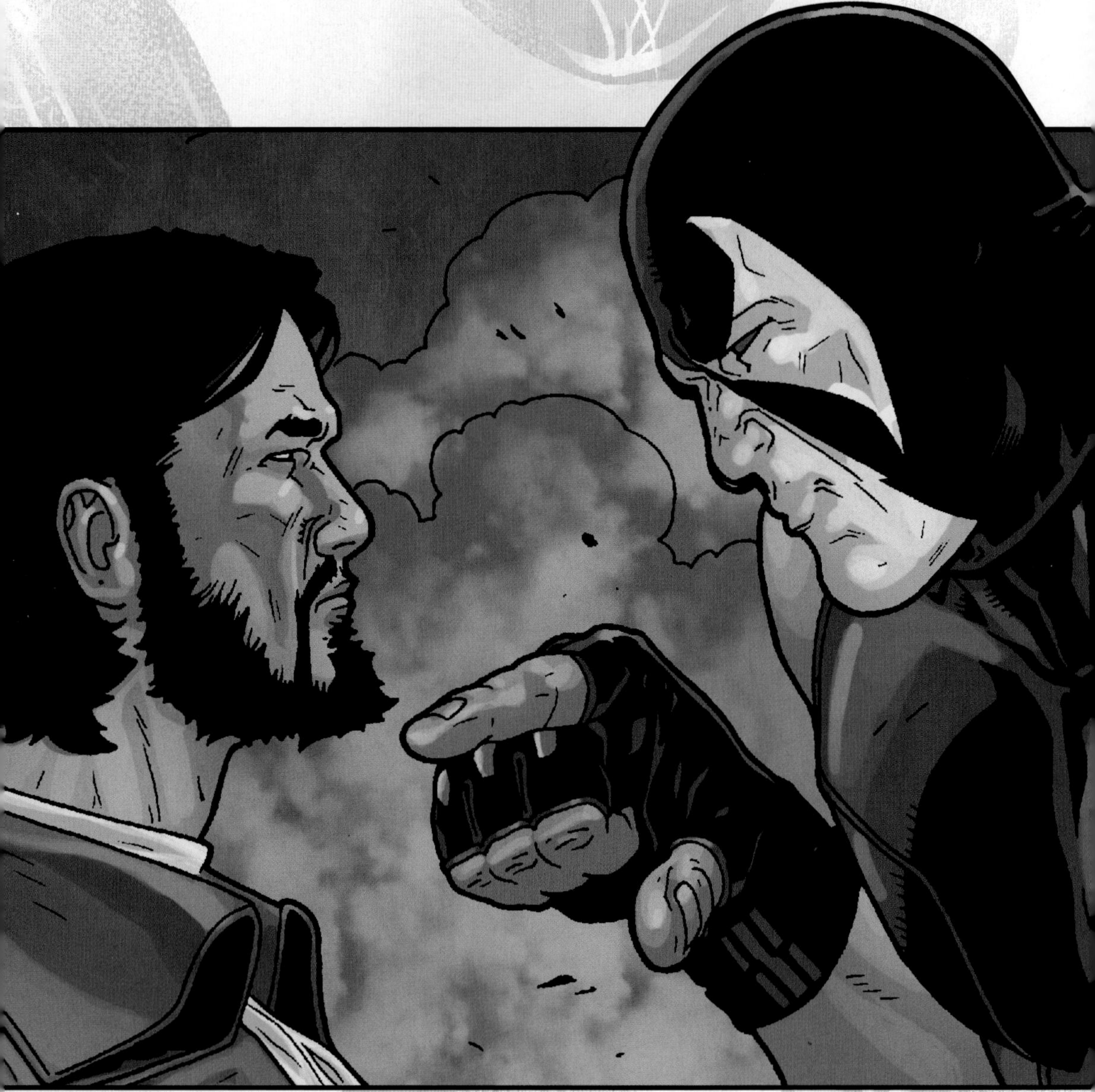

GAIL SIMONE writer
MARCOS **MARZ** penciller
LUCIANA **DELNEGRO** inker

cover by
DANIEL **LUVISI**

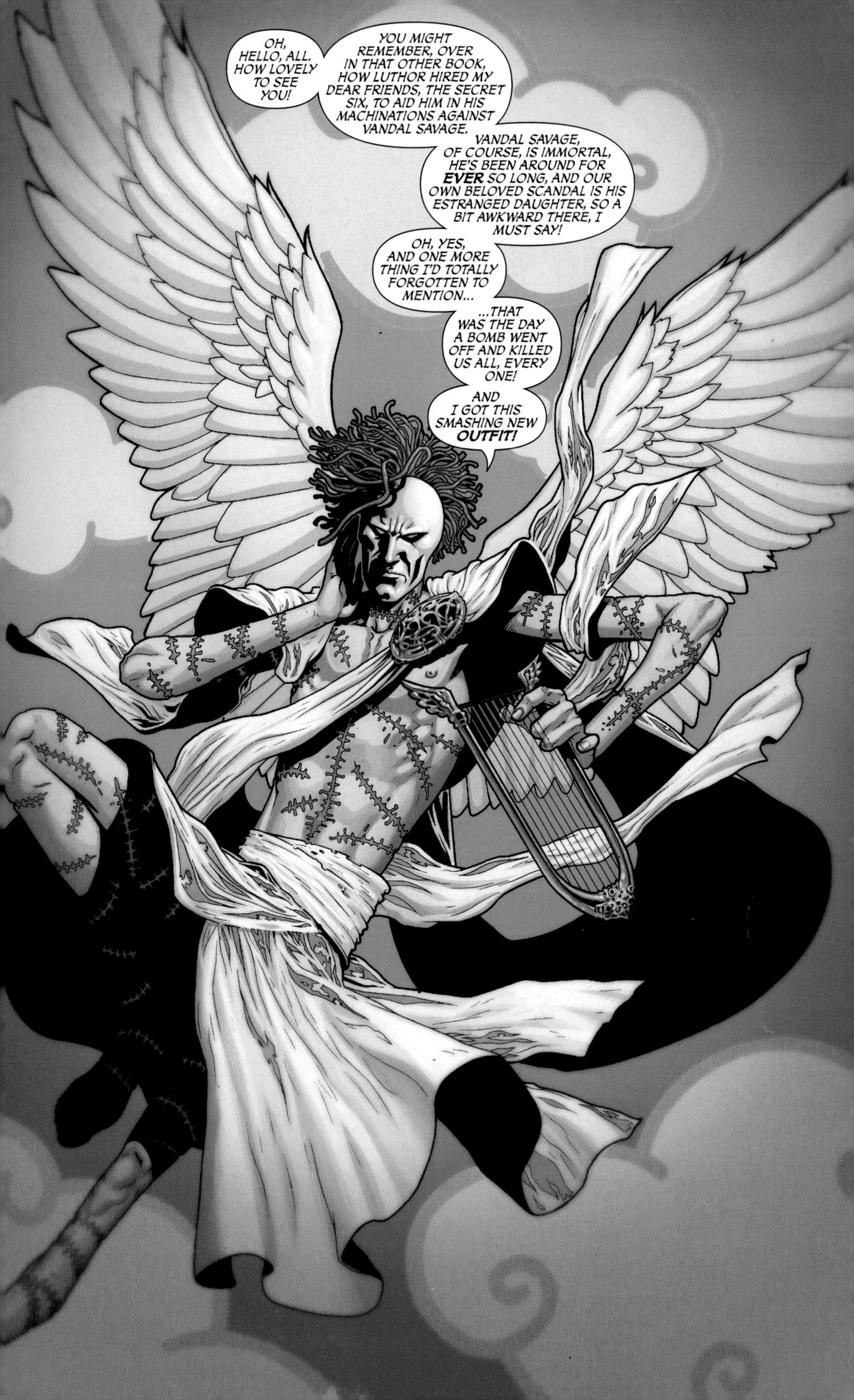
OH, HELLO, ALL. HOW LOVELY TO SEE YOU!
YOU MIGHT REMEMBER, OVER IN THAT OTHER BOOK, HOW LUTHOR HIRED MY DEAR FRIENDS, THE SECRET SIX, TO AID HIM IN HIS MACHINATIONS AGAINST VANDAL SAVAGE.
VANDAL SAVAGE, OF COURSE, IS IMMORTAL, HE'S BEEN AROUND FOR **EVER** SO LONG, AND OUR OWN BELOVED SCANDAL IS HIS ESTRANGED DAUGHTER, SO A BIT AWKWARD THERE, I MUST SAY!
OH, YES, AND ONE MORE THING I'D TOTALLY FORGOTTEN TO MENTION...
...THAT WAS THE DAY A BOMB WENT OFF AND KILLED US ALL, EVERY ONE!
AND I GOT THIS SMASHING NEW **OUTFIT!**

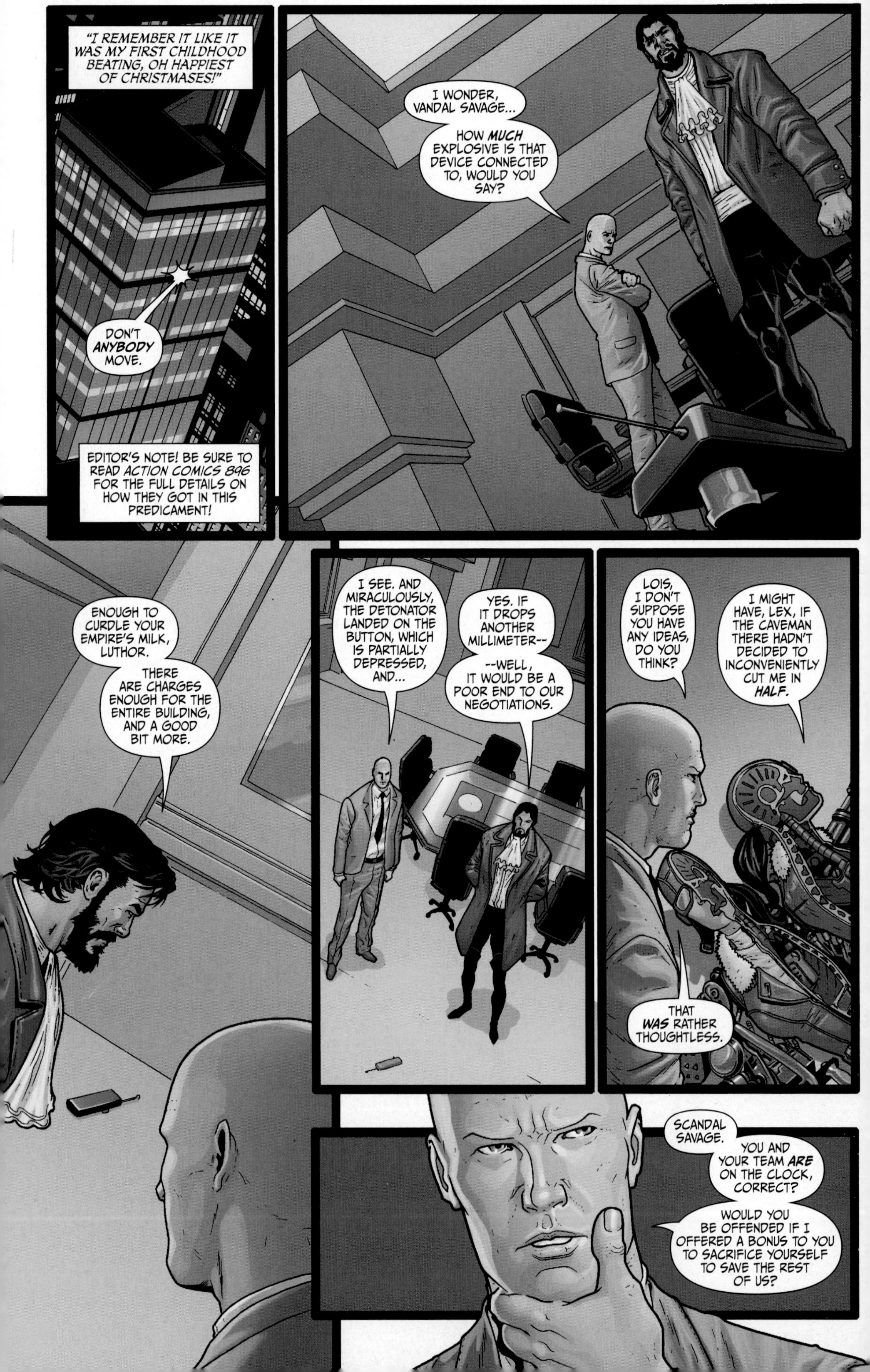
"I REMEMBER IT LIKE IT WAS MY FIRST CHILDHOOD BEATING, OH HAPPIEST OF CHRISTMASES!"
DON'T ANYBODY MOVE.
EDITOR'S NOTE! BE SURE TO READ ACTION COMICS 896 FOR THE FULL DETAILS ON HOW THEY GOT IN THIS PREDICAMENT!
I WONDER, VANDAL SAVAGE...
HOW MUCH EXPLOSIVE IS THAT DEVICE CONNECTED TO, WOULD YOU SAY?
ENOUGH TO CURDLE YOUR EMPIRE'S MILK, LUTHOR.
THERE ARE CHARGES ENOUGH FOR THE ENTIRE BUILDING, AND A GOOD BIT MORE.
I SEE. AND MIRACULOUSLY, THE DETONATOR LANDED ON THE BUTTON, WHICH IS PARTIALLY DEPRESSED, AND...
YES. IF IT DROPS ANOTHER MILLIMETER--
--WELL, IT WOULD BE A POOR END TO OUR NEGOTIATIONS.
LOIS, I DON'T SUPPOSE YOU HAVE ANY IDEAS, DO YOU THINK?
I MIGHT HAVE, LEX, IF THE CAVEMAN THERE HADN'T DECIDED TO INCONVENIENTLY CUT ME IN HALF.
THAT WAS RATHER THOUGHTLESS.
SCANDAL SAVAGE.
YOU AND YOUR TEAM ARE ON THE CLOCK, CORRECT?
WOULD YOU BE OFFENDED IF I OFFERED A BONUS TO YOU TO SACRIFICE YOURSELF TO SAVE THE REST OF US?

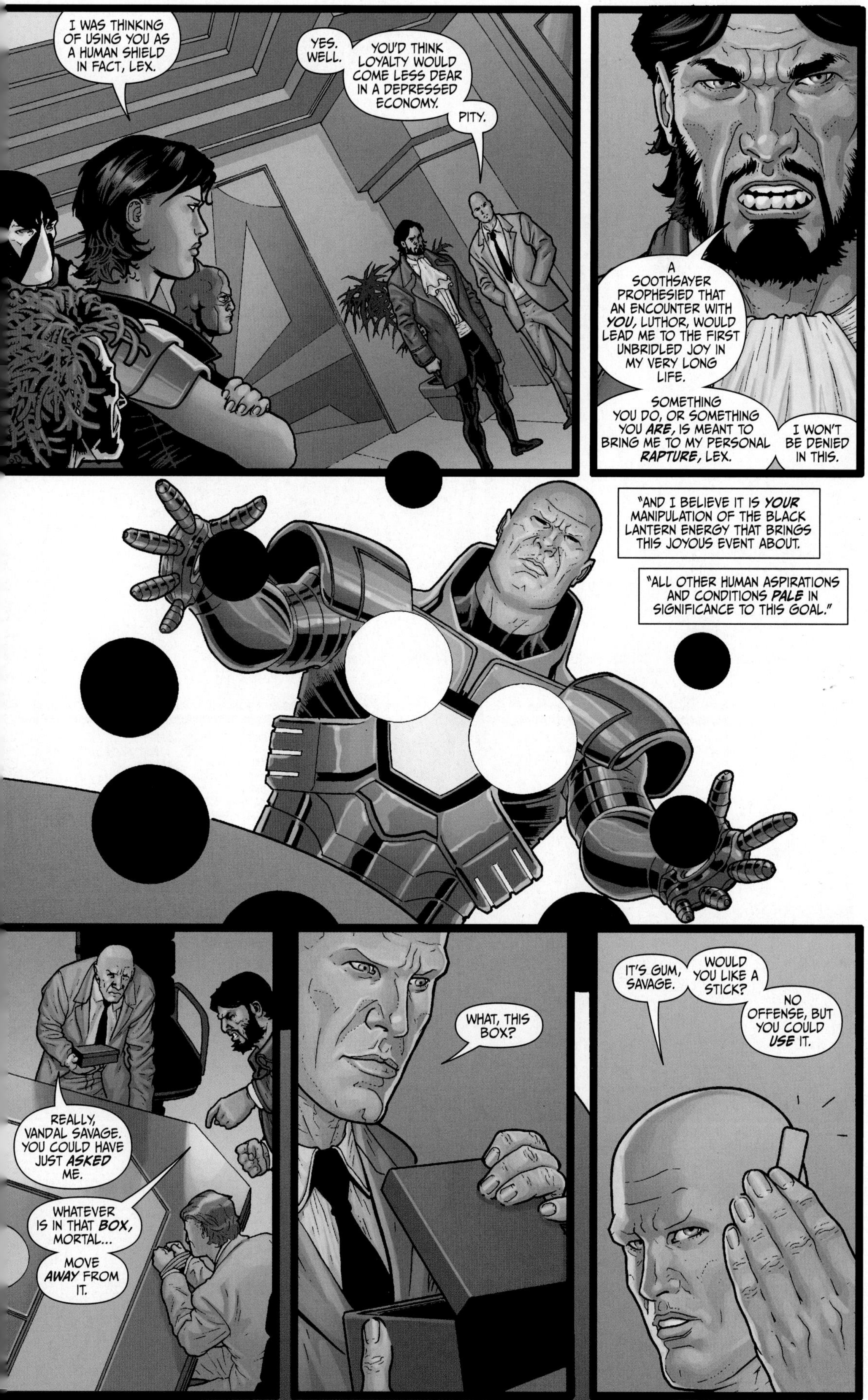
I WAS THINKING OF USING YOU AS A HUMAN SHIELD IN FACT, LEX.
YES. WELL.
YOU'D THINK LOYALTY WOULD COME LESS DEAR IN A DEPRESSED ECONOMY.
PITY.
A SOOTHSAYER PROPHESIED THAT AN ENCOUNTER WITH YOU, LUTHOR, WOULD LEAD ME TO THE FIRST UNBRIDLED JOY IN MY VERY LONG LIFE.
SOMETHING YOU DO, OR SOMETHING YOU ARE, IS MEANT TO BRING ME TO MY PERSONAL RAPTURE, LEX.
I WON'T BE DENIED IN THIS.
"AND I BELIEVE IT IS YOUR MANIPULATION OF THE BLACK LANTERN ENERGY THAT BRINGS THIS JOYOUS EVENT ABOUT.
"ALL OTHER HUMAN ASPIRATIONS AND CONDITIONS PALE IN SIGNIFICANCE TO THIS GOAL."
REALLY, VANDAL SAVAGE. YOU COULD HAVE JUST ASKED ME.
WHATEVER IS IN THAT BOX, MORTAL...
MOVE AWAY FROM IT.
WHAT, THIS BOX?
IT'S GUM, SAVAGE.
WOULD YOU LIKE A STICK?
NO OFFENSE, BUT YOU COULD USE IT.

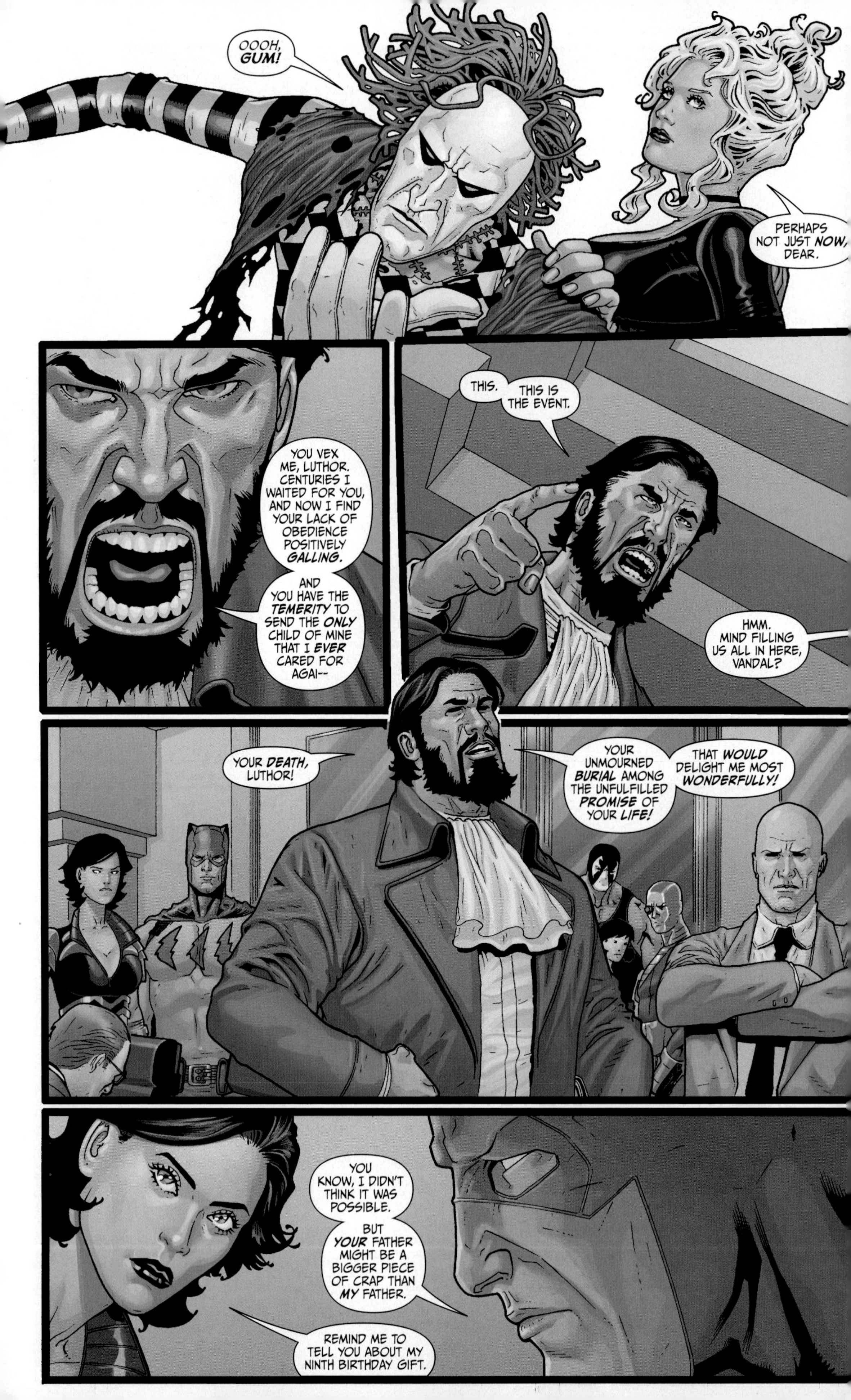
OOOH, GUM!
PERHAPS NOT JUST NOW, DEAR.
YOU VEX ME, LUTHOR. CENTURIES I WAITED FOR YOU, AND NOW I FIND YOUR LACK OF OBEDIENCE POSITIVELY GALLING.
AND YOU HAVE THE TEMERITY TO SEND THE ONLY CHILD OF MINE THAT I EVER CARED FOR AGAI--
THIS.
THIS IS THE EVENT.
HMM. MIND FILLING US ALL IN HERE, VANDAL?
YOUR DEATH, LUTHOR!
YOUR UNMOURNED BURIAL AMONG THE UNFULFILLED PROMISE OF YOUR LIFE!
THAT WOULD DELIGHT ME MOST WONDERFULLY!
YOU KNOW, I DIDN'T THINK IT WAS POSSIBLE.
BUT YOUR FATHER MIGHT BE A BIGGER PIECE OF CRAP THAN MY FATHER.
REMIND ME TO TELL YOU ABOUT MY NINTH BIRTHDAY GIFT.

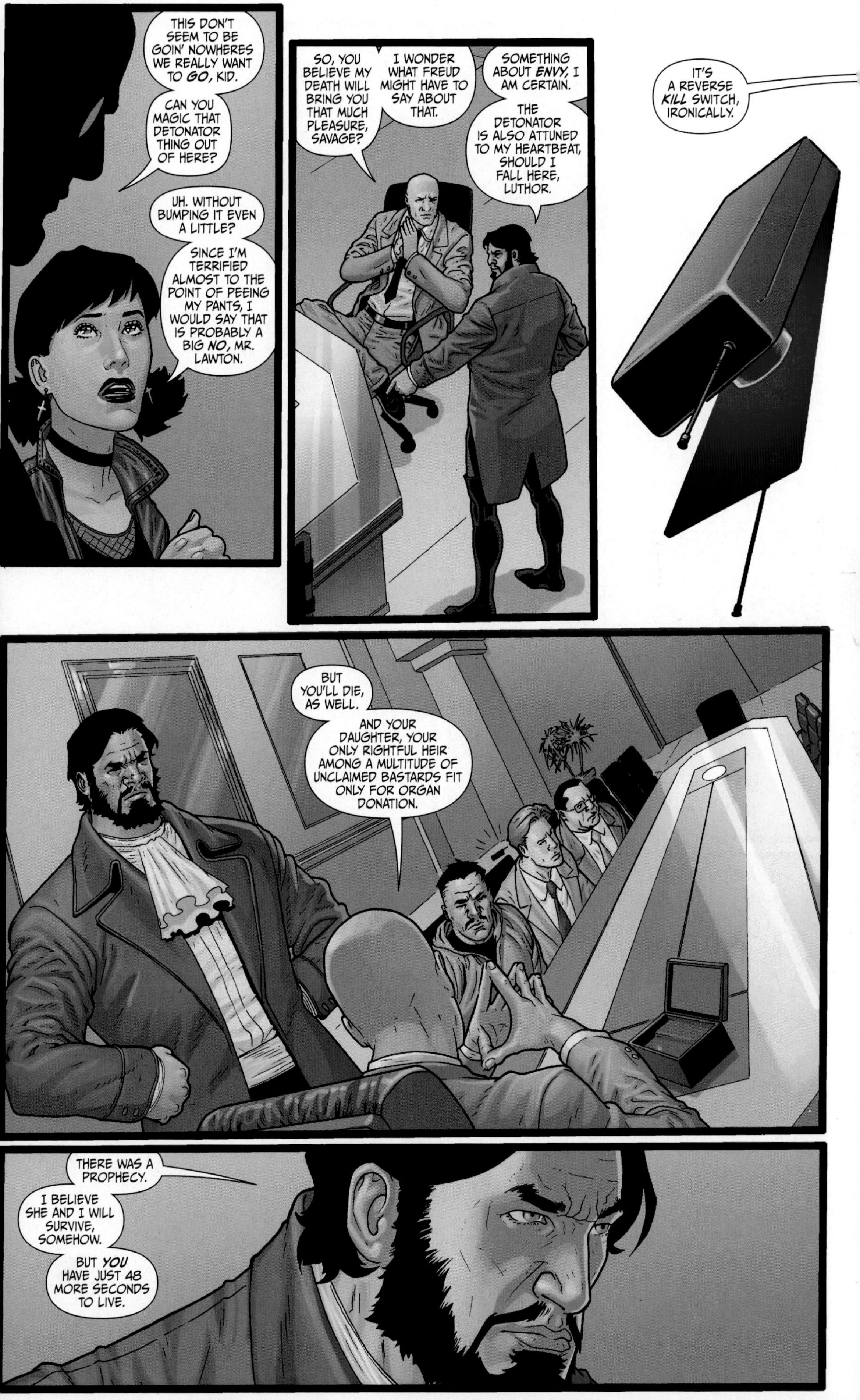
THIS DON'T SEEM TO BE GOIN' NOWHERES WE REALLY WANT TO GO, KID.
CAN YOU MAGIC THAT DETONATOR THING OUT OF HERE?
UH. WITHOUT BUMPING IT EVEN A LITTLE?
SINCE I'M TERRIFIED ALMOST TO THE POINT OF PEEING MY PANTS, I WOULD SAY THAT IS PROBABLY A BIG NO, MR. LAWTON.
SO, YOU BELIEVE MY DEATH WILL BRING YOU THAT MUCH PLEASURE, SAVAGE?
I WONDER WHAT FREUD MIGHT HAVE TO SAY ABOUT THAT.
SOMETHING ABOUT ENVY, I AM CERTAIN.
THE DETONATOR IS ALSO ATTUNED TO MY HEARTBEAT, SHOULD I FALL HERE, LUTHOR.
IT'S A REVERSE KILL SWITCH, IRONICALLY.
BUT YOU'LL DIE, AS WELL.
AND YOUR DAUGHTER, YOUR ONLY RIGHTFUL HEIR AMONG A MULTITUDE OF UNCLAIMED BASTARDS FIT ONLY FOR ORGAN DONATION.
THERE WAS A PROPHECY.
I BELIEVE SHE AND I WILL SURVIVE, SOMEHOW.
BUT YOU HAVE JUST 48 MORE SECONDS TO LIVE.

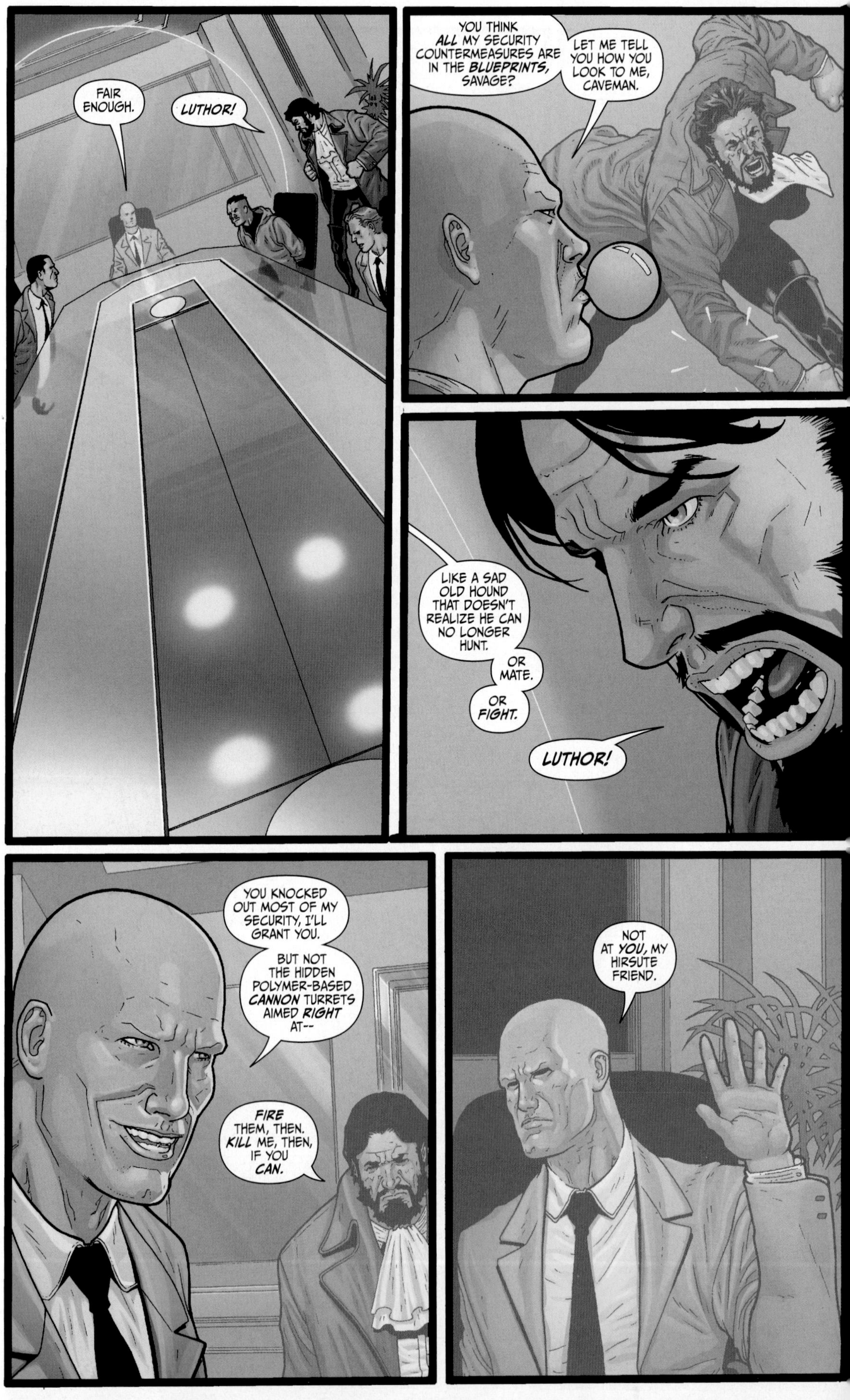

FAIR ENOUGH.
LUTHOR!
YOU THINK ALL MY SECURITY COUNTERMEASURES ARE IN THE BLUEPRINTS, SAVAGE?
LET ME TELL YOU HOW YOU LOOK TO ME, CAVEMAN.
LIKE A SAD OLD HOUND THAT DOESN'T REALIZE HE CAN NO LONGER HUNT.
OR MATE.
OR FIGHT.
LUTHOR!
YOU KNOCKED OUT MOST OF MY SECURITY, I'LL GRANT YOU.
BUT NOT THE HIDDEN POLYMER-BASED CANNON TURRETS AIMED RIGHT AT--
FIRE THEM, THEN. KILL ME, THEN, IF YOU CAN.
NOT AT YOU, MY HIRSUTE FRIEND.

AT *SCANDAL SAVAGE*. YOUR *DAUGHTER*.

:30

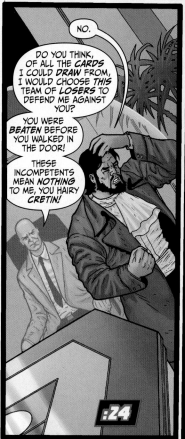

NO.

DO YOU THINK, OF ALL THE *CARDS* I COULD *DRAW* FROM, I WOULD CHOOSE *THIS* TEAM OF *LOSERS* TO DEFEND ME AGAINST YOU?

YOU WERE *BEATEN* BEFORE YOU WALKED IN THE DOOR!

THESE INCOMPETENTS MEAN *NOTHING* TO ME, YOU HAIRY *CRETIN!*

NO OFFENSE *INTENDED.*

HEY, YOU'RE ROLLING, STUFF GETS SAID.

:24

NO SKIN OFF *MY* FULL, LUSTROUS HEAD OF HAIR, MAN.

TURN OFF THE DETONATOR, SAVAGE. AND YOUR DAUGHTER *LIVES*, EVEN IF YOU DO *NOT*.

DAMN YOU, LEX. YOU'LL PAY FOR THIS. YOU'LL *PAY*.

I TAKE THIS RISK FOR *HER*, THEN.

UH. I'M AFRAID IT'S *STUCK*.

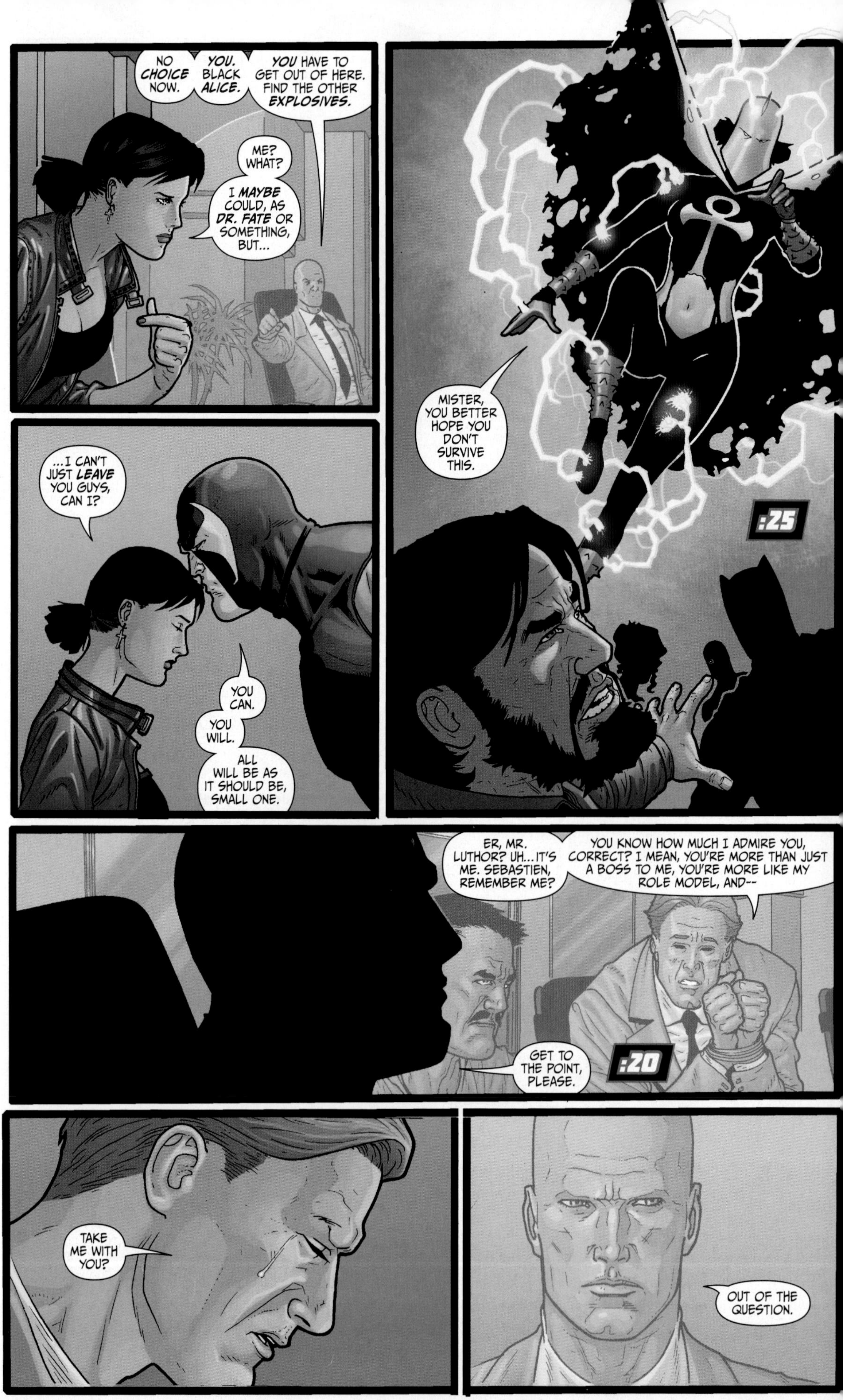
NO CHOICE NOW.
YOU. BLACK ALICE.
YOU HAVE TO GET OUT OF HERE. FIND THE OTHER EXPLOSIVES.
ME? WHAT?
I MAYBE COULD, AS DR. FATE OR SOMETHING, BUT...
...I CAN'T JUST LEAVE YOU GUYS, CAN I?
YOU CAN.
YOU WILL.
ALL WILL BE AS IT SHOULD BE, SMALL ONE.
MISTER, YOU BETTER HOPE YOU DON'T SURVIVE THIS.
:25
ER, MR. LUTHOR? UH...IT'S ME. SEBASTIEN, REMEMBER ME?
YOU KNOW HOW MUCH I ADMIRE YOU, CORRECT? I MEAN, YOU'RE MORE THAN JUST A BOSS TO ME, YOU'RE MORE LIKE MY ROLE MODEL, AND--
GET TO THE POINT, PLEASE.
:20
TAKE ME WITH YOU?
OUT OF THE QUESTION.

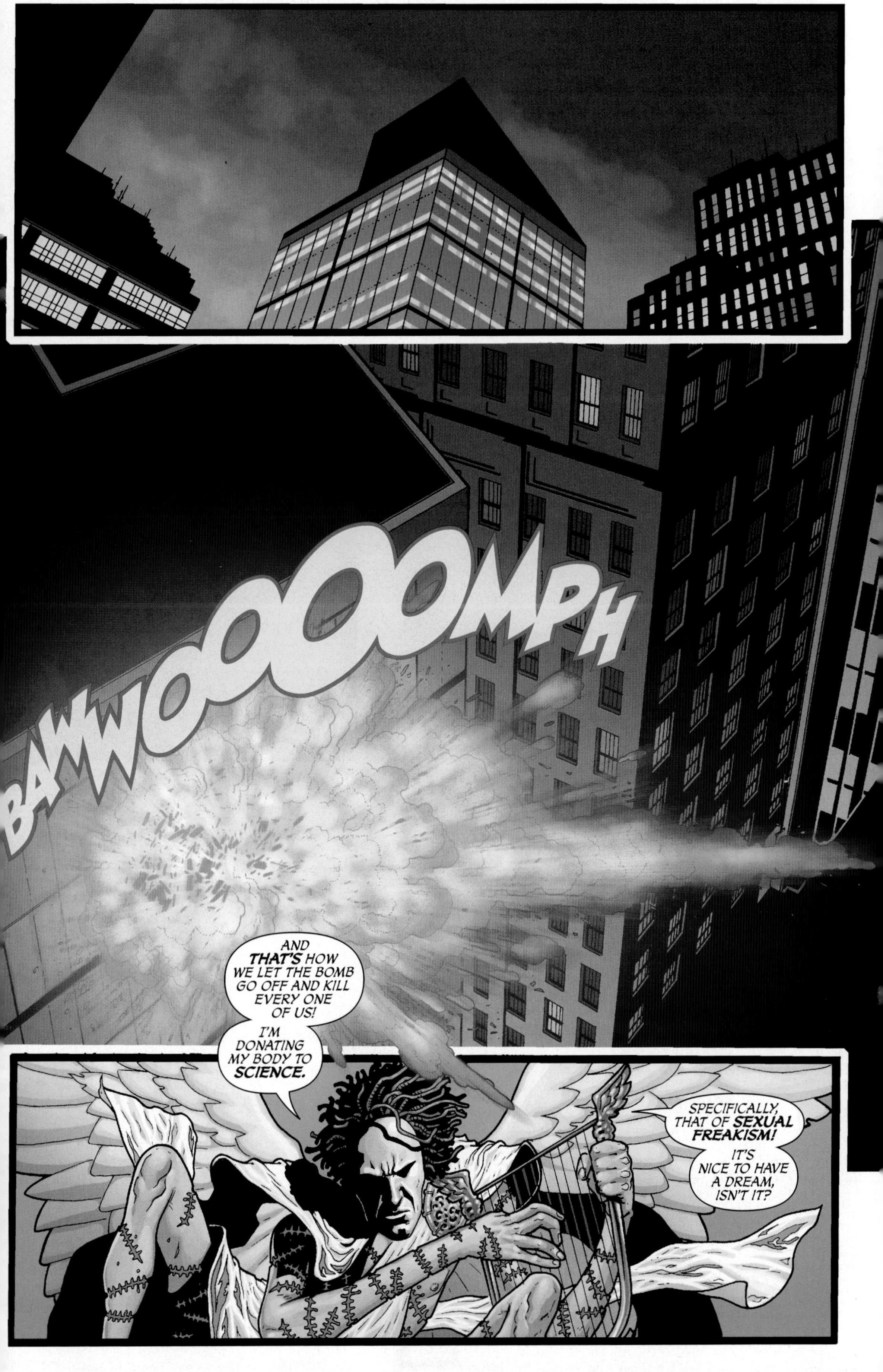
BAWOOOOOMPH
AND THAT'S HOW WE LET THE BOMB GO OFF AND KILL EVERY ONE OF US!
I'M DONATING MY BODY TO SCIENCE.
SPECIFICALLY, THAT OF SEXUAL FREAKISM!
IT'S NICE TO HAVE A DREAM, ISN'T IT?

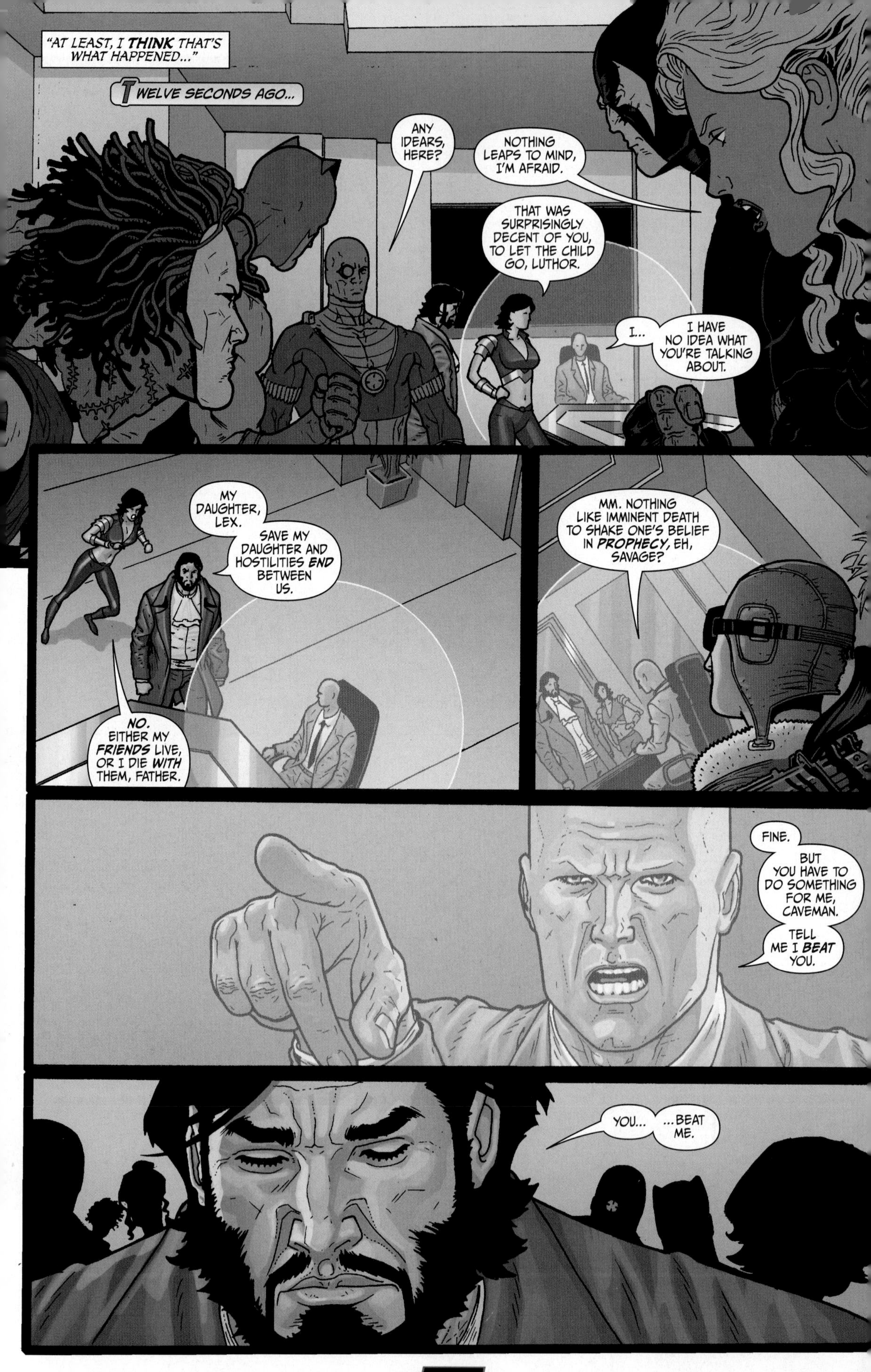
"AT LEAST, I THINK THAT'S WHAT HAPPENED..."
TWELVE SECONDS AGO...
ANY IDEARS, HERE?
NOTHING LEAPS TO MIND, I'M AFRAID.
THAT WAS SURPRISINGLY DECENT OF YOU, TO LET THE CHILD GO, LUTHOR.
I...
I HAVE NO IDEA WHAT YOU'RE TALKING ABOUT.
MY DAUGHTER, LEX.
SAVE MY DAUGHTER AND HOSTILITIES END BETWEEN US.
NO. EITHER MY FRIENDS LIVE, OR I DIE WITH THEM, FATHER.
MM. NOTHING LIKE IMMINENT DEATH TO SHAKE ONE'S BELIEF IN PROPHECY, EH, SAVAGE?
FINE.
BUT YOU HAVE TO DO SOMETHING FOR ME, CAVEMAN.
TELL ME I BEAT YOU.
YOU...
...BEAT ME.

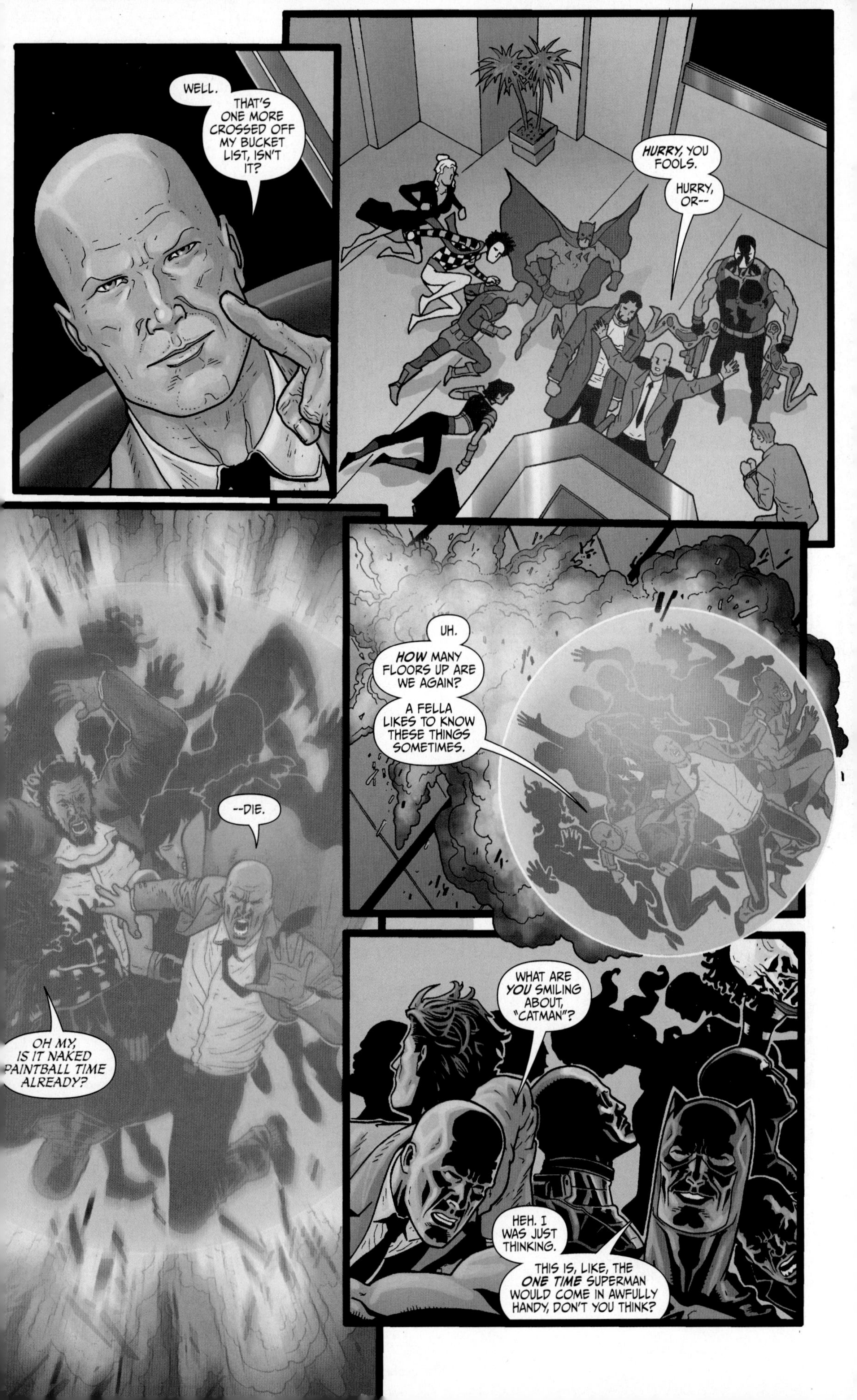
WELL.
THAT'S ONE MORE CROSSED OFF MY BUCKET LIST, ISN'T IT?
HURRY, YOU FOOLS.
HURRY, OR--
--DIE.
OH MY, IS IT NAKED PAINTBALL TIME ALREADY?
UH.
HOW MANY FLOORS UP ARE WE AGAIN?
A FELLA LIKES TO KNOW THESE THINGS SOMETIMES.
WHAT ARE *YOU* SMILING ABOUT, "CATMAN"?
HEH. I WAS JUST THINKING.
THIS IS, LIKE, THE *ONE TIME* SUPERMAN WOULD COME IN AWFULLY HANDY, DON'T YOU THINK?

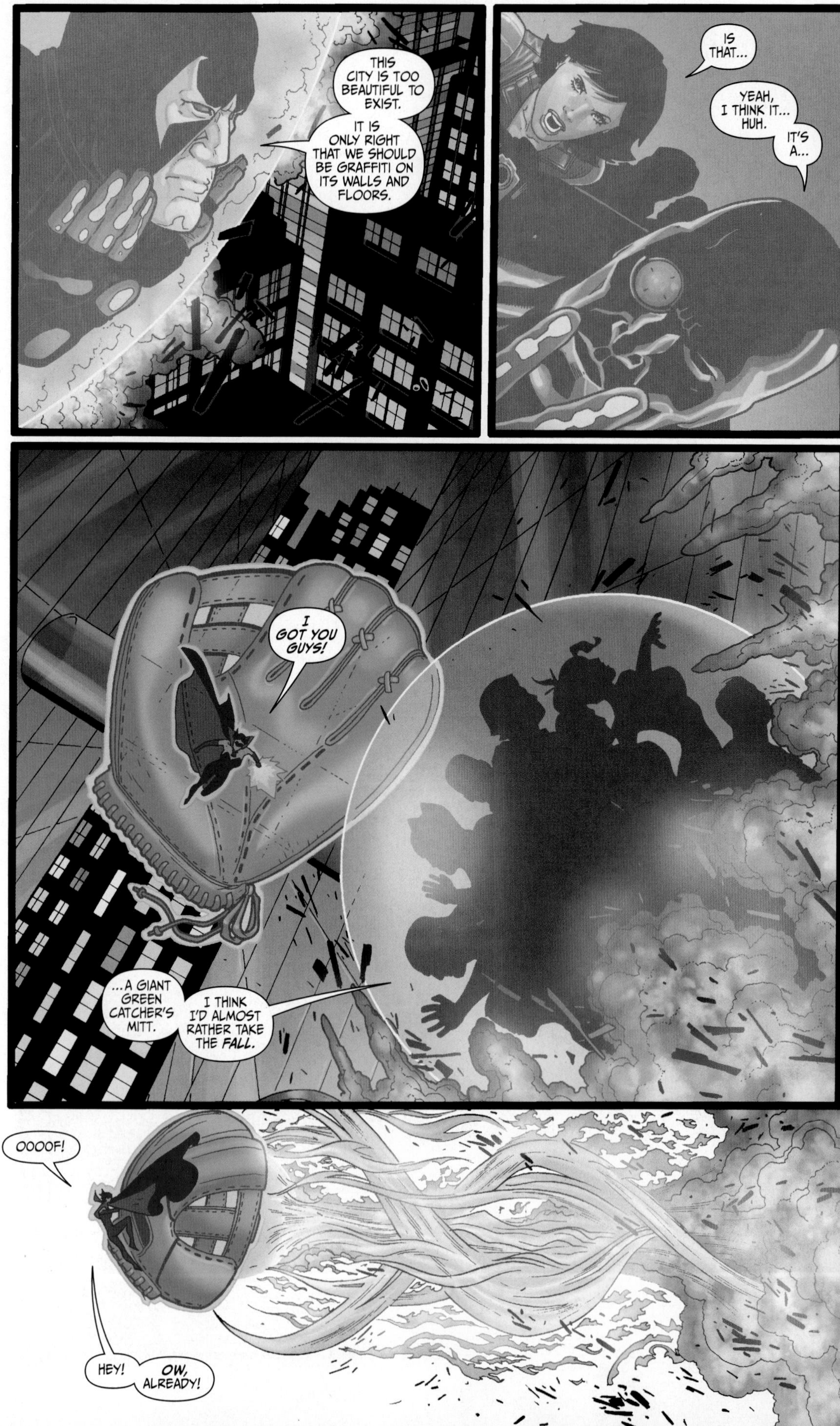
THIS CITY IS TOO BEAUTIFUL TO EXIST.
IT IS ONLY RIGHT THAT WE SHOULD BE GRAFFITI ON ITS WALLS AND FLOORS.
IS THAT...
YEAH, I THINK IT... HUH.
IT'S A...
I GOT YOU GUYS!
...A GIANT GREEN CATCHER'S MITT.
I THINK I'D ALMOST RATHER TAKE THE *FALL.*
OOOOF!
HEY!
OW, ALREADY!

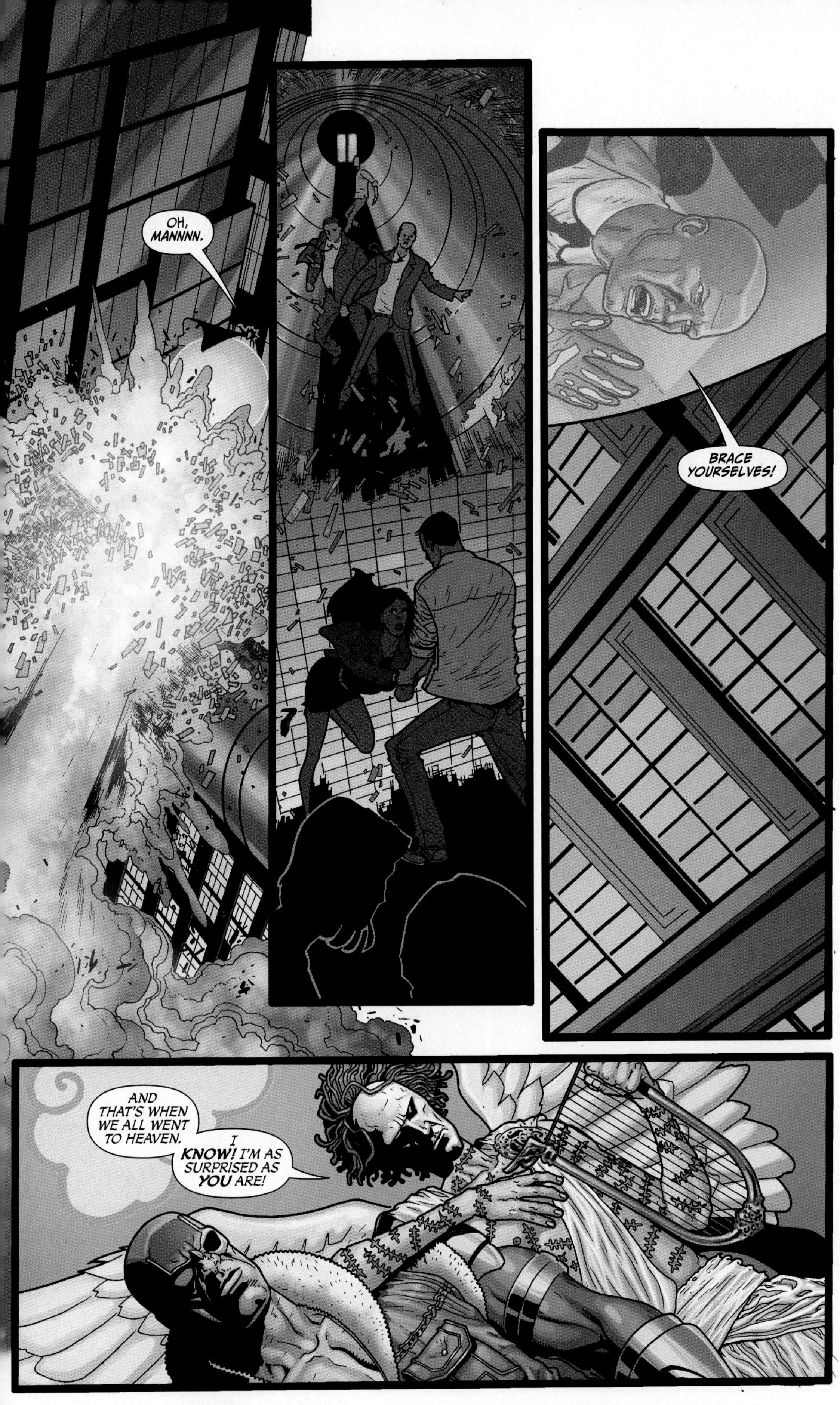

OH, MANNNN.
BRACE YOURSELVES!
AND THAT'S WHEN WE ALL WENT TO HEAVEN.
I **KNOW!** I'M AS SURPRISED AS **YOU** ARE!

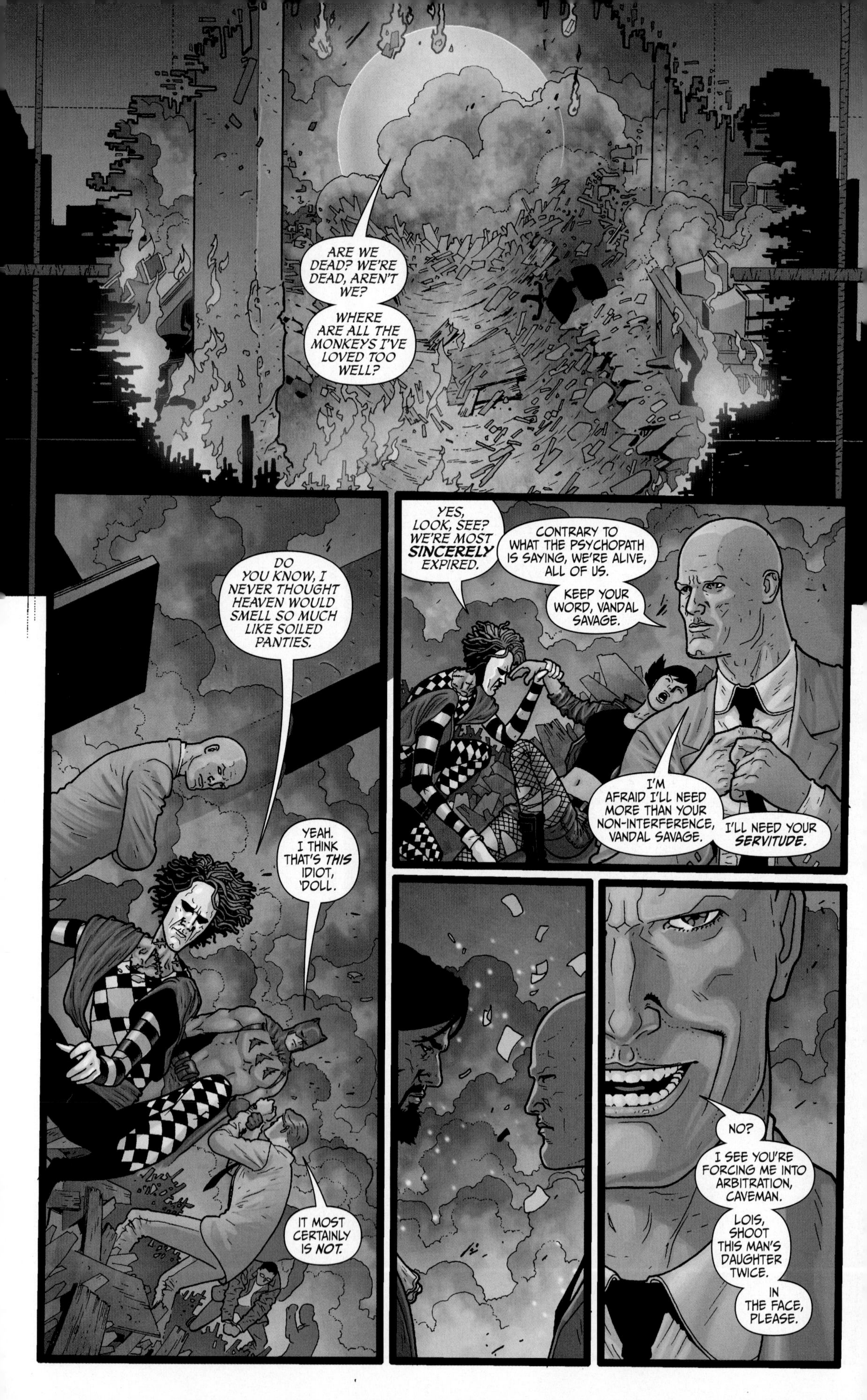
ARE WE DEAD? WE'RE DEAD, AREN'T WE?
WHERE ARE ALL THE MONKEYS I'VE LOVED TOO WELL?
DO YOU KNOW, I NEVER THOUGHT HEAVEN WOULD SMELL SO MUCH LIKE SOILED PANTIES.
YEAH. I THINK THAT'S THIS IDIOT, 'DOLL.
IT MOST CERTAINLY IS NOT.
YES, LOOK, SEE? WE'RE MOST SINCERELY EXPIRED.
CONTRARY TO WHAT THE PSYCHOPATH IS SAYING, WE'RE ALIVE, ALL OF US.
KEEP YOUR WORD, VANDAL SAVAGE.
I'M AFRAID I'LL NEED MORE THAN YOUR NON-INTERFERENCE, VANDAL SAVAGE.
I'LL NEED YOUR SERVITUDE.
NO?
I SEE YOU'RE FORCING ME INTO ARBITRATION, CAVEMAN.
LOIS, SHOOT THIS MAN'S DAUGHTER TWICE.
IN THE FACE, PLEASE.

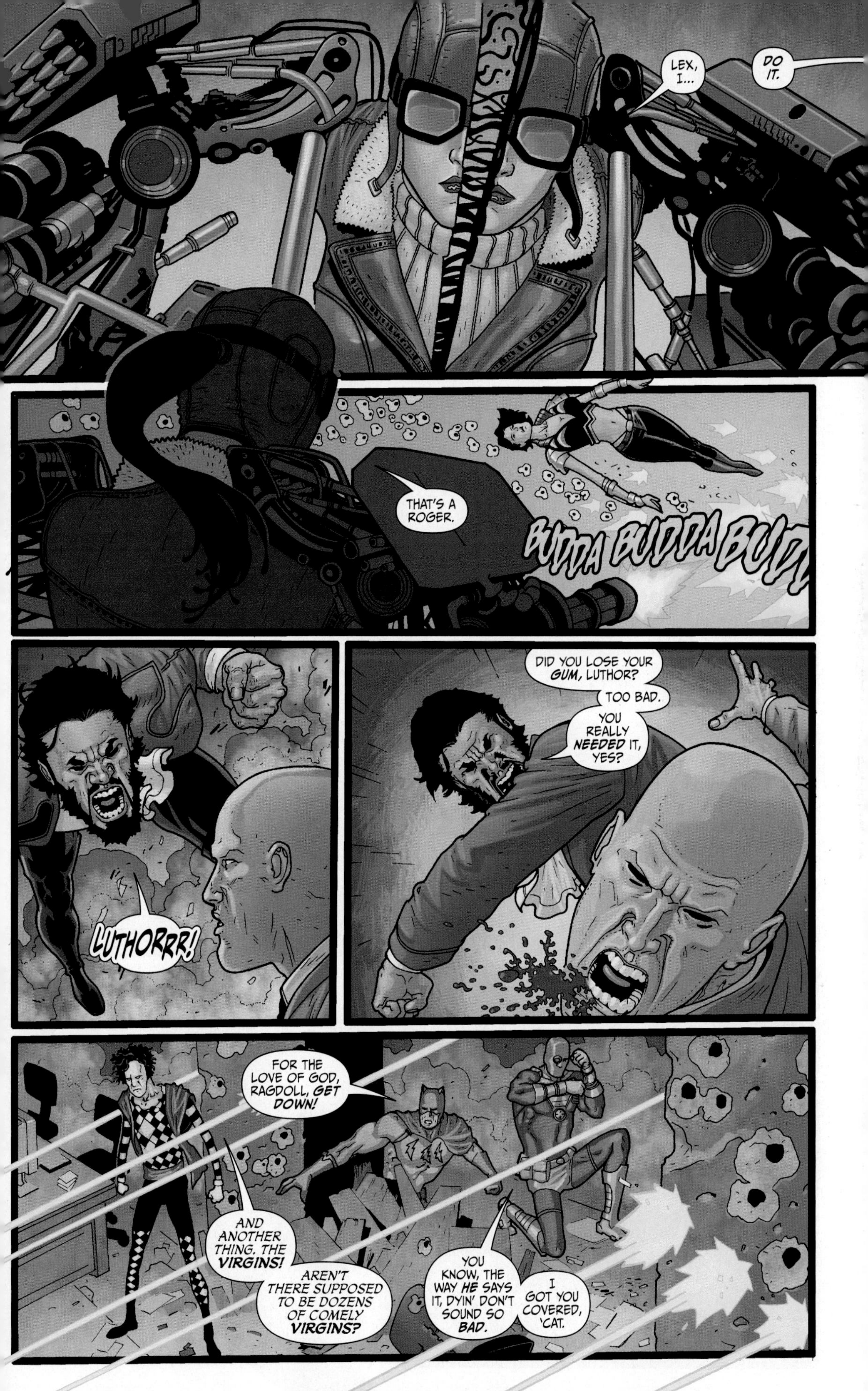
LEX, I...
DO IT.
THAT'S A ROGER.
BUDDA BUDDA BUDD
LUTHORRR!
DID YOU LOSE YOUR GUM, LUTHOR?
TOO BAD.
YOU REALLY NEEDED IT, YES?
FOR THE LOVE OF GOD, RAGDOLL, GET DOWN!
AND ANOTHER THING. THE VIRGINS!
AREN'T THERE SUPPOSED TO BE DOZENS OF COMELY VIRGINS?
YOU KNOW, THE WAY HE SAYS IT, DYIN' DON'T SOUND SO BAD.
I GOT YOU COVERED, 'CAT.

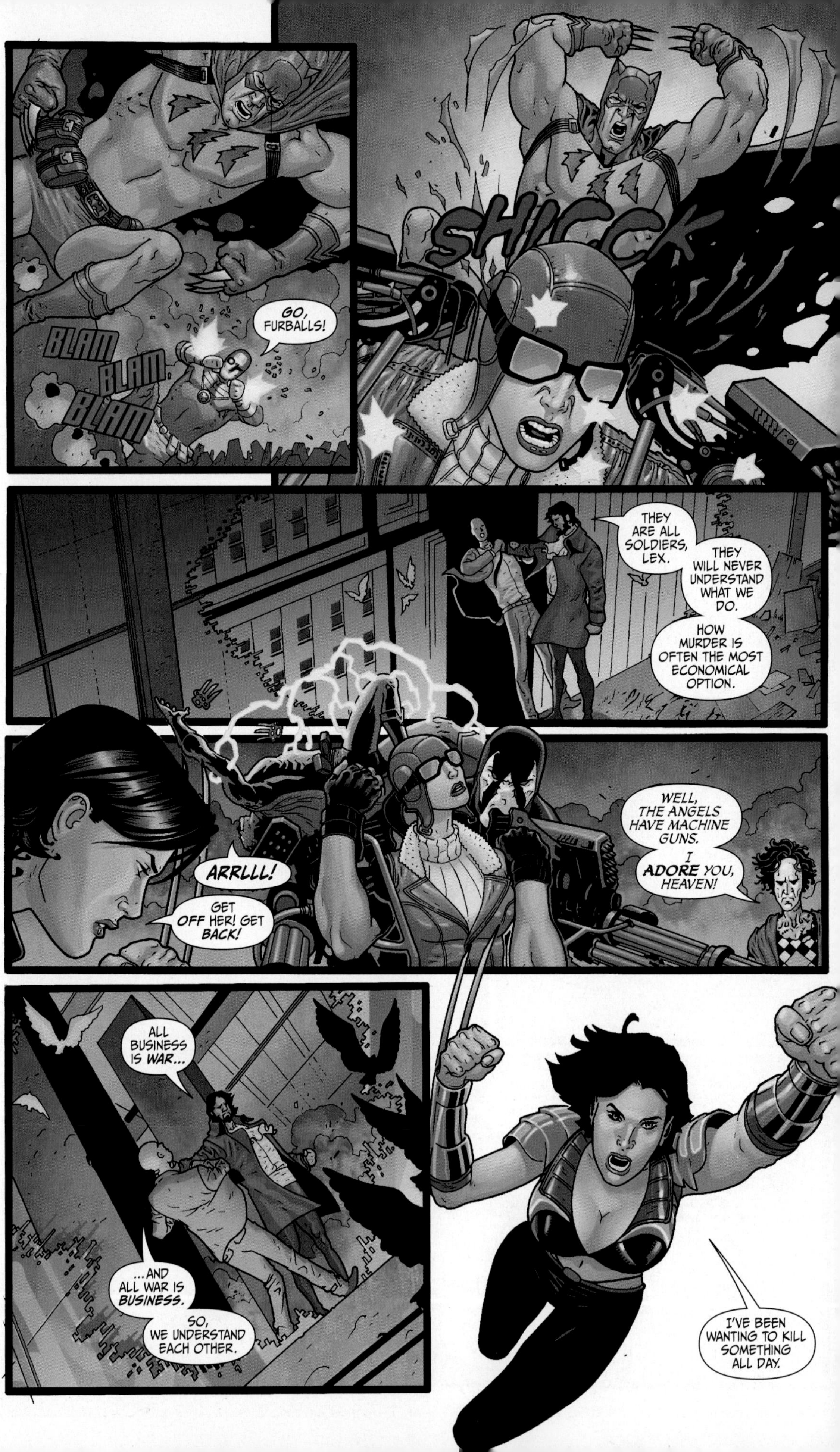
GO, FURBALLS!
BLAM BLAM BLAM
SHICCK
THEY ARE ALL SOLDIERS, LEX.
THEY WILL NEVER UNDERSTAND WHAT WE DO.
HOW MURDER IS OFTEN THE MOST ECONOMICAL OPTION.
ARRLLL!
GET OFF HER! GET BACK!
WELL, THE ANGELS HAVE MACHINE GUNS.
I ADORE YOU, HEAVEN!
ALL BUSINESS IS WAR...
...AND ALL WAR IS BUSINESS.
SO, WE UNDERSTAND EACH OTHER.
I'VE BEEN WANTING TO KILL SOMETHING ALL DAY.

WELL, *THIS* IS AWKWARD.

FAMILIES.

THEY CAN BE SO *STRESSFUL*.

FATHER.

I CAN'T ALLOW YOU TO KILL OUR EMPLOYER. THE SIX HAVING ANOTHER DEAD *EMPLOYER* WOULD *DEMOLISH* OUR REPUTATIONS.

DON'T MAKE ME LIVE OUT MY DREAMS AND SLIT YOUR CAROTID.

FINE. MY DAUGHTER IS SAFE. I'LL KEEP MY VOW.

I'M ASSUMING YOU HAVE A YACHT, LUTHOR?

SEVERAL. ⸸KAFF⸸

AND THERE'S *RUM* ON THIS VESSEL?

OH, YES.

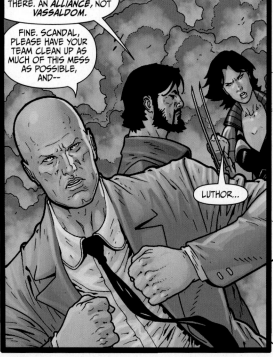

WE CAN NEGOTIATE THERE. AN *ALLIANCE*, NOT *VASSALDOM*.

FINE. SCANDAL, PLEASE HAVE YOUR TEAM CLEAN UP AS MUCH OF THIS MESS AS POSSIBLE, AND--

LUTHOR...

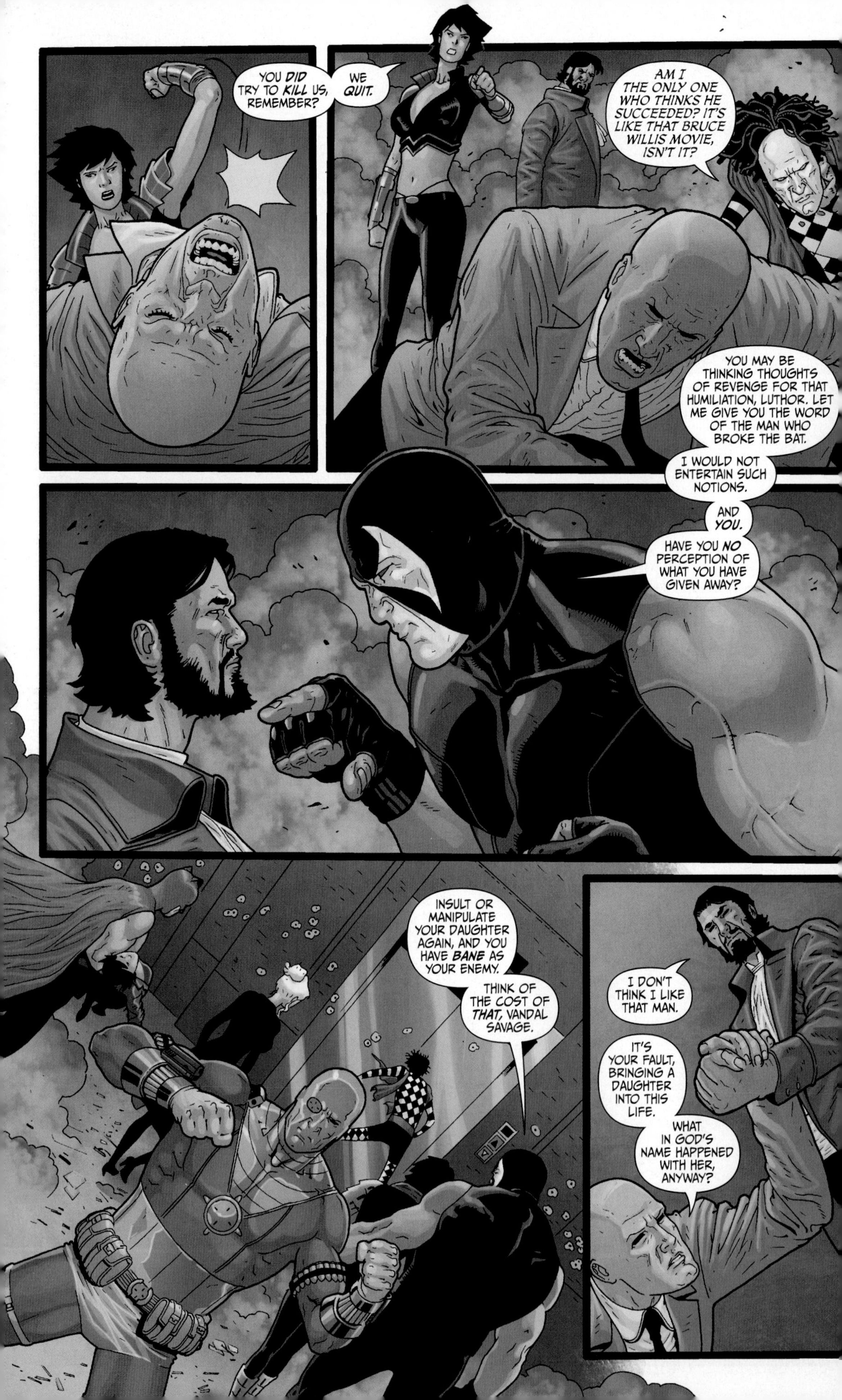

YOU DID TRY TO KILL US, REMEMBER?
WE QUIT.
AM I THE ONLY ONE WHO THINKS HE SUCCEEDED? IT'S LIKE THAT BRUCE WILLIS MOVIE, ISN'T IT?
YOU MAY BE THINKING THOUGHTS OF REVENGE FOR THAT HUMILIATION, LUTHOR. LET ME GIVE YOU THE WORD OF THE MAN WHO BROKE THE BAT.
I WOULD NOT ENTERTAIN SUCH NOTIONS.
AND YOU.
HAVE YOU NO PERCEPTION OF WHAT YOU HAVE GIVEN AWAY?
INSULT OR MANIPULATE YOUR DAUGHTER AGAIN, AND YOU HAVE BANE AS YOUR ENEMY.
THINK OF THE COST OF THAT, VANDAL SAVAGE.
I DON'T THINK I LIKE THAT MAN.
IT'S YOUR FAULT, BRINGING A DAUGHTER INTO THIS LIFE.
WHAT IN GOD'S NAME HAPPENED WITH HER, ANYWAY?

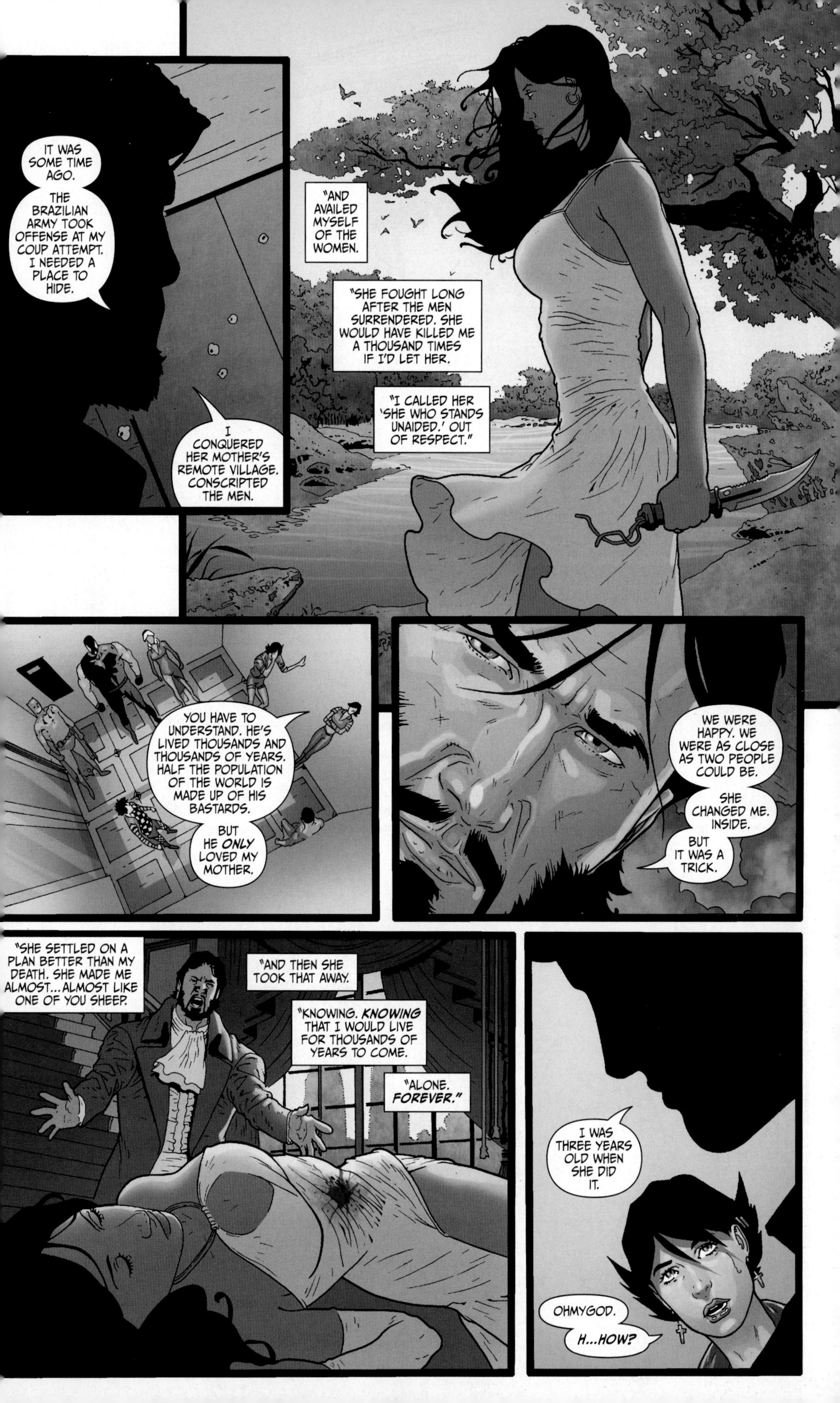
IT WAS SOME TIME AGO.
THE BRAZILIAN ARMY TOOK OFFENSE AT MY COUP ATTEMPT. I NEEDED A PLACE TO HIDE.
I CONQUERED HER MOTHER'S REMOTE VILLAGE. CONSCRIPTED THE MEN.
"AND AVAILED MYSELF OF THE WOMEN.
"SHE FOUGHT LONG AFTER THE MEN SURRENDERED. SHE WOULD HAVE KILLED ME A THOUSAND TIMES IF I'D LET HER.
"I CALLED HER 'SHE WHO STANDS UNAIDED.' OUT OF RESPECT."
YOU HAVE TO UNDERSTAND. HE'S LIVED THOUSANDS AND THOUSANDS OF YEARS. HALF THE POPULATION OF THE WORLD IS MADE UP OF HIS BASTARDS.
BUT HE *ONLY* LOVED MY MOTHER.
WE WERE HAPPY. WE WERE AS CLOSE AS TWO PEOPLE COULD BE.
SHE CHANGED ME. INSIDE.
BUT IT WAS A TRICK.
"SHE SETTLED ON A PLAN BETTER THAN MY DEATH. SHE MADE ME ALMOST...ALMOST LIKE ONE OF YOU SHEEP.
"AND THEN SHE TOOK THAT AWAY.
"KNOWING. *KNOWING* THAT I WOULD LIVE FOR THOUSANDS OF YEARS TO COME.
"ALONE. *FOREVER.*"
I WAS THREE YEARS OLD WHEN SHE DID IT.
OHMYGOD.
H...HOW?

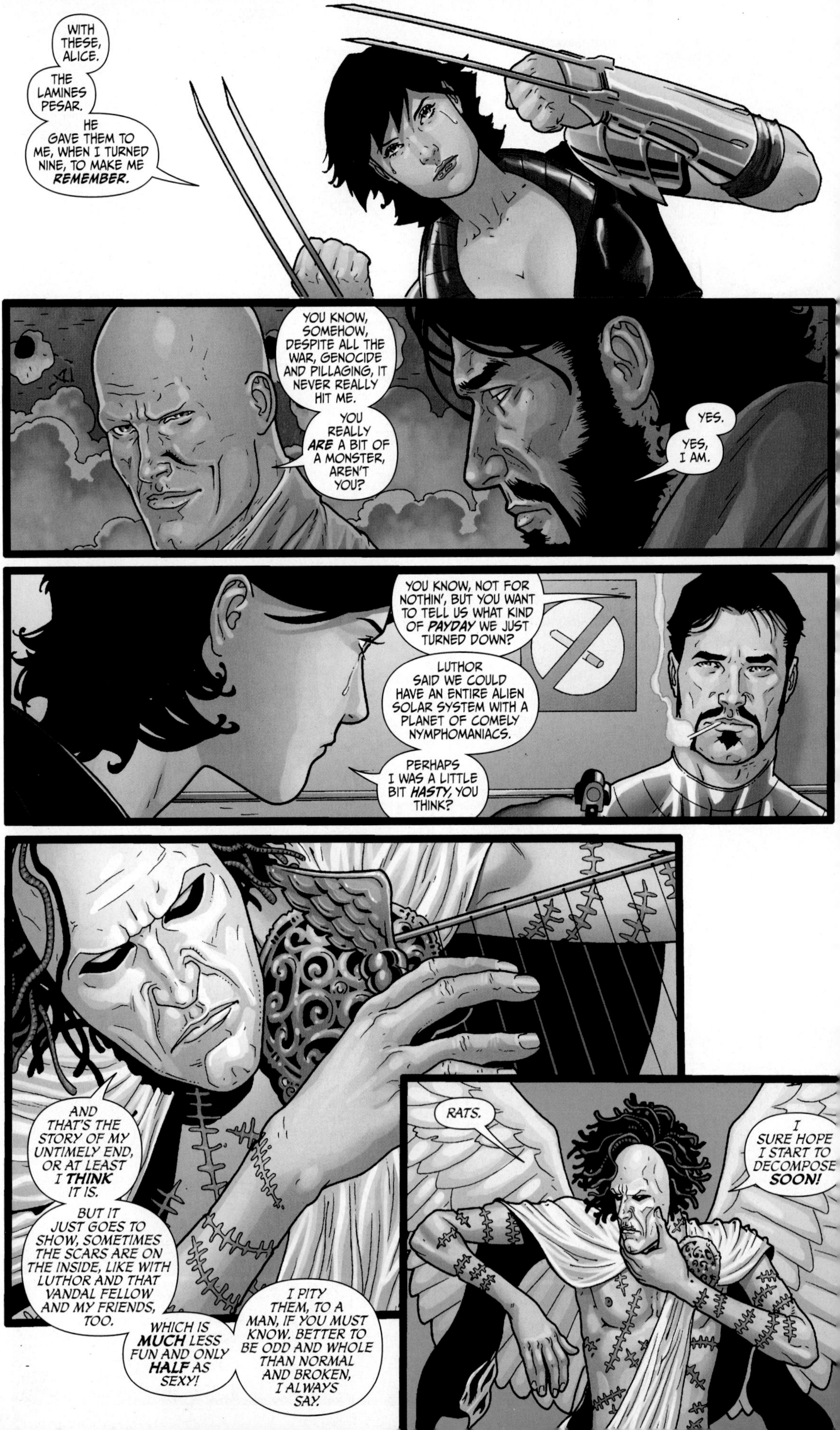

WITH THESE, ALICE.
THE LAMINES PESAR.
HE GAVE THEM TO ME, WHEN I TURNED NINE, TO MAKE ME REMEMBER.
YOU KNOW, SOMEHOW, DESPITE ALL THE WAR, GENOCIDE AND PILLAGING, IT NEVER REALLY HIT ME.
YOU REALLY ARE A BIT OF A MONSTER, AREN'T YOU?
YES.
YES, I AM.
YOU KNOW, NOT FOR NOTHIN', BUT YOU WANT TO TELL US WHAT KIND OF PAYDAY WE JUST TURNED DOWN?
LUTHOR SAID WE COULD HAVE AN ENTIRE ALIEN SOLAR SYSTEM WITH A PLANET OF COMELY NYMPHOMANIACS.
PERHAPS I WAS A LITTLE BIT HASTY, YOU THINK?
AND THAT'S THE STORY OF MY UNTIMELY END, OR AT LEAST I THINK IT IS.
BUT IT JUST GOES TO SHOW, SOMETIMES THE SCARS ARE ON THE INSIDE, LIKE WITH LUTHOR AND THAT VANDAL FELLOW AND MY FRIENDS, TOO.
WHICH IS MUCH LESS FUN AND ONLY HALF AS SEXY!
I PITY THEM, TO A MAN, IF YOU MUST KNOW. BETTER TO BE ODD AND WHOLE THAN NORMAL AND BROKEN, I ALWAYS SAY.
RATS.
I SURE HOPE I START TO DECOMPOSE SOON!

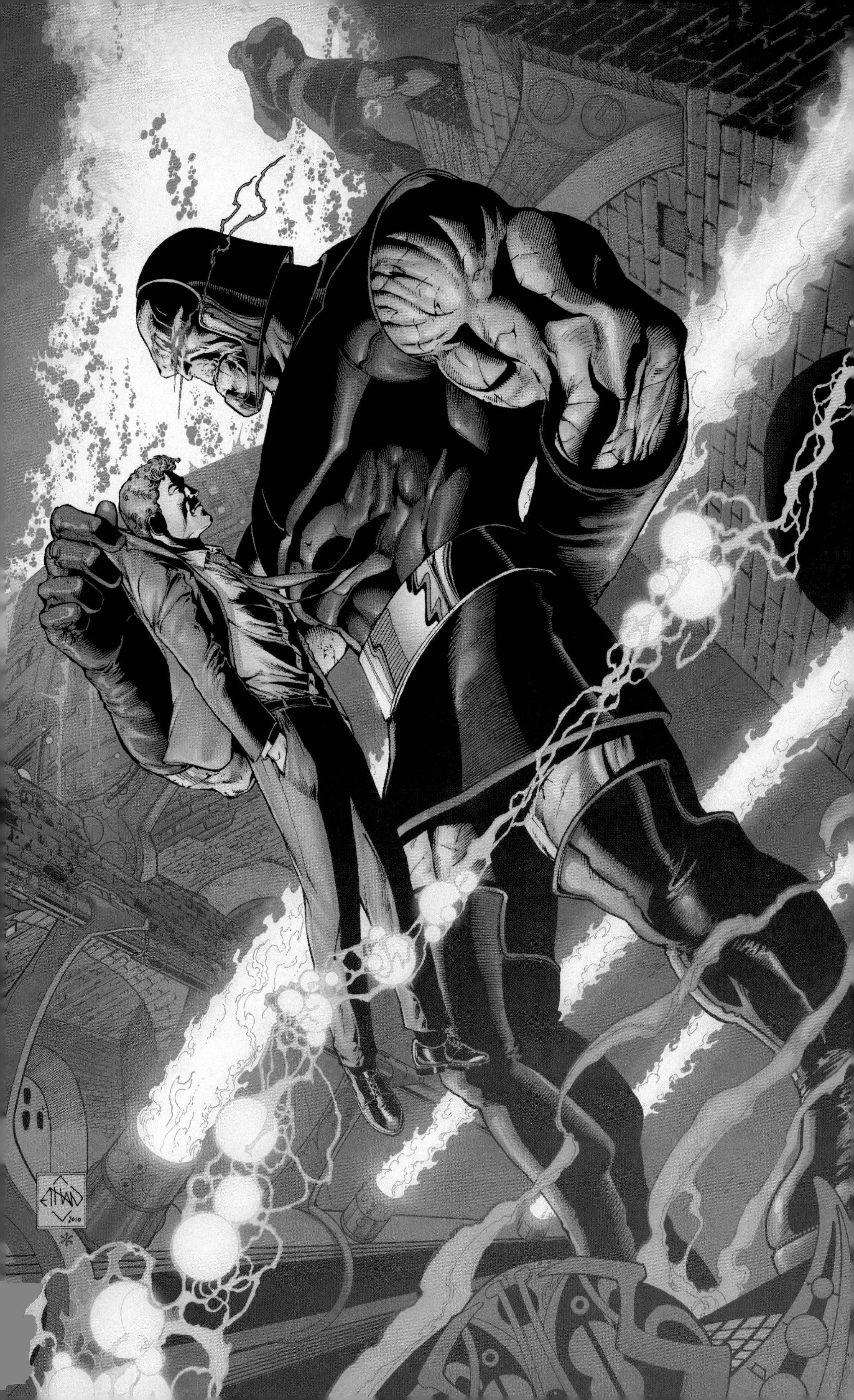

young lex luthor in:

FATHER BOX

PAUL **CORNELL** writer
MARCO **RUDY** artist

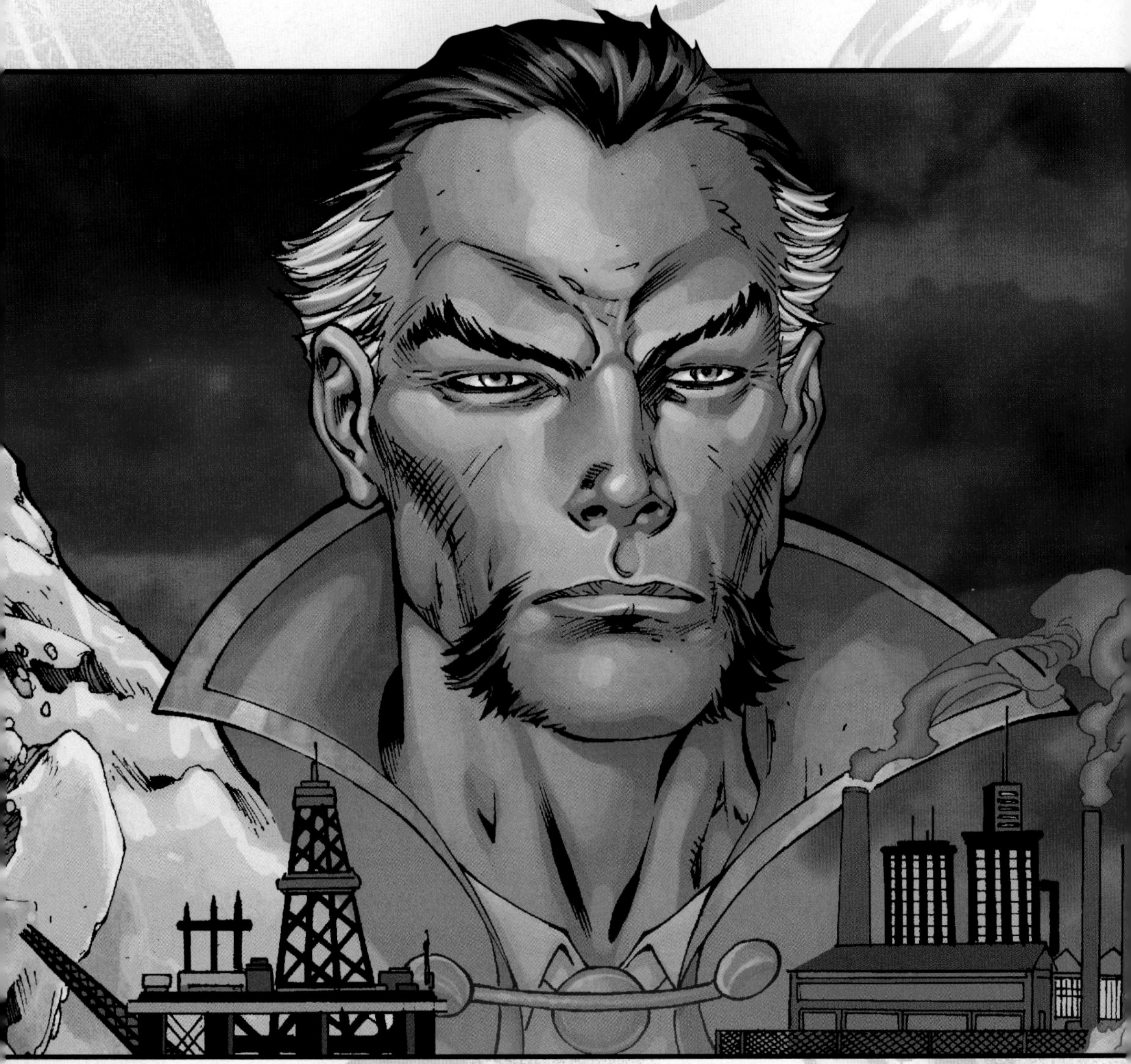

A FATHER'S BOX

PAUL **CORNELL** writer
ED **BENES** artist

cover by
ETHAN **VAN SCIVER** & **HI-FI**

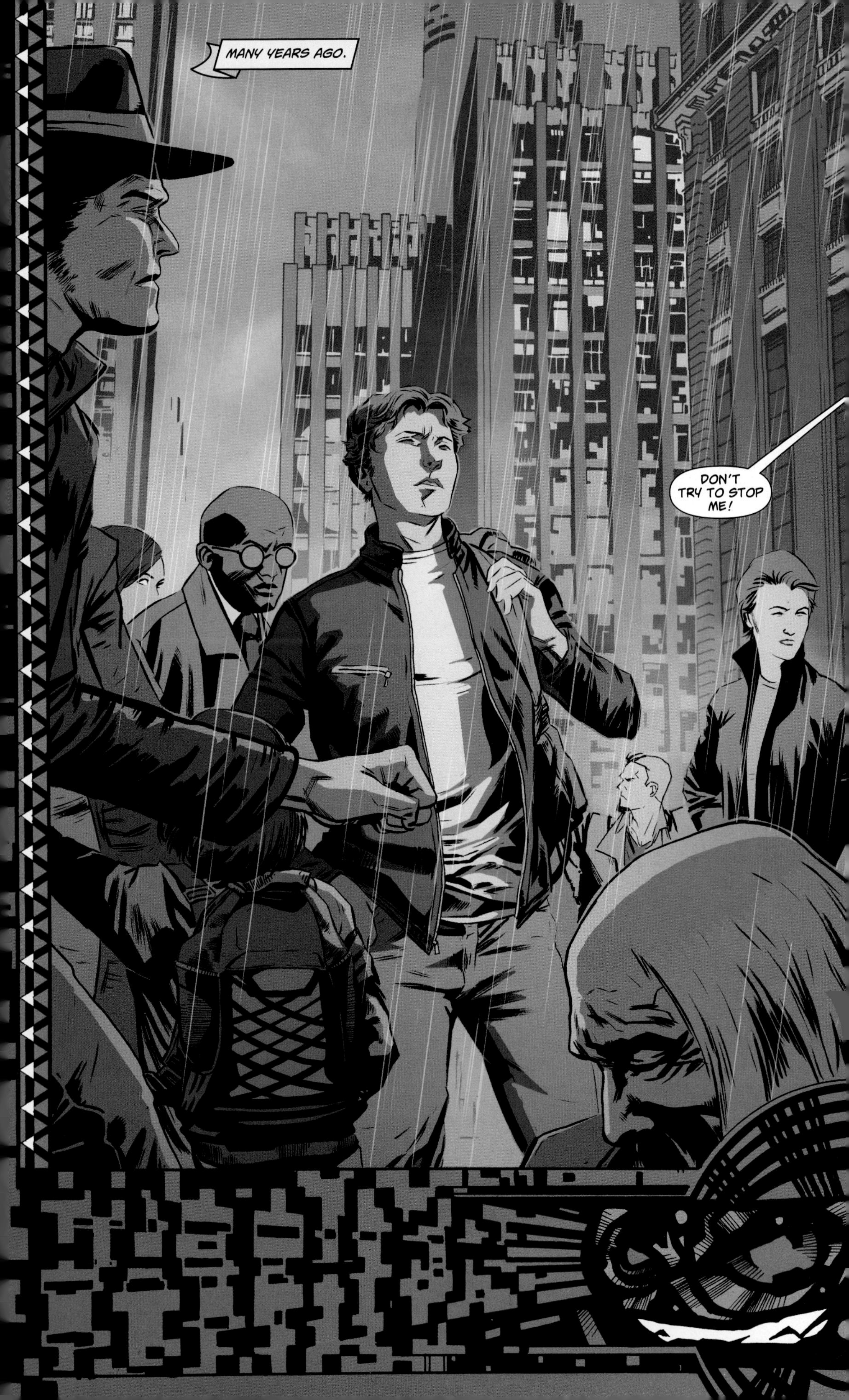
MANY YEARS AGO.
DON'T TRY TO STOP ME!

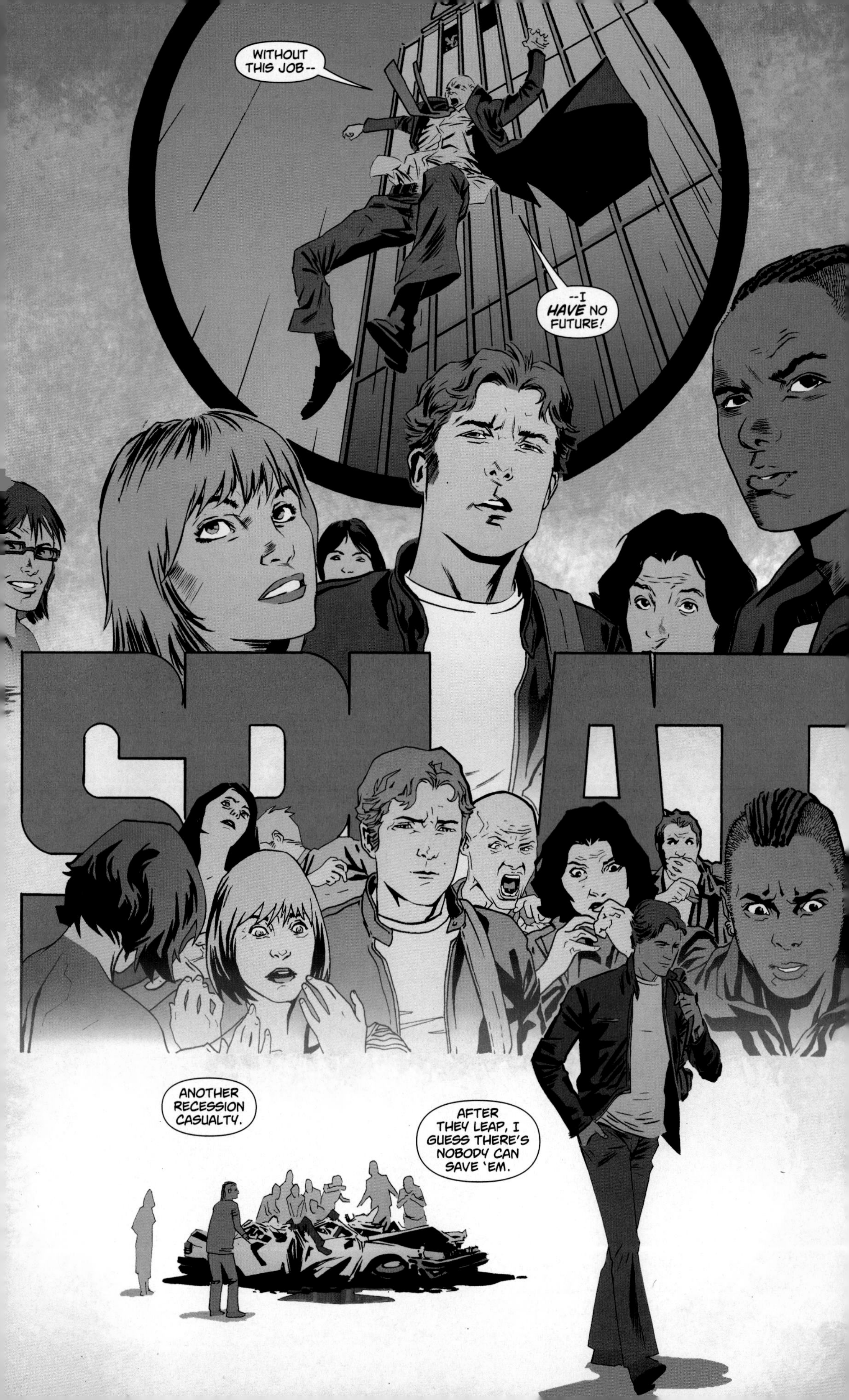
WITHOUT THIS JOB--
--I *HAVE* NO FUTURE!
ANOTHER RECESSION CASUALTY.
AFTER THEY LEAP, I GUESS THERE'S NOBODY CAN SAVE 'EM.

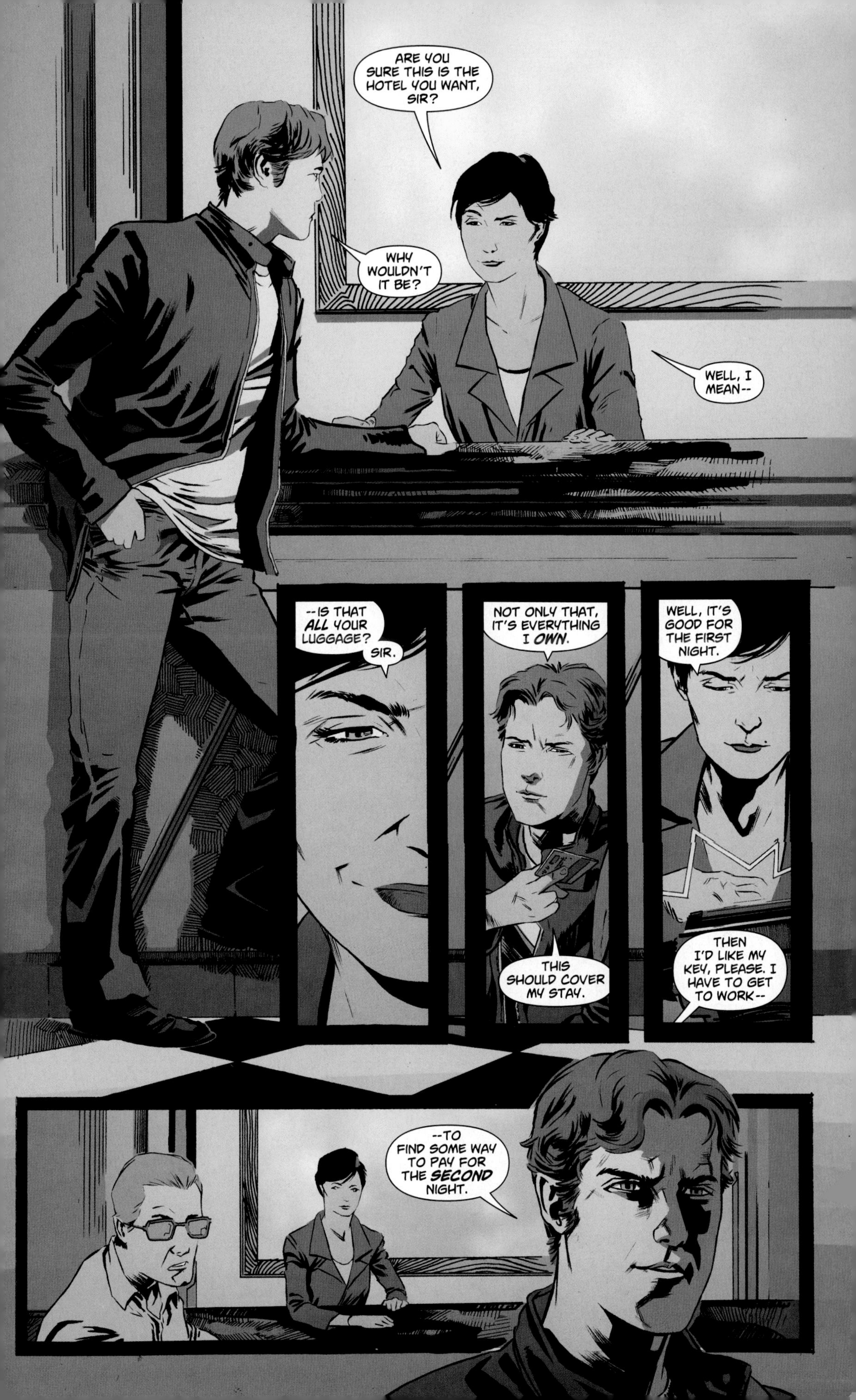
ARE YOU SURE THIS IS THE HOTEL YOU WANT, SIR?
WHY WOULDN'T IT BE?
WELL, I MEAN--
--IS THAT ALL YOUR LUGGAGE?
SIR.
NOT ONLY THAT, IT'S EVERYTHING I OWN.
THIS SHOULD COVER MY STAY.
WELL, IT'S GOOD FOR THE FIRST NIGHT.
THEN I'D LIKE MY KEY, PLEASE. I HAVE TO GET TO WORK--
--TO FIND SOME WAY TO PAY FOR THE SECOND NIGHT.

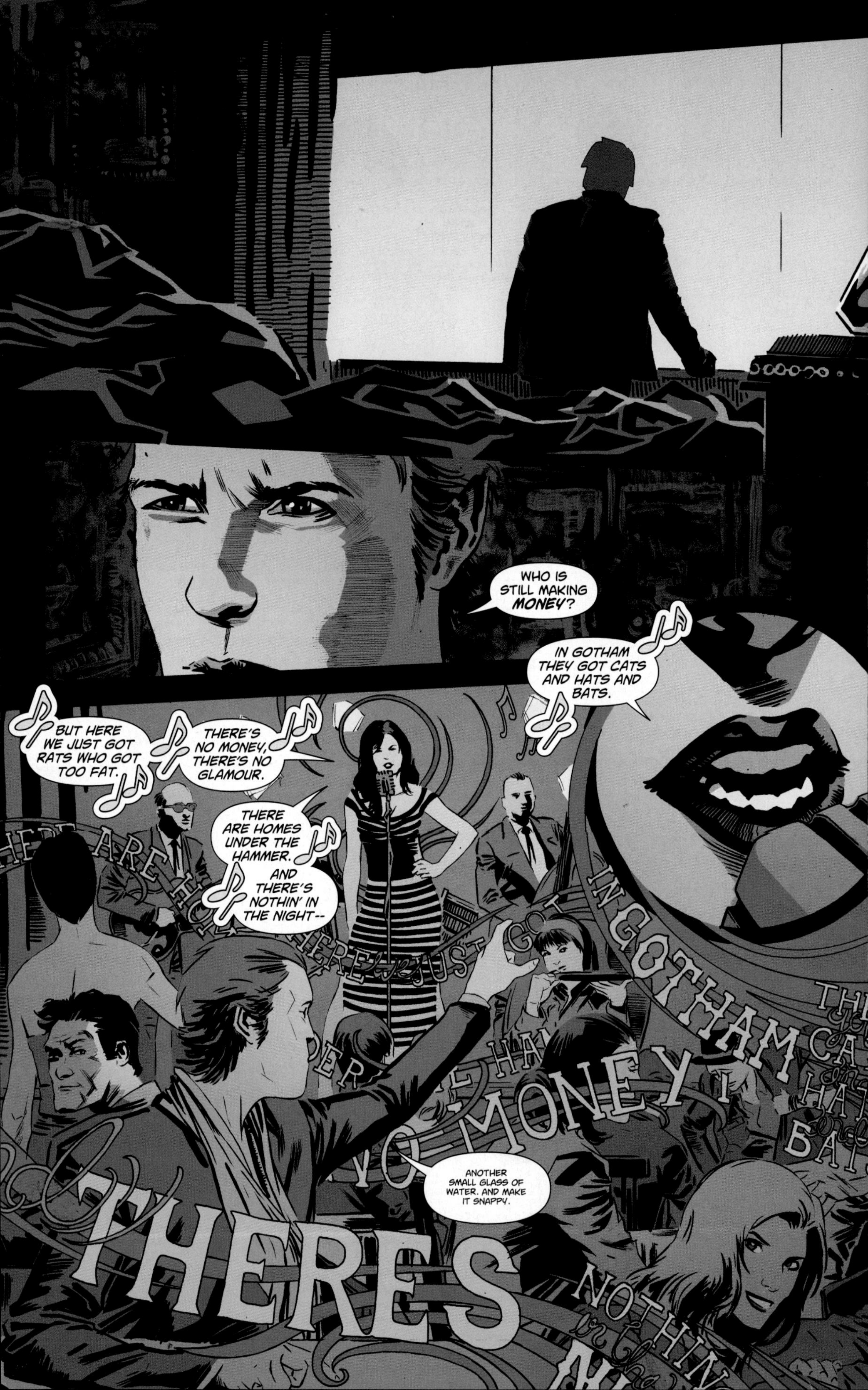
WHO IS STILL MAKING *MONEY*?
IN GOTHAM THEY GOT CATS AND HATS AND BATS.
BUT HERE WE JUST GOT RATS WHO GOT TOO FAT.
THERE'S NO MONEY, THERE'S NO GLAMOUR.
THERE ARE HOMES UNDER THE HAMMER.
AND THERE'S NOTHIN' IN THE NIGHT--
ANOTHER SMALL GLASS OF WATER. AND MAKE IT SNAPPY.
IN GOTHAM
NO MONEY
THERES

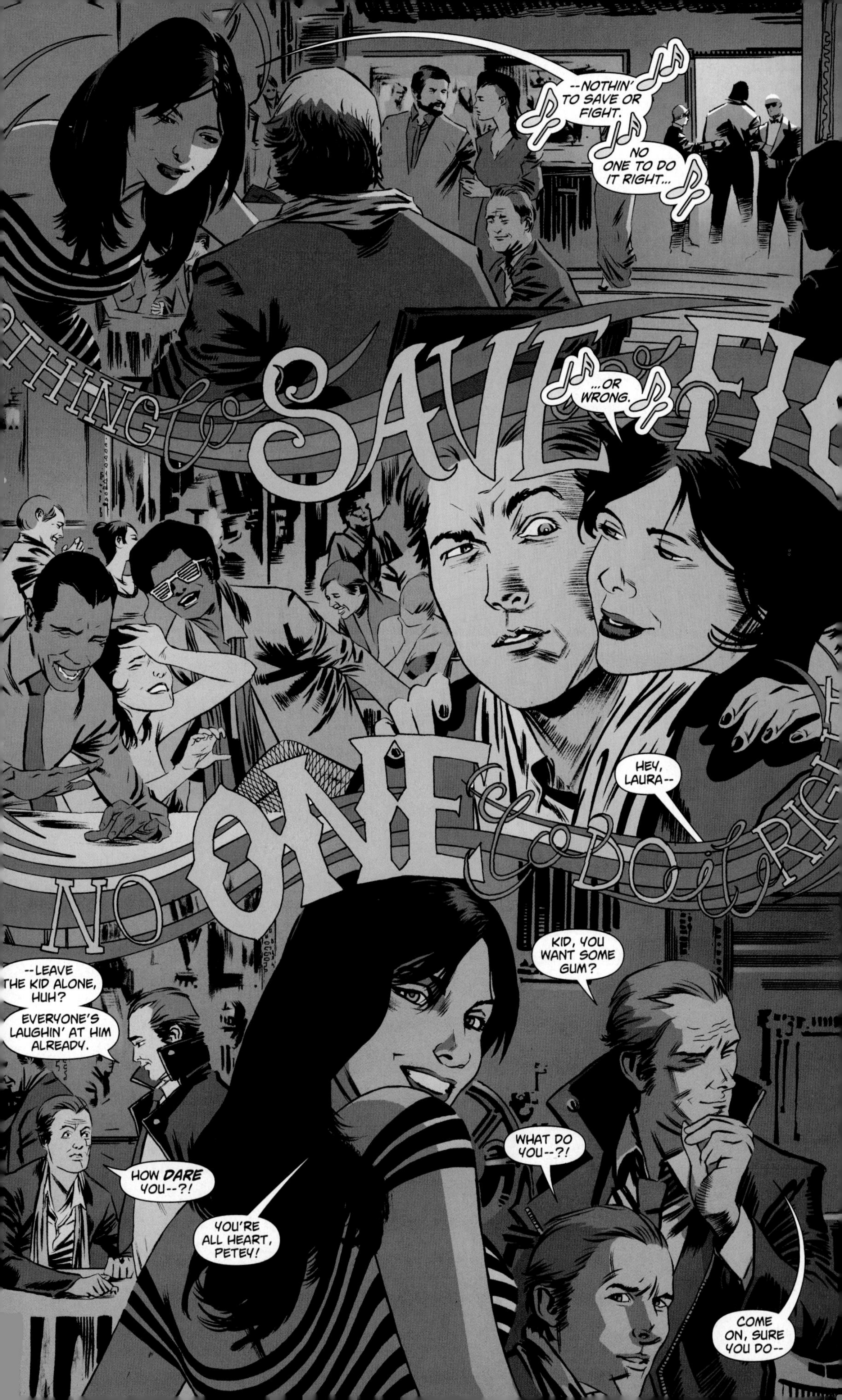
--NOTHIN' TO SAVE OR FIGHT.
NO ONE TO DO IT RIGHT...
...OR WRONG.
HEY, LAURA--
--LEAVE THE KID ALONE, HUH?
EVERYONE'S LAUGHIN' AT HIM ALREADY.
KID, YOU WANT SOME GUM?
HOW DARE YOU--?!
YOU'RE ALL HEART, PETEY!
WHAT DO YOU--?!
COME ON, SURE YOU DO--

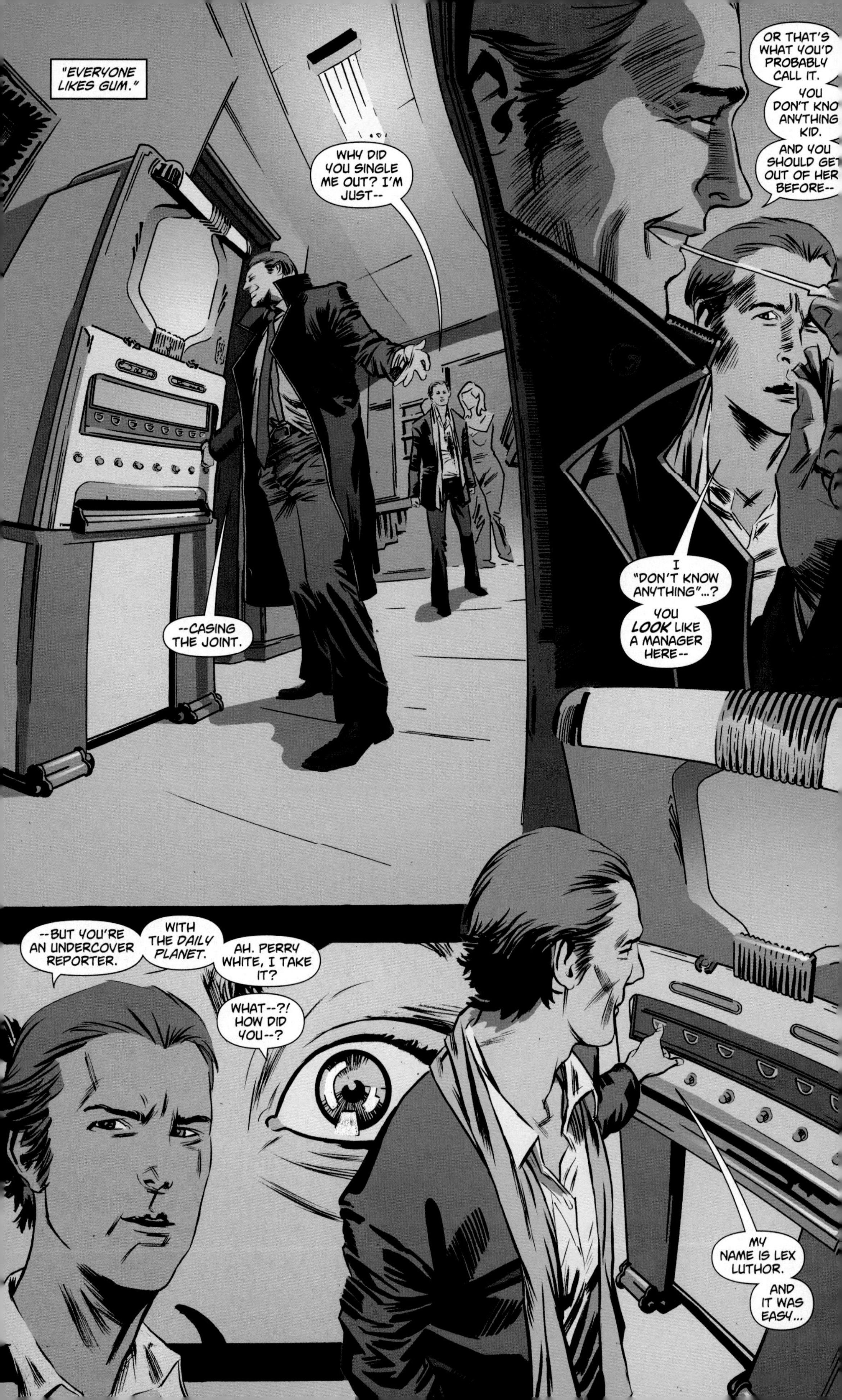
"EVERYONE LIKES GUM."
WHY DID YOU SINGLE ME OUT? I'M JUST--
--CASING THE JOINT.
OR THAT'S WHAT YOU'D PROBABLY CALL IT.
YOU DON'T KNO ANYTHING KID.
AND YOU SHOULD GET OUT OF HER BEFORE--
I "DON'T KNOW ANYTHING"...?
YOU LOOK LIKE A MANAGER HERE--
--BUT YOU'RE AN UNDERCOVER REPORTER.
WITH THE DAILY PLANET.
AH. PERRY WHITE, I TAKE IT?
WHAT--?! HOW DID YOU--?
MY NAME IS LEX LUTHOR.
AND IT WAS EASY...

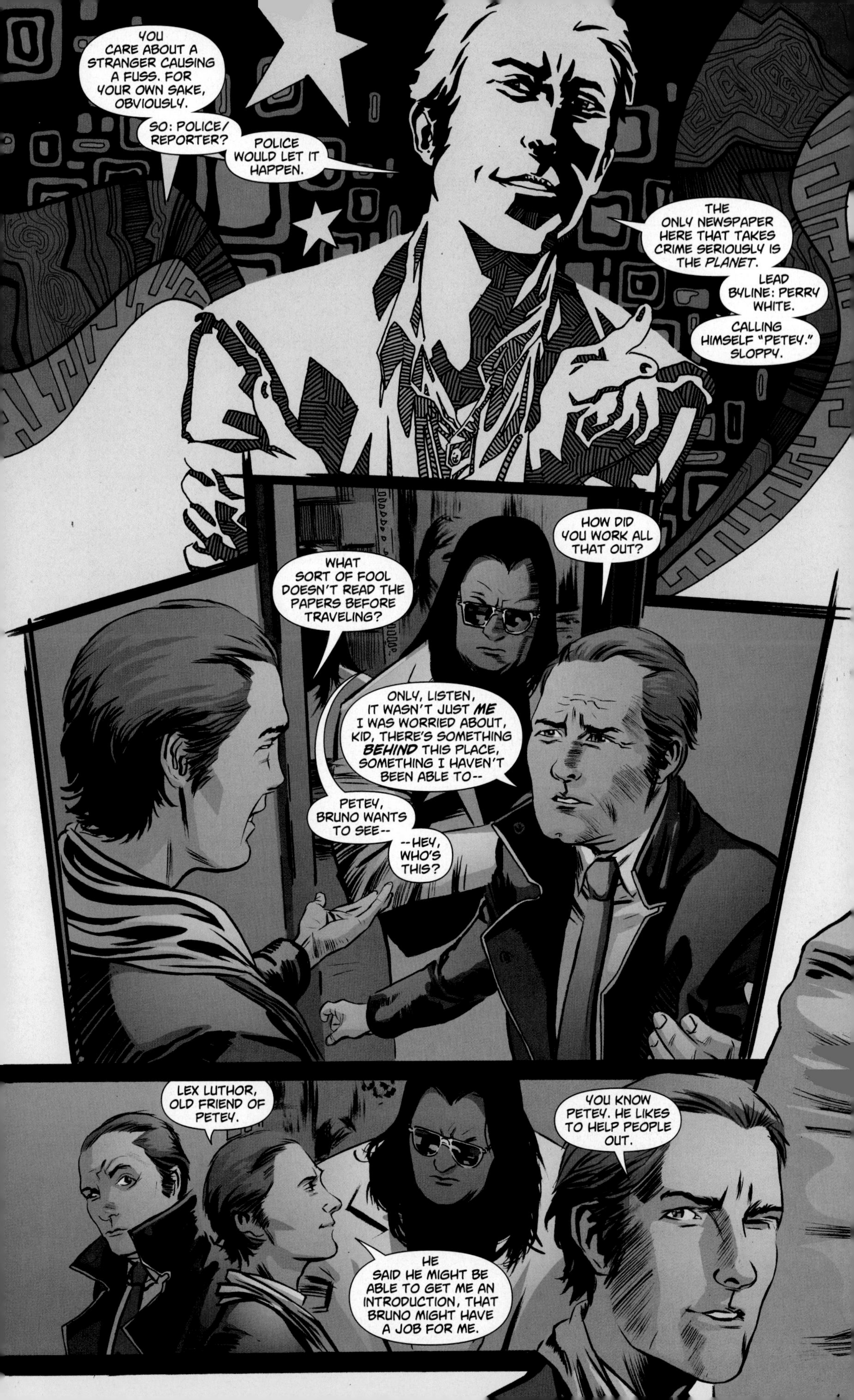

YOU CARE ABOUT A STRANGER CAUSING A FUSS. FOR YOUR OWN SAKE, OBVIOUSLY.
SO: POLICE/ REPORTER?
POLICE WOULD LET IT HAPPEN.
THE ONLY NEWSPAPER HERE THAT TAKES CRIME SERIOUSLY IS THE *PLANET*.
LEAD BYLINE: PERRY WHITE.
CALLING HIMSELF "PETEY." SLOPPY.
HOW DID YOU WORK ALL THAT OUT?
WHAT SORT OF FOOL DOESN'T READ THE PAPERS BEFORE TRAVELING?
ONLY, LISTEN, IT WASN'T JUST ***ME*** I WAS WORRIED ABOUT, KID, THERE'S SOMETHING ***BEHIND*** THIS PLACE, SOMETHING I HAVEN'T BEEN ABLE TO--
PETEY, BRUNO WANTS TO SEE--
--HEY, WHO'S THIS?
LEX LUTHOR, OLD FRIEND OF PETEY.
YOU KNOW PETEY. HE LIKES TO HELP PEOPLE OUT.
HE SAID HE MIGHT BE ABLE TO GET ME AN INTRODUCTION, THAT BRUNO MIGHT HAVE A JOB FOR ME.

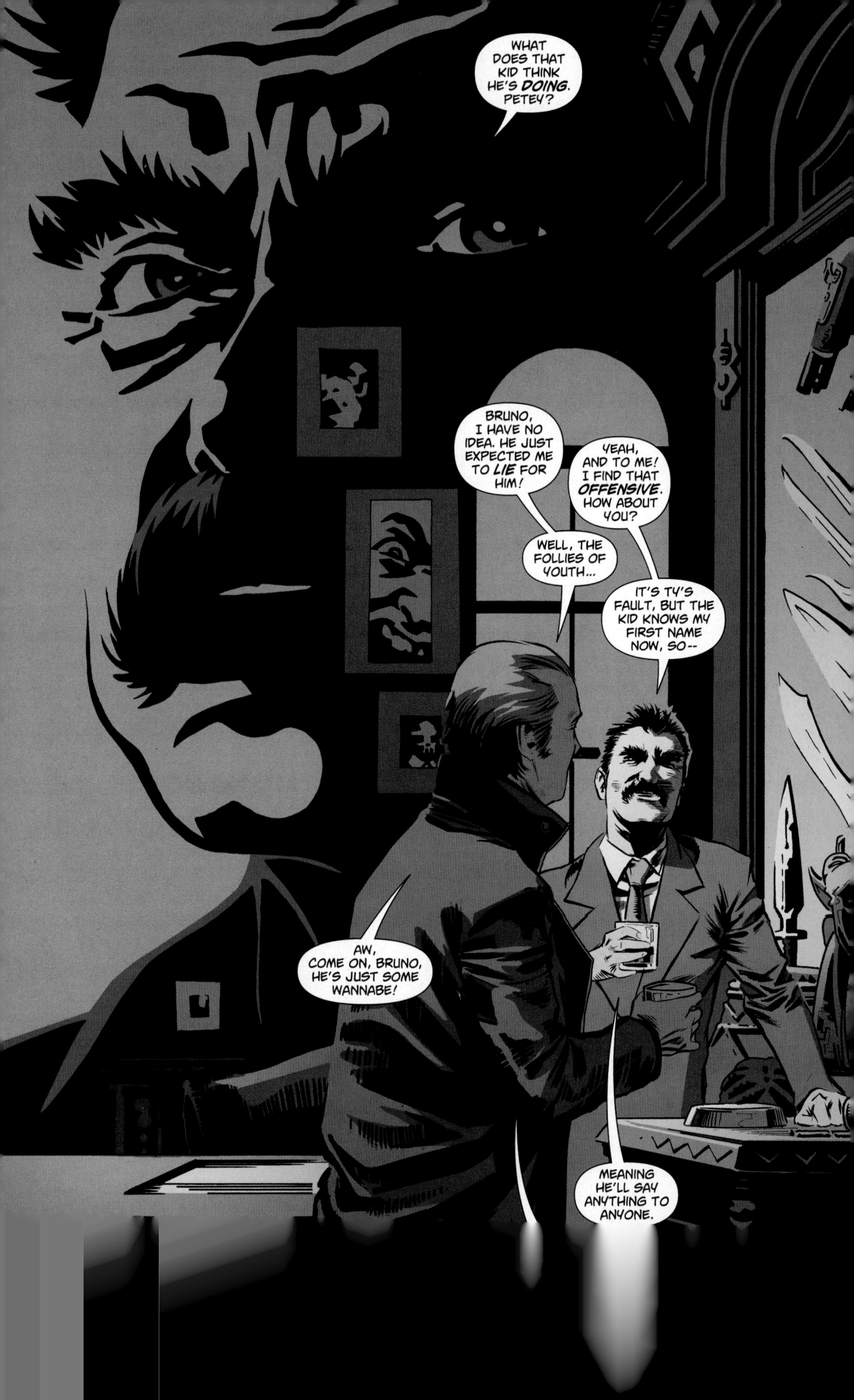
WHAT DOES THAT KID THINK HE'S DOING. PETEY?
BRUNO, I HAVE NO IDEA. HE JUST EXPECTED ME TO LIE FOR HIM!
YEAH, AND TO ME! I FIND THAT OFFENSIVE. HOW ABOUT YOU?
WELL, THE FOLLIES OF YOUTH...
IT'S TY'S FAULT, BUT THE KID KNOWS MY FIRST NAME NOW, SO--
AW, COME ON, BRUNO, HE'S JUST SOME WANNABE!
MEANING HE'LL SAY ANYTHING TO ANYONE.

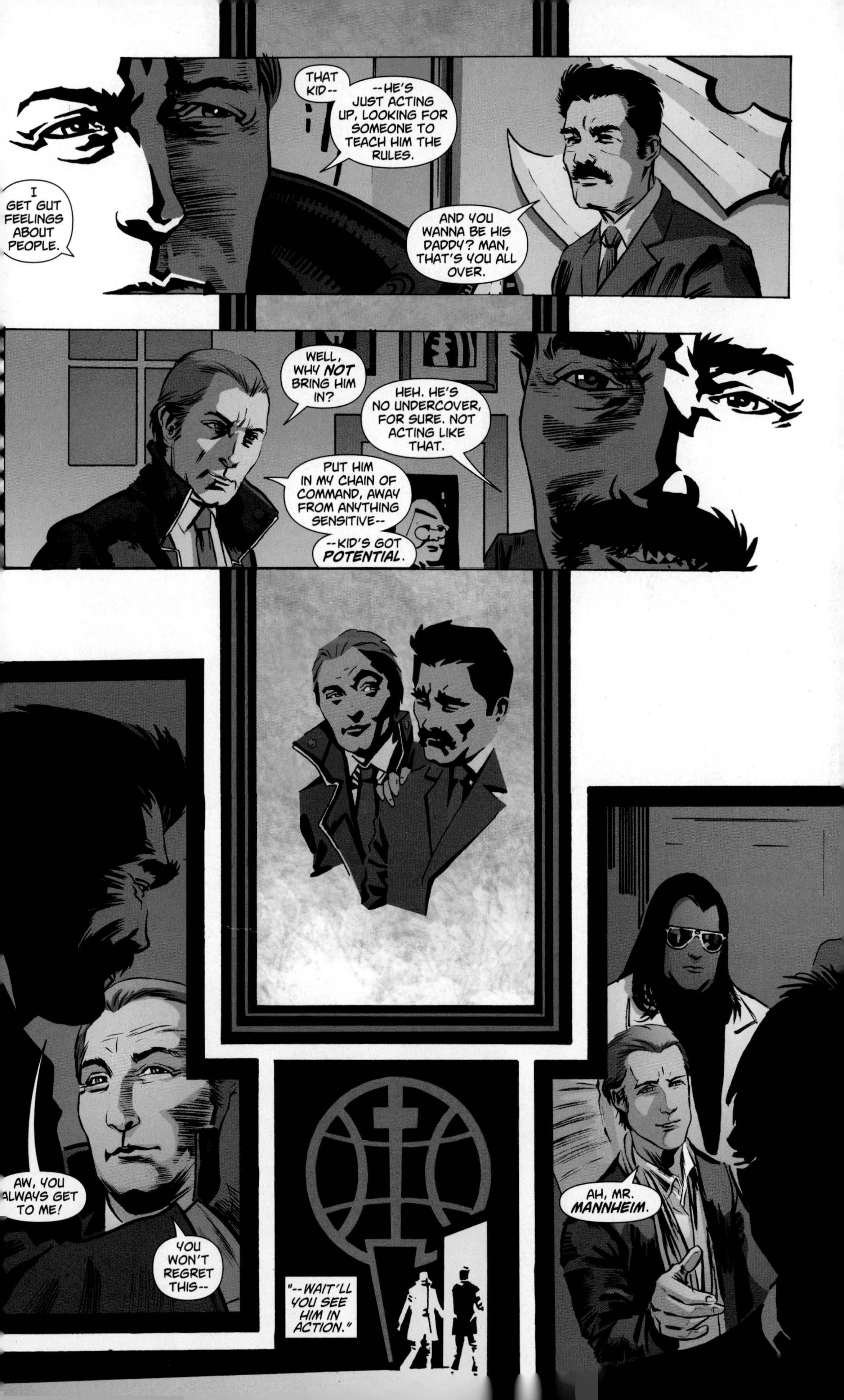
THAT KID--
--HE'S JUST ACTING UP, LOOKING FOR SOMEONE TO TEACH HIM THE RULES.
I GET GUT FEELINGS ABOUT PEOPLE.
AND YOU WANNA BE HIS DADDY? MAN, THAT'S YOU ALL OVER.
WELL, WHY NOT BRING HIM IN?
HEH. HE'S NO UNDERCOVER, FOR SURE. NOT ACTING LIKE THAT.
PUT HIM IN MY CHAIN OF COMMAND, AWAY FROM ANYTHING SENSITIVE--
--KID'S GOT POTENTIAL.
AW, YOU ALWAYS GET TO ME!
YOU WON'T REGRET THIS--
"--WAIT'LL YOU SEE HIM IN ACTION."
AH, MR. MANNHEIM.

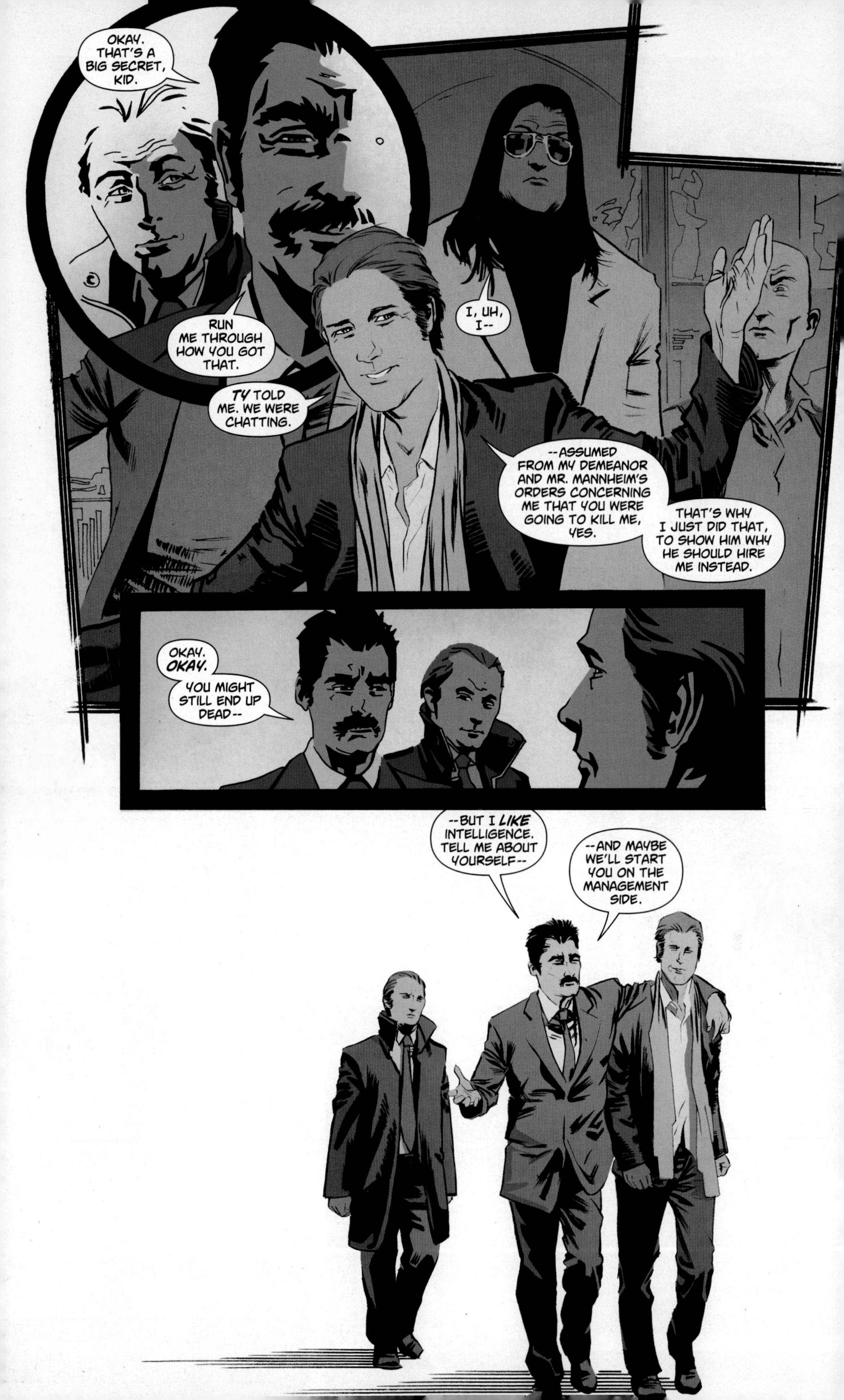
OKAY. THAT'S A BIG SECRET, KID.
RUN ME THROUGH HOW YOU GOT THAT.
TY TOLD ME. WE WERE CHATTING.
I, UH, I--
--ASSUMED FROM MY DEMEANOR AND MR. MANNHEIM'S ORDERS CONCERNING ME THAT YOU WERE GOING TO KILL ME, YES.
THAT'S WHY I JUST DID THAT, TO SHOW HIM WHY HE SHOULD HIRE ME INSTEAD.
OKAY. OKAY. YOU MIGHT STILL END UP DEAD--
--BUT I LIKE INTELLIGENCE. TELL ME ABOUT YOURSELF--
--AND MAYBE WE'LL START YOU ON THE MANAGEMENT SIDE.

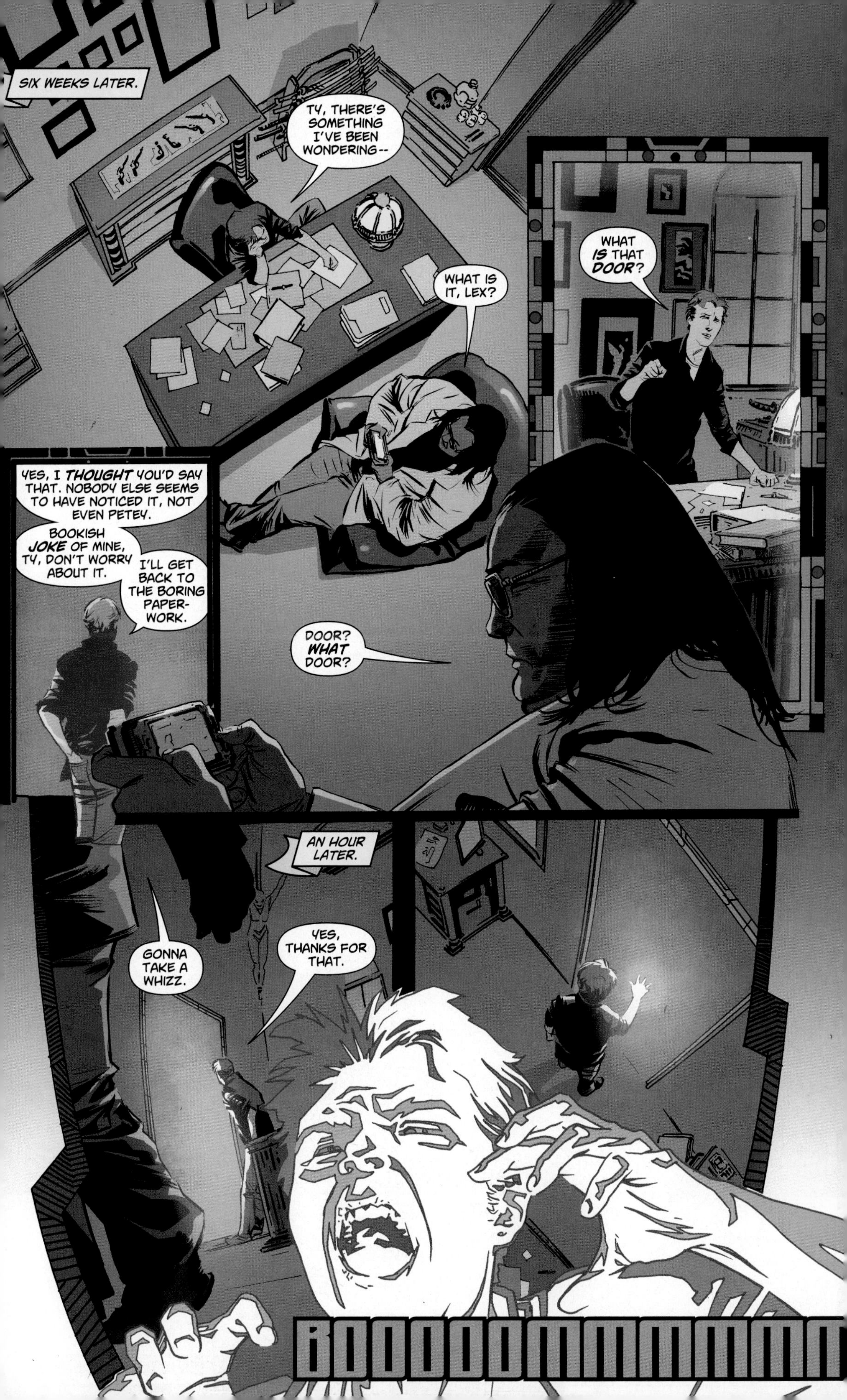
SIX WEEKS LATER.
TY, THERE'S SOMETHING I'VE BEEN WONDERING--
WHAT IS IT, LEX?
WHAT IS THAT DOOR?
DOOR? WHAT DOOR?
YES, I THOUGHT YOU'D SAY THAT. NOBODY ELSE SEEMS TO HAVE NOTICED IT, NOT EVEN PETEY.
BOOKISH JOKE OF MINE, TY, DON'T WORRY ABOUT IT.
I'LL GET BACK TO THE BORING PAPER-WORK.
AN HOUR LATER.
GONNA TAKE A WHIZZ.
YES, THANKS FOR THAT.
BOOOOOMMMMMMM

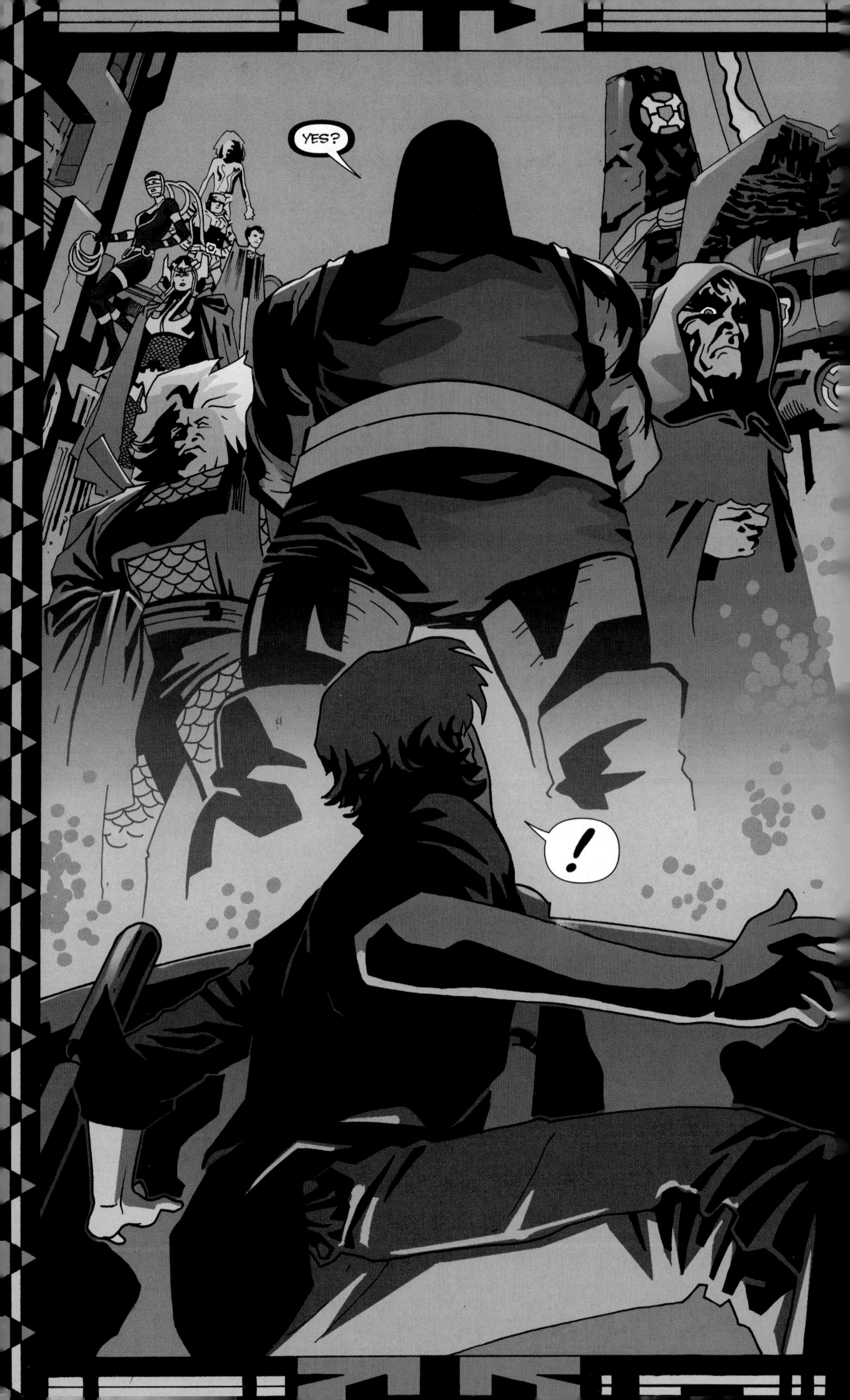
YES?
!

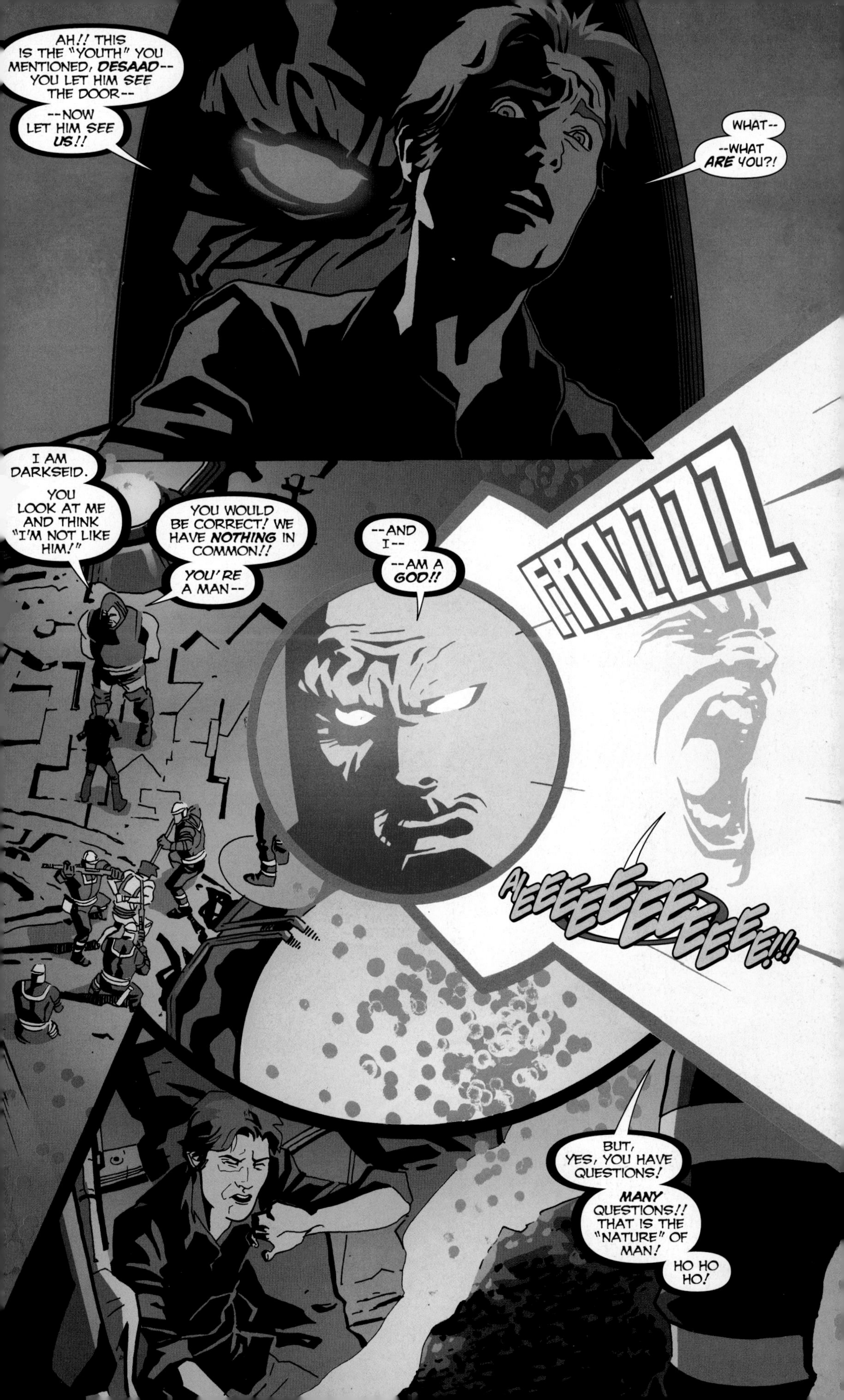

AH!! THIS IS THE "YOUTH" YOU MENTIONED, DESAAD-- YOU LET HIM SEE THE DOOR--
--NOW LET HIM SEE US!!
WHAT--
--WHAT ARE YOU?!
I AM DARKSEID.
YOU LOOK AT ME AND THINK "I'M NOT LIKE HIM!"
YOU WOULD BE CORRECT! WE HAVE NOTHING IN COMMON!!
YOU'RE A MAN--
--AND I--
--AM A GOD!!
FRAZZZZ
AEEEEEEEEEEEEEEE!!
BUT, YES, YOU HAVE QUESTIONS!
MANY QUESTIONS!! THAT IS THE "NATURE" OF MAN!
HO HO HO!

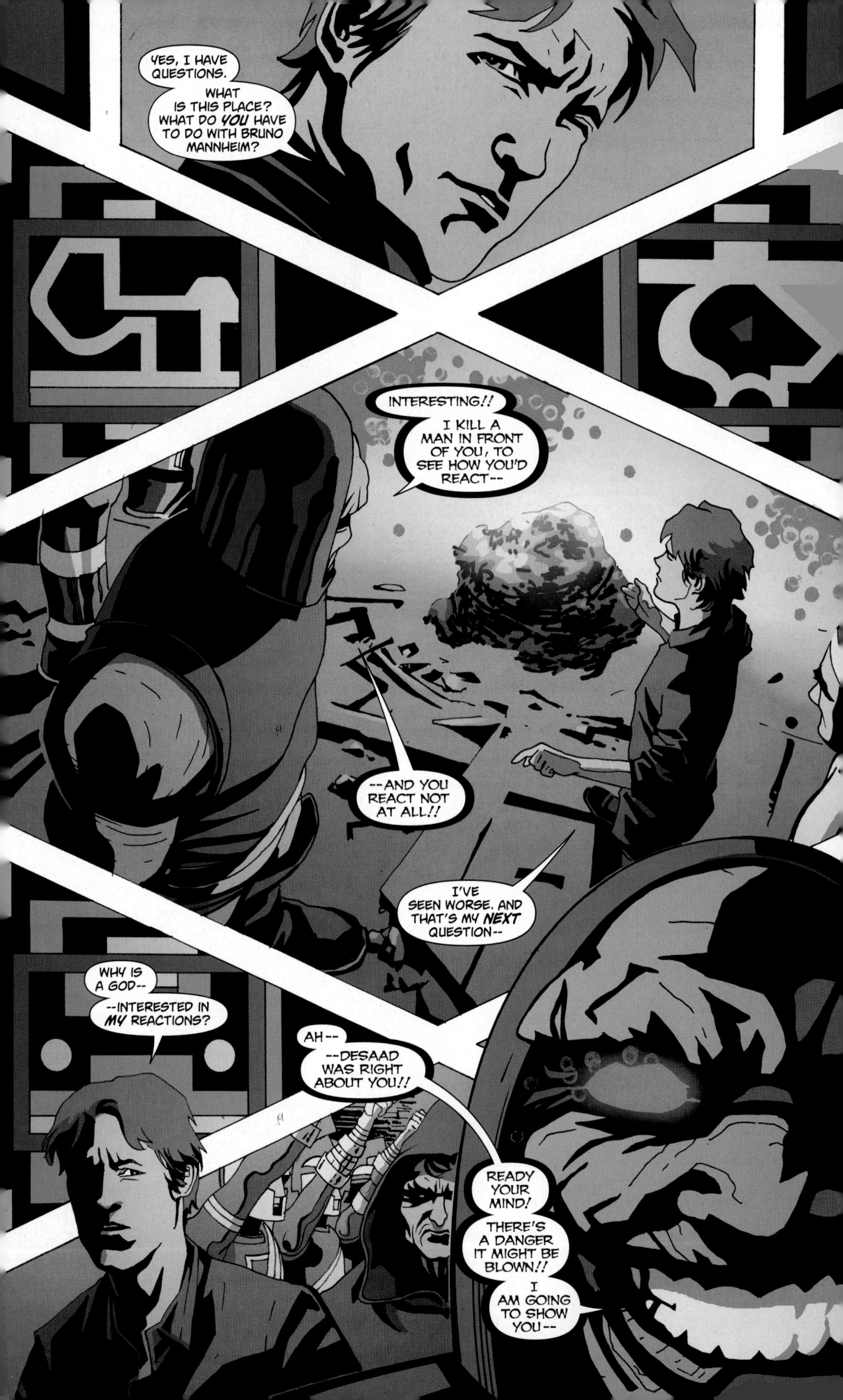
YES, I HAVE QUESTIONS.
WHAT IS THIS PLACE? WHAT DO *YOU* HAVE TO DO WITH BRUNO MANNHEIM?
INTERESTING!!
I KILL A MAN IN FRONT OF YOU, TO SEE HOW YOU'D REACT--
--AND YOU REACT NOT AT ALL!!
I'VE SEEN WORSE. AND THAT'S MY *NEXT* QUESTION--
WHY IS A GOD--
--INTERESTED IN *MY* REACTIONS?
AH--
--DESAAD WAS RIGHT ABOUT YOU!!
READY YOUR MIND!
THERE'S A DANGER IT MIGHT BE BLOWN!!
I AM GOING TO SHOW YOU--

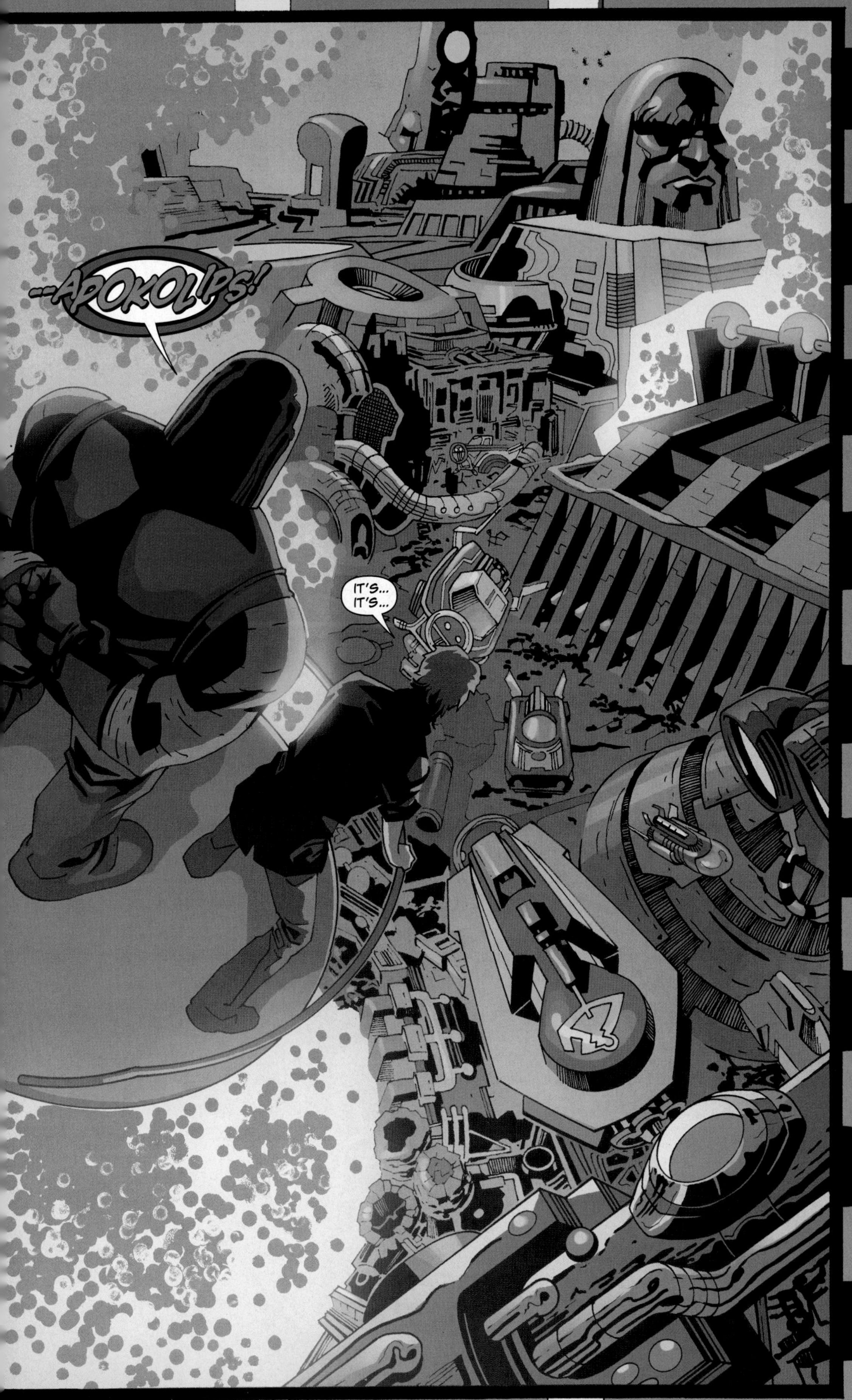
--APOKOLIPS!
IT'S... IT'S...

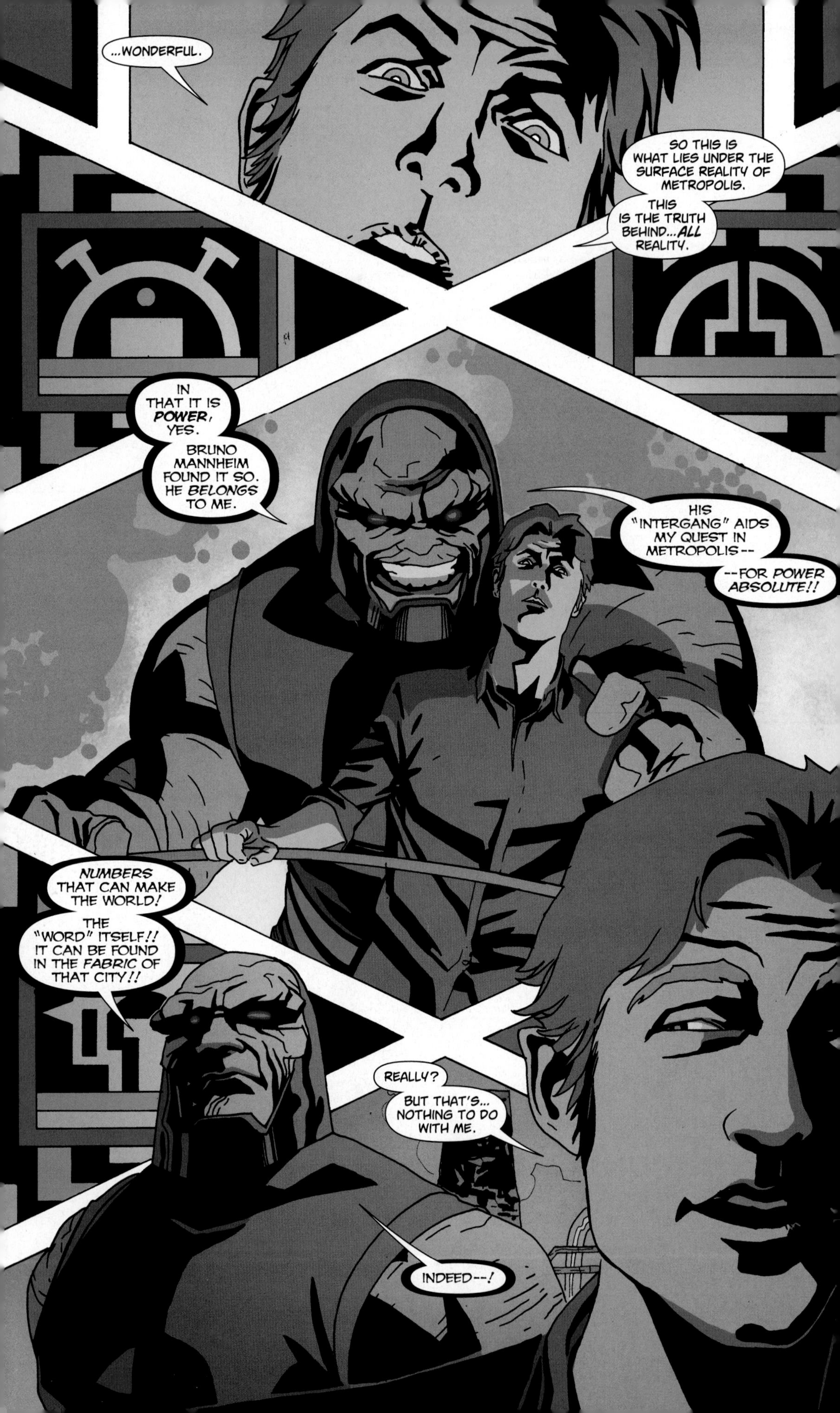

...WONDERFUL.
SO THIS IS WHAT LIES UNDER THE SURFACE REALITY OF METROPOLIS.
THIS IS THE TRUTH BEHIND...*ALL* REALITY.
IN THAT IT IS ***POWER***, YES.
BRUNO MANNHEIM FOUND IT SO. HE *BELONGS* TO ME.
HIS "INTERGANG" AIDS MY QUEST IN METROPOLIS--
--FOR *POWER ABSOLUTE!!*
NUMBERS THAT CAN MAKE THE WORLD!
THE "WORD" ITSELF!! IT CAN BE FOUND IN THE *FABRIC* OF THAT CITY!!
REALLY?
BUT THAT'S... NOTHING TO DO WITH ME.
INDEED--!

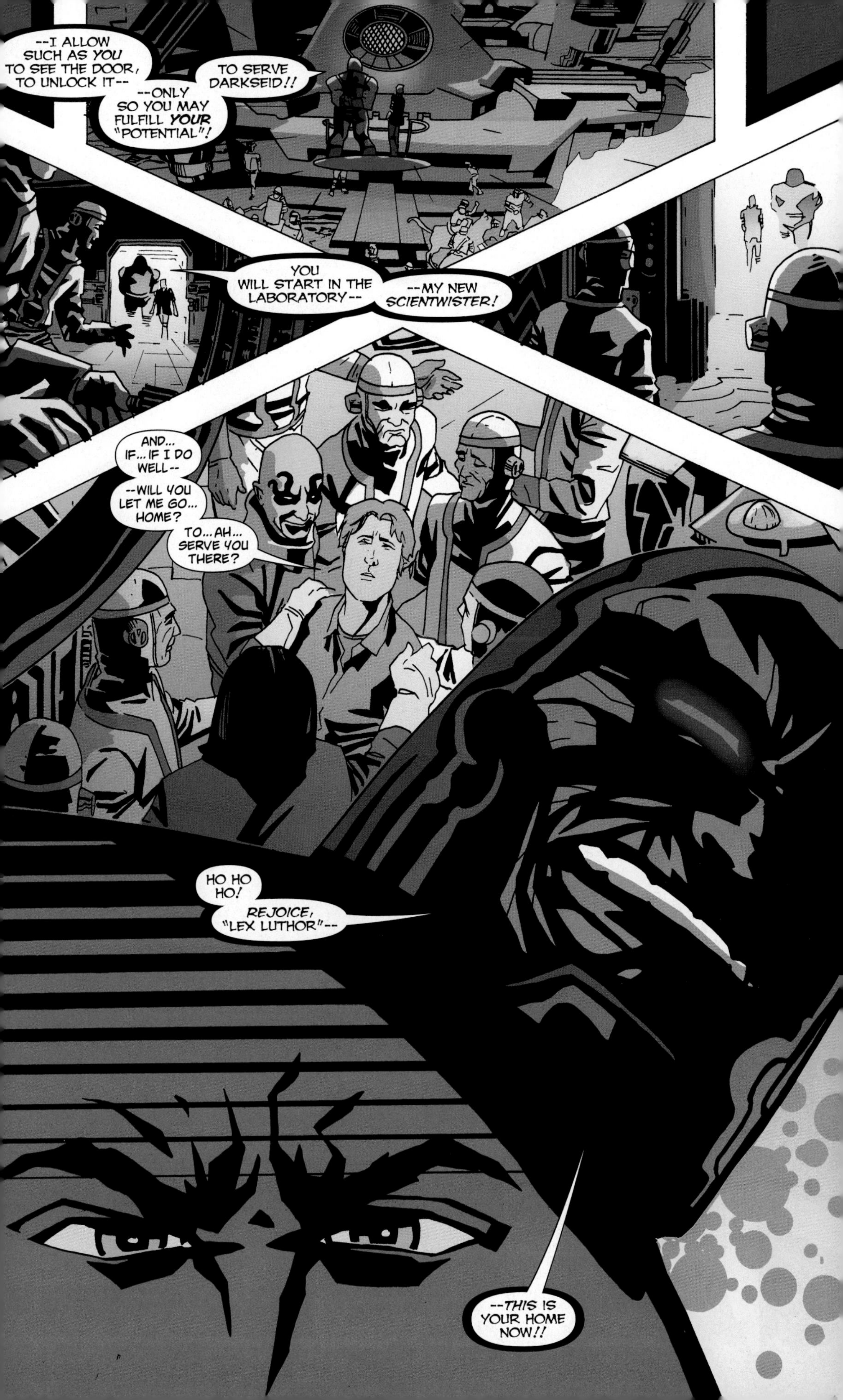
--I ALLOW SUCH AS YOU TO SEE THE DOOR, TO UNLOCK IT--
--ONLY SO YOU MAY FULFILL YOUR "POTENTIAL"!
TO SERVE DARKSEID!!
YOU WILL START IN THE LABORATORY--
--MY NEW SCIENTWISTER!
AND... IF... IF I DO WELL--
--WILL YOU LET ME GO... HOME?
TO... AH... SERVE YOU THERE?
HO HO HO!
REJOICE, "LEX LUTHOR"--
--THIS IS YOUR HOME NOW!!

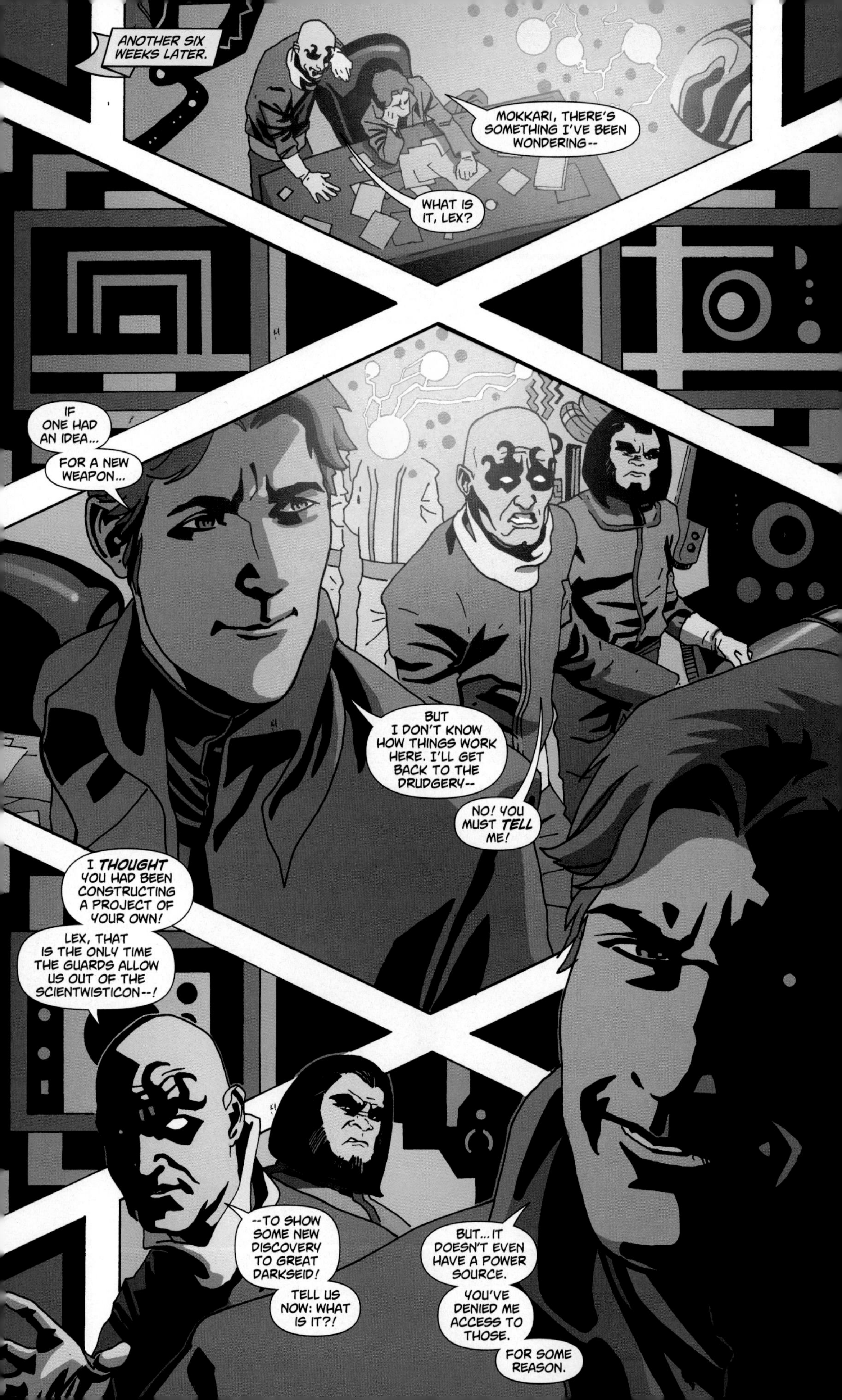
ANOTHER SIX WEEKS LATER.
MOKKARI, THERE'S SOMETHING I'VE BEEN WONDERING--
WHAT IS IT, LEX?
IF ONE HAD AN IDEA...
FOR A NEW WEAPON...
BUT I DON'T KNOW HOW THINGS WORK HERE. I'LL GET BACK TO THE DRUDGERY--
NO! YOU MUST TELL ME!
I THOUGHT YOU HAD BEEN CONSTRUCTING A PROJECT OF YOUR OWN!
LEX, THAT IS THE ONLY TIME THE GUARDS ALLOW US OUT OF THE SCIENTWISTICON--!
--TO SHOW SOME NEW DISCOVERY TO GREAT DARKSEID!
TELL US NOW: WHAT IS IT?!
BUT... IT DOESN'T EVEN HAVE A POWER SOURCE.
YOU'VE DENIED ME ACCESS TO THOSE.
FOR SOME REASON.

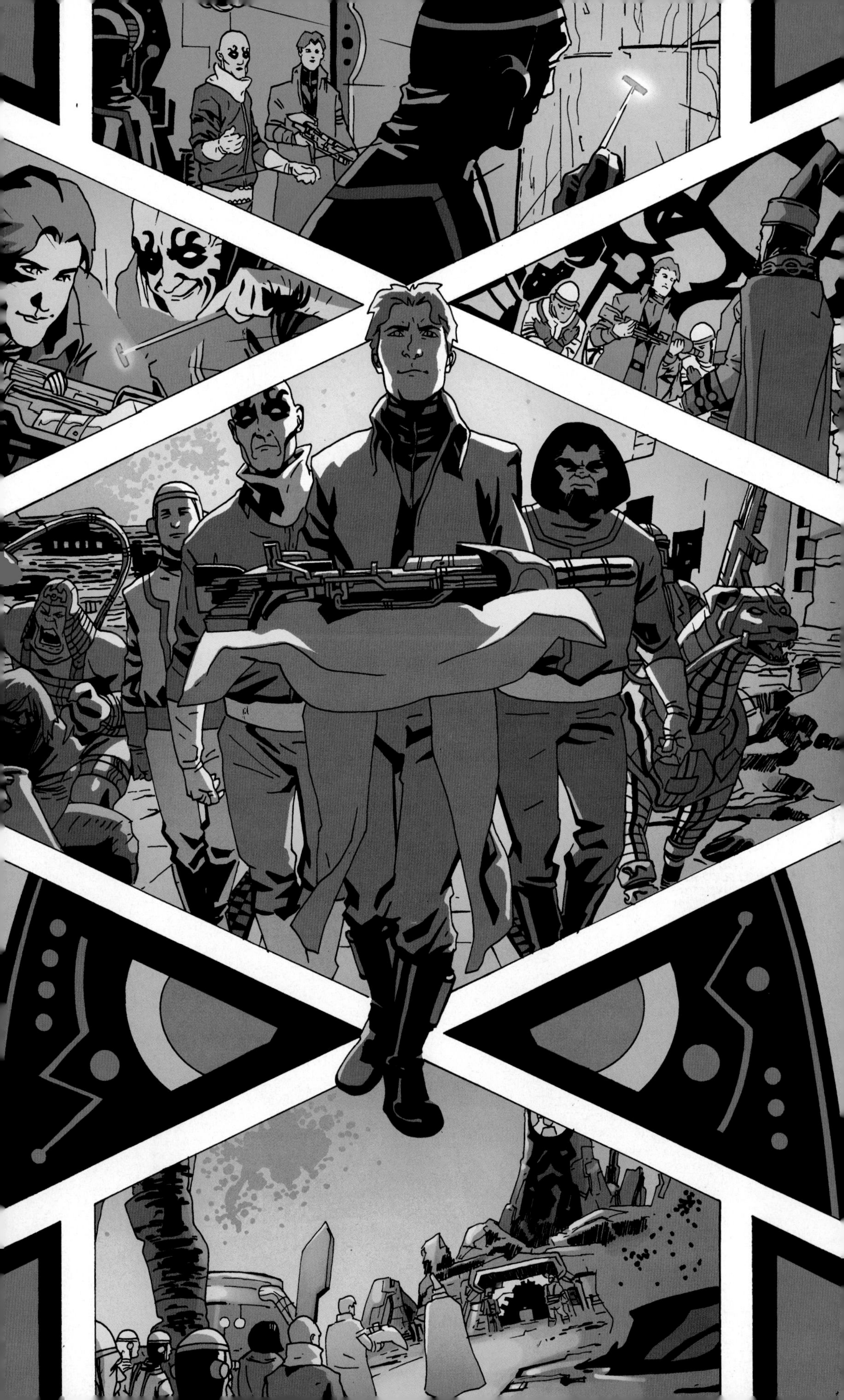

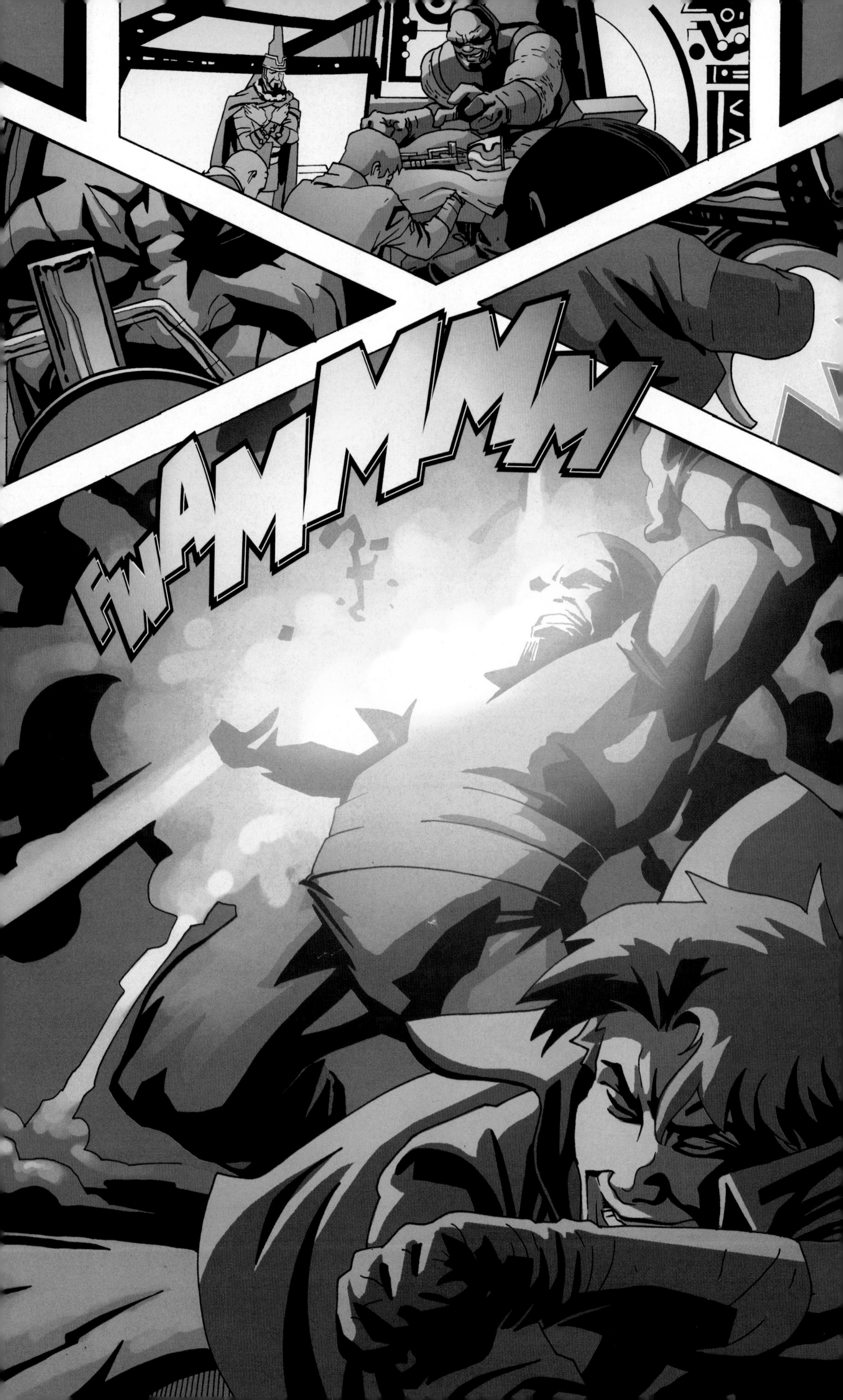
FWAMMMM

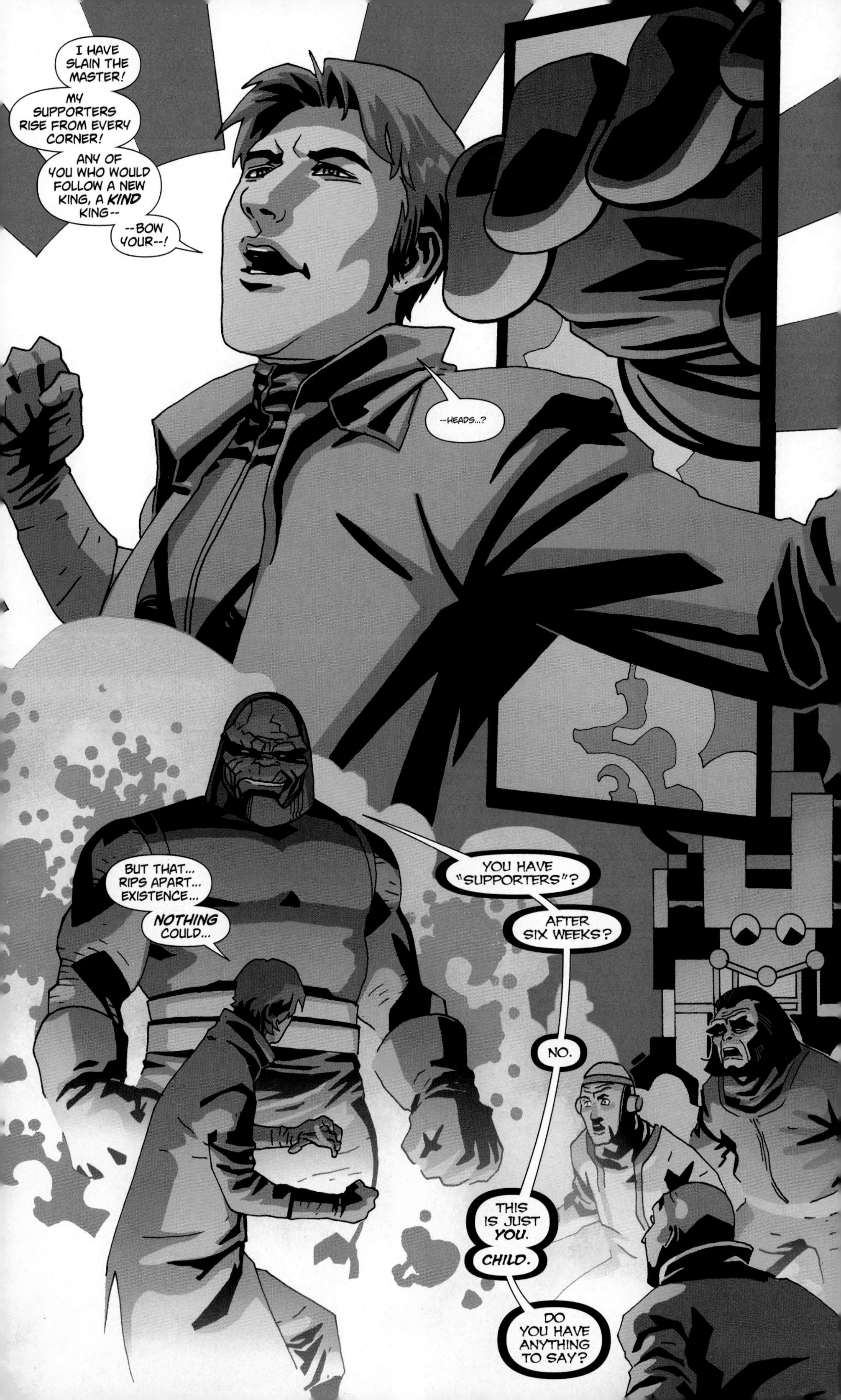
I HAVE SLAIN THE MASTER!
MY SUPPORTERS RISE FROM EVERY CORNER!
ANY OF YOU WHO WOULD FOLLOW A NEW KING, A *KIND* KING--
--BOW YOUR--!
--HEADS...?
BUT THAT... RIPS APART... EXISTENCE...
NOTHING COULD...
YOU HAVE "SUPPORTERS"?
AFTER SIX WEEKS?
NO.
THIS IS JUST *YOU*.
CHILD.
DO YOU HAVE ANYTHING TO SAY?

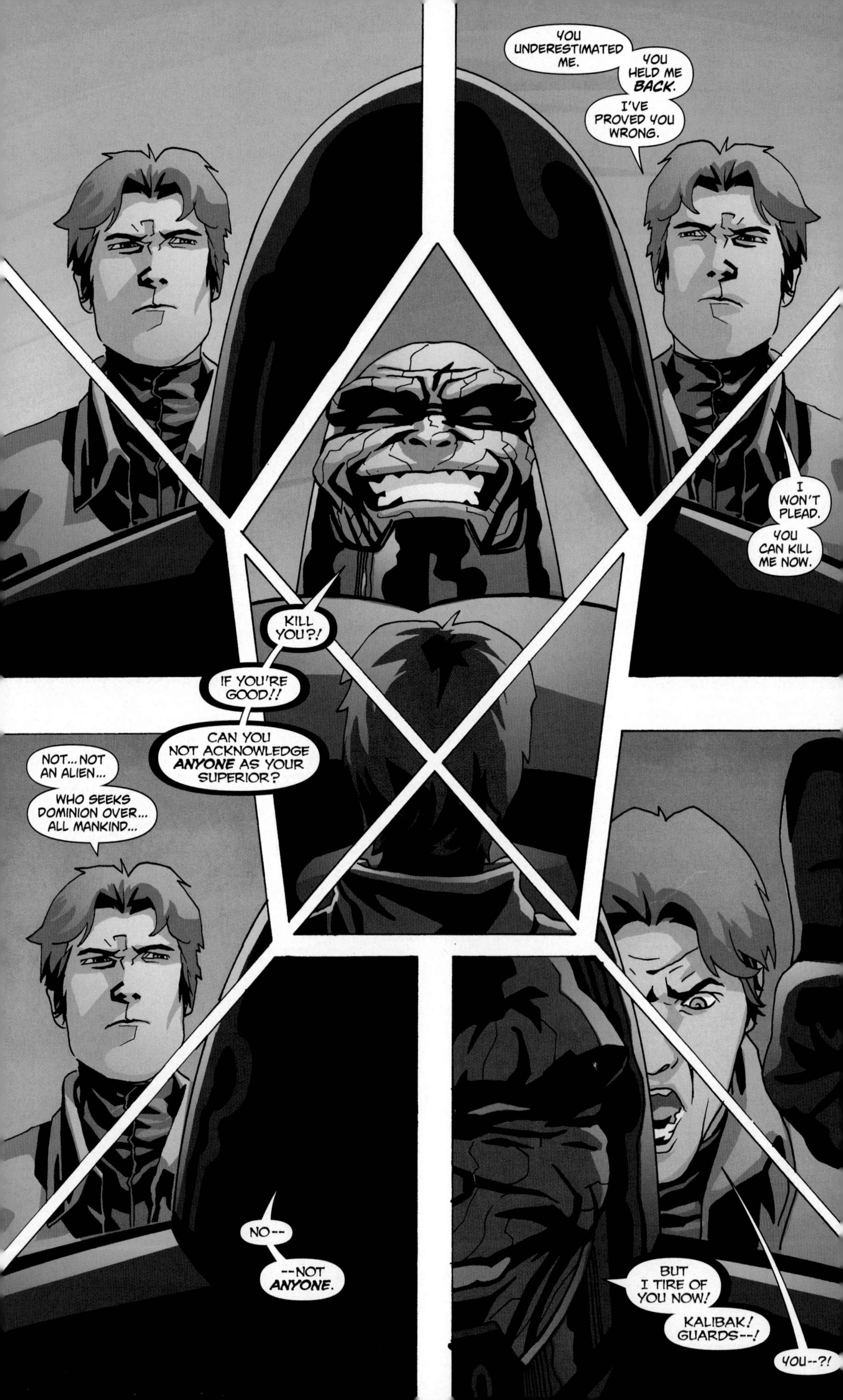
YOU UNDERESTIMATED ME.
YOU HELD ME BACK.
I'VE PROVED YOU WRONG.
I WON'T PLEAD.
YOU CAN KILL ME NOW.
KILL YOU?!
IF YOU'RE GOOD!!
CAN YOU NOT ACKNOWLEDGE ANYONE AS YOUR SUPERIOR?
NOT...NOT AN ALIEN...
WHO SEEKS DOMINION OVER... ALL MANKIND...
NO--
--NOT ANYONE.
BUT I TIRE OF YOU NOW!
KALIBAK! GUARDS--!
YOU--?!

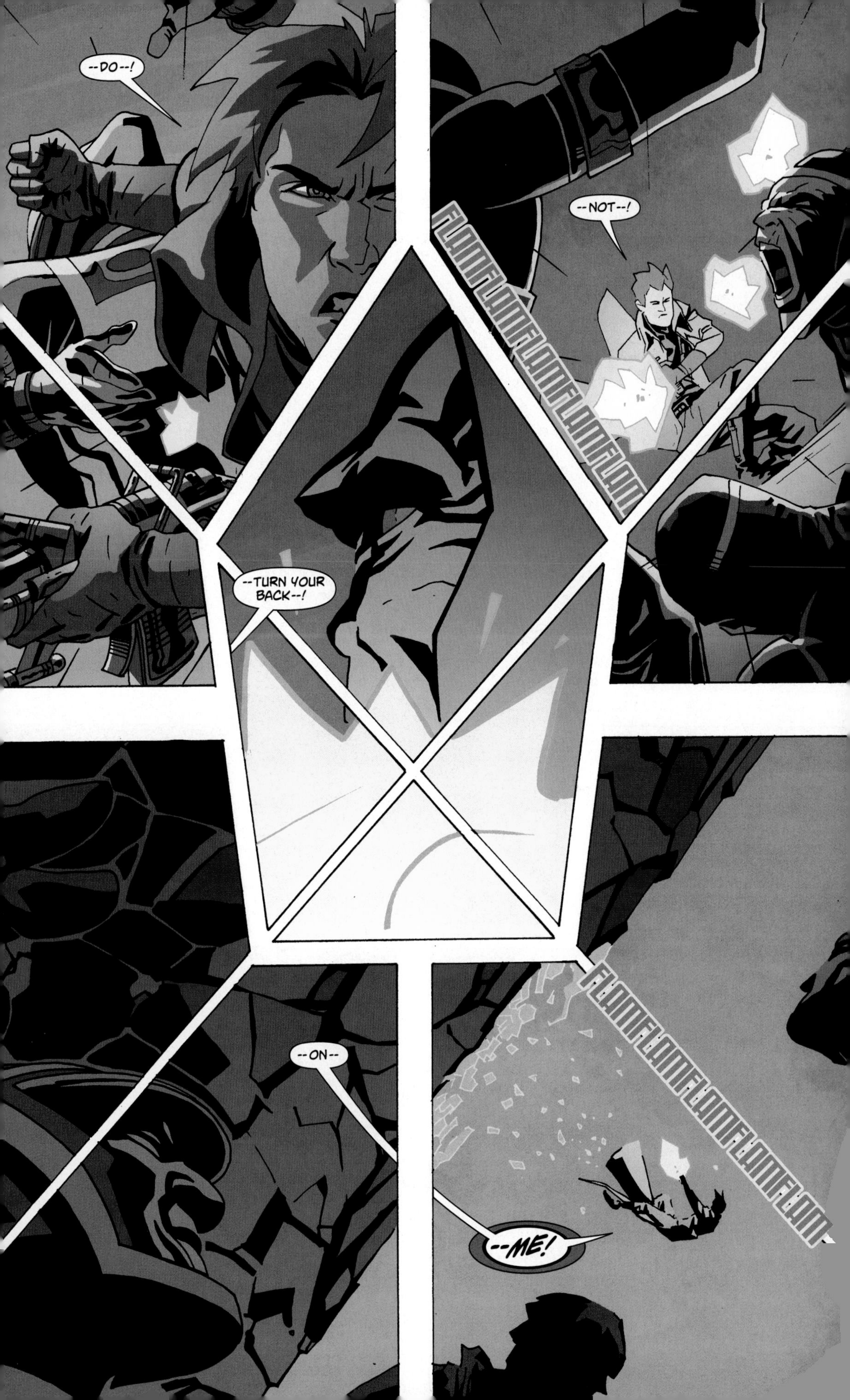
--DO--!
--NOT--!
FLAMFLAMFLAMFLAM
--TURN YOUR BACK--!
--ON--
FLAMFLAMFLAMFLAM
--ME!

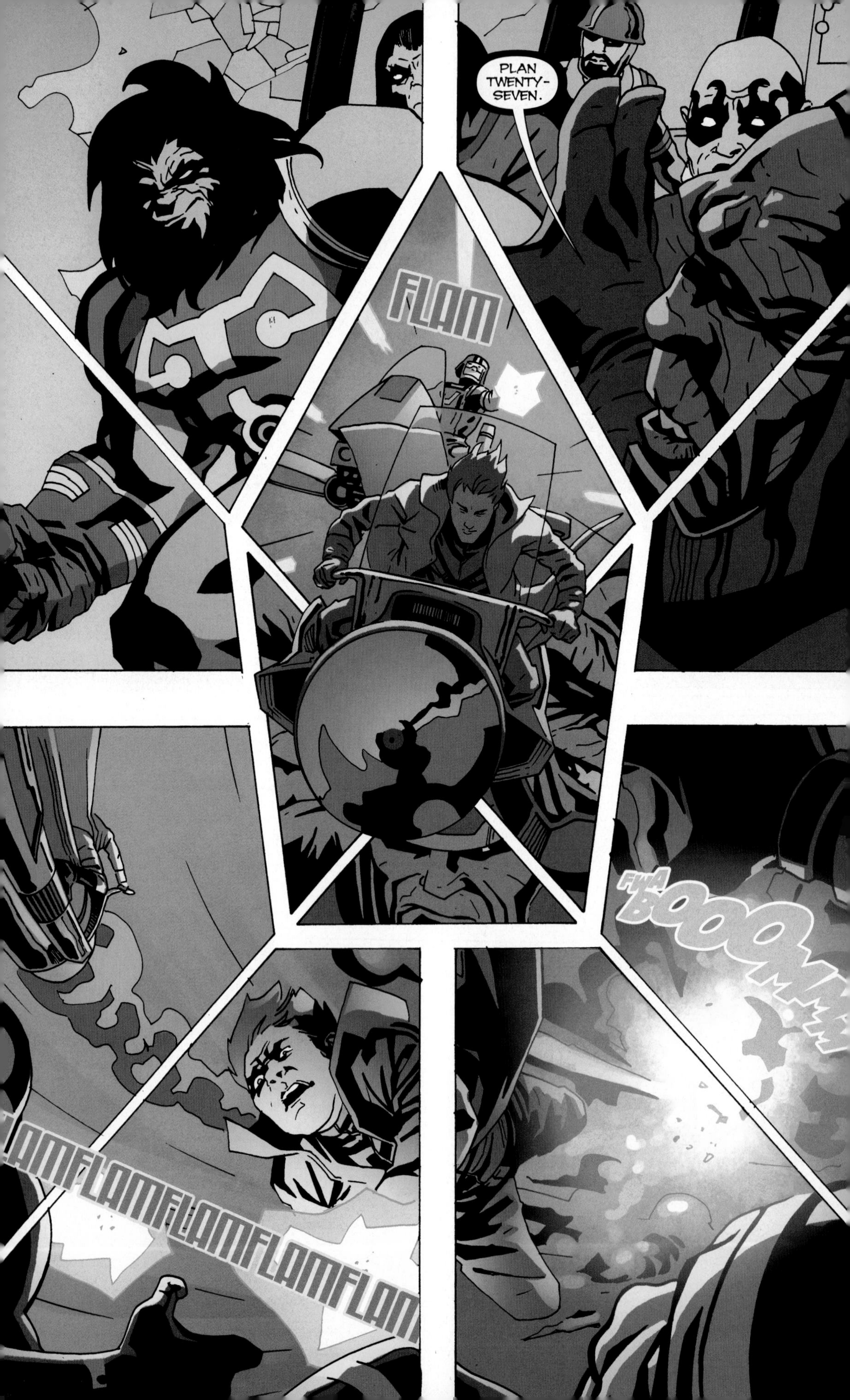
PLAN TWENTY-SEVEN.
FLAM
FWA BOOOM
FLAMFLAMFLAMFLAMFLAM

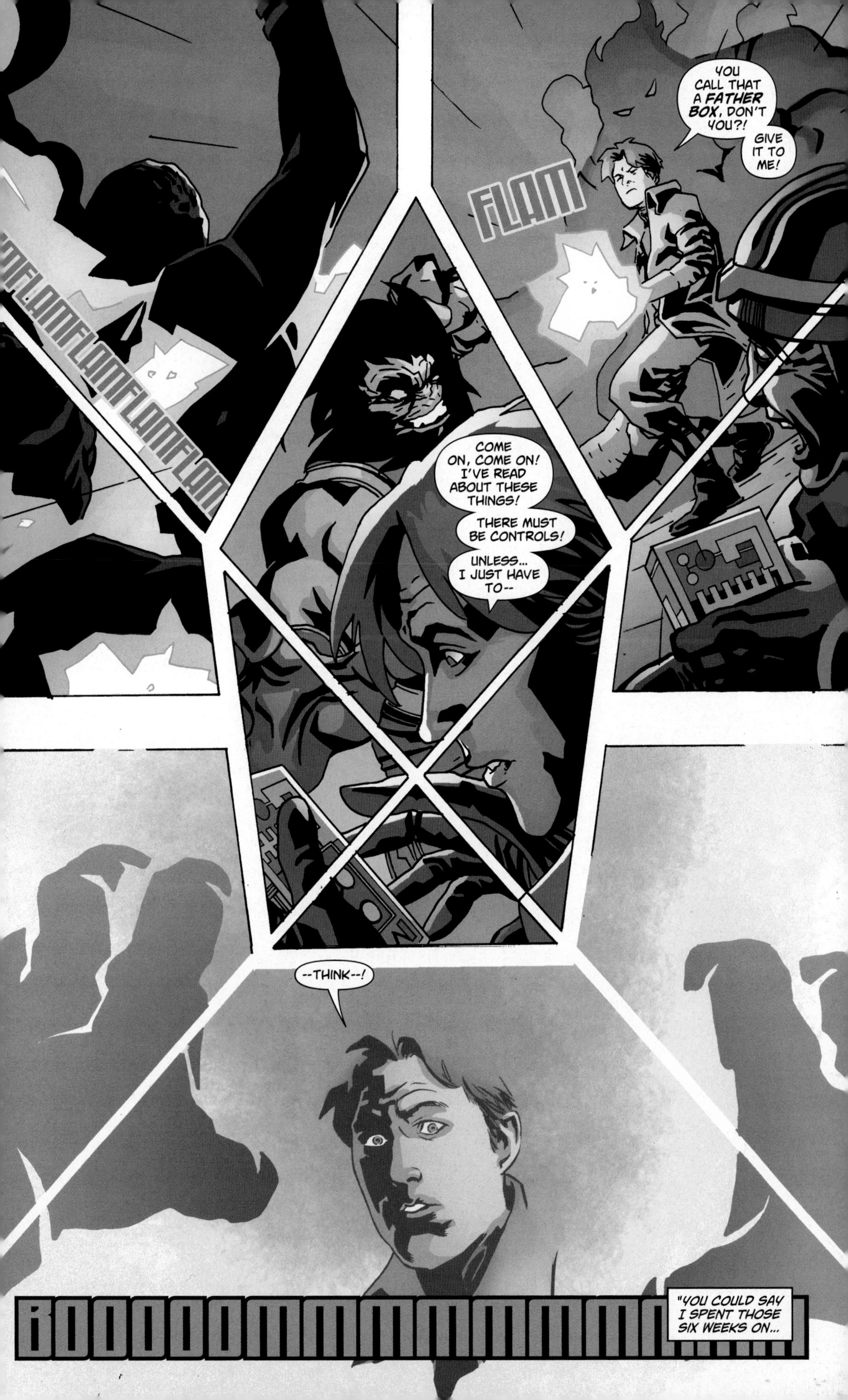
FLAMFLAMFLAMFLAMFLAM
YOU CALL THAT A FATHER BOX, DON'T YOU?!
GIVE IT TO ME!
FLAM
COME ON, COME ON! I'VE READ ABOUT THESE THINGS!
THERE MUST BE CONTROLS!
UNLESS... I JUST HAVE TO--
--THINK--!
BOOOOOMMMMMMMMMMMM......
"YOU COULD SAY I SPENT THOSE SIX WEEKS ON...

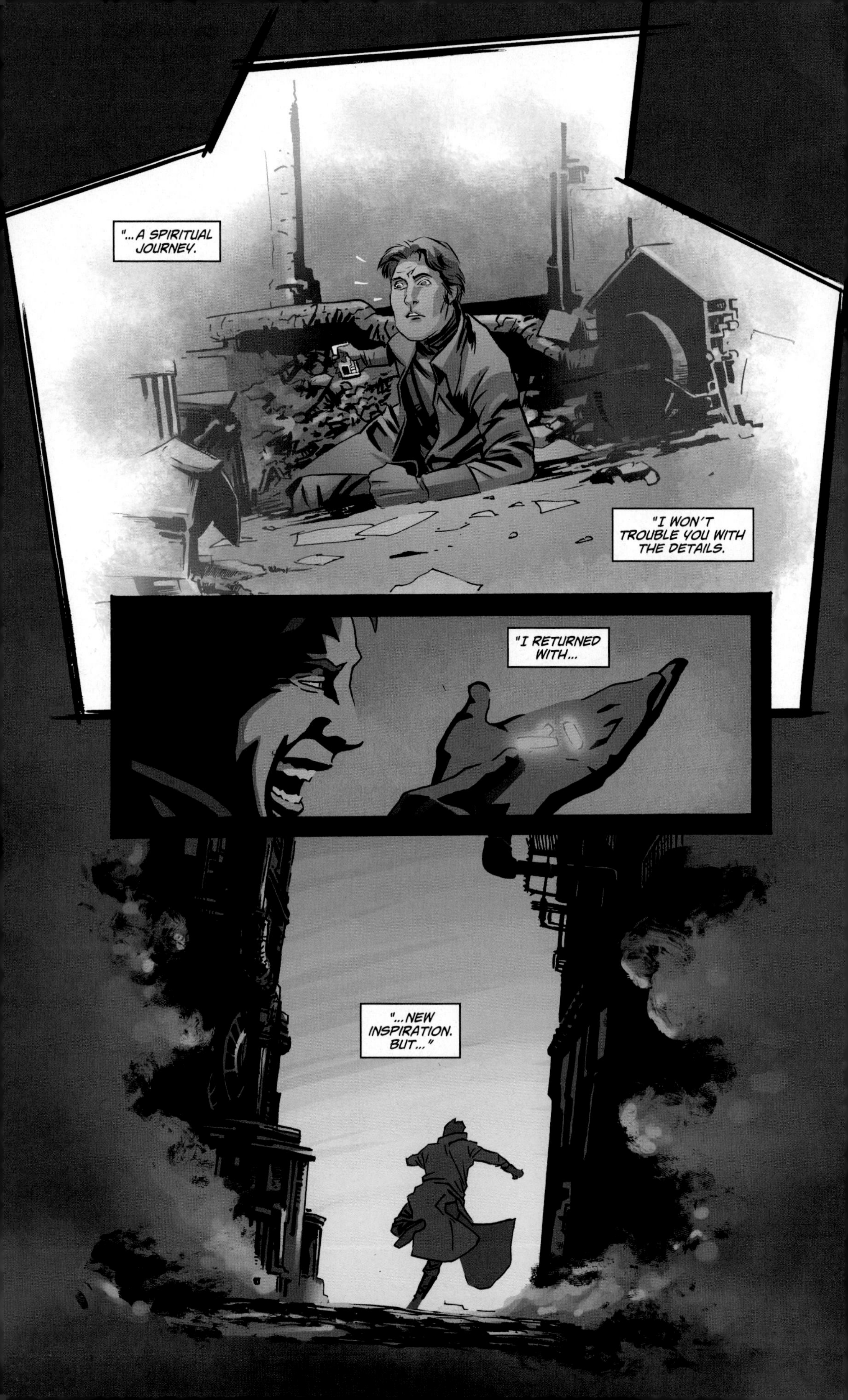
"...A SPIRITUAL JOURNEY.
"I WON'T TROUBLE YOU WITH THE DETAILS.
"I RETURNED WITH...
"...NEW INSPIRATION. BUT..."

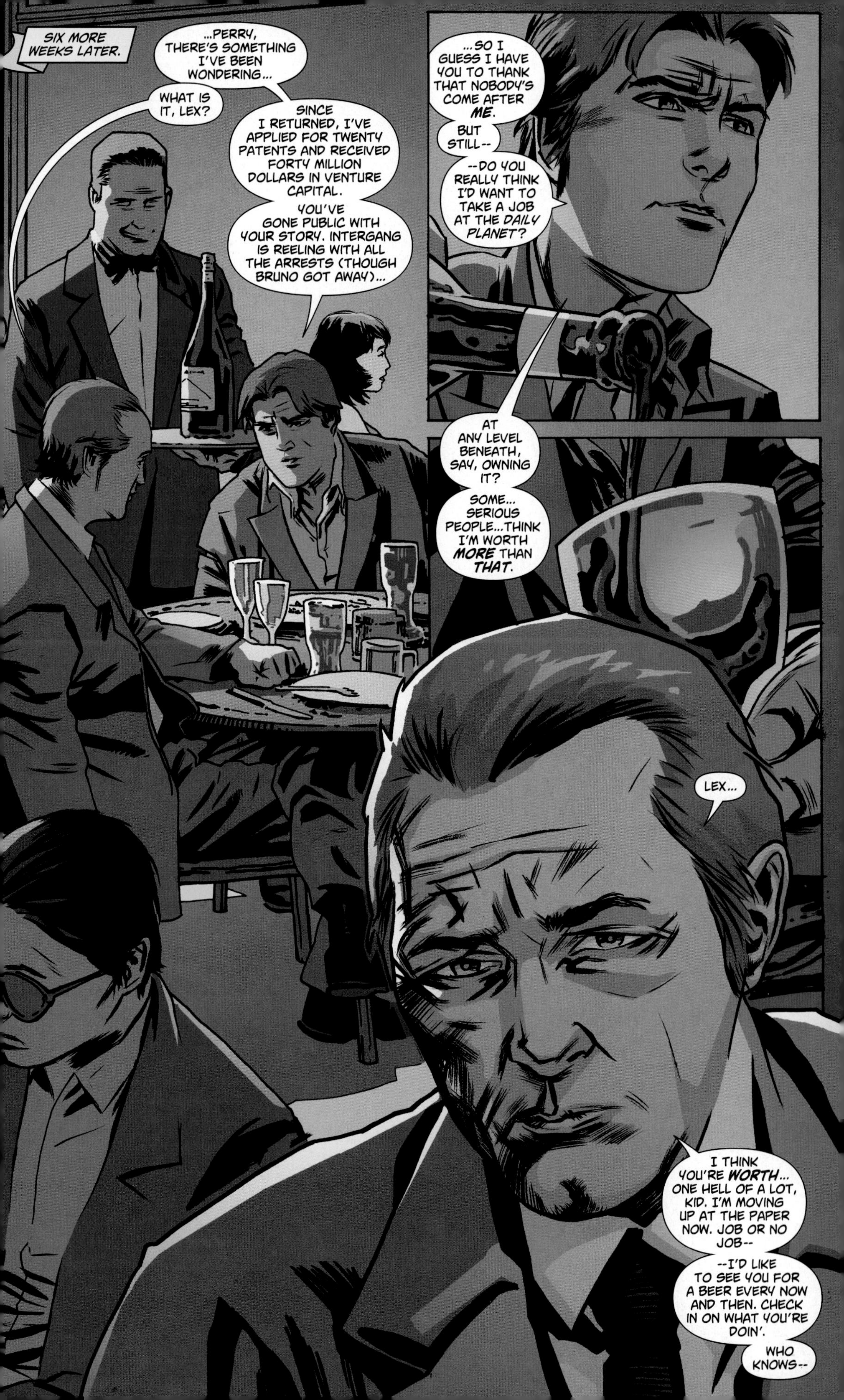
SIX MORE WEEKS LATER.
...PERRY, THERE'S SOMETHING I'VE BEEN WONDERING...
WHAT IS IT, LEX?
SINCE I RETURNED, I'VE APPLIED FOR TWENTY PATENTS AND RECEIVED FORTY MILLION DOLLARS IN VENTURE CAPITAL.
YOU'VE GONE PUBLIC WITH YOUR STORY. INTERGANG IS REELING WITH ALL THE ARRESTS (THOUGH BRUNO GOT AWAY)...
...SO I GUESS I HAVE YOU TO THANK THAT NOBODY'S COME AFTER ***ME***.
BUT STILL--
--DO YOU REALLY THINK I'D WANT TO TAKE A JOB AT THE *DAILY PLANET*?
AT ANY LEVEL BENEATH, SAY, OWNING IT?
SOME... SERIOUS PEOPLE...THINK I'M WORTH ***MORE*** THAN ***THAT***.
LEX...
I THINK YOU'RE ***WORTH***... ONE HELL OF A LOT, KID. I'M MOVING UP AT THE PAPER NOW. JOB OR NO JOB--
--I'D LIKE TO SEE YOU FOR A BEER EVERY NOW AND THEN. CHECK IN ON WHAT YOU'RE DOIN'.
WHO KNOWS--

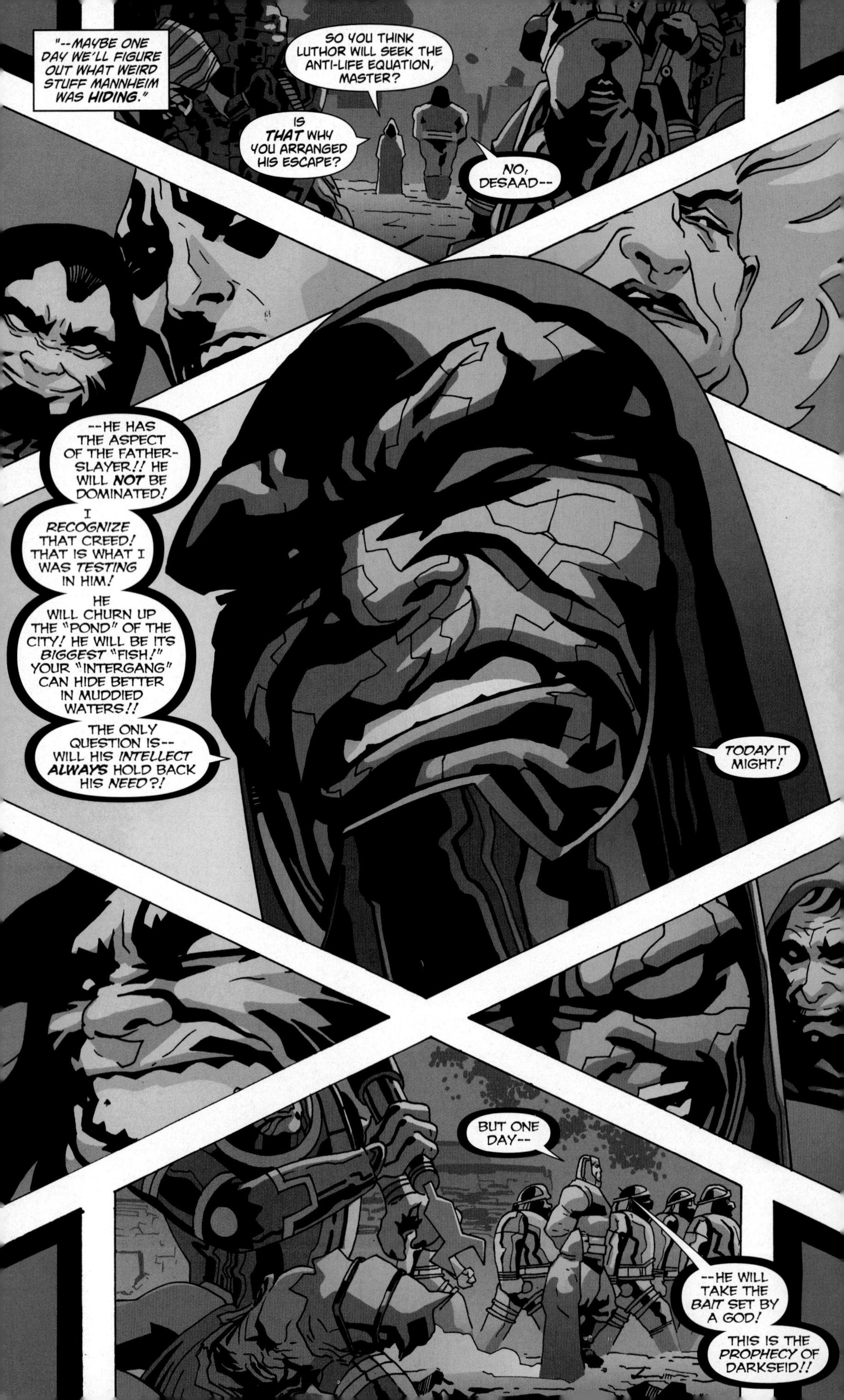
"--MAYBE ONE DAY WE'LL FIGURE OUT WHAT WEIRD STUFF MANNHEIM WAS HIDING."
SO YOU THINK LUTHOR WILL SEEK THE ANTI-LIFE EQUATION, MASTER?
IS THAT WHY YOU ARRANGED HIS ESCAPE?
NO, DESAAD--
--HE HAS THE ASPECT OF THE FATHER-SLAYER!! HE WILL NOT BE DOMINATED!
I RECOGNIZE THAT CREED! THAT IS WHAT I WAS TESTING IN HIM!
HE WILL CHURN UP THE "POND" OF THE CITY! HE WILL BE ITS BIGGEST "FISH!" YOUR "INTERGANG" CAN HIDE BETTER IN MUDDIED WATERS!!
THE ONLY QUESTION IS-- WILL HIS INTELLECT ALWAYS HOLD BACK HIS NEED?!
TODAY IT MIGHT!
BUT ONE DAY--
--HE WILL TAKE THE BAIT SET BY A GOD!
THIS IS THE PROPHECY OF DARKSEID!!

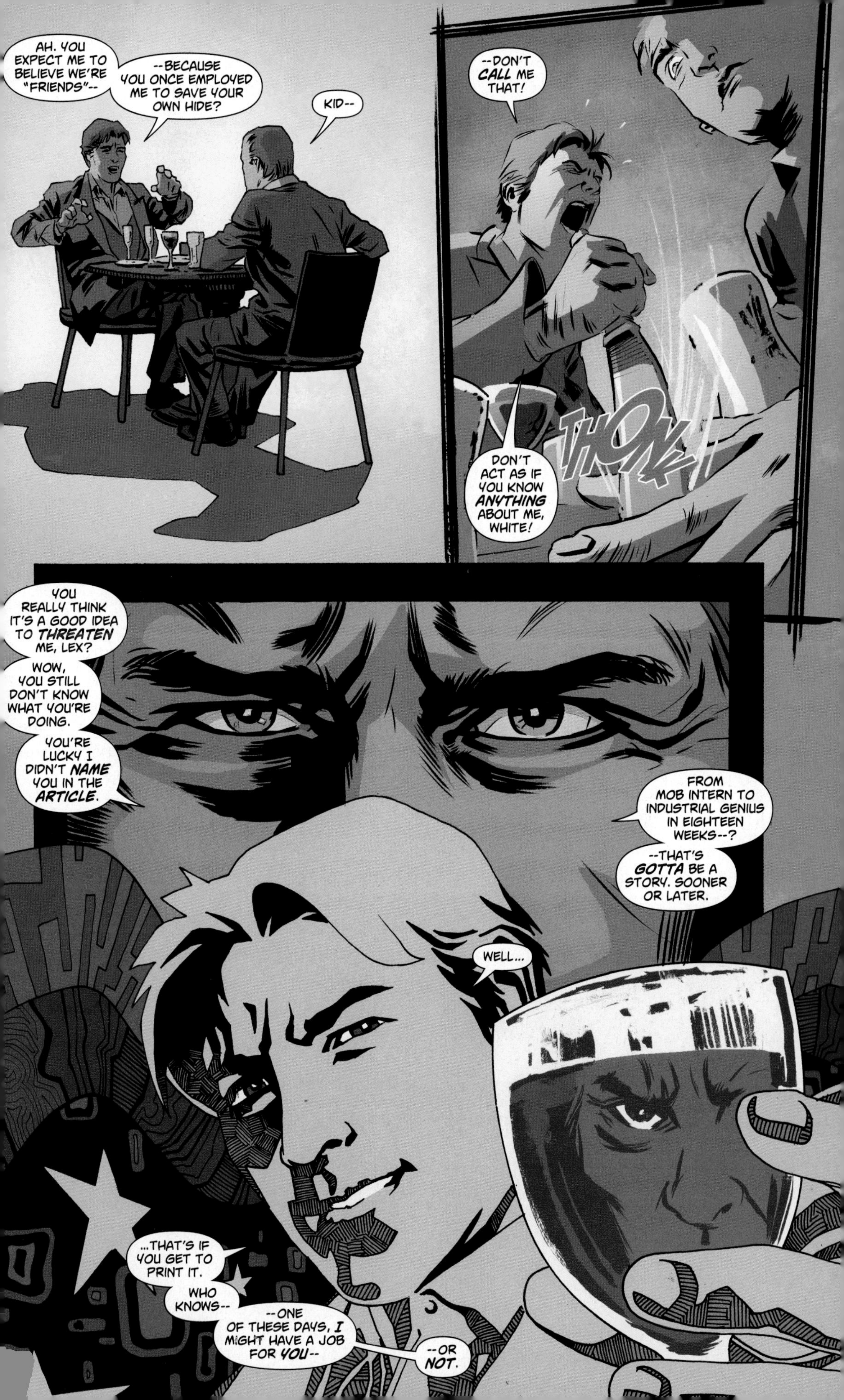
AH. YOU EXPECT ME TO BELIEVE WE'RE "FRIENDS"--
--BECAUSE YOU ONCE EMPLOYED ME TO SAVE YOUR OWN HIDE?
KID--
--DON'T CALL ME THAT!
THONK
DON'T ACT AS IF YOU KNOW ANYTHING ABOUT ME, WHITE!
YOU REALLY THINK IT'S A GOOD IDEA TO THREATEN ME, LEX?
WOW, YOU STILL DON'T KNOW WHAT YOU'RE DOING.
YOU'RE LUCKY I DIDN'T NAME YOU IN THE ARTICLE.
FROM MOB INTERN TO INDUSTRIAL GENIUS IN EIGHTEEN WEEKS--?
--THAT'S GOTTA BE A STORY. SOONER OR LATER.
WELL...
...THAT'S IF YOU GET TO PRINT IT.
WHO KNOWS--
--ONE OF THESE DAYS, I MIGHT HAVE A JOB FOR YOU--
--OR NOT.

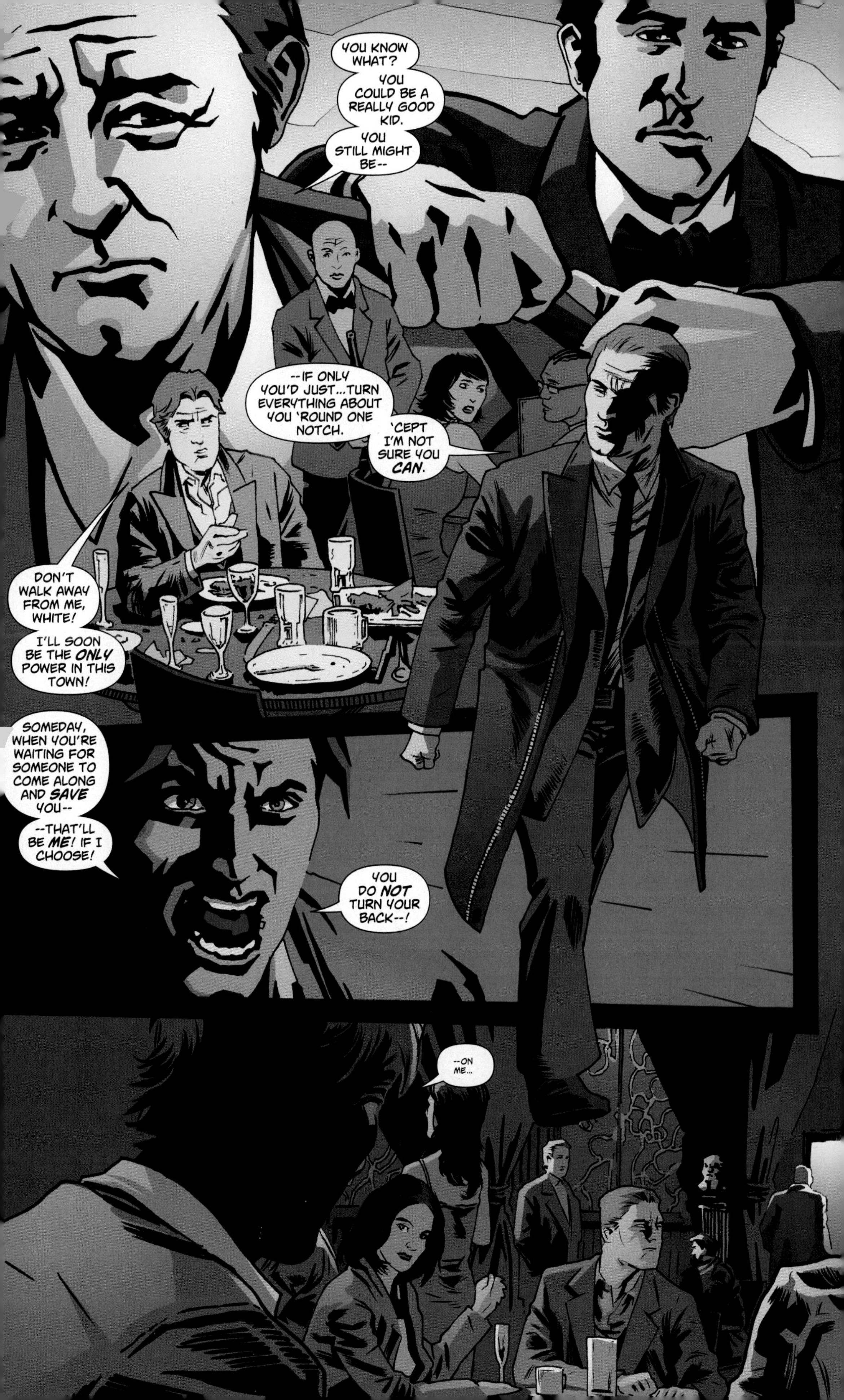
YOU KNOW WHAT?
YOU COULD BE A REALLY GOOD KID.
YOU STILL MIGHT BE--
--IF ONLY YOU'D JUST...TURN EVERYTHING ABOUT YOU 'ROUND ONE NOTCH.
'CEPT I'M NOT SURE YOU CAN.
DON'T WALK AWAY FROM ME, WHITE!
I'LL SOON BE THE ONLY POWER IN THIS TOWN!
SOMEDAY, WHEN YOU'RE WAITING FOR SOMEONE TO COME ALONG AND SAVE YOU--
--THAT'LL BE ME! IF I CHOOSE!
YOU DO NOT TURN YOUR BACK--!
--ON ME...

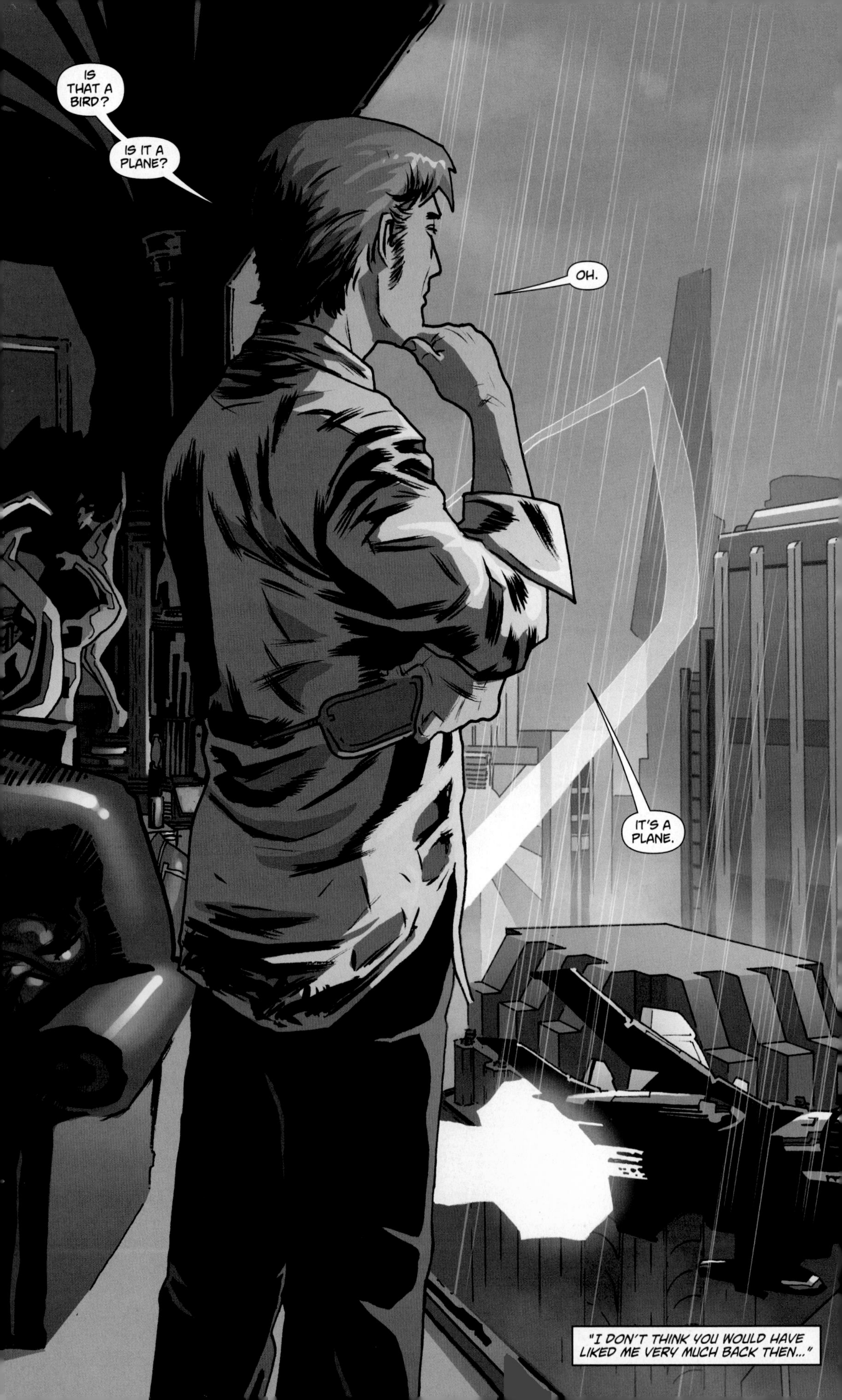
IS THAT A BIRD?
IS IT A PLANE?
OH.
IT'S A PLANE.
"I DON'T THINK YOU WOULD HAVE LIKED ME VERY MUCH BACK THEN..."

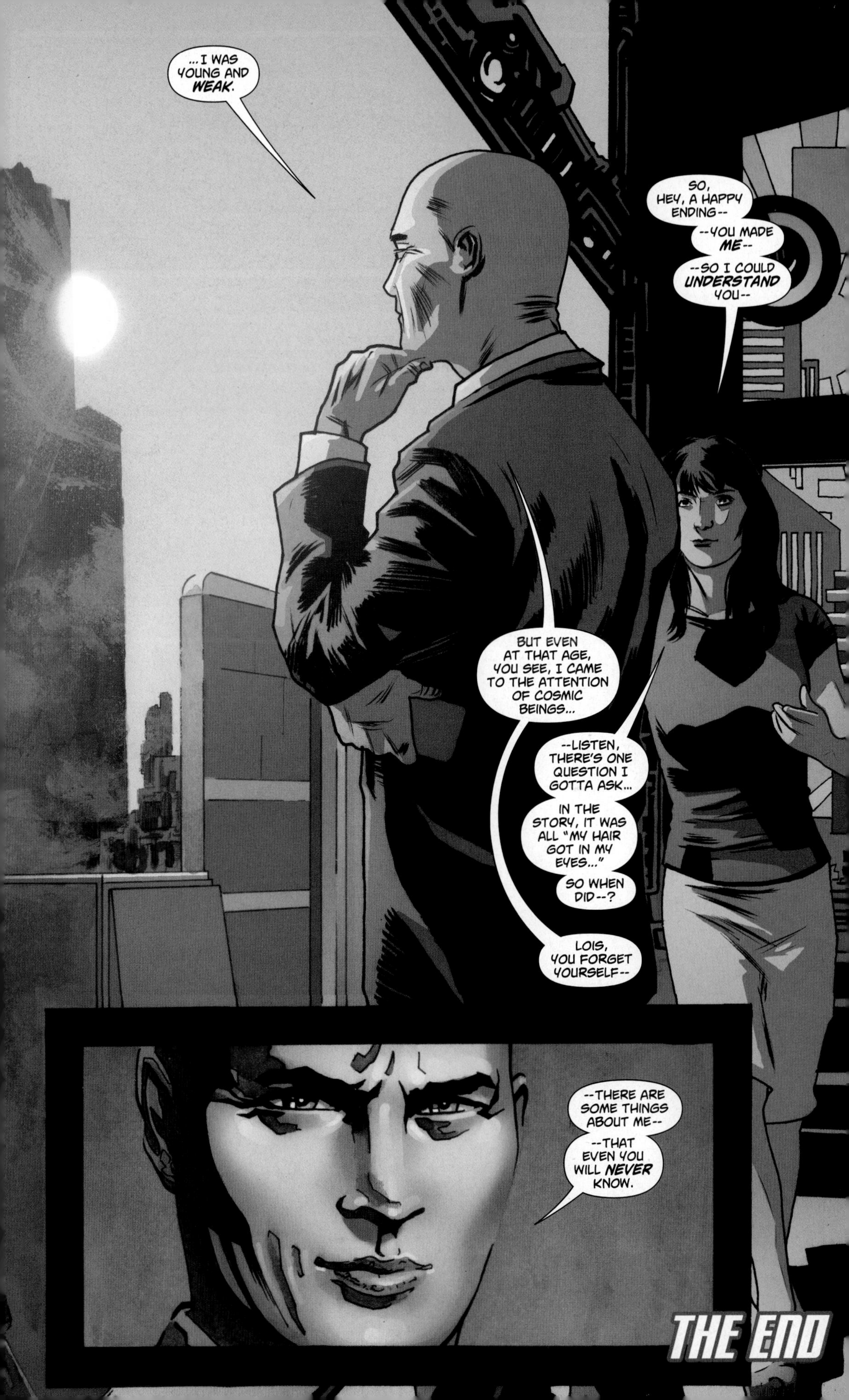
...I WAS YOUNG AND WEAK.
SO, HEY, A HAPPY ENDING--
--YOU MADE ME--
--SO I COULD UNDERSTAND YOU--
BUT EVEN AT THAT AGE, YOU SEE, I CAME TO THE ATTENTION OF COSMIC BEINGS...
--LISTEN, THERE'S ONE QUESTION I GOTTA ASK...
IN THE STORY, IT WAS ALL "MY HAIR GOT IN MY EYES..."
SO WHEN DID--?
LOIS, YOU FORGET YOURSELF--
--THERE ARE SOME THINGS ABOUT ME--
--THAT EVEN YOU WILL NEVER KNOW.
THE END

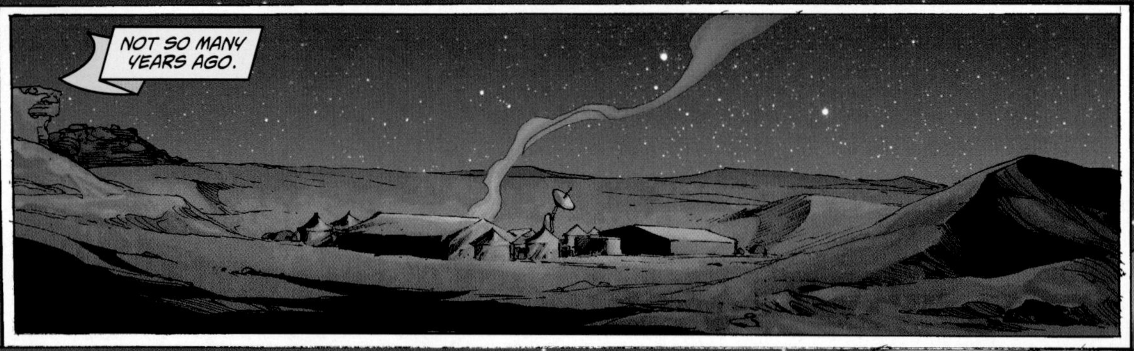
NOT SO MANY
YEARS AGO.

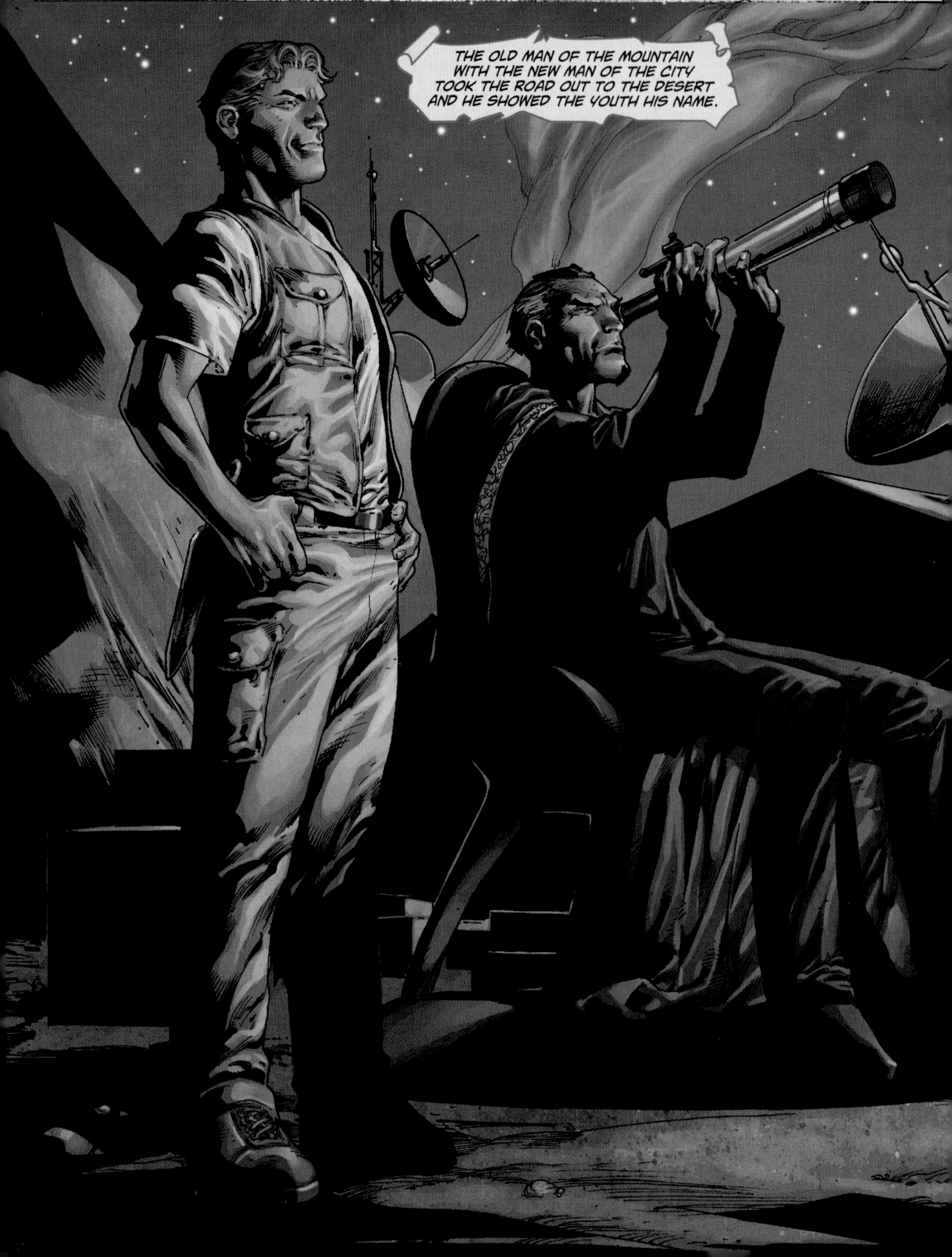
THE OLD MAN OF THE MOUNTAIN
WITH THE NEW MAN OF THE CITY
TOOK THE ROAD OUT TO THE DESERT
AND HE SHOWED THE YOUTH HIS NAME.

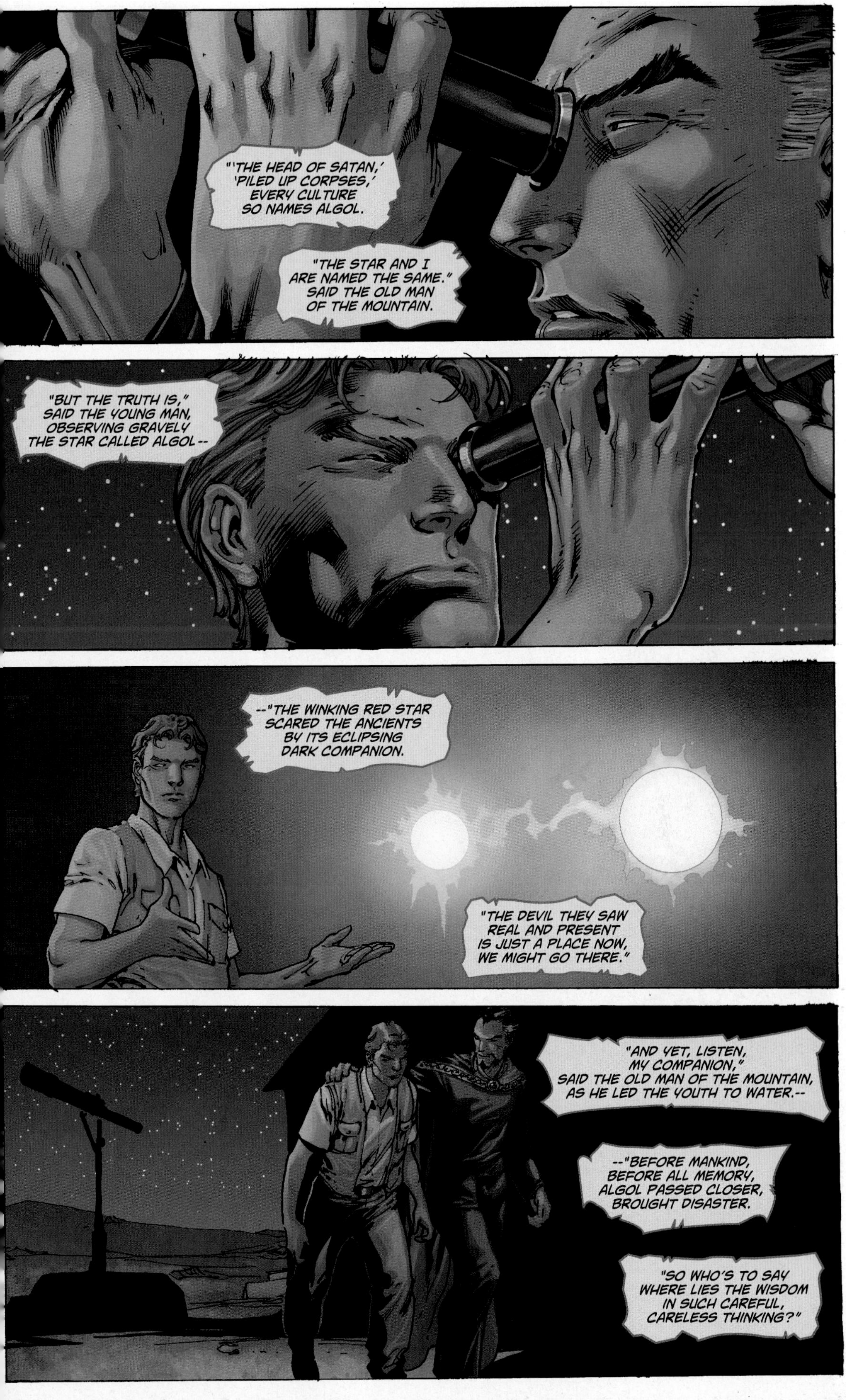
"'THE HEAD OF SATAN,' 'PILED UP CORPSES,' EVERY CULTURE SO NAMES ALGOL.
"THE STAR AND I ARE NAMED THE SAME." SAID THE OLD MAN OF THE MOUNTAIN.
"BUT THE TRUTH IS," SAID THE YOUNG MAN, OBSERVING GRAVELY THE STAR CALLED ALGOL--
--"THE WINKING RED STAR SCARED THE ANCIENTS BY ITS ECLIPSING DARK COMPANION.
"THE DEVIL THEY SAW REAL AND PRESENT IS JUST A PLACE NOW, WE MIGHT GO THERE."
"AND YET, LISTEN, MY COMPANION," SAID THE OLD MAN OF THE MOUNTAIN, AS HE LED THE YOUTH TO WATER.--
--"BEFORE MANKIND, BEFORE ALL MEMORY, ALGOL PASSED CLOSER, BROUGHT DISASTER.
"SO WHO'S TO SAY WHERE LIES THE WISDOM IN SUCH CAREFUL, CARELESS THINKING?"

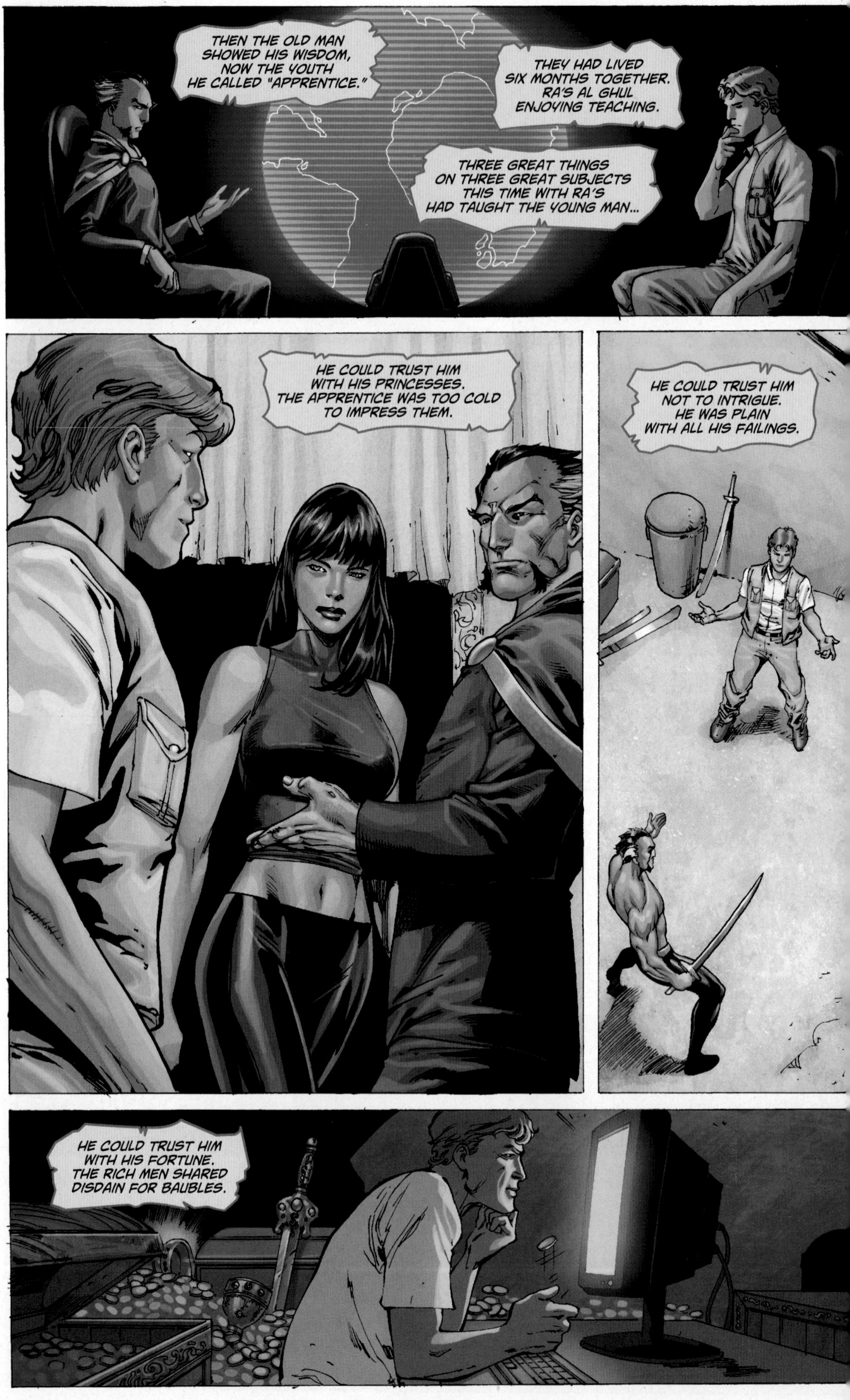
THEN THE OLD MAN SHOWED HIS WISDOM, NOW THE YOUTH HE CALLED "APPRENTICE."
THEY HAD LIVED SIX MONTHS TOGETHER. RA'S AL GHUL ENJOYING TEACHING.
THREE GREAT THINGS ON THREE GREAT SUBJECTS THIS TIME WITH RA'S HAD TAUGHT THE YOUNG MAN...
HE COULD TRUST HIM WITH HIS PRINCESSES. THE APPRENTICE WAS TOO COLD TO IMPRESS THEM.
HE COULD TRUST HIM NOT TO INTRIGUE. HE WAS PLAIN WITH ALL HIS FAILINGS.
HE COULD TRUST HIM WITH HIS FORTUNE. THE RICH MEN SHARED DISDAIN FOR BAUBLES.

HE'D LOVED THE WORLD FOR MANY CENTURIES, OLD MAN OF RIVERS, FIELDS AND MOUNTAIN.

IT BROKE HIS HEART TO SEE IT BREAKING. HE KNEW ITS VALUE: MORE THAN MORTALS.

AND SO HE KILLED AND KILLED AND KILLED AND WOULD HAVE THINNED THE POPULATION.

THROUGH MASS AND NOT CAPRICIOUS KILLING. THROUGH CULLING PEOPLES, WITH THEIR LEADERS.

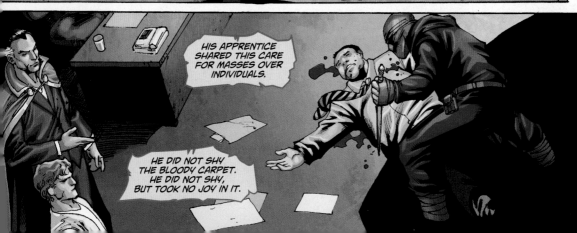

HIS APPRENTICE SHARED THIS CARE FOR MASSES OVER INDIVIDUALS.

HE DID NOT SHY THE BLOODY CARPET. HE DID NOT SHY, BUT TOOK NO JOY IN IT.

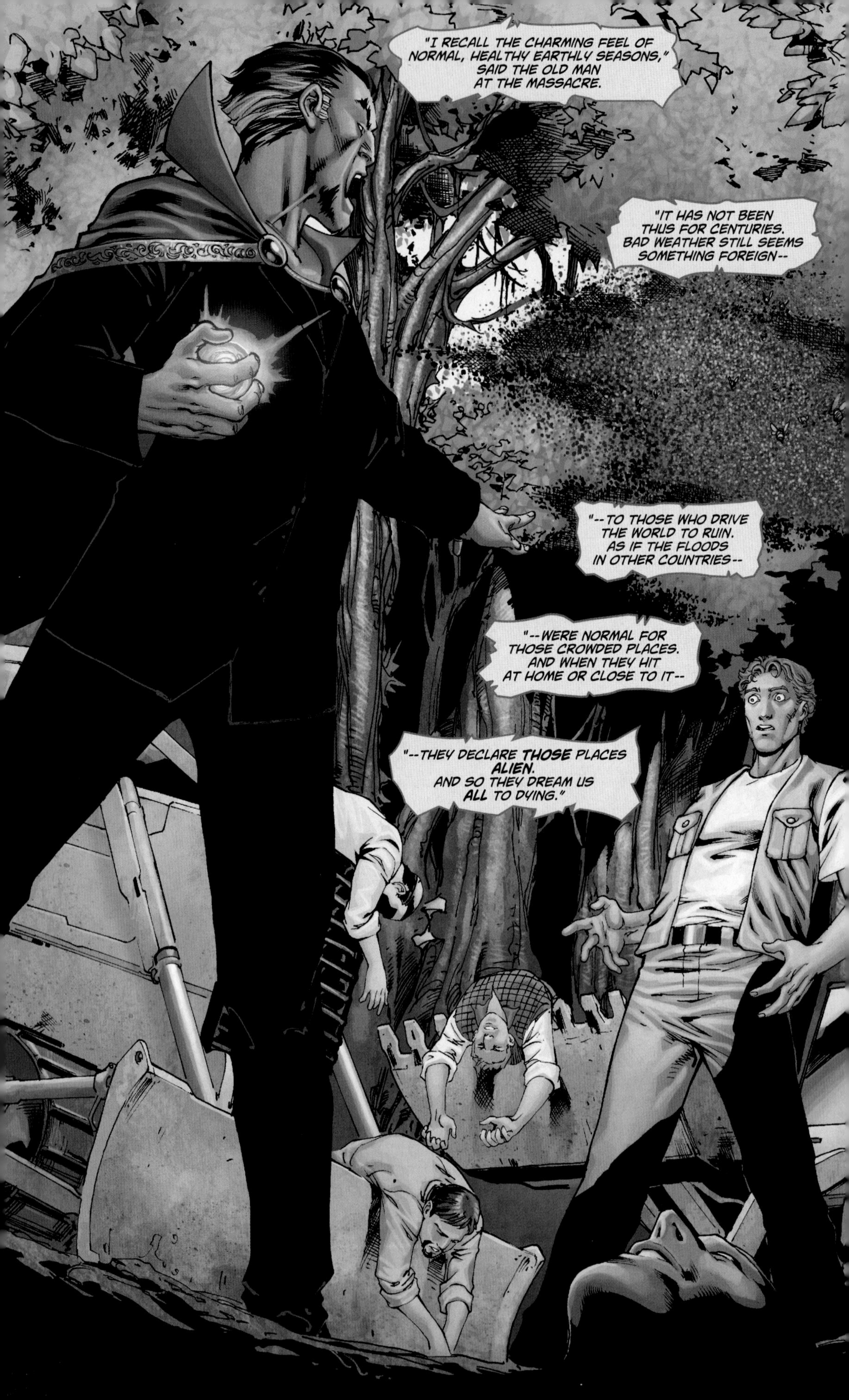
"I RECALL THE CHARMING FEEL OF NORMAL, HEALTHY EARTHLY SEASONS," SAID THE OLD MAN AT THE MASSACRE.
"IT HAS NOT BEEN THUS FOR CENTURIES. BAD WEATHER STILL SEEMS SOMETHING FOREIGN--
"--TO THOSE WHO DRIVE THE WORLD TO RUIN. AS IF THE FLOODS IN OTHER COUNTRIES--
"--WERE NORMAL FOR THOSE CROWDED PLACES. AND WHEN THEY HIT AT HOME OR CLOSE TO IT--
"--THEY DECLARE **THOSE** PLACES **ALIEN**. AND SO THEY DREAM US **ALL** TO DYING."

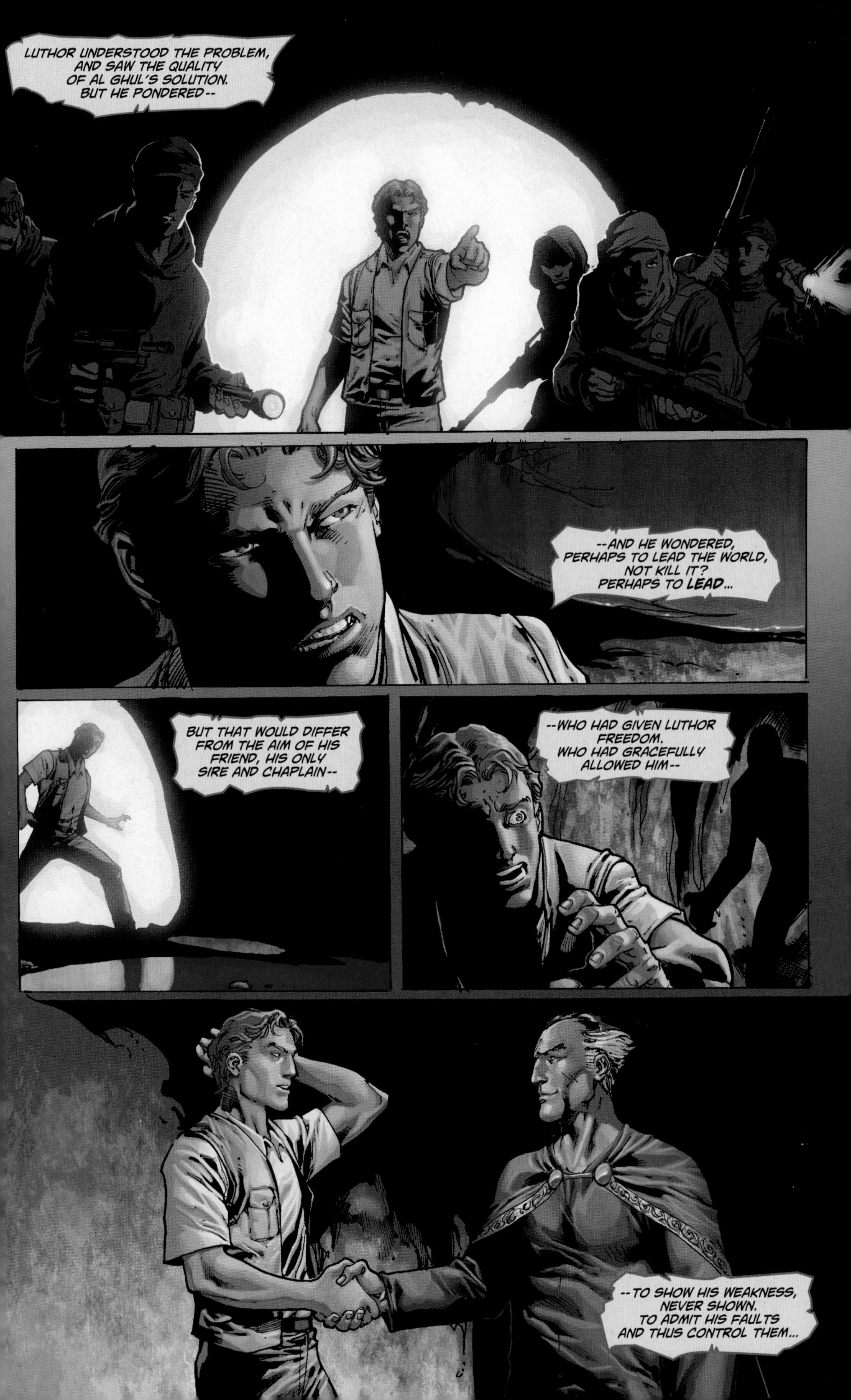
LUTHOR UNDERSTOOD THE PROBLEM, AND SAW THE QUALITY OF AL GHUL'S SOLUTION. BUT HE PONDERED--
--AND HE WONDERED, PERHAPS TO LEAD THE WORLD, NOT KILL IT? PERHAPS TO LEAD...
BUT THAT WOULD DIFFER FROM THE AIM OF HIS FRIEND, HIS ONLY SIRE AND CHAPLAIN--
--WHO HAD GIVEN LUTHOR FREEDOM. WHO HAD GRACEFULLY ALLOWED HIM--
--TO SHOW HIS WEAKNESS, NEVER SHOWN. TO ADMIT HIS FAULTS AND THUS CONTROL THEM...

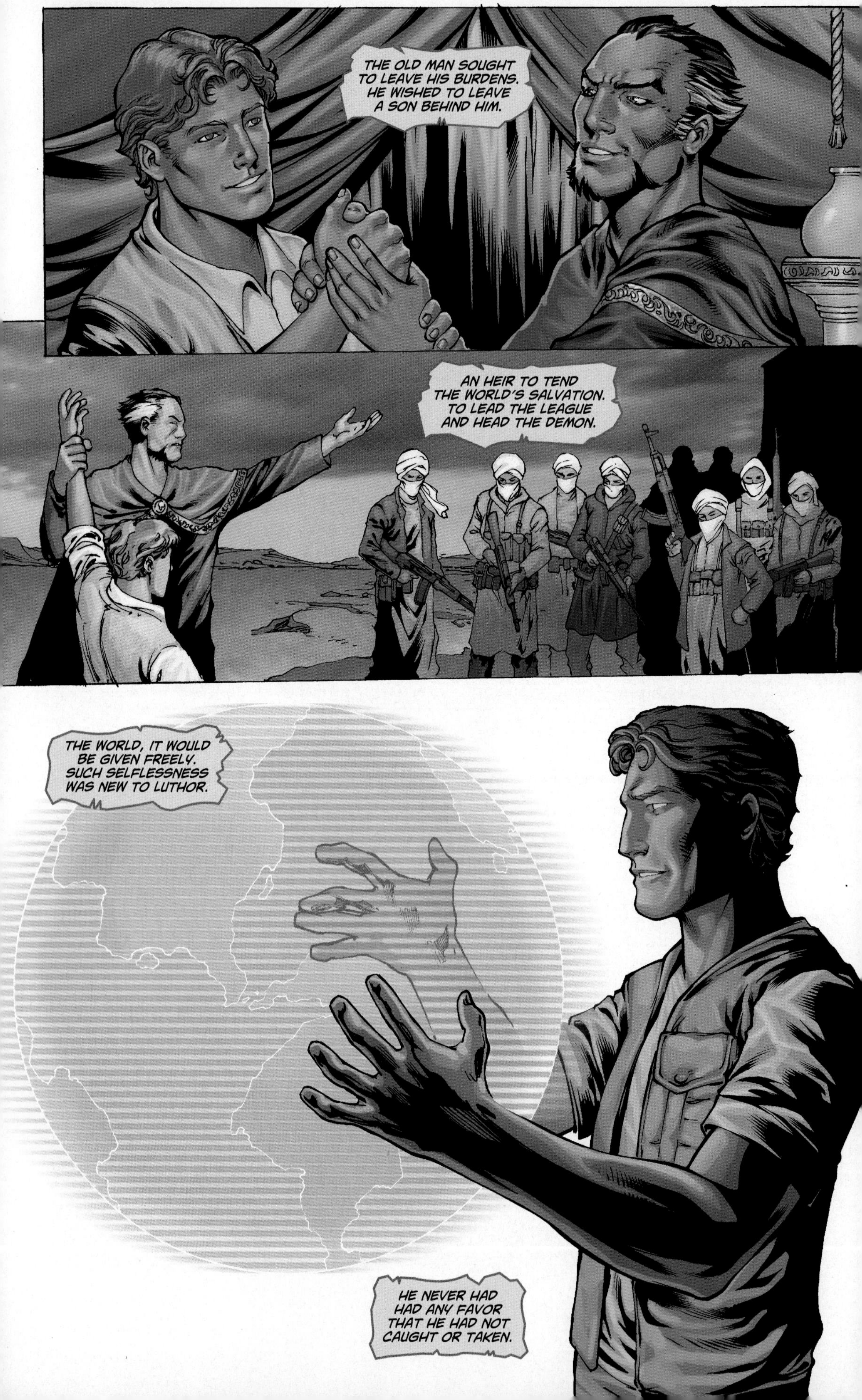
THE OLD MAN SOUGHT TO LEAVE HIS BURDENS. HE WISHED TO LEAVE A SON BEHIND HIM.
AN HEIR TO TEND THE WORLD'S SALVATION. TO LEAD THE LEAGUE AND HEAD THE DEMON.
THE WORLD, IT WOULD BE GIVEN FREELY. SUCH SELFLESSNESS WAS NEW TO LUTHOR.
HE NEVER HAD HAD ANY FAVOR THAT HE HAD NOT CAUGHT OR TAKEN.

BUT COULD HE TRUST THIS UNKNOWN FEELING? HE HAD NOTHING TO WHICH TO COMPARE IT.

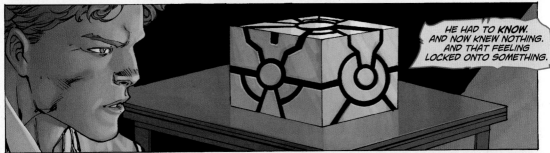

HE HAD TO KNOW. AND NOW KNEW NOTHING. AND THAT FEELING LOCKED ONTO SOMETHING.

RA'S HAD TOLD HIM NOT TO LOOK IN THE MOST PUZZLING, TROUBLING CASKET.

"IN THERE'S A BOOK. IN THERE'S THE SECRET OF ALL OUR LIVES AND ALL OUR QUESTING."

HE'D MADE A LOCKPICK FROM APOKOLIPS. HE'D MADE SCIENCE AGAINST AL GHUL'S ART.

HE SOUGHT THE ANSWER TO THE ABSENCE THAT SAT INSIDE HIM LIKE A HEART.

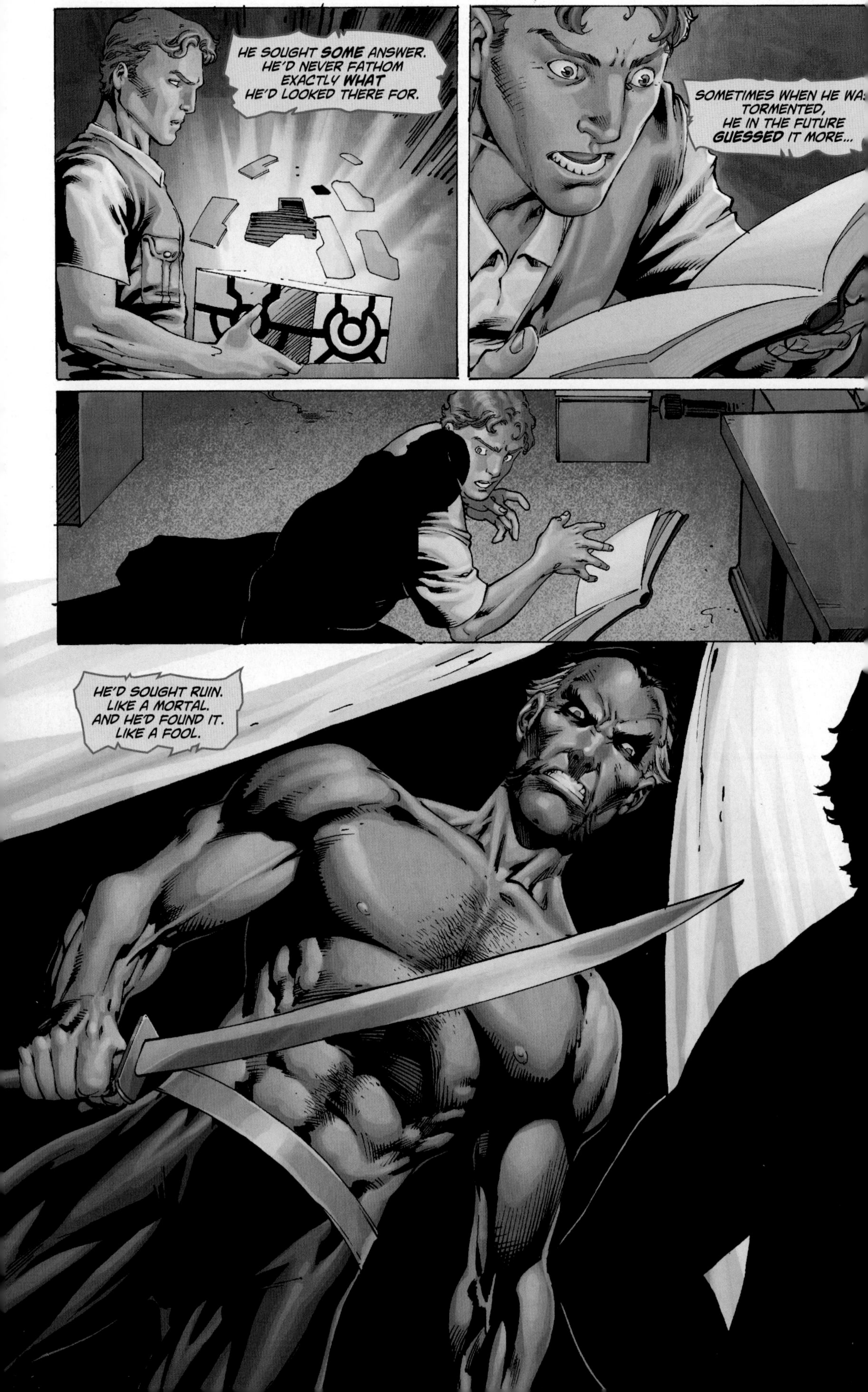
HE SOUGHT SOME ANSWER. HE'D NEVER FATHOM EXACTLY WHAT HE'D LOOKED THERE FOR.
SOMETIMES WHEN HE WAS TORMENTED, HE IN THE FUTURE GUESSED IT MORE...
HE'D SOUGHT RUIN. LIKE A MORTAL. AND HE'D FOUND IT. LIKE A FOOL.

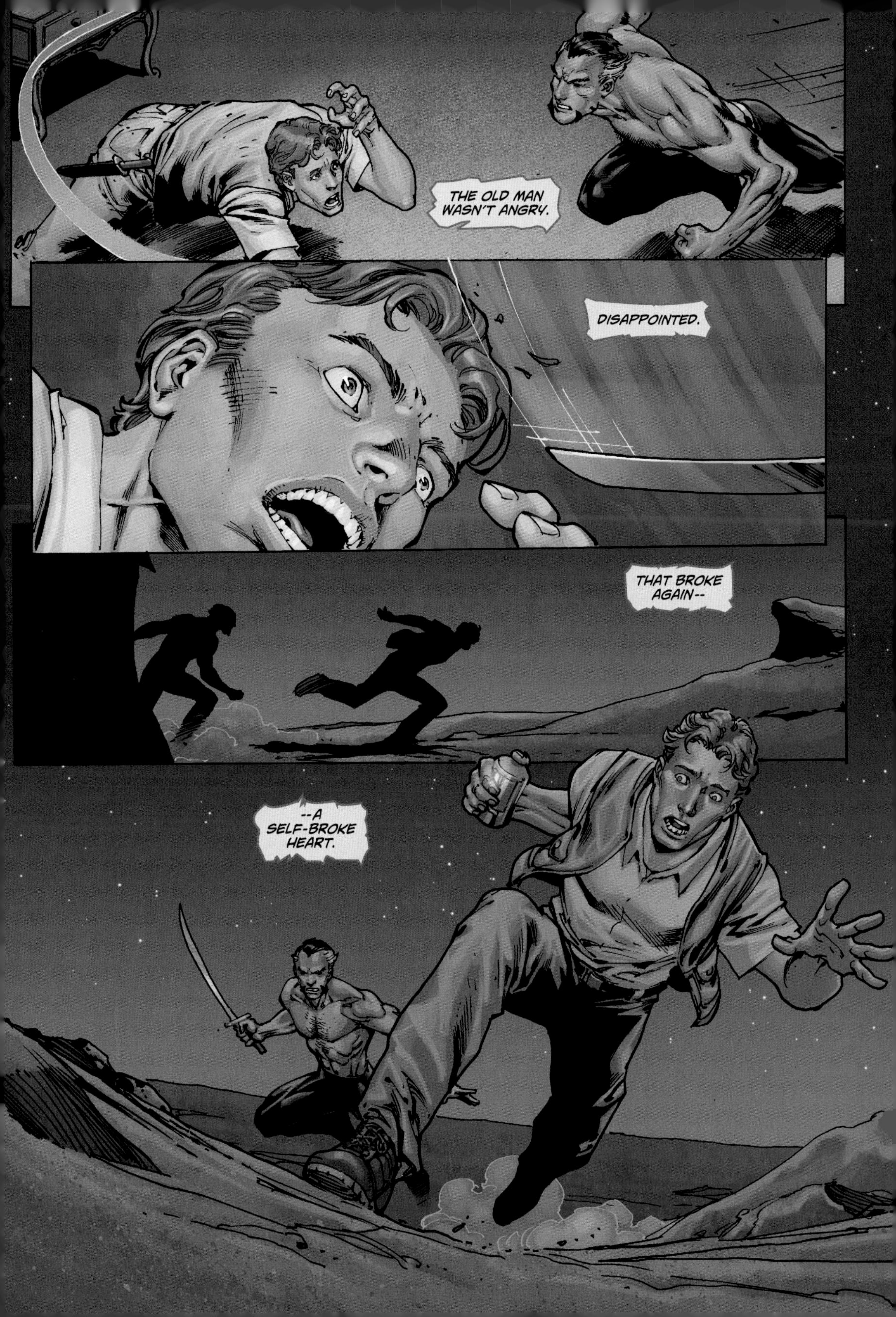
THE OLD MAN WASN'T ANGRY.
DISAPPOINTED.
THAT BROKE AGAIN--
--A SELF-BROKE HEART.

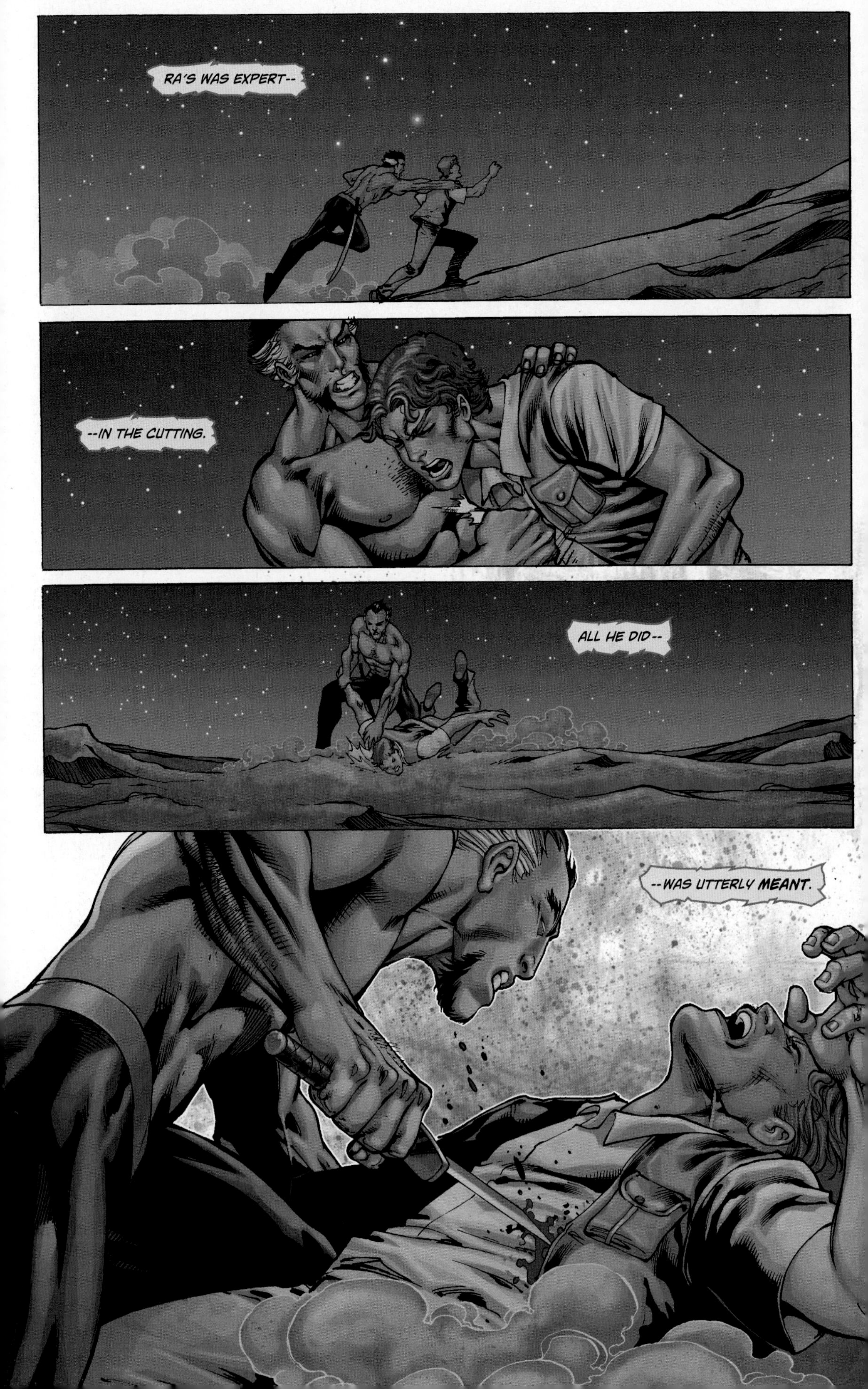
RA'S WAS EXPERT--
--IN THE CUTTING.
ALL HE DID--
--WAS UTTERLY MEANT.

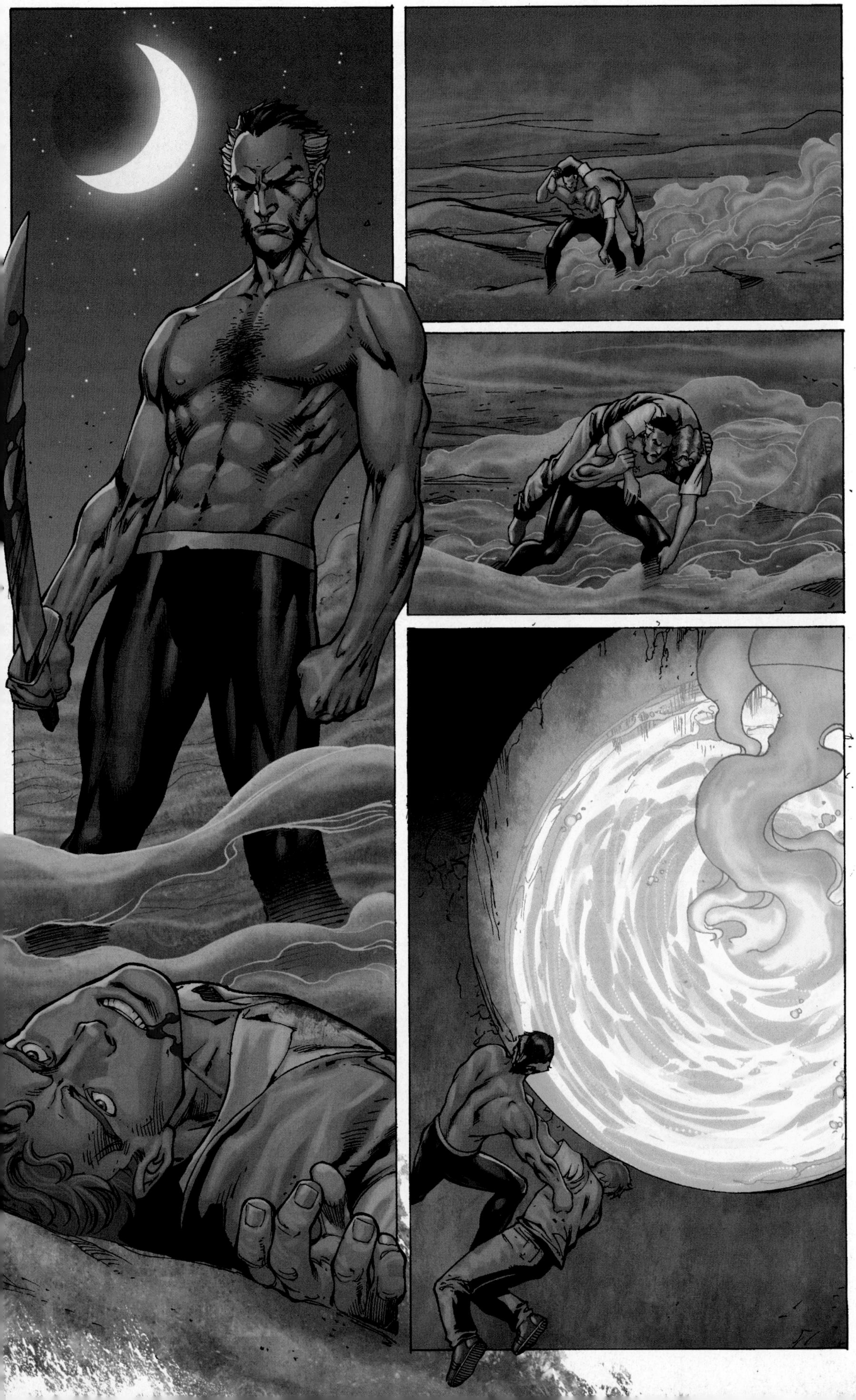

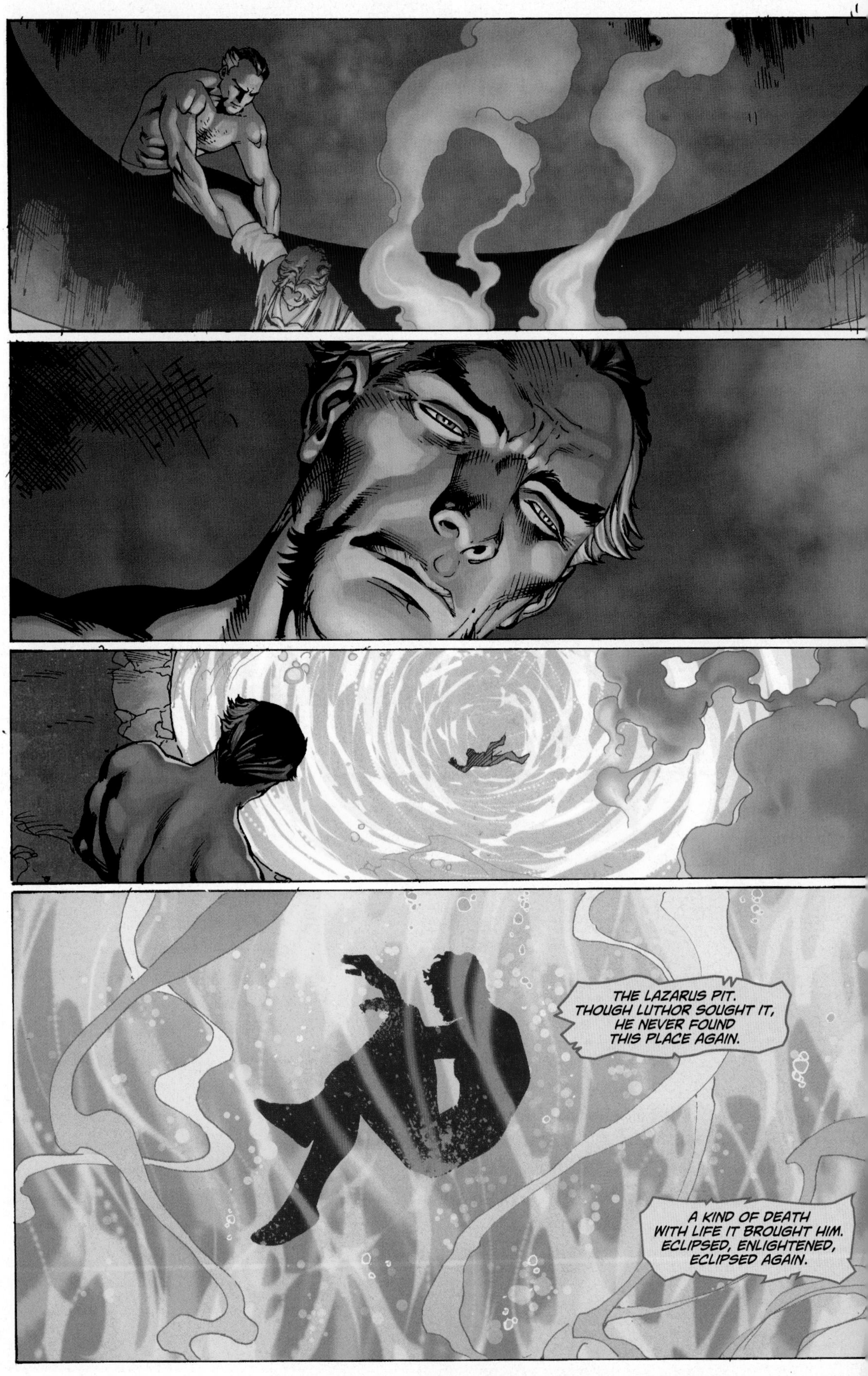
THE LAZARUS PIT.
THOUGH LUTHOR SOUGHT IT,
HE NEVER FOUND
THIS PLACE AGAIN.
A KIND OF DEATH
WITH LIFE IT BROUGHT HIM.
ECLIPSED, ENLIGHTENED,
ECLIPSED AGAIN.

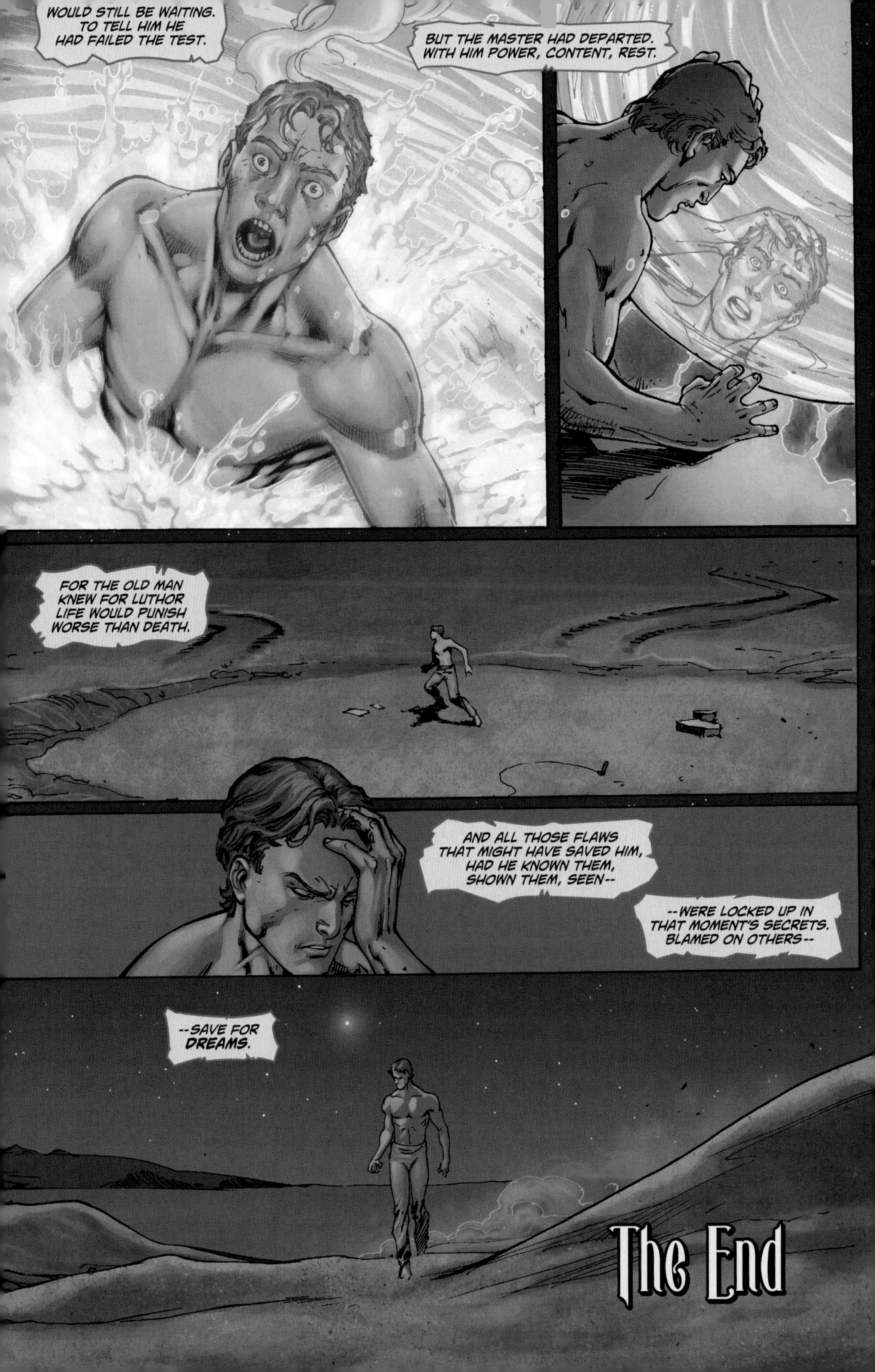
WOULD STILL BE WAITING. TO TELL HIM HE HAD FAILED THE TEST.
BUT THE MASTER HAD DEPARTED. WITH HIM POWER, CONTENT, REST.
FOR THE OLD MAN KNEW FOR LUTHOR LIFE WOULD PUNISH WORSE THAN DEATH.
AND ALL THOSE FLAWS THAT MIGHT HAVE SAVED HIM, HAD HE KNOWN THEM, SHOWN THEM, SEEN--
--WERE LOCKED UP IN THAT MOMENT'S SECRETS. BLAMED ON OTHERS--
--SAVE FOR DREAMS.
The End

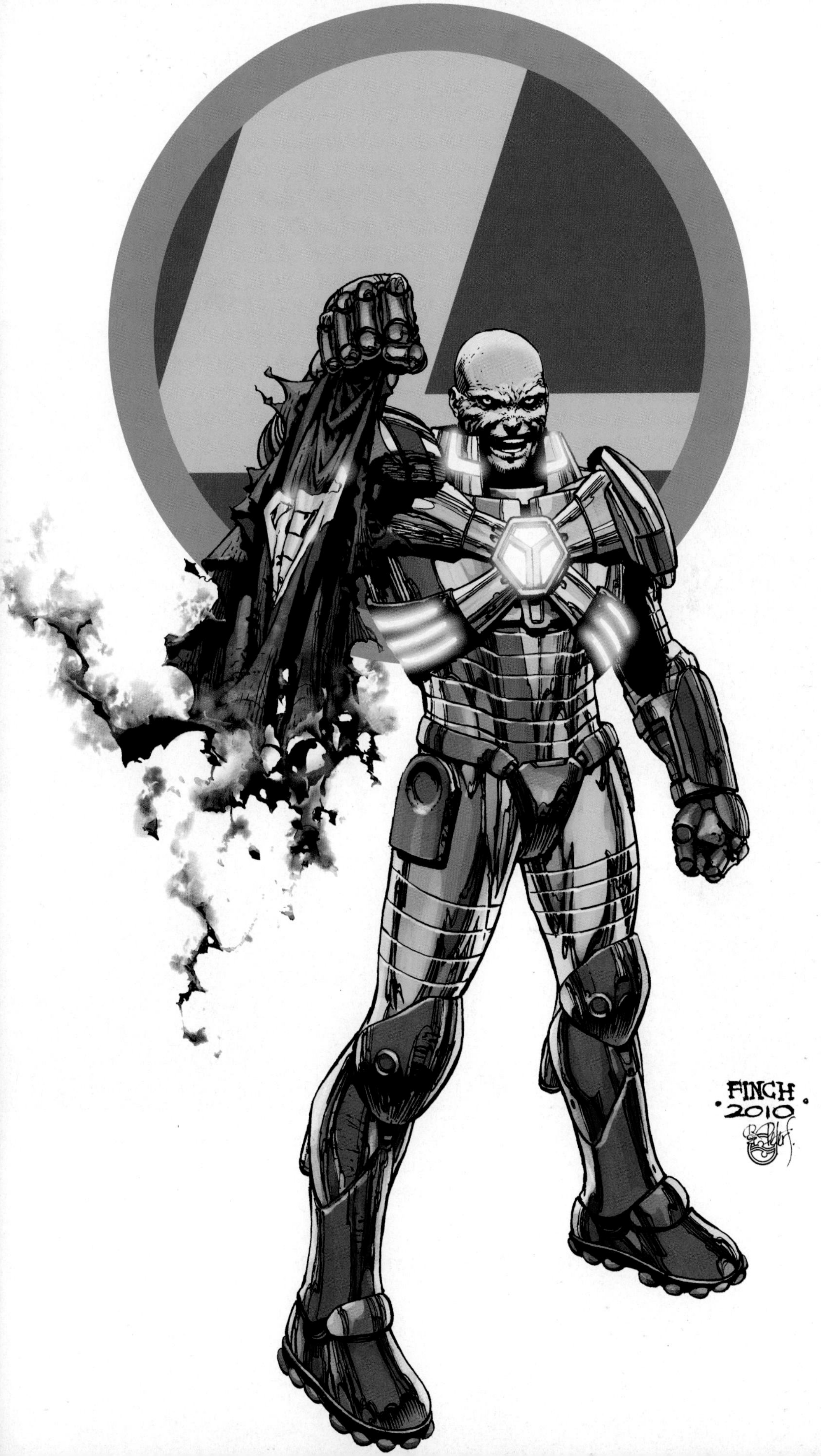
FINCH
2010

THE BLACK RING
part eight

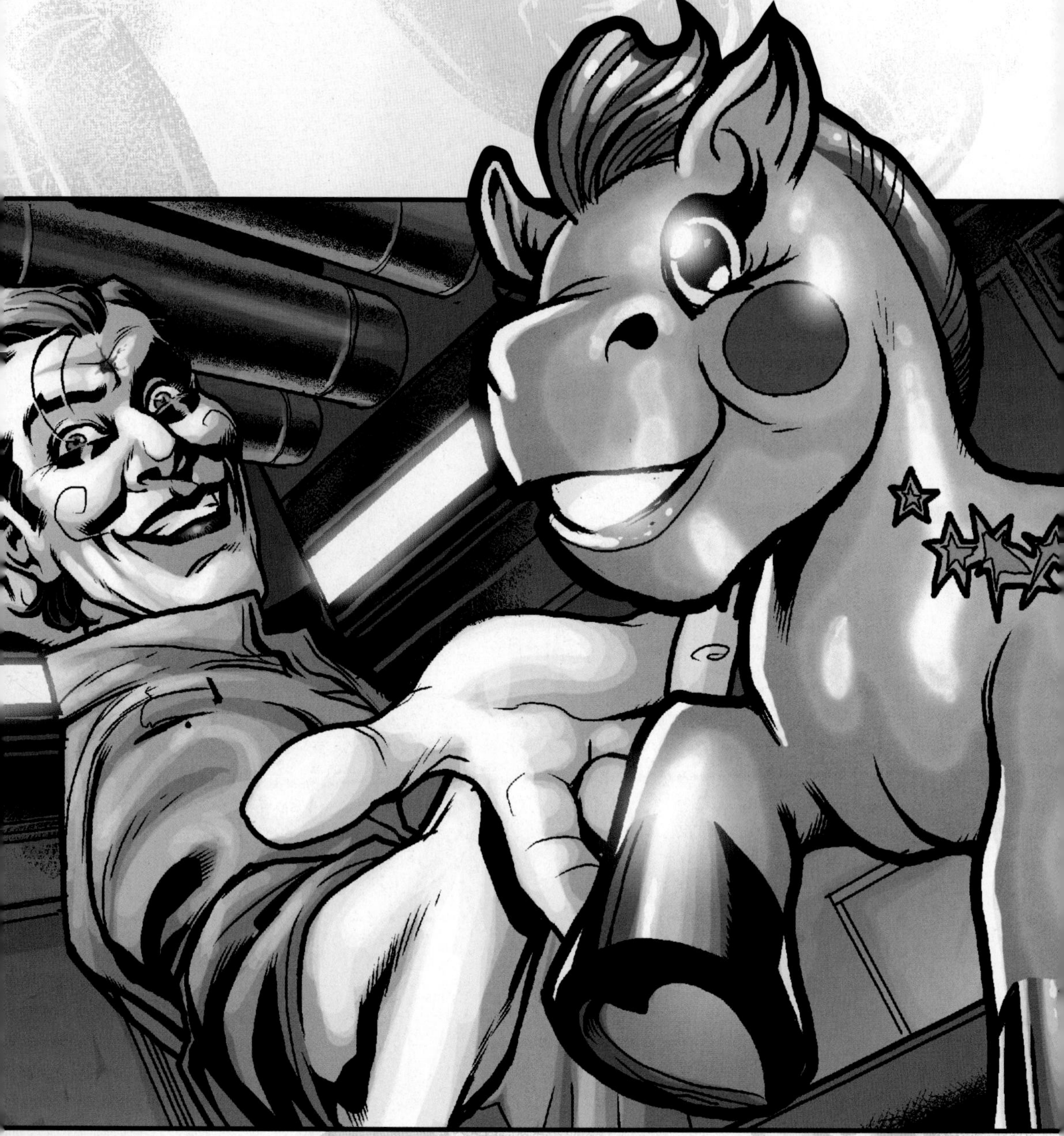

PAUL **CORNELL** writer
PETE **WOODS** artist

cover by
DAVID **FINCH** & PETER **STEIGERWALD**

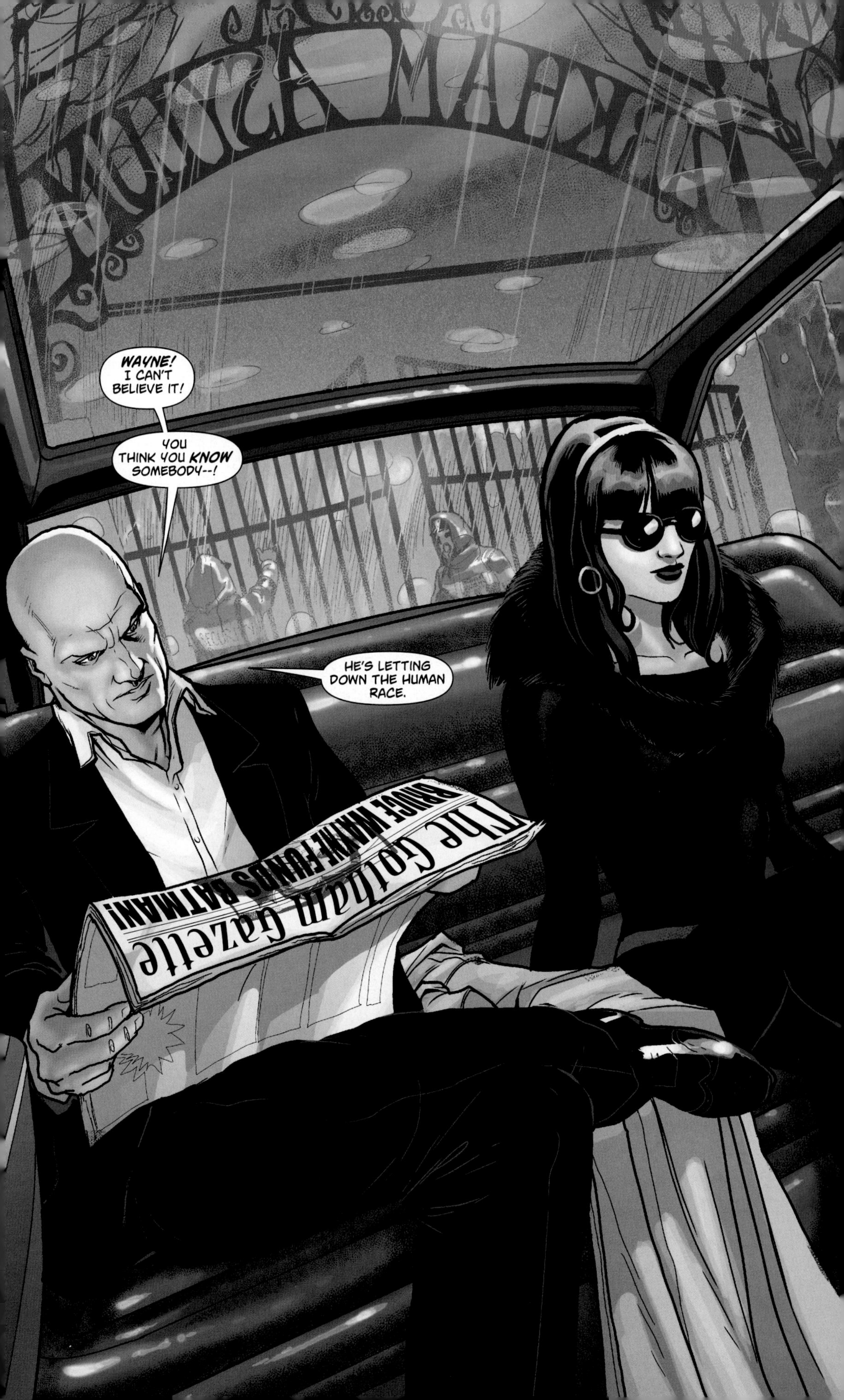
WAYNE! I CAN'T BELIEVE IT!
YOU THINK YOU KNOW SOMEBODY--!
HE'S LETTING DOWN THE HUMAN RACE.
The Gotham Gazette
BRUCE WAYNE FUNDS BATMAN!

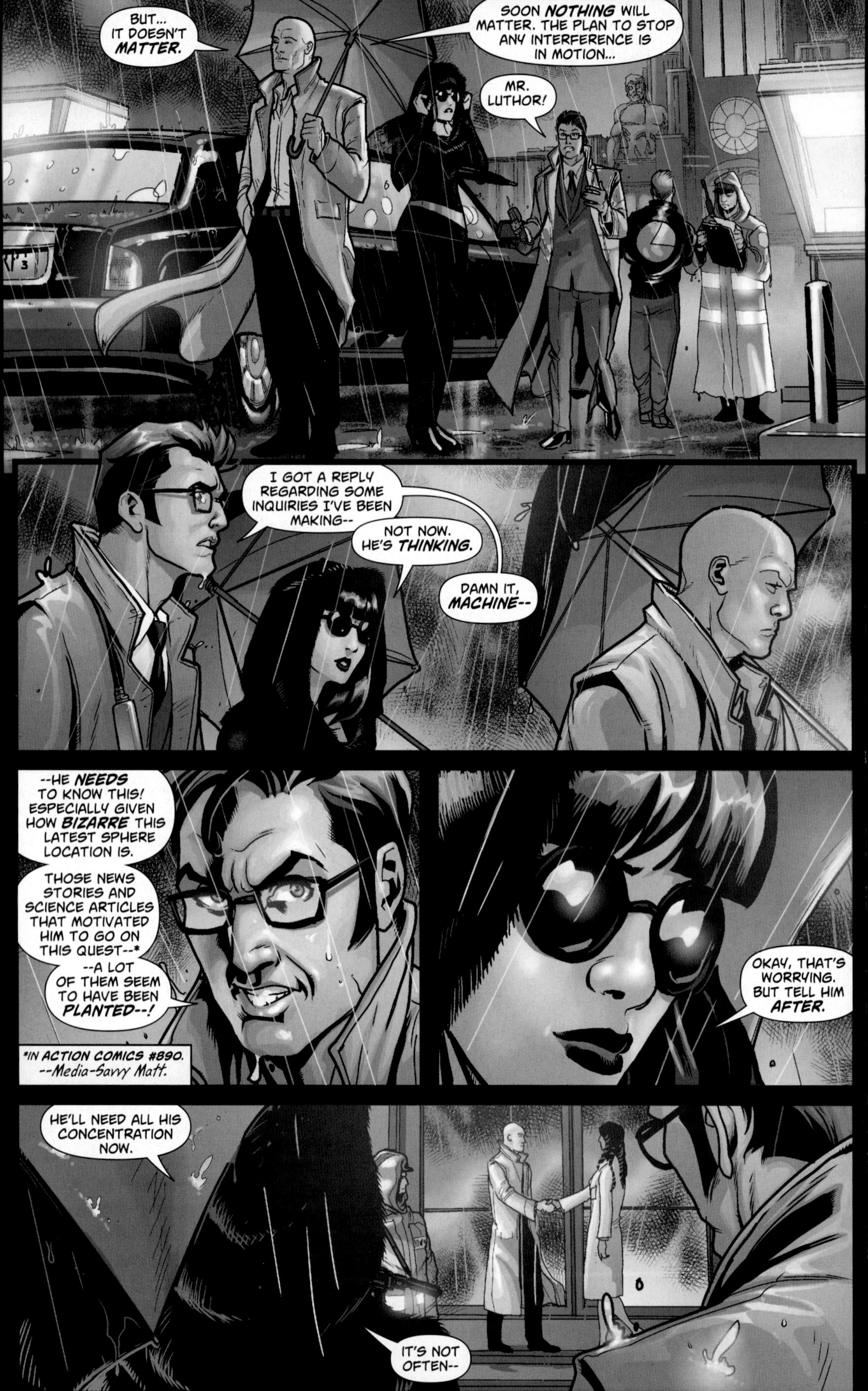
BUT... IT DOESN'T MATTER.
SOON NOTHING WILL MATTER. THE PLAN TO STOP ANY INTERFERENCE IS IN MOTION...
MR. LUTHOR!
I GOT A REPLY REGARDING SOME INQUIRIES I'VE BEEN MAKING--
NOT NOW. HE'S THINKING.
DAMN IT, MACHINE--
--HE NEEDS TO KNOW THIS! ESPECIALLY GIVEN HOW BIZARRE THIS LATEST SPHERE LOCATION IS.
THOSE NEWS STORIES AND SCIENCE ARTICLES THAT MOTIVATED HIM TO GO ON THIS QUEST--*
--A LOT OF THEM SEEM TO HAVE BEEN PLANTED--!
*IN ACTION COMICS #890. --Media-Savvy Matt.
OKAY, THAT'S WORRYING. BUT TELL HIM AFTER.
HE'LL NEED ALL HIS CONCENTRATION NOW.
IT'S NOT OFTEN--

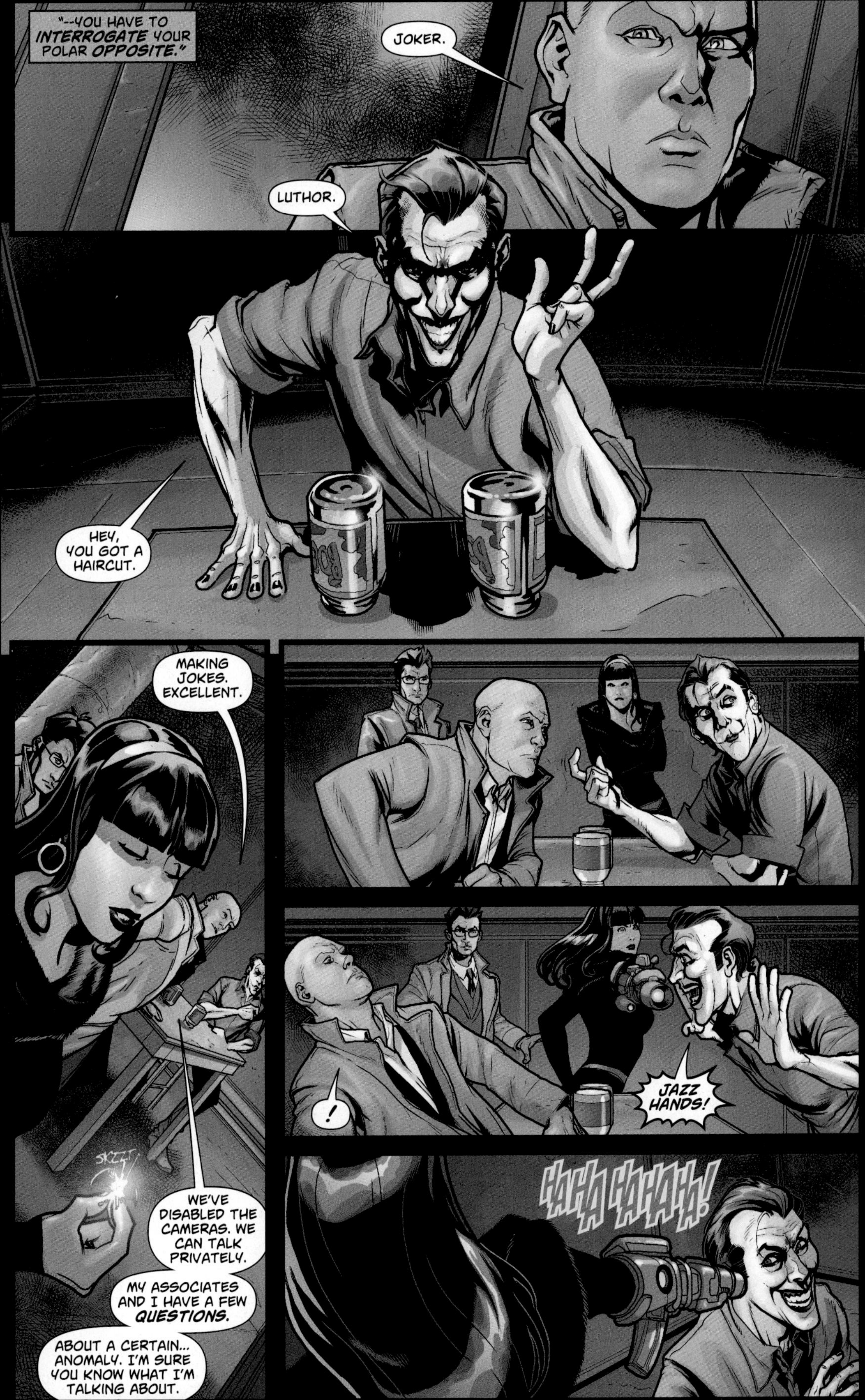
"--YOU HAVE TO INTERROGATE YOUR POLAR OPPOSITE."
JOKER.
LUTHOR.
HEY, YOU GOT A HAIRCUT.
MAKING JOKES. EXCELLENT.
SKZZT
WE'VE DISABLED THE CAMERAS. WE CAN TALK PRIVATELY.
MY ASSOCIATES AND I HAVE A FEW QUESTIONS.
ABOUT A CERTAIN... ANOMALY. I'M SURE YOU KNOW WHAT I'M TALKING ABOUT.
!
JAZZ HANDS!
HAHA HAHAHA!

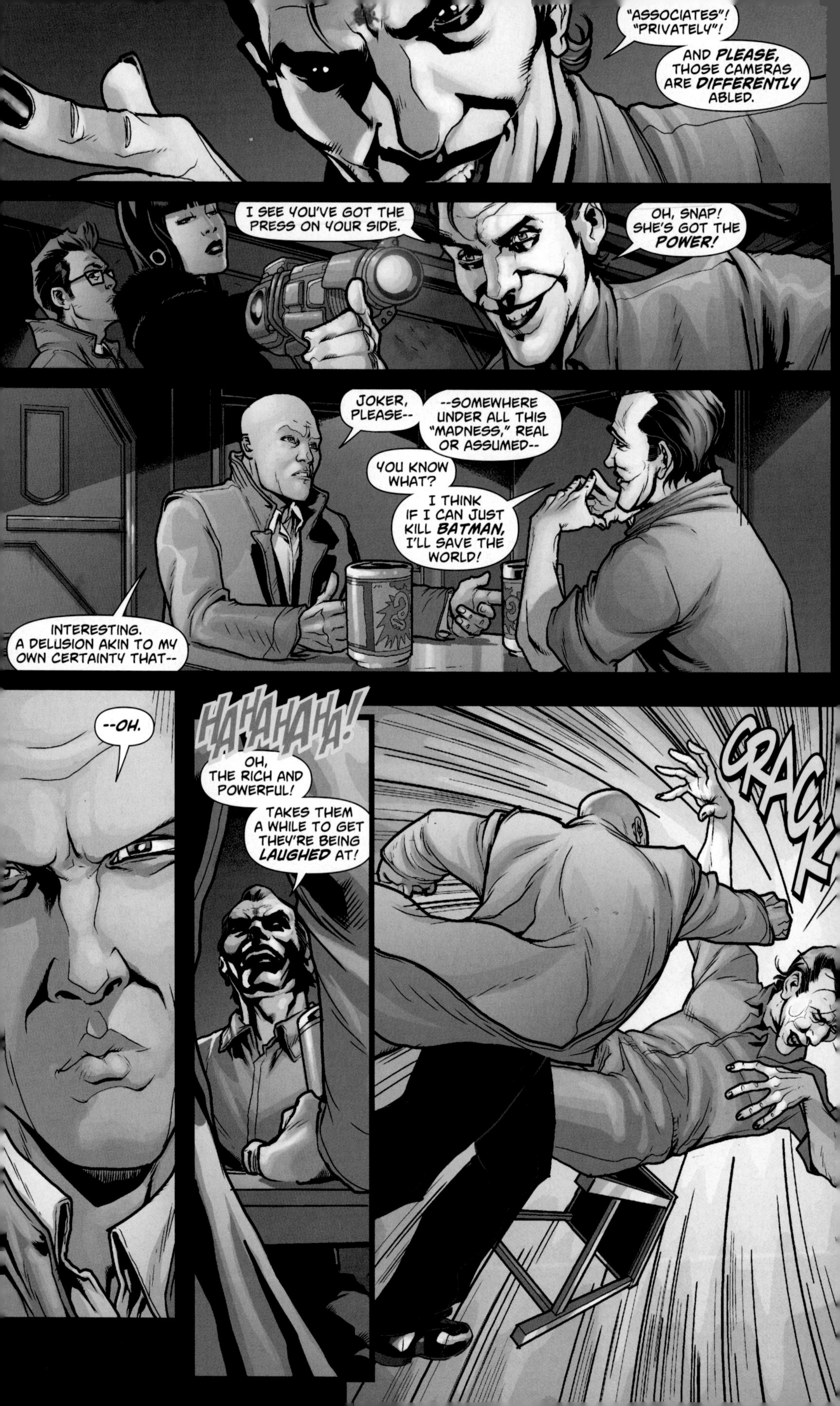
"ASSOCIATES"! "PRIVATELY"!
AND PLEASE, THOSE CAMERAS ARE DIFFERENTLY ABLED.
I SEE YOU'VE GOT THE PRESS ON YOUR SIDE.
OH, SNAP! SHE'S GOT THE POWER!
JOKER, PLEASE--
--SOMEWHERE UNDER ALL THIS "MADNESS," REAL OR ASSUMED--
YOU KNOW WHAT?
I THINK IF I CAN JUST KILL BATMAN, I'LL SAVE THE WORLD!
INTERESTING. A DELUSION AKIN TO MY OWN CERTAINTY THAT--
--OH.
HAHAHAHA!
OH, THE RICH AND POWERFUL!
TAKES THEM A WHILE TO GET THEY'RE BEING LAUGHED AT!
CRACK!

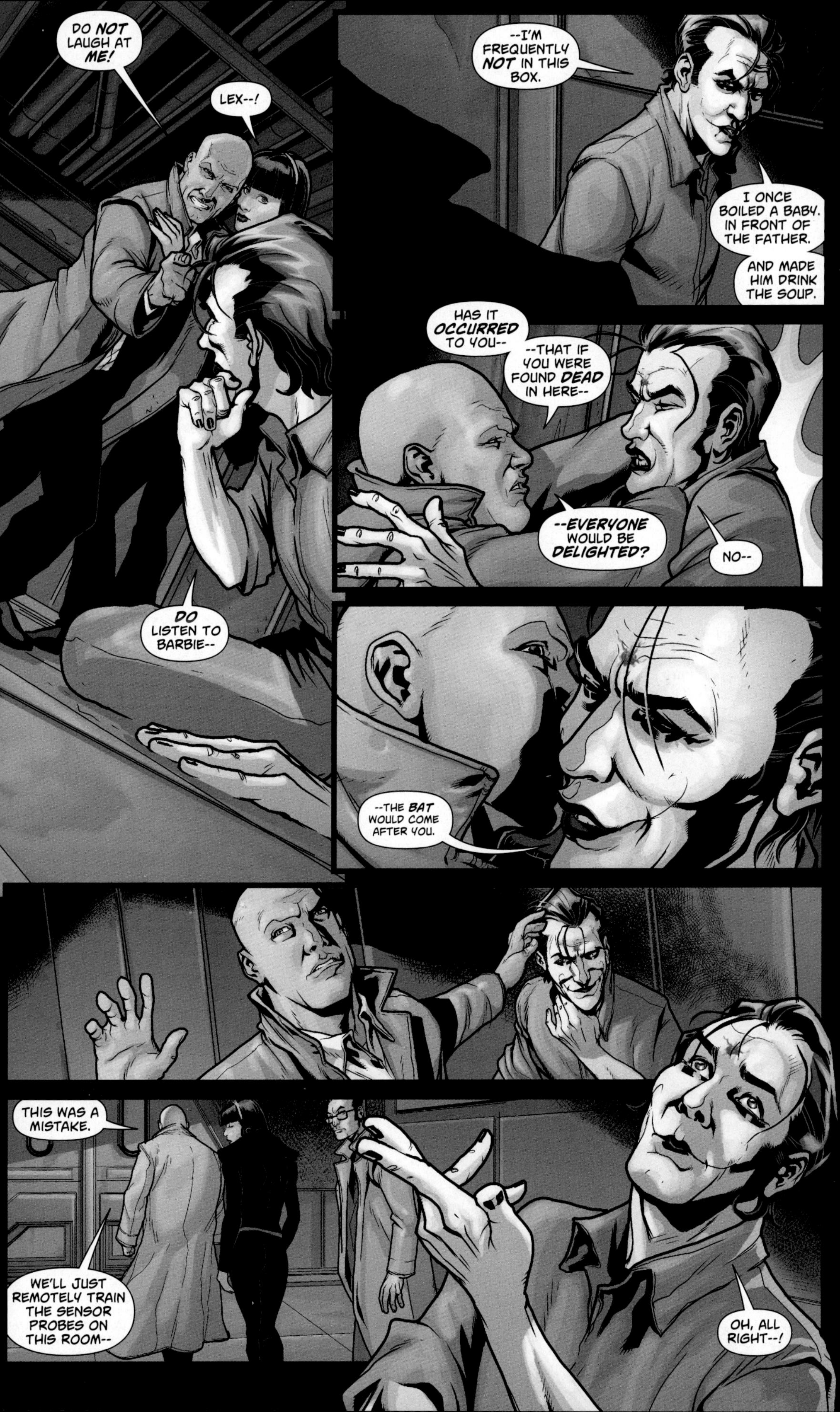
DO NOT LAUGH AT ME!
LEX--!
DO LISTEN TO BARBIE--
--I'M FREQUENTLY NOT IN THIS BOX.
I ONCE BOILED A BABY. IN FRONT OF THE FATHER.
AND MADE HIM DRINK THE SOUP.
HAS IT OCCURRED TO YOU--
--THAT IF YOU WERE FOUND DEAD IN HERE--
--EVERYONE WOULD BE DELIGHTED?
NO--
--THE BAT WOULD COME AFTER YOU.
THIS WAS A MISTAKE.
WE'LL JUST REMOTELY TRAIN THE SENSOR PROBES ON THIS ROOM--
OH, ALL RIGHT--!

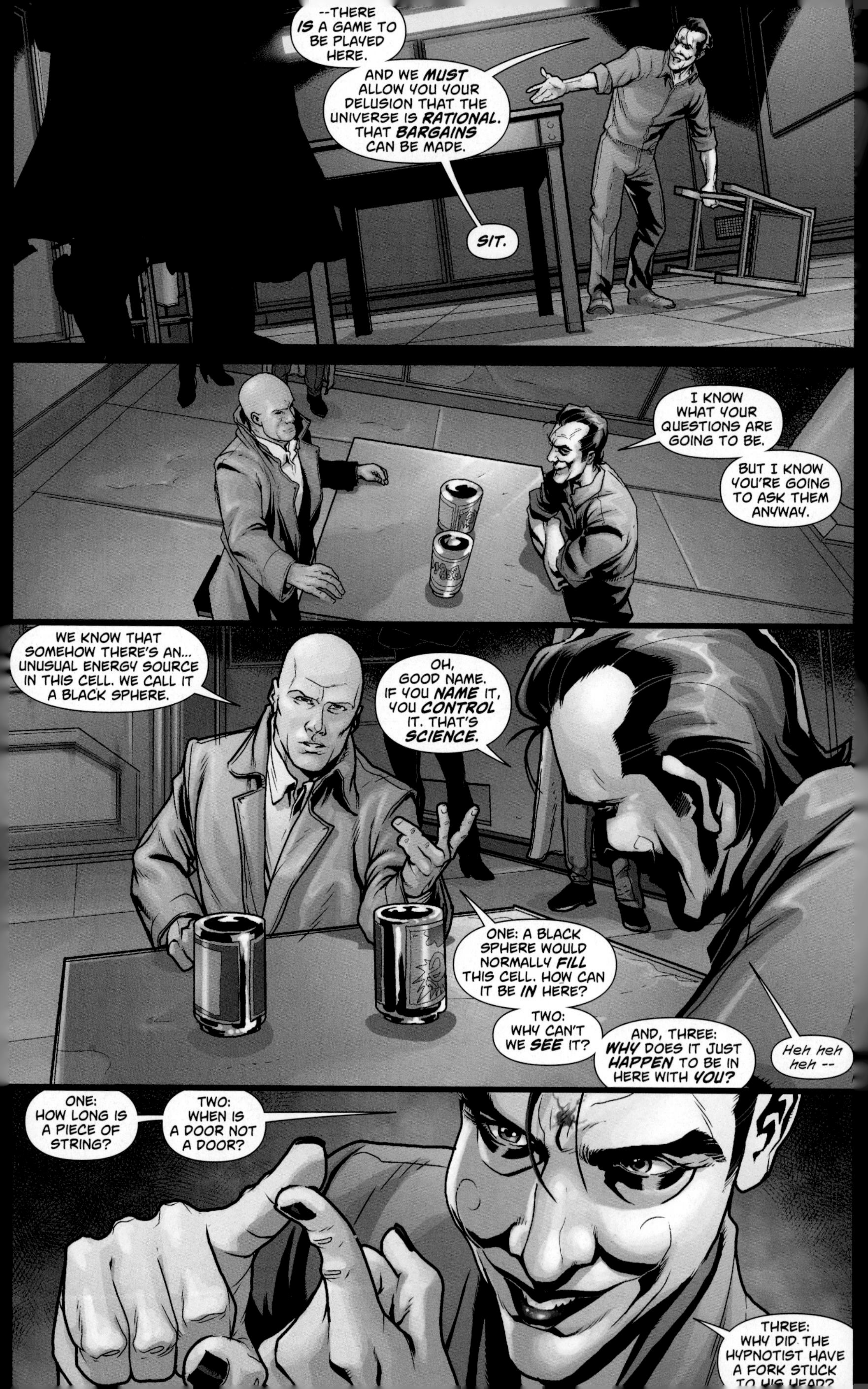
--THERE IS A GAME TO BE PLAYED HERE.
AND WE MUST ALLOW YOU YOUR DELUSION THAT THE UNIVERSE IS RATIONAL. THAT BARGAINS CAN BE MADE.
SIT.
I KNOW WHAT YOUR QUESTIONS ARE GOING TO BE.
BUT I KNOW YOU'RE GOING TO ASK THEM ANYWAY.
WE KNOW THAT SOMEHOW THERE'S AN... UNUSUAL ENERGY SOURCE IN THIS CELL. WE CALL IT A BLACK SPHERE.
OH, GOOD NAME. IF YOU NAME IT, YOU CONTROL IT. THAT'S SCIENCE.
ONE: A BLACK SPHERE WOULD NORMALLY FILL THIS CELL. HOW CAN IT BE IN HERE?
TWO: WHY CAN'T WE SEE IT?
AND, THREE: WHY DOES IT JUST HAPPEN TO BE IN HERE WITH YOU?
Heh heh heh --
ONE: HOW LONG IS A PIECE OF STRING?
TWO: WHEN IS A DOOR NOT A DOOR?
THREE: WHY DID THE HYPNOTIST HAVE A FORK STUCK

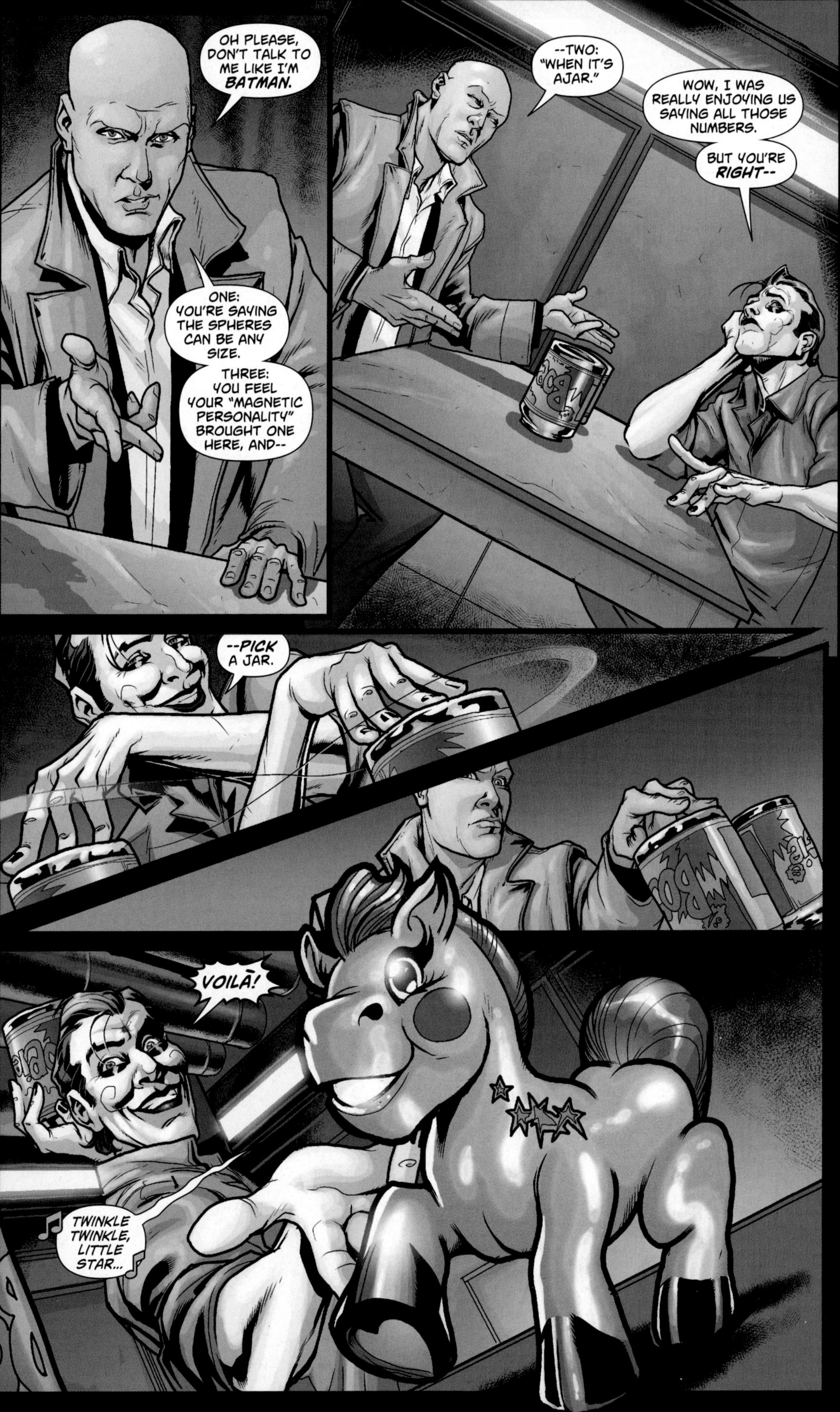
OH PLEASE, DON'T TALK TO ME LIKE I'M BATMAN.
ONE: YOU'RE SAYING THE SPHERES CAN BE ANY SIZE.
THREE: YOU FEEL YOUR "MAGNETIC PERSONALITY" BROUGHT ONE HERE, AND--
--TWO: "WHEN IT'S AJAR."
WOW, I WAS REALLY ENJOYING US SAYING ALL THOSE NUMBERS.
BUT YOU'RE RIGHT--
--PICK A JAR.
VOILÀ!
TWINKLE TWINKLE, LITTLE STAR...

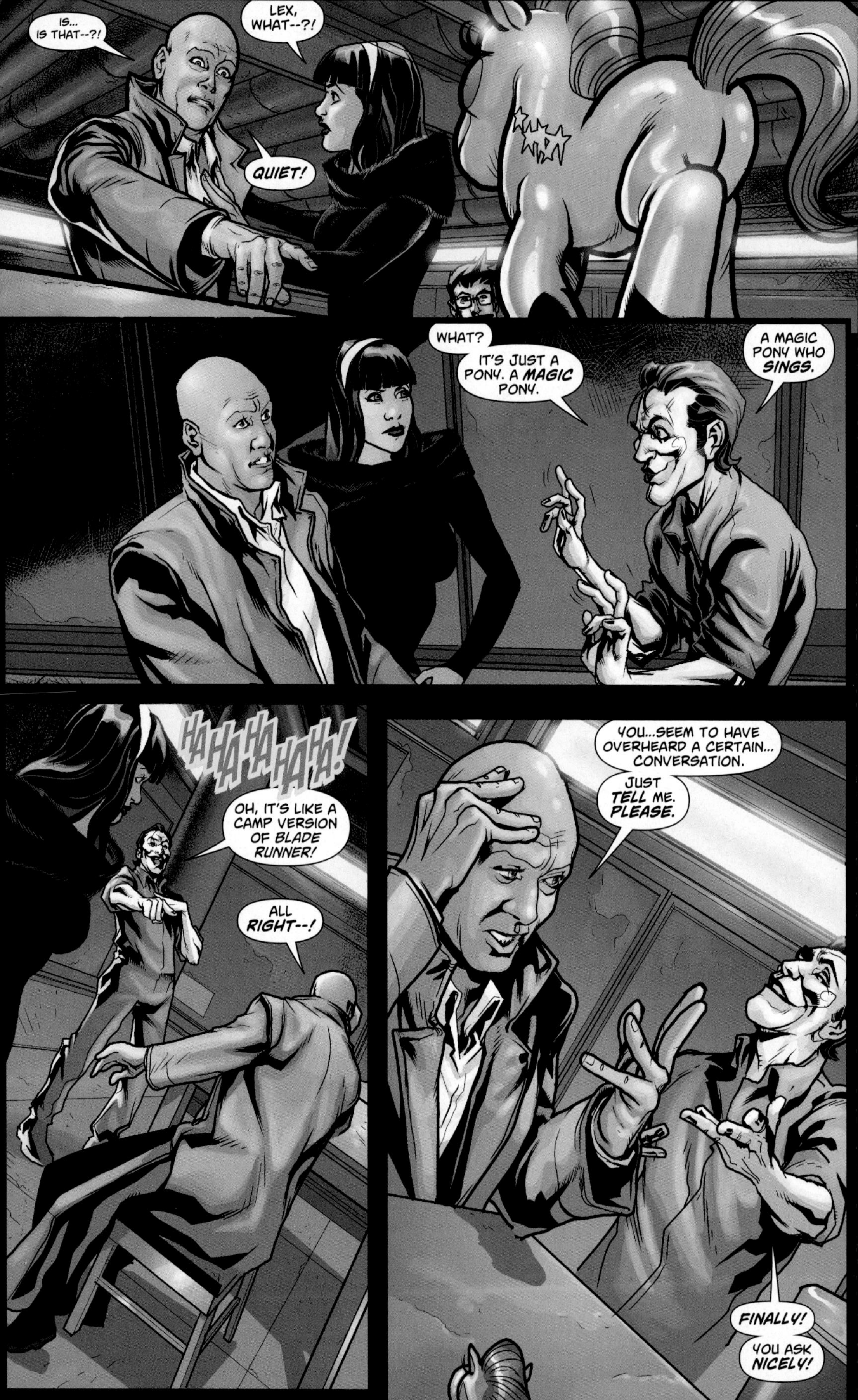
IS... IS THAT--?!
LEX, WHAT--?!
QUIET!
WHAT?
IT'S JUST A PONY. A MAGIC PONY.
A MAGIC PONY WHO SINGS.
HA HA HA HA HA HA HA!
OH, IT'S LIKE A CAMP VERSION OF BLADE RUNNER!
ALL RIGHT--!
YOU...SEEM TO HAVE OVERHEARD A CERTAIN... CONVERSATION.
JUST TELL ME. PLEASE.
FINALLY!
YOU ASK NICELY!

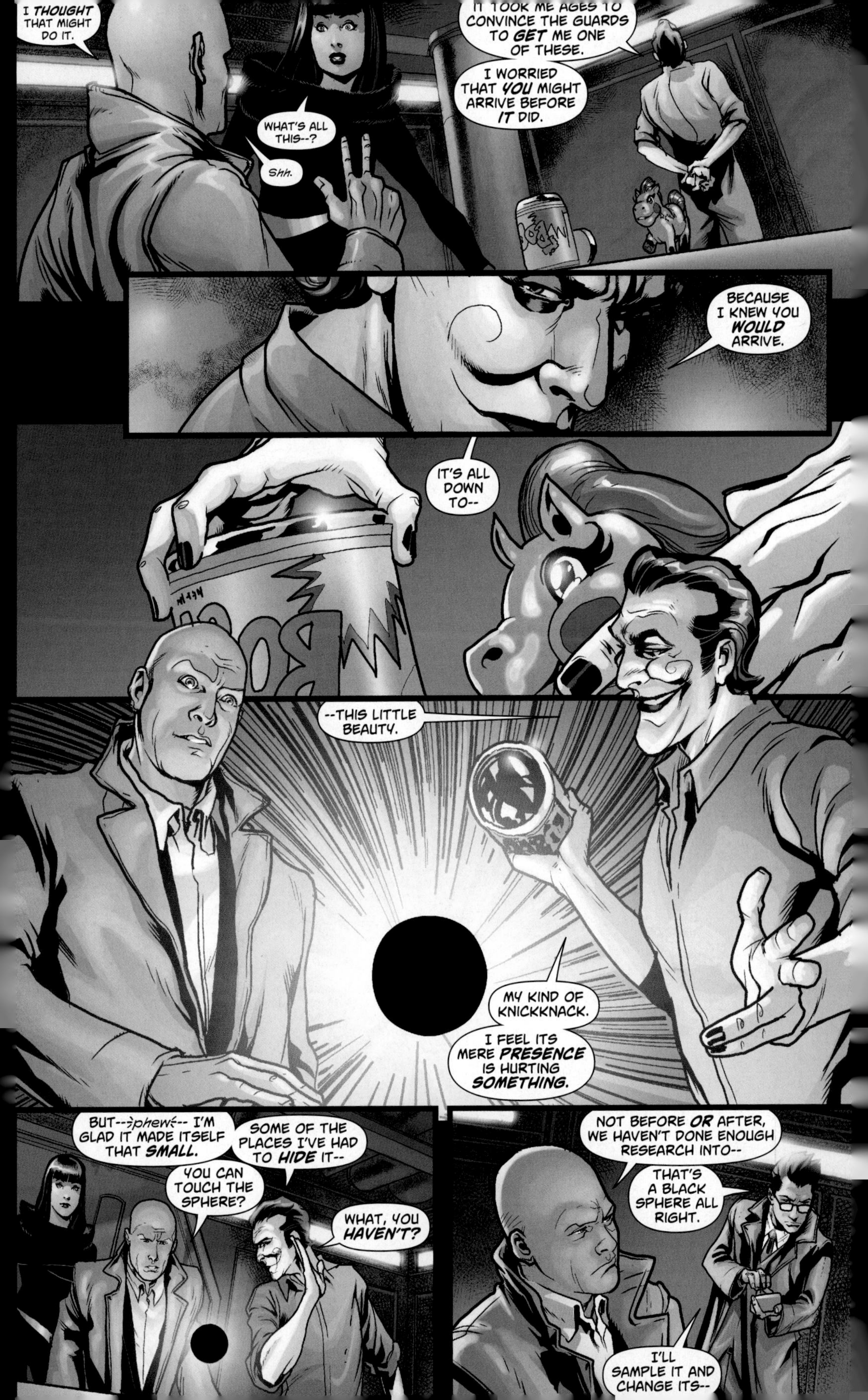
I THOUGHT THAT MIGHT DO IT.
WHAT'S ALL THIS--?
Shh.
IT TOOK ME AGES TO CONVINCE THE GUARDS TO GET ME ONE OF THESE.
I WORRIED THAT YOU MIGHT ARRIVE BEFORE IT DID.
BECAUSE I KNEW YOU WOULD ARRIVE.
IT'S ALL DOWN TO--
--THIS LITTLE BEAUTY.
MY KIND OF KNICKKNACK.
I FEEL ITS MERE PRESENCE IS HURTING SOMETHING.
BUT-- phew -- I'M GLAD IT MADE ITSELF THAT SMALL.
SOME OF THE PLACES I'VE HAD TO HIDE IT--
YOU CAN TOUCH THE SPHERE?
WHAT, YOU HAVEN'T?
NOT BEFORE OR AFTER, WE HAVEN'T DONE ENOUGH RESEARCH INTO--
THAT'S A BLACK SPHERE ALL RIGHT.
I'LL SAMPLE IT AND CHANGE ITS--

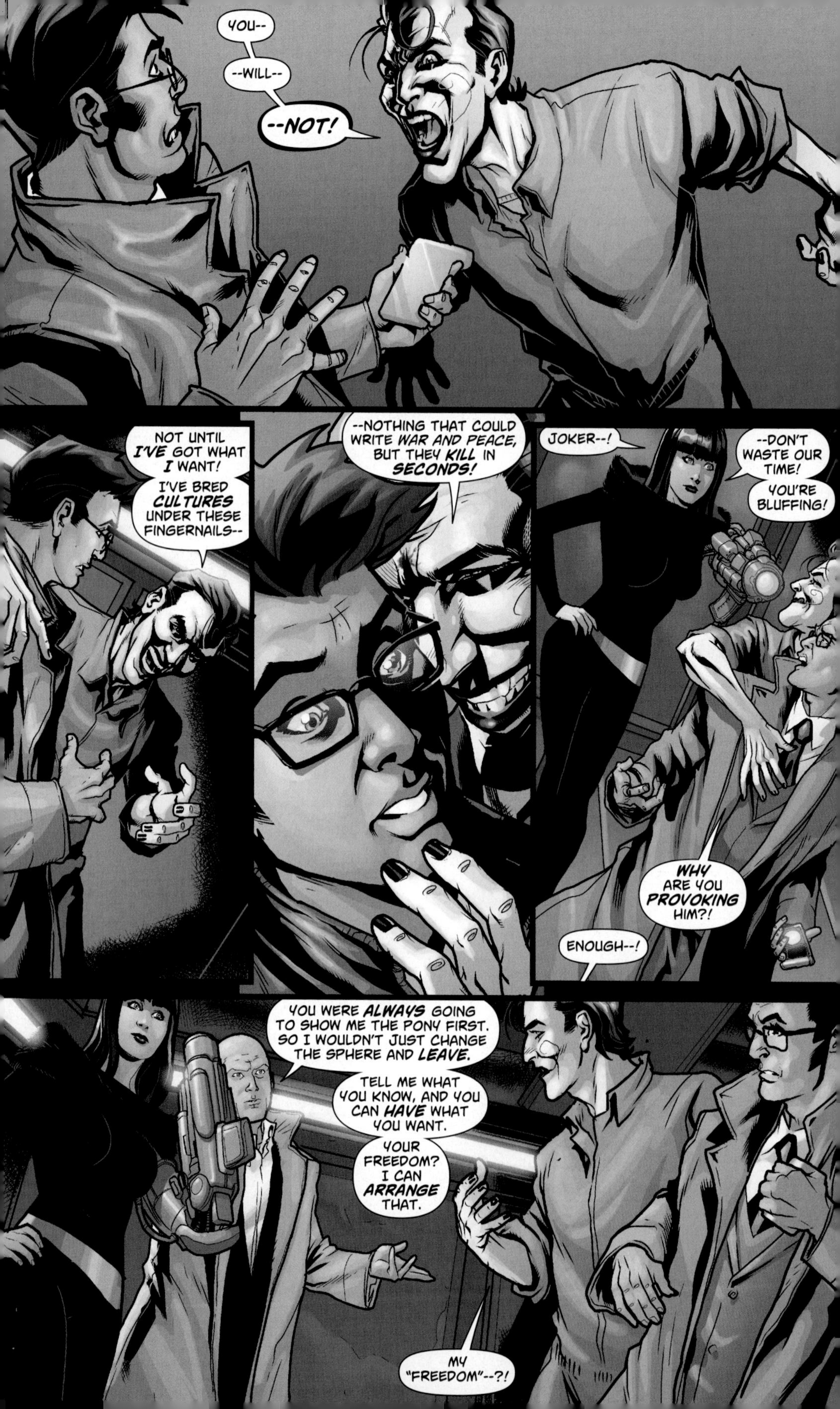

YOU--
--WILL--
--NOT!
NOT UNTIL I'VE GOT WHAT I WANT!
I'VE BRED CULTURES UNDER THESE FINGERNAILS--
--NOTHING THAT COULD WRITE WAR AND PEACE, BUT THEY KILL IN SECONDS!
JOKER--!
--DON'T WASTE OUR TIME!
YOU'RE BLUFFING!
WHY ARE YOU PROVOKING HIM?!
ENOUGH--!
YOU WERE ALWAYS GOING TO SHOW ME THE PONY FIRST. SO I WOULDN'T JUST CHANGE THE SPHERE AND LEAVE.
TELL ME WHAT YOU KNOW, AND YOU CAN HAVE WHAT YOU WANT.
YOUR FREEDOM? I CAN ARRANGE THAT.
MY "FREEDOM"--?!

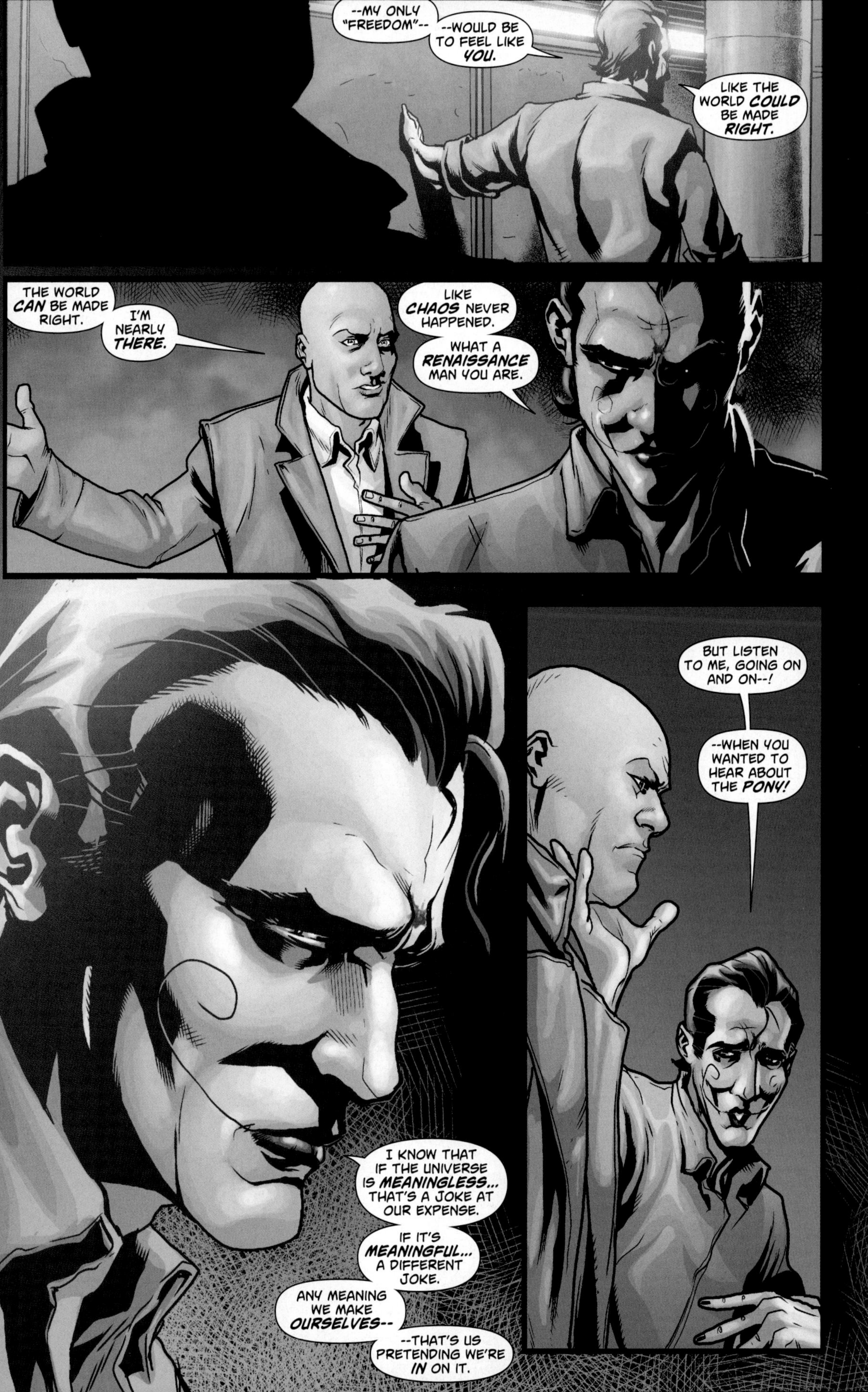
--MY ONLY "FREEDOM"--
--WOULD BE TO FEEL LIKE *YOU*.
LIKE THE WORLD *COULD* BE MADE *RIGHT*.
THE WORLD *CAN* BE MADE RIGHT.
I'M NEARLY *THERE*.
LIKE *CHAOS* NEVER HAPPENED.
WHAT A *RENAISSANCE* MAN YOU ARE.
BUT LISTEN TO ME, GOING ON AND ON--!
--WHEN YOU WANTED TO HEAR ABOUT THE *PONY*!
I KNOW THAT IF THE UNIVERSE IS *MEANINGLESS*... THAT'S A JOKE AT OUR EXPENSE.
IF IT'S *MEANINGFUL*... A DIFFERENT JOKE.
ANY MEANING WE MAKE *OURSELVES*--
--THAT'S US PRETENDING WE'RE *IN* ON IT.

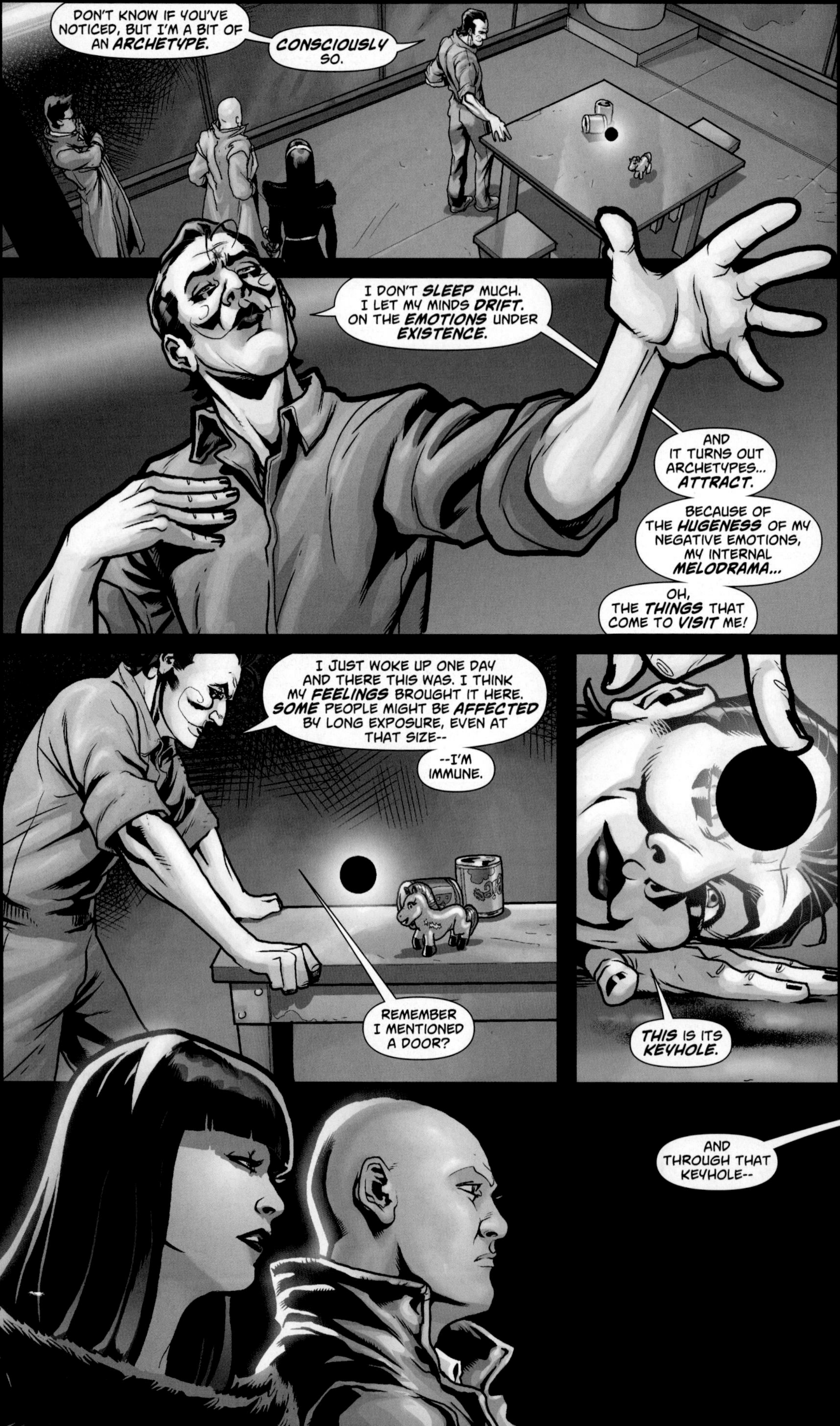
DON'T KNOW IF YOU'VE NOTICED, BUT I'M A BIT OF AN ARCHETYPE.
CONSCIOUSLY SO.
I DON'T SLEEP MUCH. I LET MY MINDS DRIFT. ON THE EMOTIONS UNDER EXISTENCE.
AND IT TURNS OUT ARCHETYPES... ATTRACT.
BECAUSE OF THE HUGENESS OF MY NEGATIVE EMOTIONS, MY INTERNAL MELODRAMA...
OH, THE THINGS THAT COME TO VISIT ME!
I JUST WOKE UP ONE DAY AND THERE THIS WAS. I THINK MY FEELINGS BROUGHT IT HERE. SOME PEOPLE MIGHT BE AFFECTED BY LONG EXPOSURE, EVEN AT THAT SIZE--
--I'M IMMUNE.
REMEMBER I MENTIONED A DOOR?
THIS IS ITS KEYHOLE.
AND THROUGH THAT KEYHOLE--

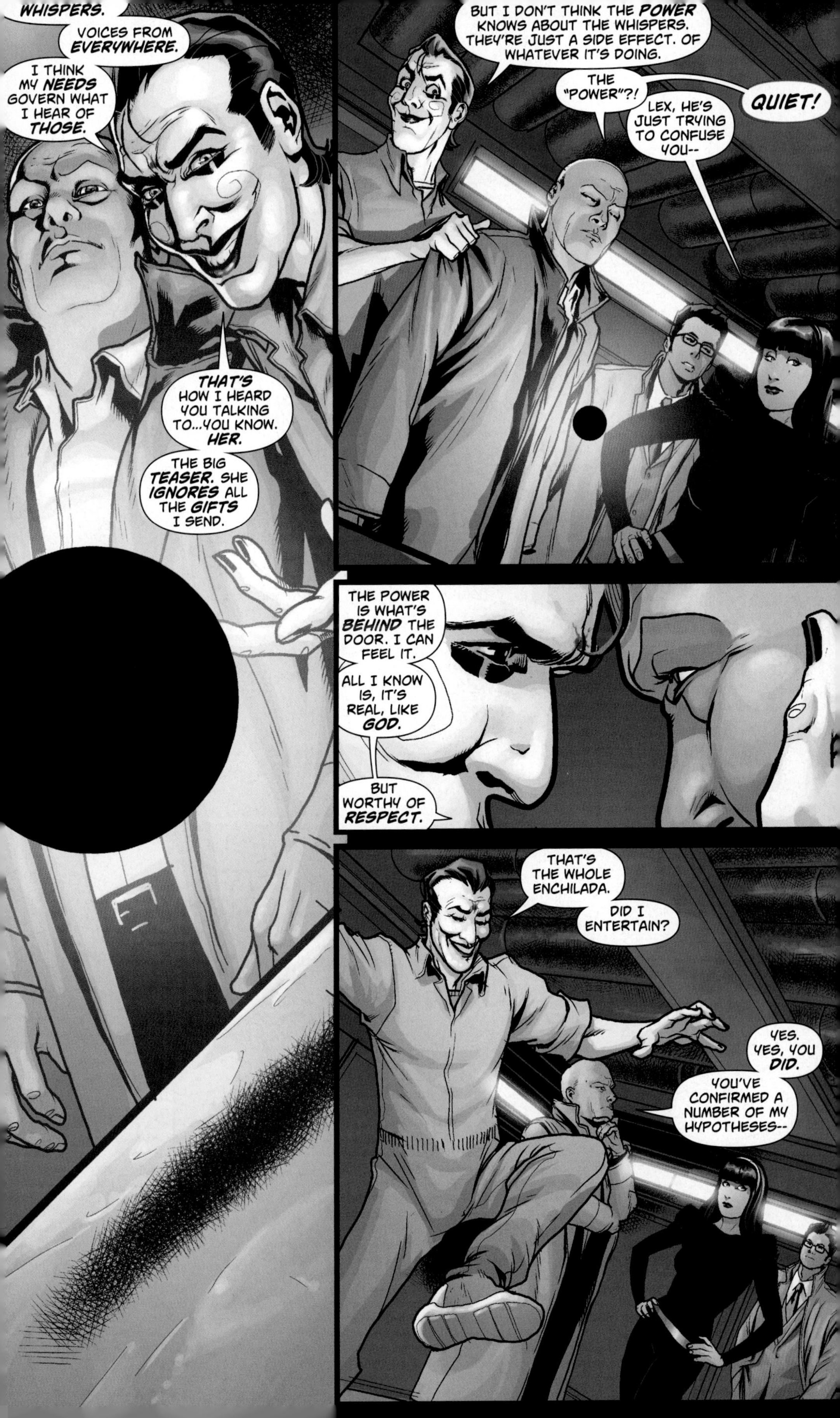
WHISPERS.
VOICES FROM EVERYWHERE.
I THINK MY NEEDS GOVERN WHAT I HEAR OF THOSE.
THAT'S HOW I HEARD YOU TALKING TO...YOU KNOW. HER.
THE BIG TEASER. SHE IGNORES ALL THE GIFTS I SEND.
BUT I DON'T THINK THE POWER KNOWS ABOUT THE WHISPERS. THEY'RE JUST A SIDE EFFECT. OF WHATEVER IT'S DOING.
THE "POWER"?!
LEX, HE'S JUST TRYING TO CONFUSE YOU--
QUIET!
THE POWER IS WHAT'S BEHIND THE DOOR. I CAN FEEL IT.
ALL I KNOW IS, IT'S REAL, LIKE GOD.
BUT WORTHY OF RESPECT.
THAT'S THE WHOLE ENCHILADA.
DID I ENTERTAIN?
YES. YES, YOU DID.
YOU'VE CONFIRMED A NUMBER OF MY HYPOTHESES--

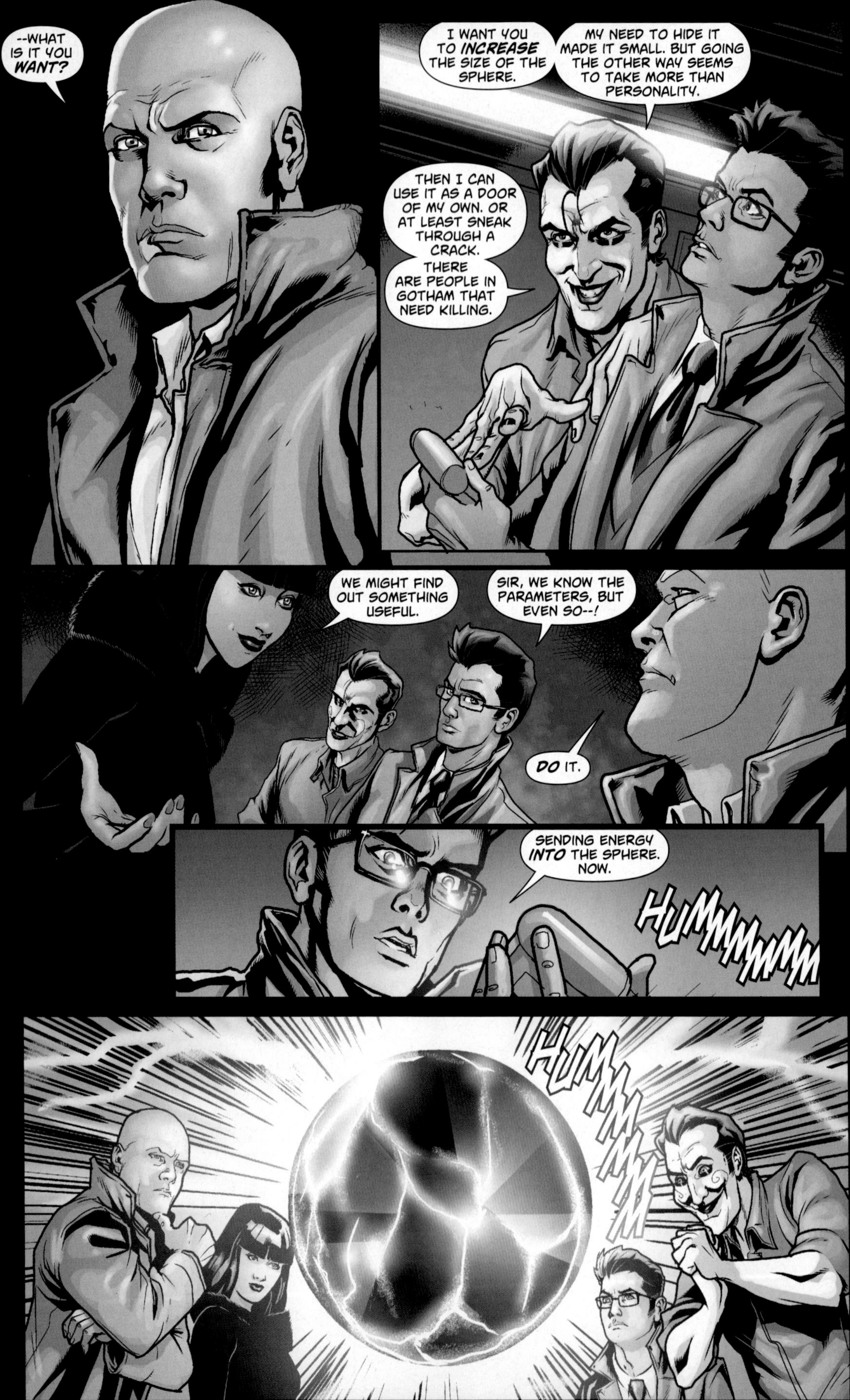
--WHAT IS IT YOU WANT?
I WANT YOU TO INCREASE THE SIZE OF THE SPHERE.
MY NEED TO HIDE IT MADE IT SMALL. BUT GOING THE OTHER WAY SEEMS TO TAKE MORE THAN PERSONALITY.
THEN I CAN USE IT AS A DOOR OF MY OWN. OR AT LEAST SNEAK THROUGH A CRACK.
THERE ARE PEOPLE IN GOTHAM THAT NEED KILLING.
WE MIGHT FIND OUT SOMETHING USEFUL.
SIR, WE KNOW THE PARAMETERS, BUT EVEN SO--!
DO IT.
SENDING ENERGY INTO THE SPHERE. NOW.
HUMMMMMMMM
HUMMMMMMM

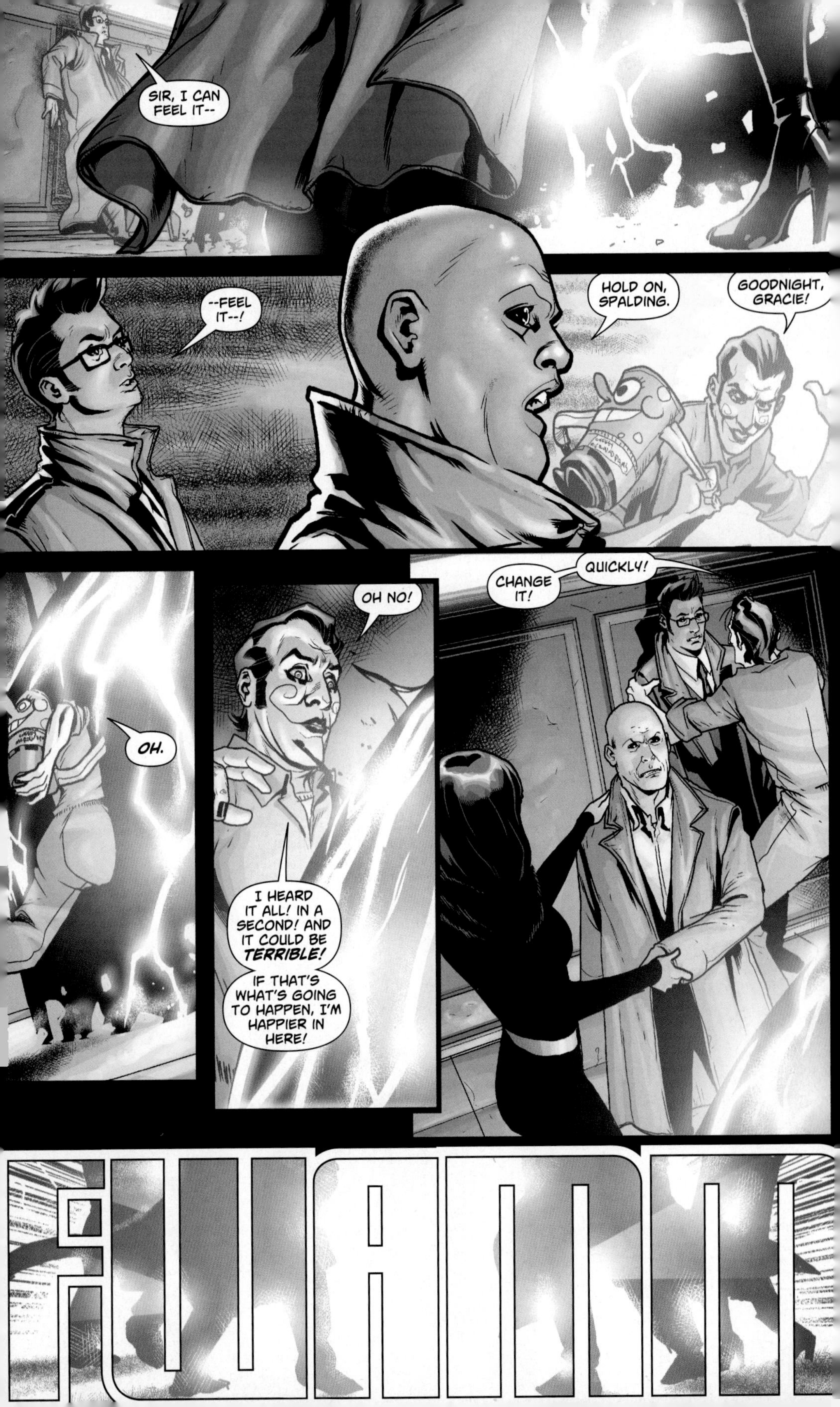
SIR, I CAN FEEL IT--
--FEEL IT--!
HOLD ON, SPALDING.
GOODNIGHT, GRACIE!
OH.
OH NO!
I HEARD IT ALL! IN A SECOND! AND IT COULD BE *TERRIBLE!*
IF THAT'S WHAT'S GOING TO HAPPEN, I'M HAPPIER IN HERE!
CHANGE IT!
QUICKLY!
FWANN

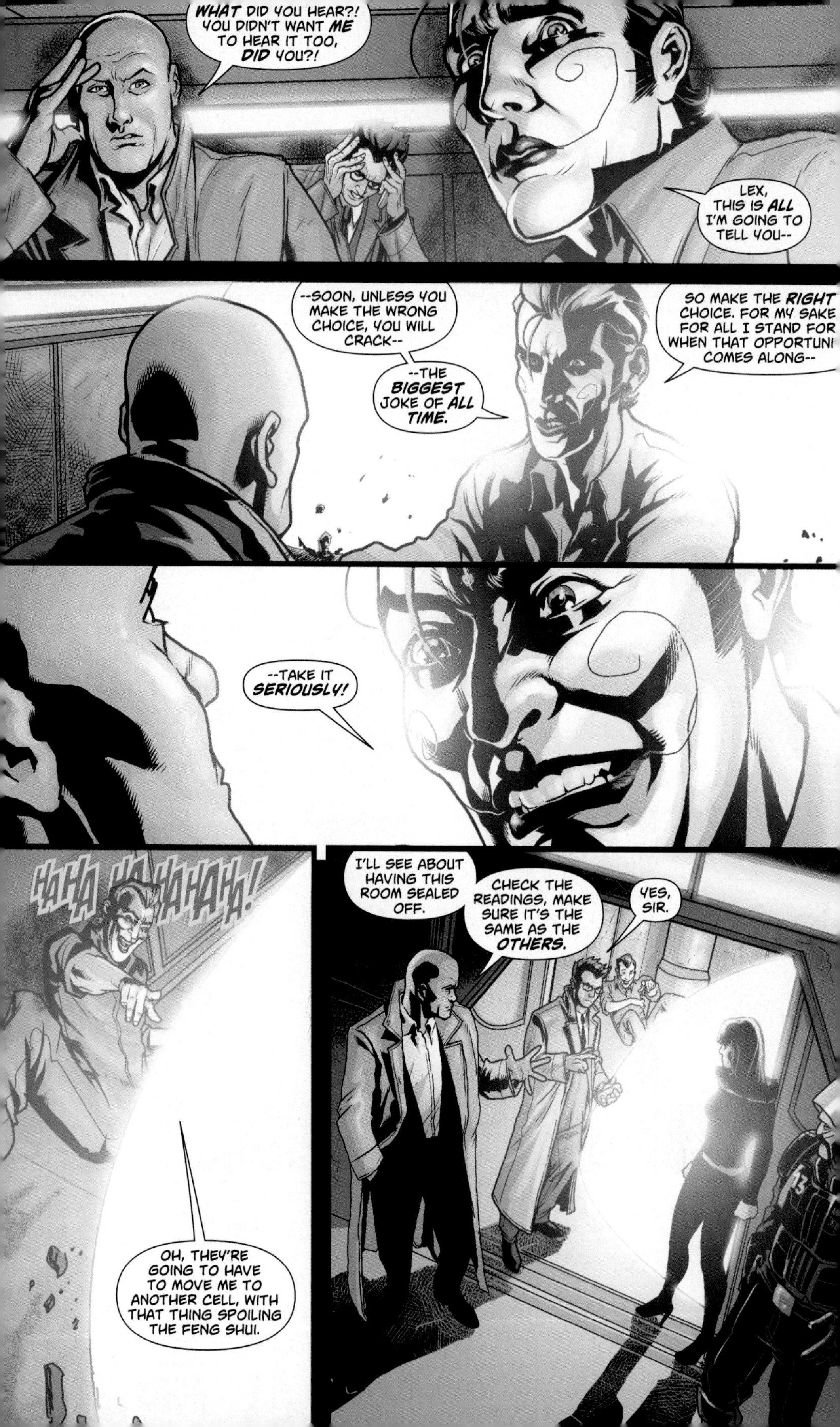
WHAT DID YOU HEAR?! YOU DIDN'T WANT ME TO HEAR IT TOO, DID YOU?!
LEX, THIS IS ALL I'M GOING TO TELL YOU--
--SOON, UNLESS YOU MAKE THE WRONG CHOICE, YOU WILL CRACK--
--THE BIGGEST JOKE OF ALL TIME.
SO MAKE THE RIGHT CHOICE. FOR MY SAKE FOR ALL I STAND FOR WHEN THAT OPPORTUNI COMES ALONG--
--TAKE IT SERIOUSLY!
HAHA HA HAHAHA!
OH, THEY'RE GOING TO HAVE TO MOVE ME TO ANOTHER CELL, WITH THAT THING SPOILING THE FENG SHUI.
I'LL SEE ABOUT HAVING THIS ROOM SEALED OFF.
CHECK THE READINGS, MAKE SURE IT'S THE SAME AS THE OTHERS.
YES, SIR.

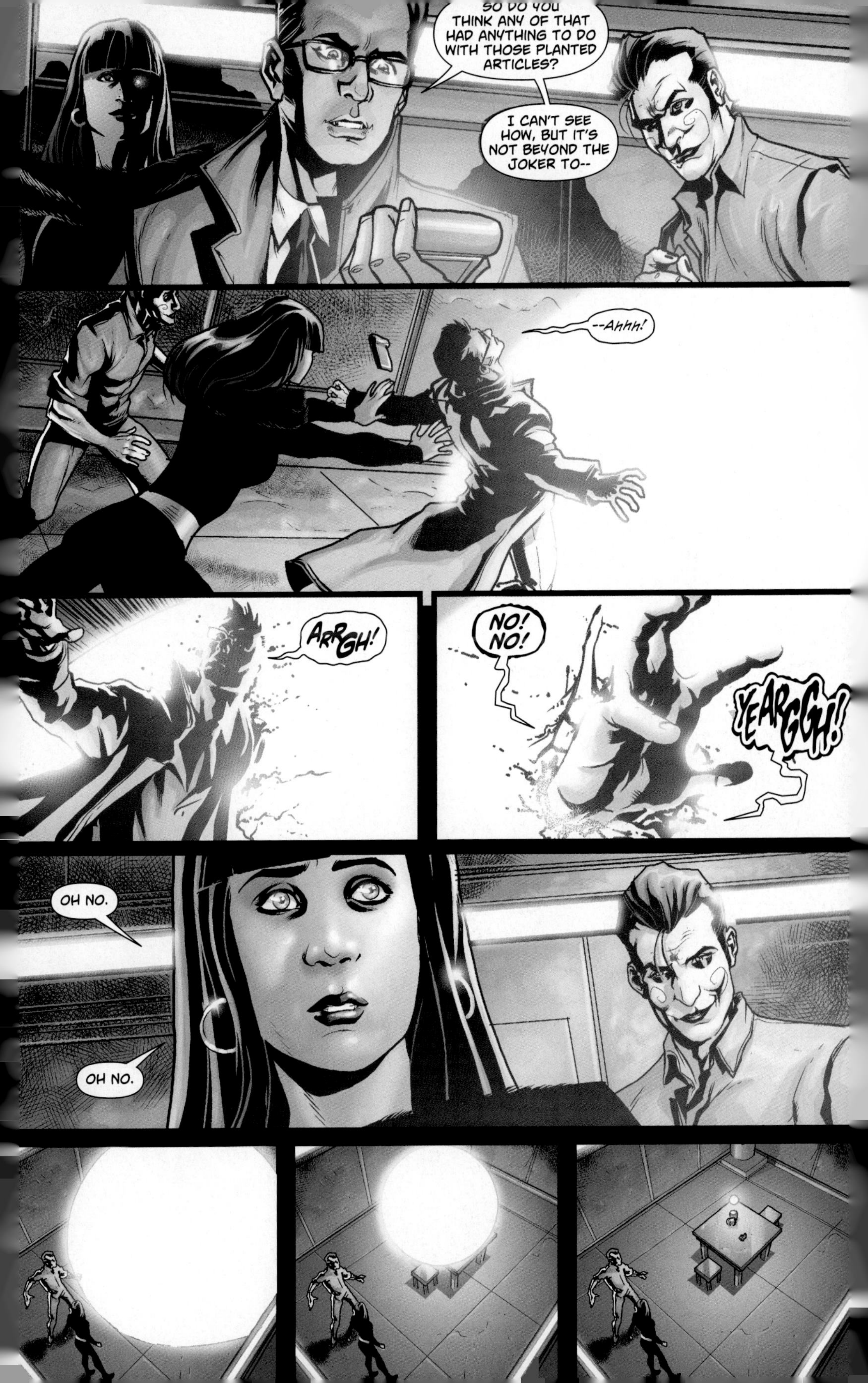
SO DO YOU THINK ANY OF THAT HAD ANYTHING TO DO WITH THOSE PLANTED ARTICLES?
I CAN'T SEE HOW, BUT IT'S NOT BEYOND THE JOKER TO--
--Ahhh!
ARRGH!
NO! NO!
YEARGGH!
OH NO.
OH NO.

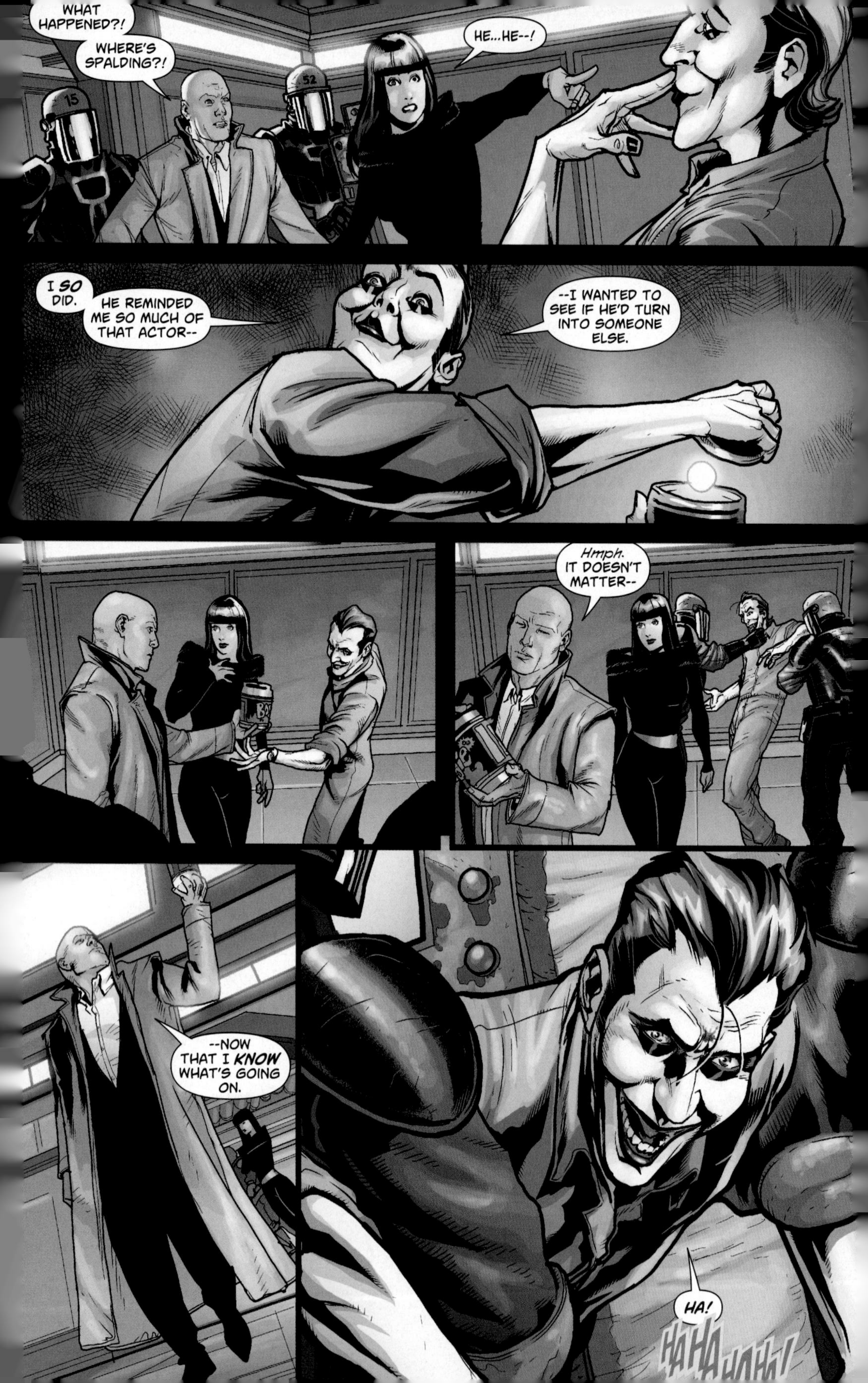
WHAT HAPPENED?!
WHERE'S SPALDING?!
HE...HE--!
I *SO* DID.
HE REMINDED ME SO MUCH OF THAT ACTOR--
--I WANTED TO SEE IF HE'D TURN INTO SOMEONE ELSE.
Hmph. IT DOESN'T MATTER--
--NOW THAT I *KNOW* WHAT'S GOING ON.
HA!
HAHA HAHA!

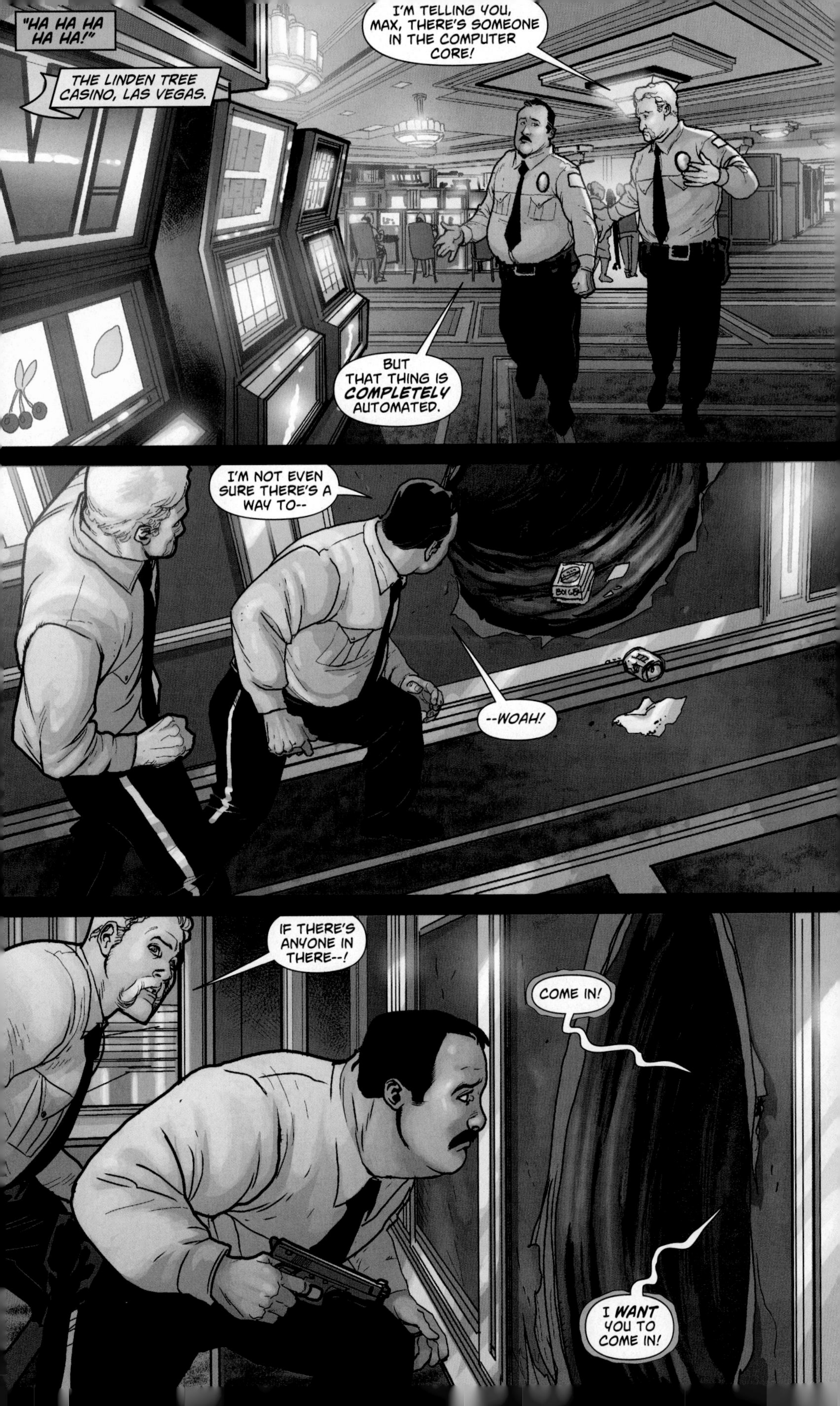
"HA HA HA HA HA!"
THE LINDEN TREE CASINO, LAS VEGAS.
I'M TELLING YOU, MAX, THERE'S SOMEONE IN THE COMPUTER CORE!
BUT THAT THING IS COMPLETELY AUTOMATED.
I'M NOT EVEN SURE THERE'S A WAY TO--
--WOAH!
IF THERE'S ANYONE IN THERE--!
COME IN!
I WANT YOU TO COME IN!

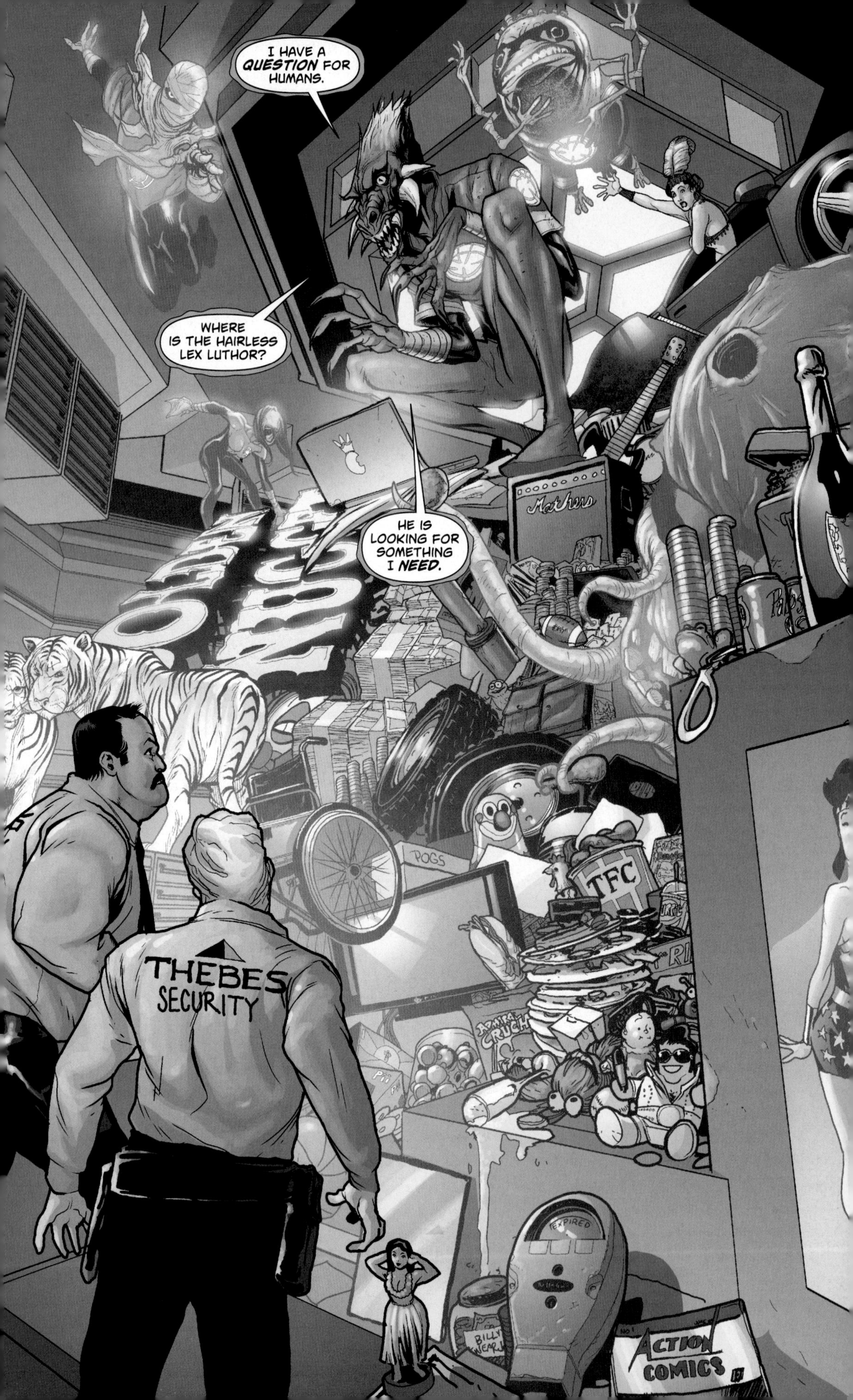
I HAVE A *QUESTION* FOR HUMANS.
WHERE IS THE HAIRLESS LEX LUTHOR?
HE IS LOOKING FOR SOMETHING I *NEED*.
Mathers
POGS
TFC
THEBES SECURITY
EXPIRED
ACTION COMICS

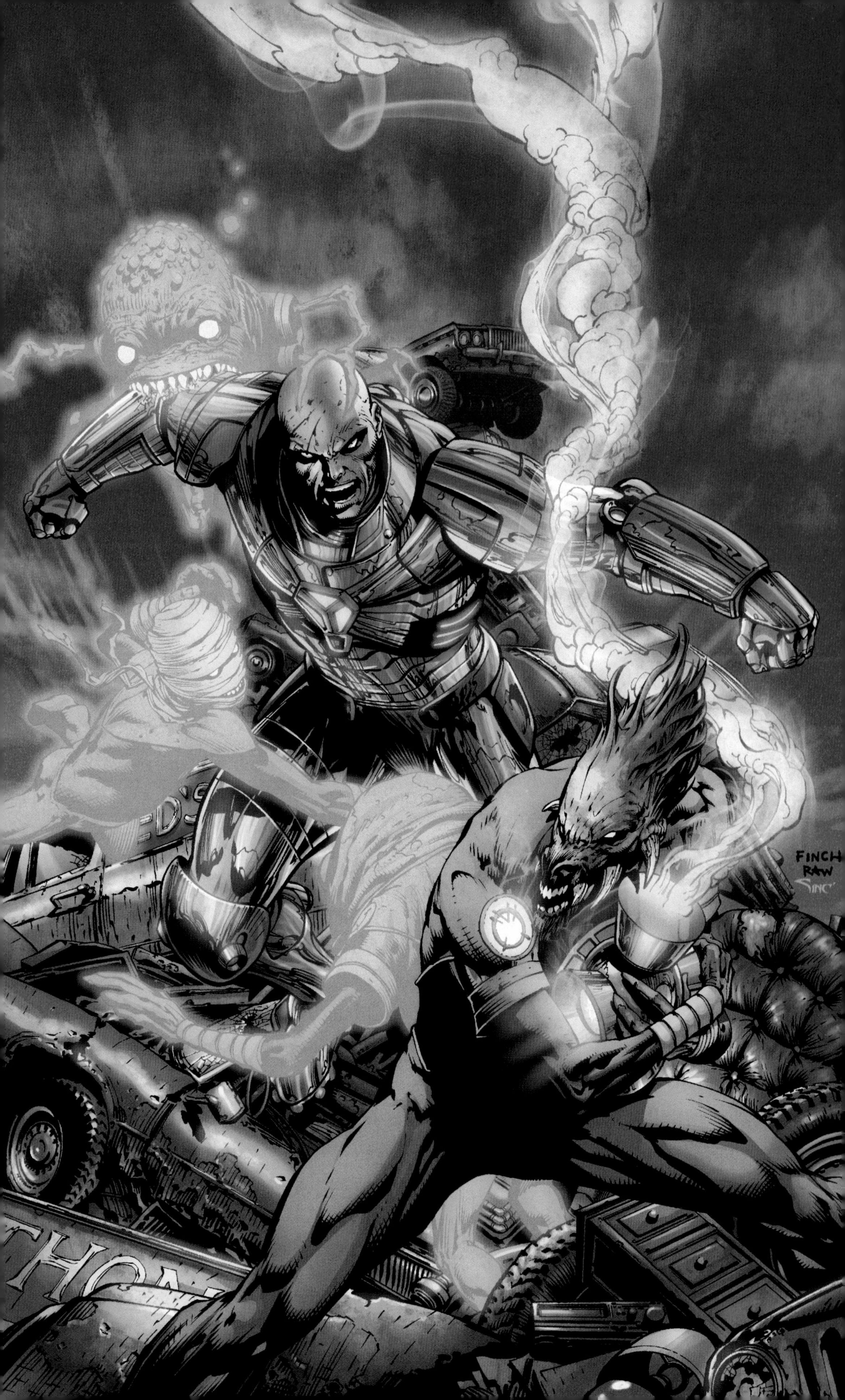
FINCH
RAW

THE BLACK RING
part nine

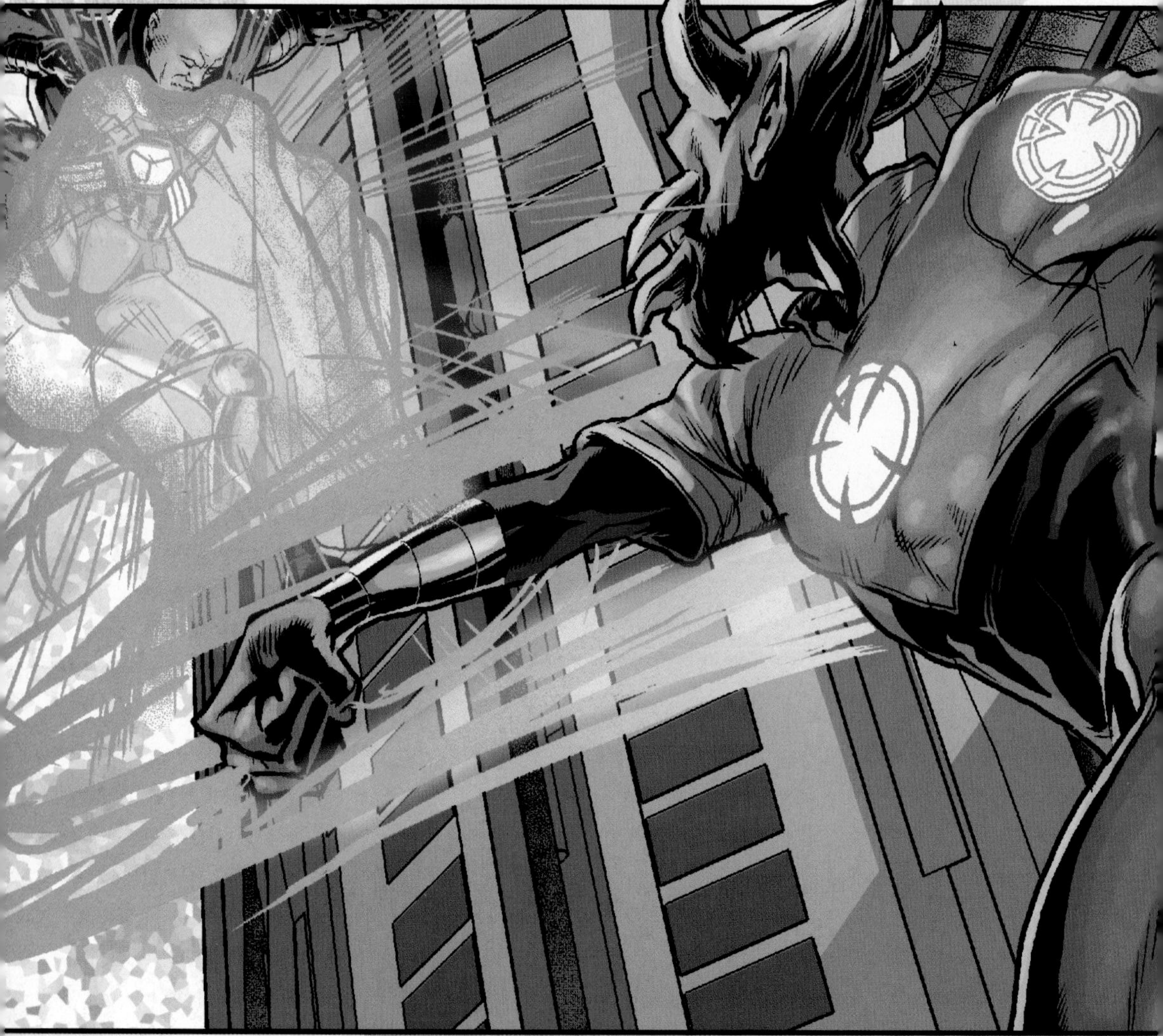

PAUL CORNELL writer
PETE WOODS artist

cover by
DAVID **FINCH**, RYAN **WINN** & ALEX **SINCLAIR**

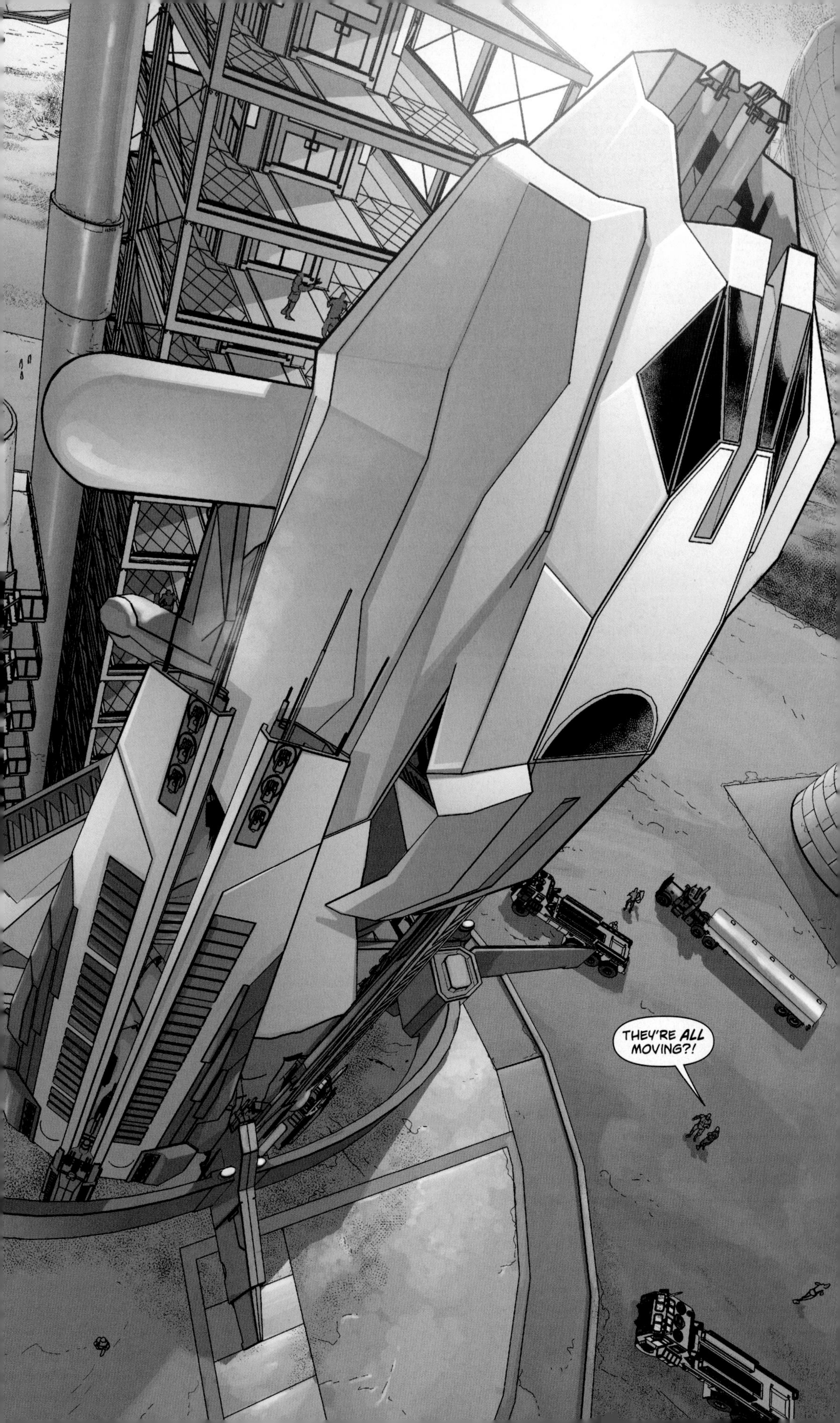
THEY'RE ALL MOVING?!

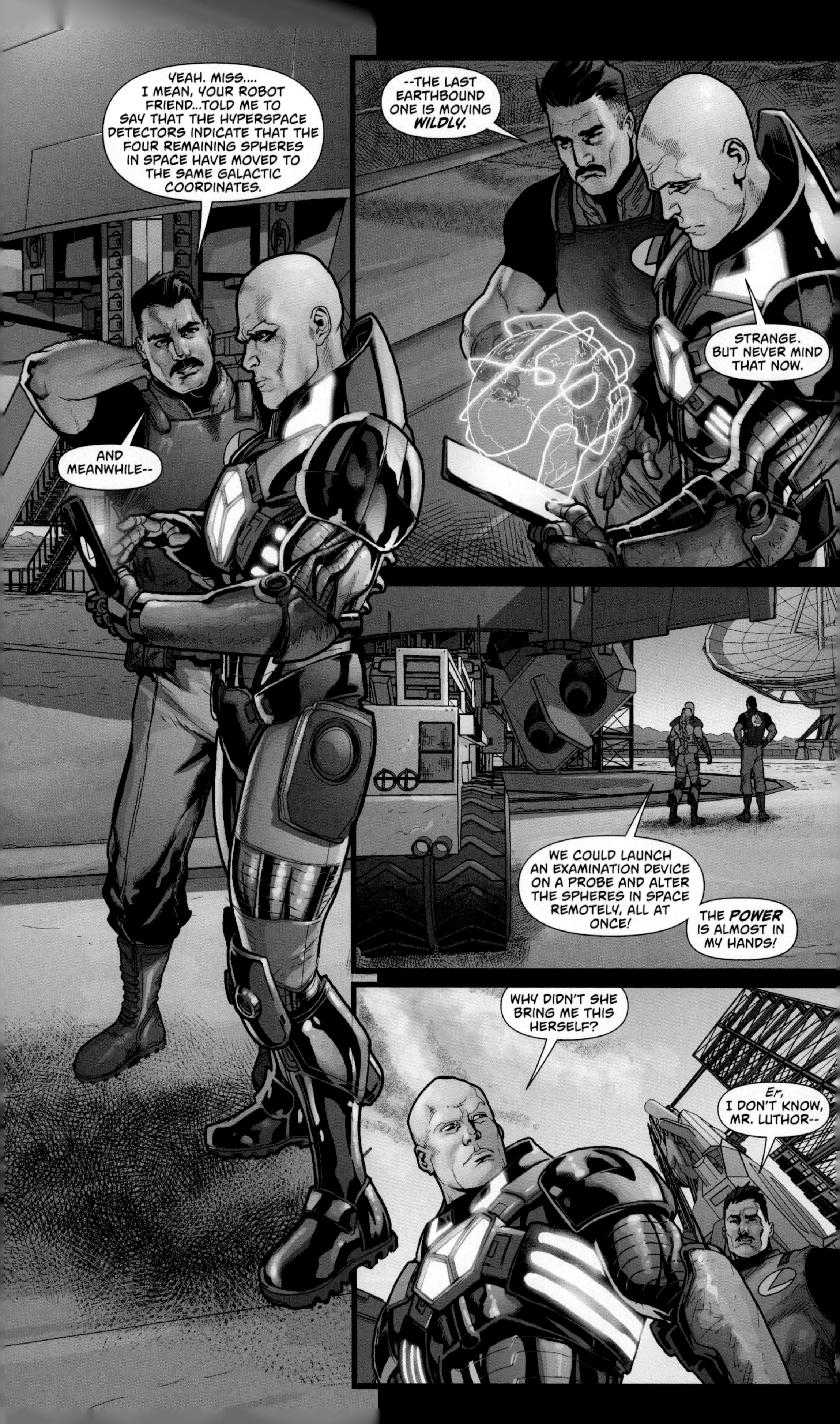
YEAH. MISS.... I MEAN, YOUR ROBOT FRIEND...TOLD ME TO SAY THAT THE HYPERSPACE DETECTORS INDICATE THAT THE FOUR REMAINING SPHERES IN SPACE HAVE MOVED TO THE SAME GALACTIC COORDINATES.
AND MEANWHILE--
--THE LAST EARTHBOUND ONE IS MOVING *WILDLY.*
STRANGE. BUT NEVER MIND THAT NOW.
WE COULD LAUNCH AN EXAMINATION DEVICE ON A PROBE AND ALTER THE SPHERES IN SPACE REMOTELY, ALL AT ONCE!
THE *POWER* IS ALMOST IN MY HANDS!
WHY DIDN'T SHE BRING ME THIS HERSELF?
Er, I DON'T KNOW, MR. LUTHOR--

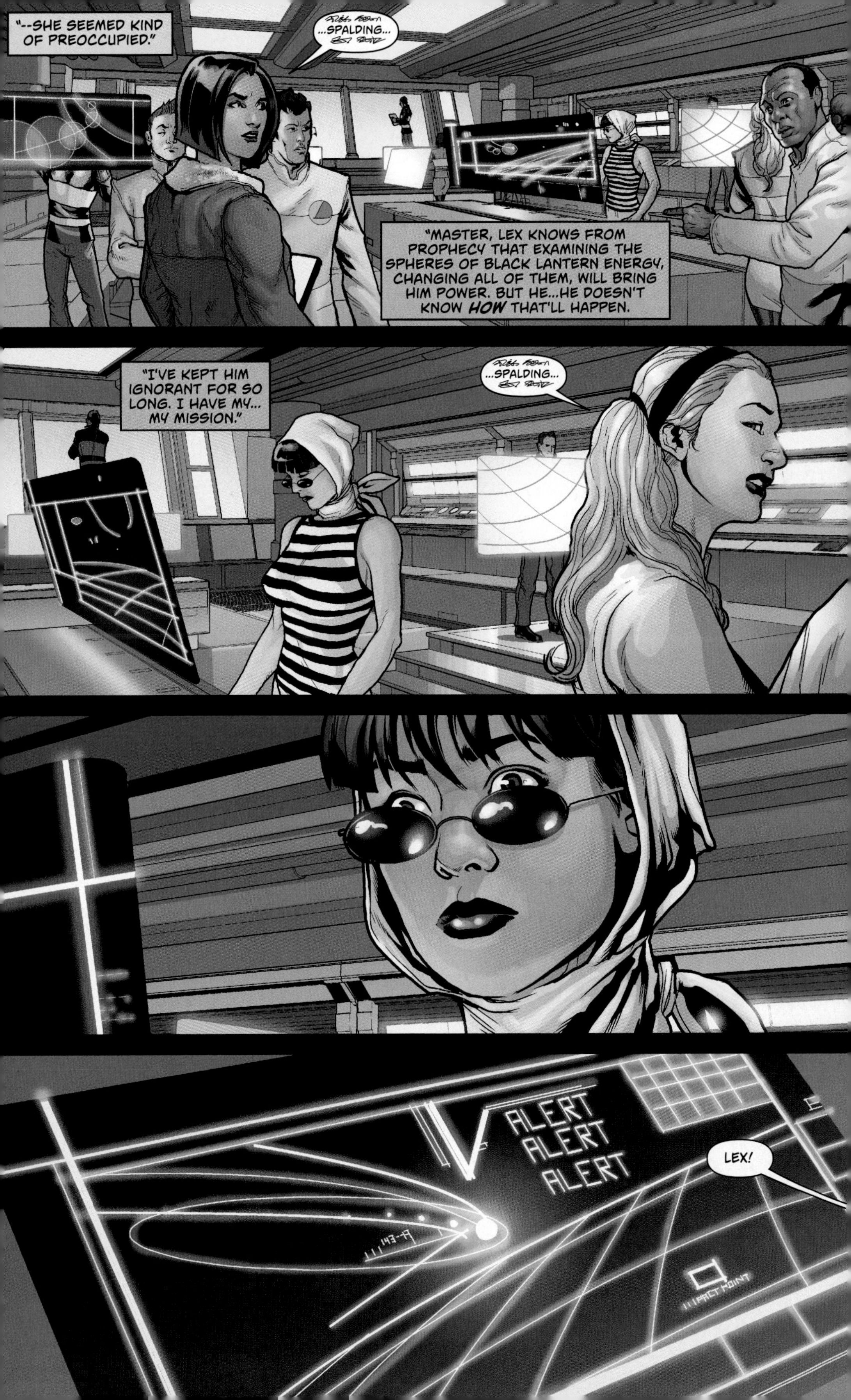
"--SHE SEEMED KIND OF PREOCCUPIED."
...SPALDING...
"MASTER, LEX KNOWS FROM PROPHECY THAT EXAMINING THE SPHERES OF BLACK LANTERN ENERGY, CHANGING ALL OF THEM, WILL BRING HIM POWER. BUT HE...HE DOESN'T KNOW *HOW* THAT'LL HAPPEN.
"I'VE KEPT HIM IGNORANT FOR SO LONG. I HAVE MY... MY MISSION."
...SPALDING...
ALERT
ALERT
ALERT
LEX!
IMPACT POINT

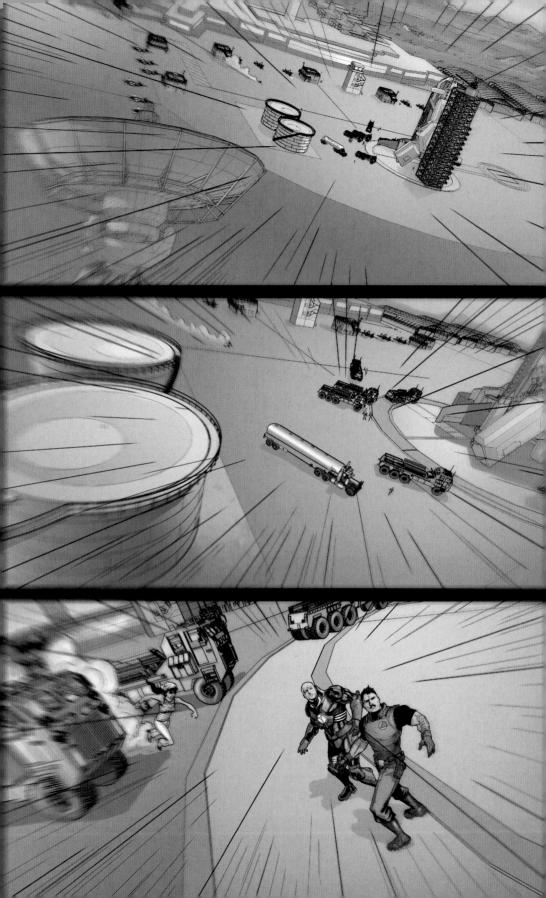

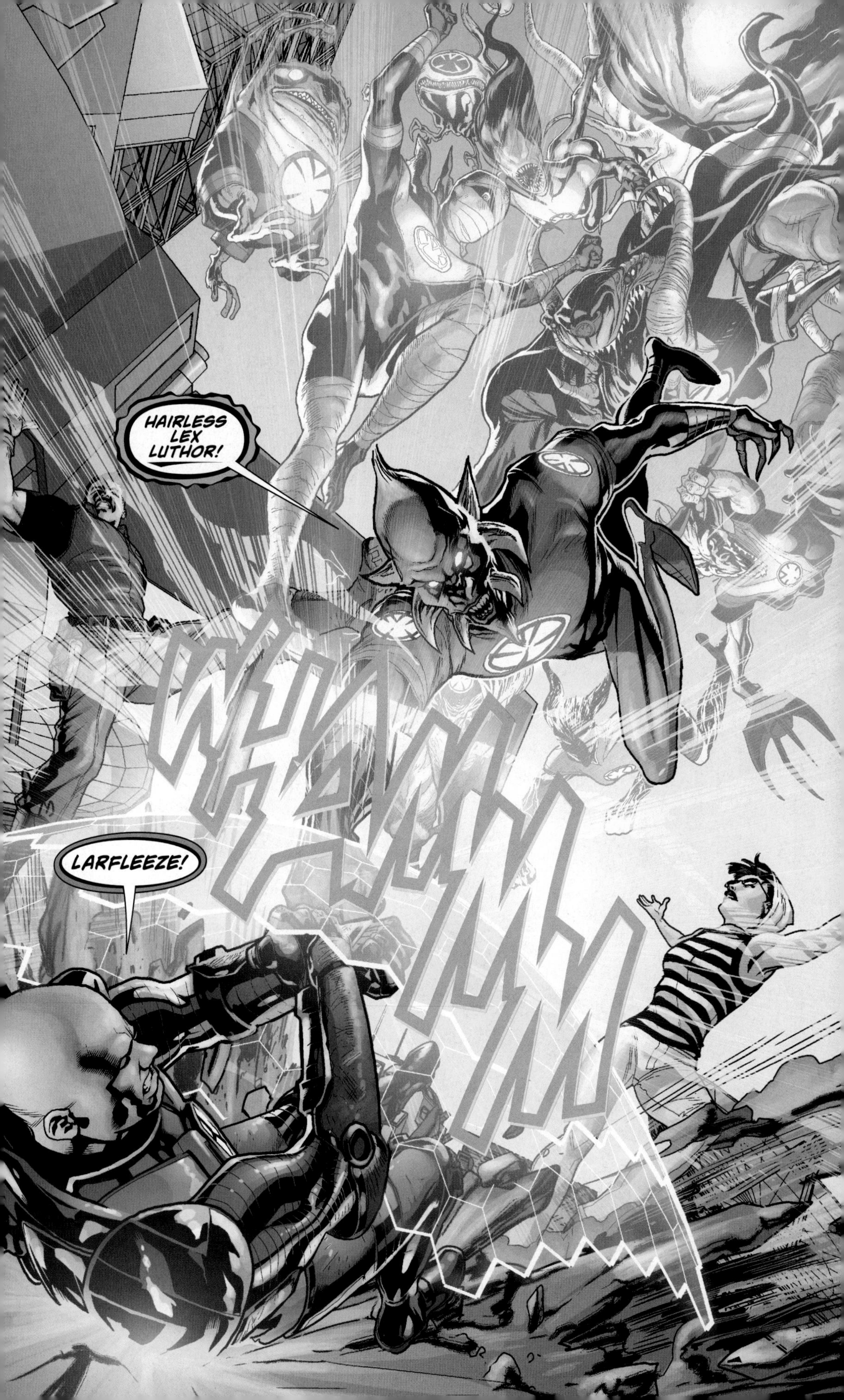
HAIRLESS LEX LUTHOR!
WHAM
LARFLEEZE!

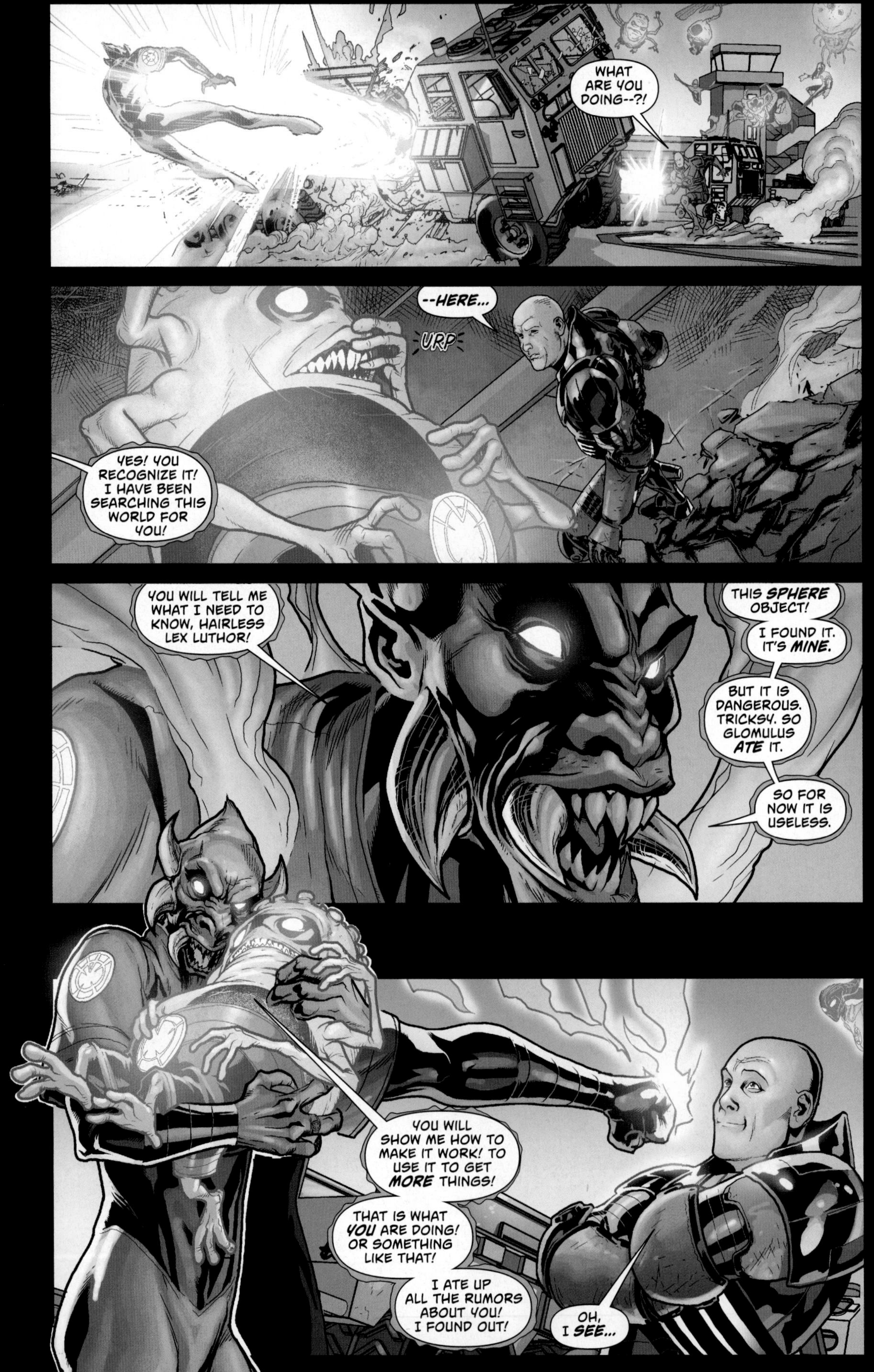
WHAT ARE YOU DOING--?!
--HERE...
URP
YES! YOU RECOGNIZE IT! I HAVE BEEN SEARCHING THIS WORLD FOR YOU!
YOU WILL TELL ME WHAT I NEED TO KNOW, HAIRLESS LEX LUTHOR!
THIS SPHERE OBJECT!
I FOUND IT. IT'S MINE.
BUT IT IS DANGEROUS. TRICKSY. SO GLOMULUS ATE IT.
SO FOR NOW IT IS USELESS.
YOU WILL SHOW ME HOW TO MAKE IT WORK! TO USE IT TO GET MORE THINGS!
THAT IS WHAT YOU ARE DOING! OR SOMETHING LIKE THAT!
I ATE UP ALL THE RUMORS ABOUT YOU! I FOUND OUT!
OH, I SEE...

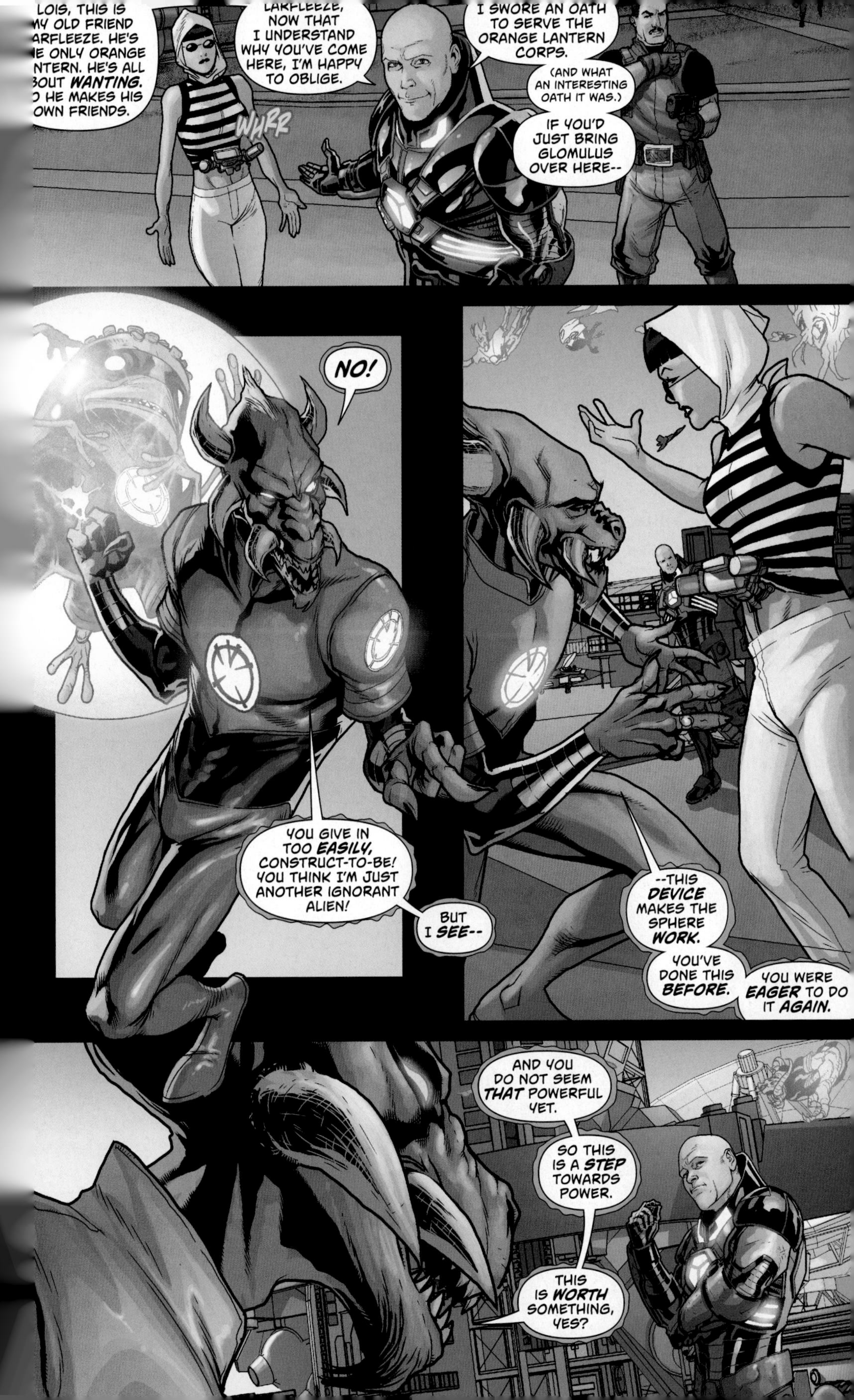
LOIS, THIS IS MY OLD FRIEND ARFLEEZE. HE'S E ONLY ORANGE NTERN. HE'S ALL OUT WANTING. D HE MAKES HIS OWN FRIENDS.
LARFLEEZE, NOW THAT I UNDERSTAND WHY YOU'VE COME HERE, I'M HAPPY TO OBLIGE.
I SWORE AN OATH TO SERVE THE ORANGE LANTERN CORPS.
(AND WHAT AN INTERESTING OATH IT WAS.)
IF YOU'D JUST BRING GLOMULUS OVER HERE--
WHRR
NO!
YOU GIVE IN TOO EASILY, CONSTRUCT-TO-BE! YOU THINK I'M JUST ANOTHER IGNORANT ALIEN!
BUT I SEE--
--THIS DEVICE MAKES THE SPHERE WORK.
YOU'VE DONE THIS BEFORE.
YOU WERE EAGER TO DO IT AGAIN.
AND YOU DO NOT SEEM THAT POWERFUL YET.
SO THIS IS A STEP TOWARDS POWER.
THIS IS WORTH SOMETHING, YES?

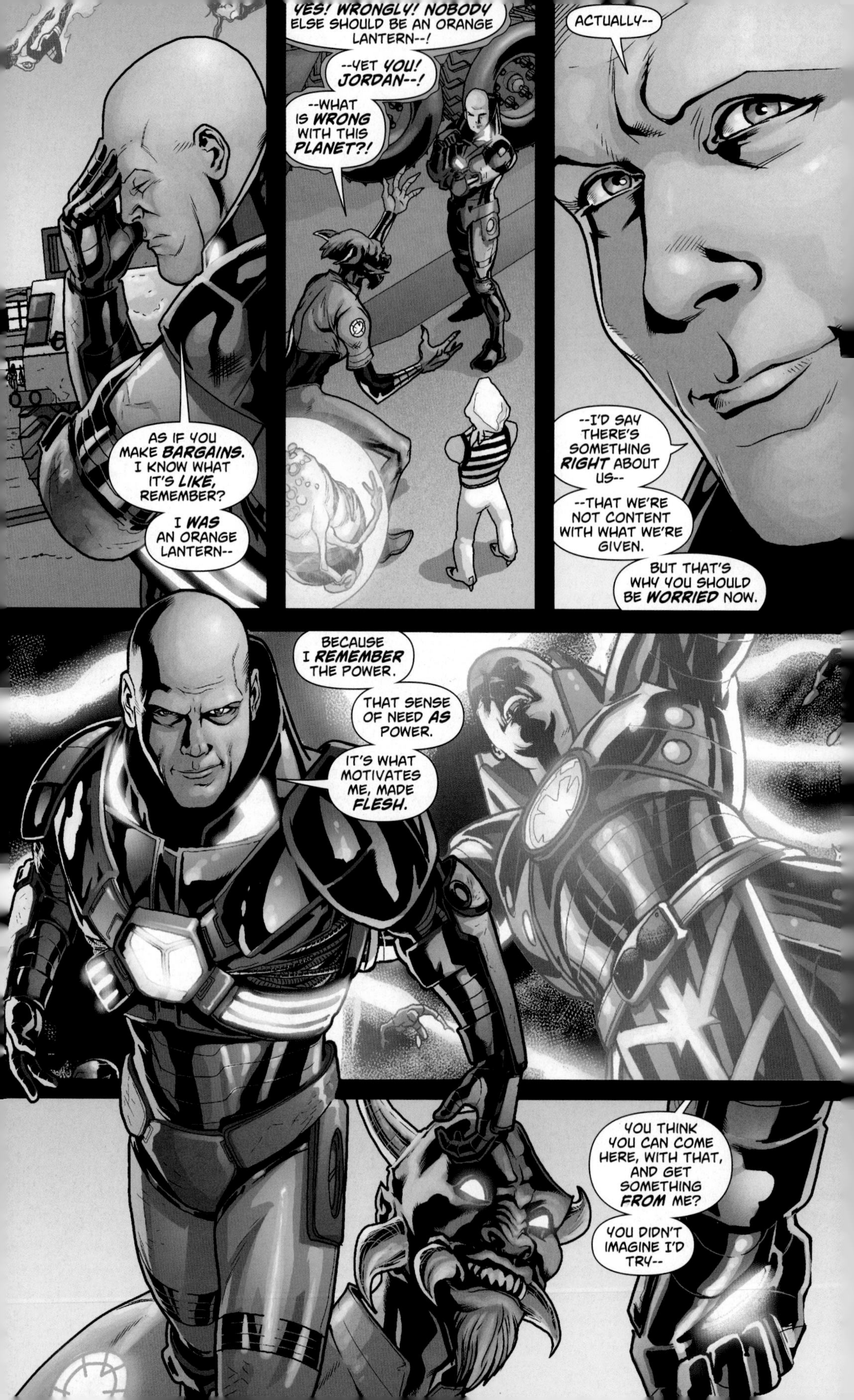
AS IF YOU MAKE BARGAINS. I KNOW WHAT IT'S LIKE, REMEMBER?
I WAS AN ORANGE LANTERN--
YES! WRONGLY! NOBODY ELSE SHOULD BE AN ORANGE LANTERN--!
--YET YOU! JORDAN--!
--WHAT IS WRONG WITH THIS PLANET?!
ACTUALLY--
--I'D SAY THERE'S SOMETHING RIGHT ABOUT US--
--THAT WE'RE NOT CONTENT WITH WHAT WE'RE GIVEN.
BUT THAT'S WHY YOU SHOULD BE WORRIED NOW.
BECAUSE I REMEMBER THE POWER.
THAT SENSE OF NEED AS POWER.
IT'S WHAT MOTIVATES ME, MADE FLESH.
YOU THINK YOU CAN COME HERE, WITH THAT, AND GET SOMETHING FROM ME?
YOU DIDN'T IMAGINE I'D TRY--

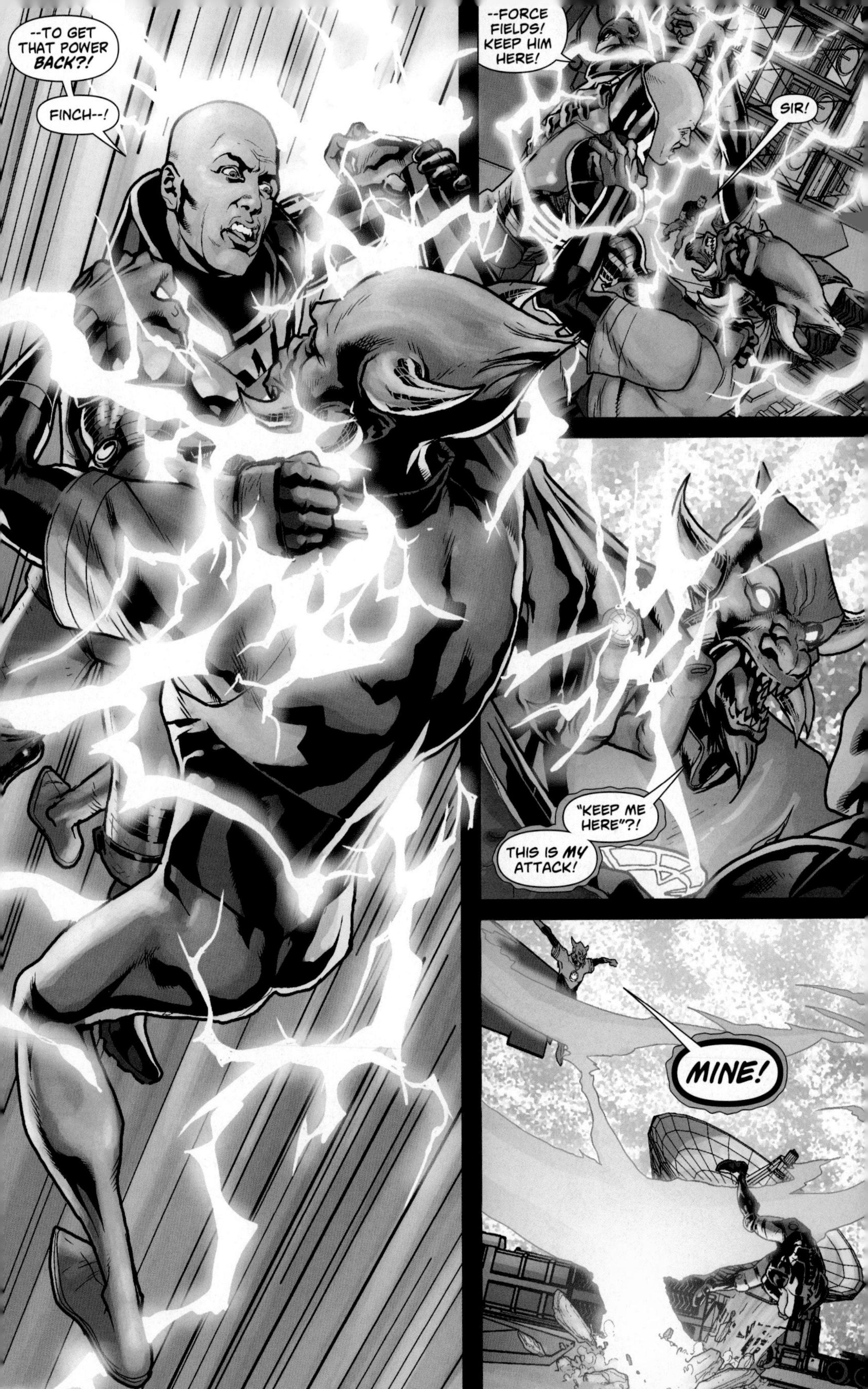
--TO GET THAT POWER BACK?!
FINCH--!
--FORCE FIELDS! KEEP HIM HERE!
SIR!
"KEEP ME HERE"?!
THIS IS MY ATTACK!
MINE!

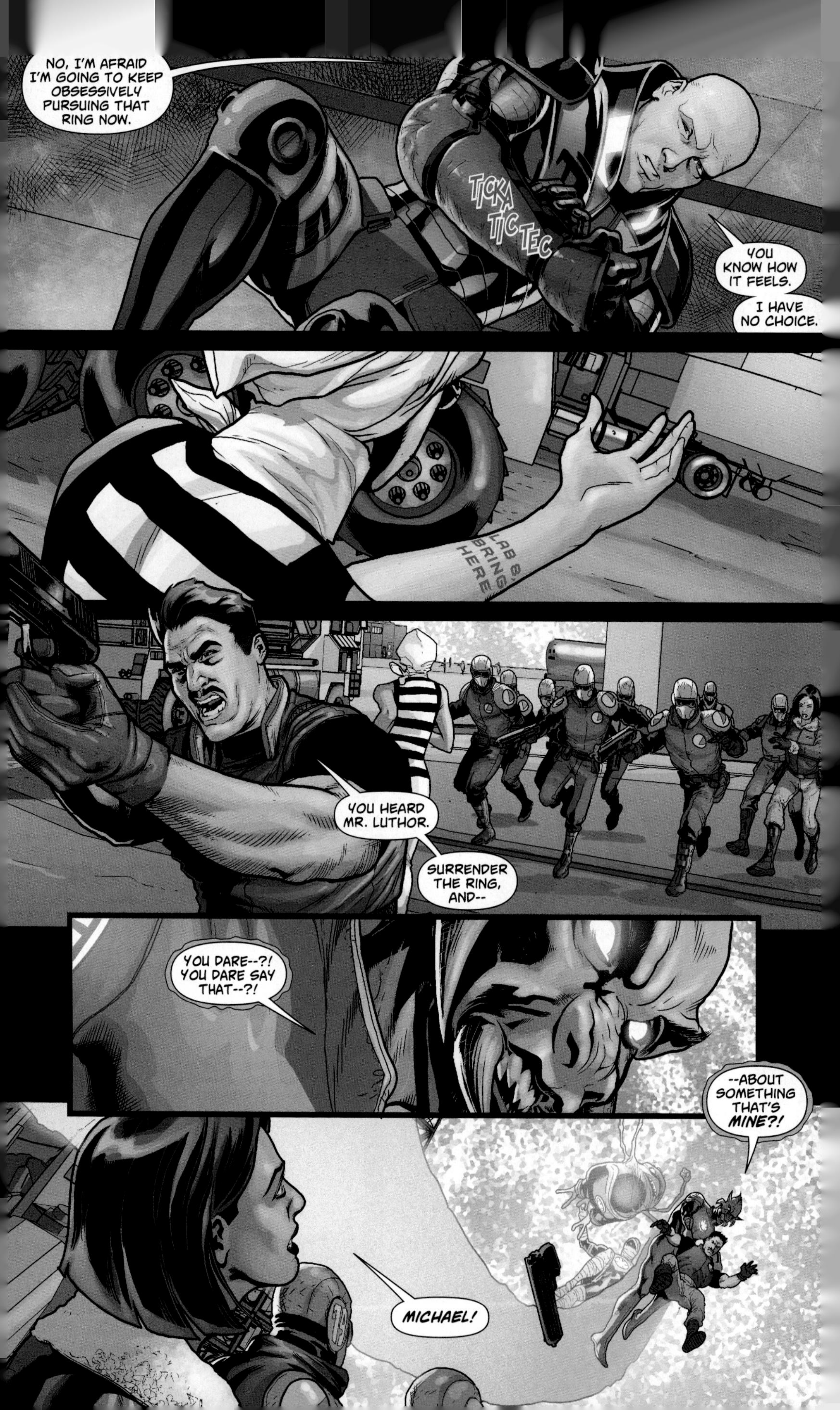
NO, I'M AFRAID I'M GOING TO KEEP OBSESSIVELY PURSUING THAT RING NOW.
TICKA TIC TEC
YOU KNOW HOW IT FEELS.
I HAVE NO CHOICE.
LAB 8. BRING HERE
YOU HEARD MR. LUTHOR.
SURRENDER THE RING, AND--
YOU DARE--?! YOU DARE SAY THAT--?!
--ABOUT SOMETHING THAT'S MINE?!
MICHAEL!

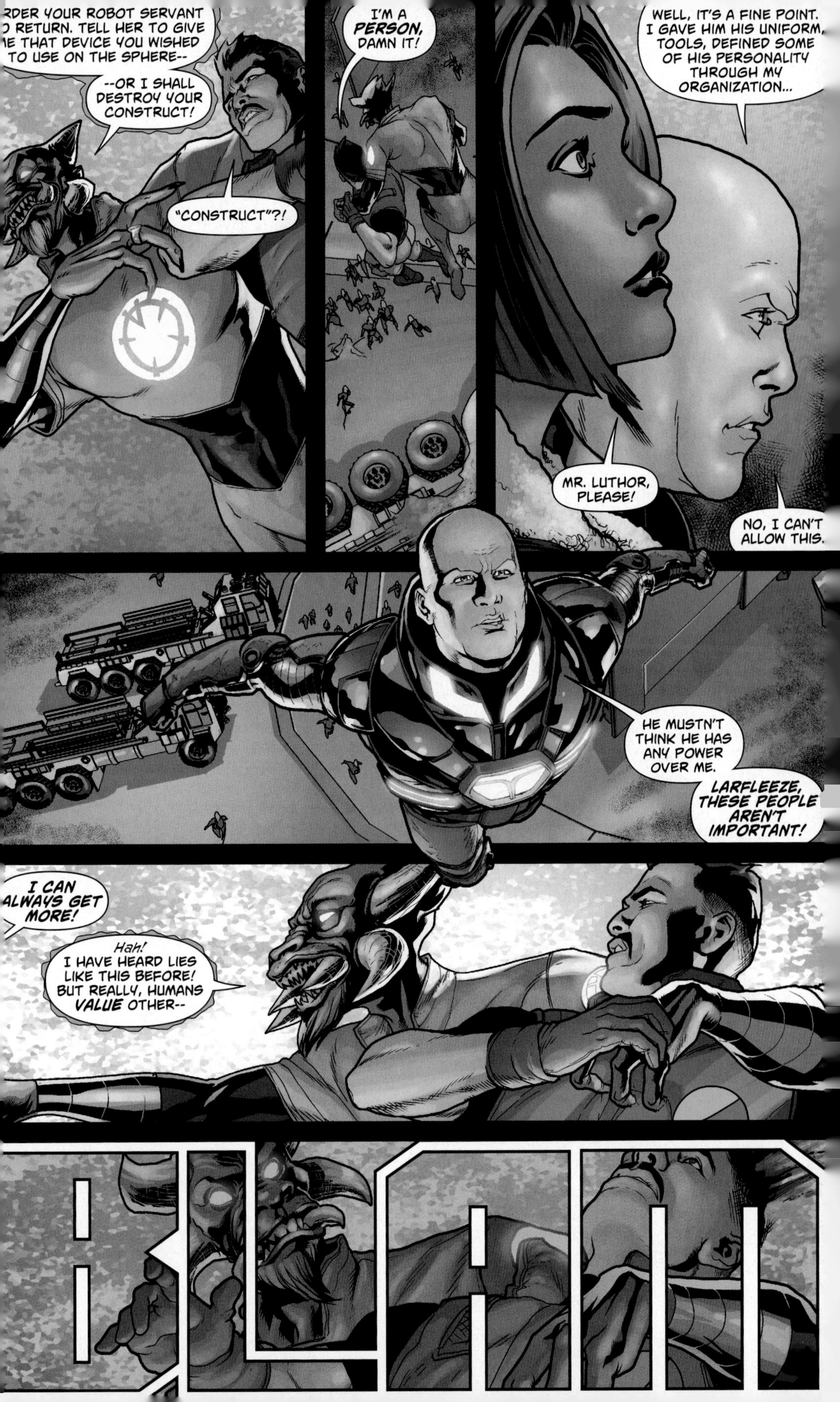

RDER YOUR ROBOT SERVANT
O RETURN. TELL HER TO GIVE
E THAT DEVICE YOU WISHED
TO USE ON THE SPHERE--
--OR I SHALL DESTROY YOUR CONSTRUCT!
"CONSTRUCT"?!
I'M A *PERSON,* DAMN IT!
WELL, IT'S A FINE POINT. I GAVE HIM HIS UNIFORM, TOOLS, DEFINED SOME OF HIS PERSONALITY THROUGH MY ORGANIZATION...
MR. LUTHOR, PLEASE!
NO, I CAN'T ALLOW THIS.
HE MUSTN'T THINK HE HAS ANY POWER OVER ME.
LARFLEEZE, THESE PEOPLE AREN'T IMPORTANT!
I CAN ALWAYS GET MORE!
Hah! I HAVE HEARD LIES LIKE THIS BEFORE! BUT REALLY, HUMANS *VALUE* OTHER--

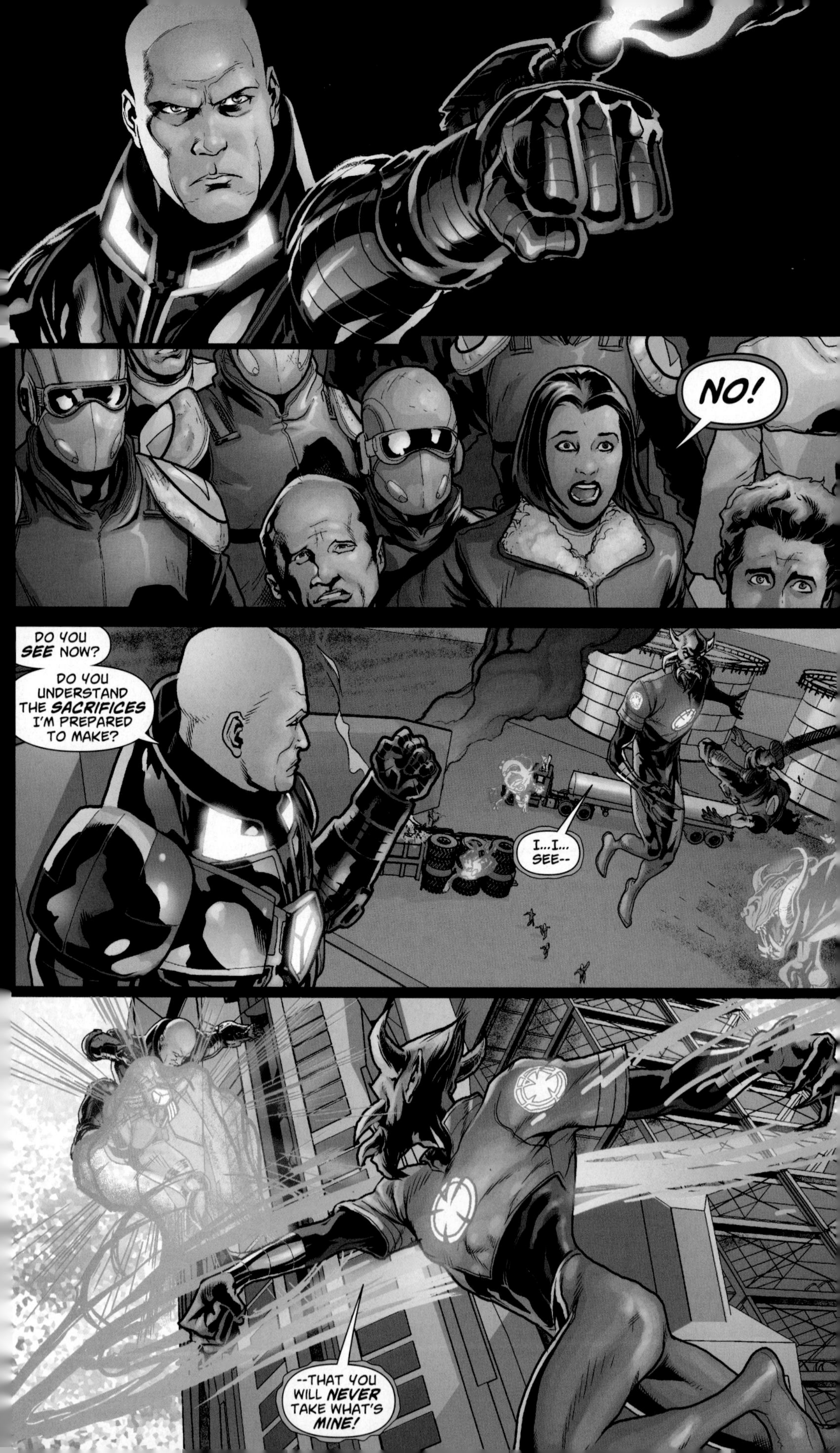
NO!
DO YOU SEE NOW?
DO YOU UNDERSTAND THE SACRIFICES I'M PREPARED TO MAKE?
I...I... SEE--
--THAT YOU WILL NEVER TAKE WHAT'S MINE!

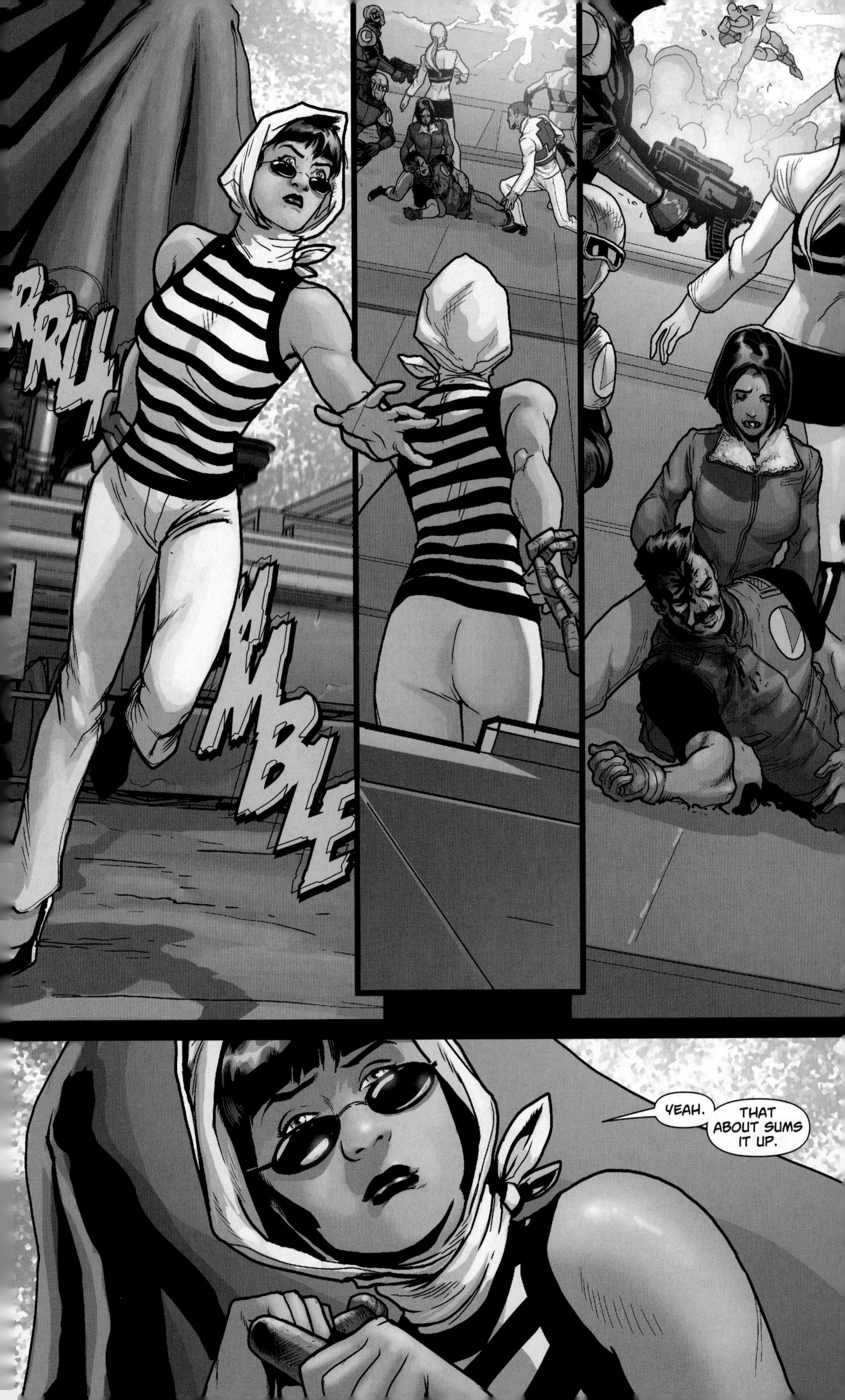
RRUMBLE
YEAH.
THAT ABOUT SUMS IT UP.

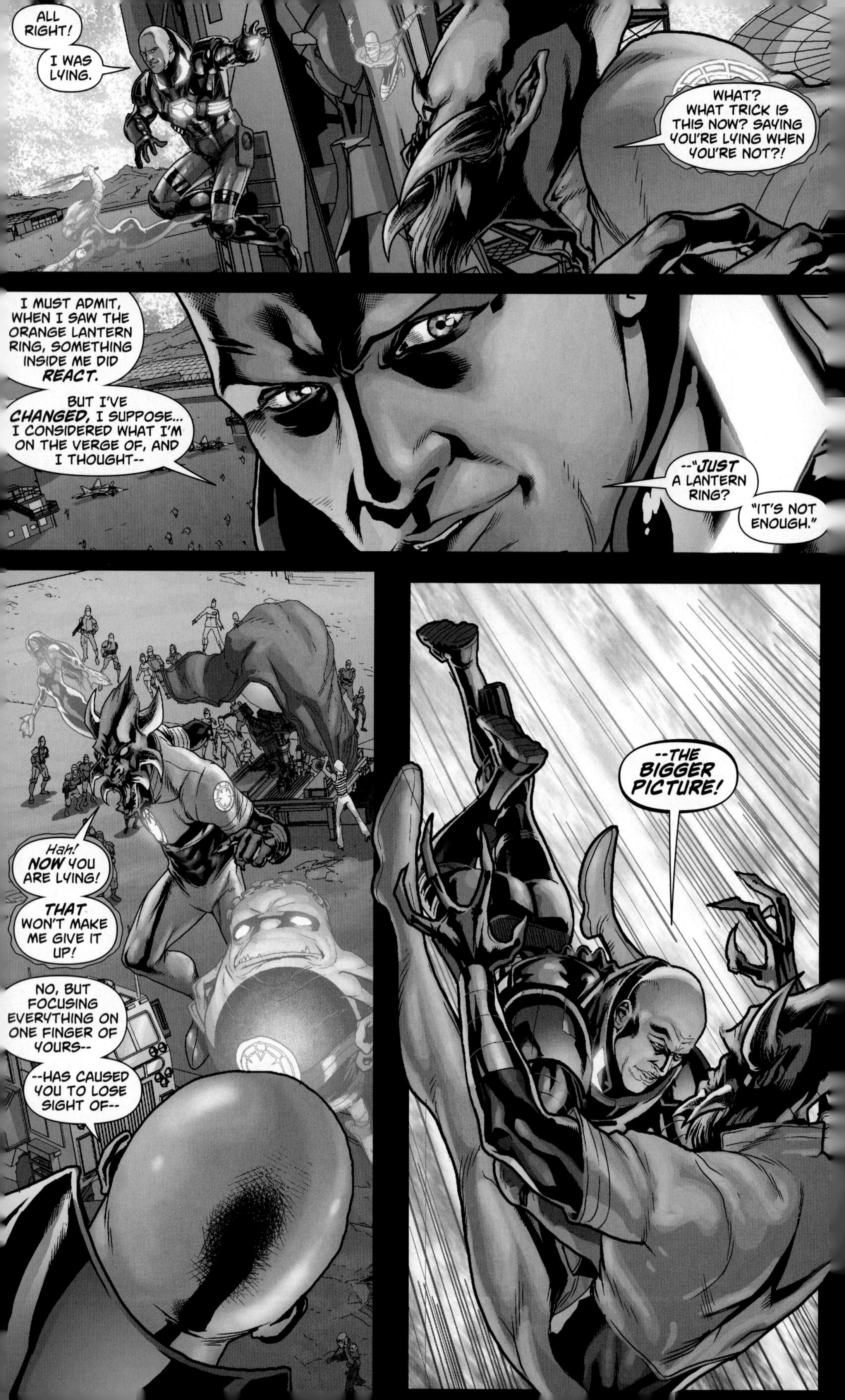

ALL RIGHT!
I WAS LYING.
WHAT? WHAT TRICK IS THIS NOW? SAYING YOU'RE LYING WHEN YOU'RE NOT?!
I MUST ADMIT, WHEN I SAW THE ORANGE LANTERN RING, SOMETHING INSIDE ME DID REACT.
BUT I'VE CHANGED, I SUPPOSE... I CONSIDERED WHAT I'M ON THE VERGE OF, AND I THOUGHT--
--"JUST A LANTERN RING?
"IT'S NOT ENOUGH."
Hah! NOW YOU ARE LYING!
THAT WON'T MAKE ME GIVE IT UP!
NO, BUT FOCUSING EVERYTHING ON ONE FINGER OF YOURS--
--HAS CAUSED YOU TO LOSE SIGHT OF--
--THE BIGGER PICTURE!

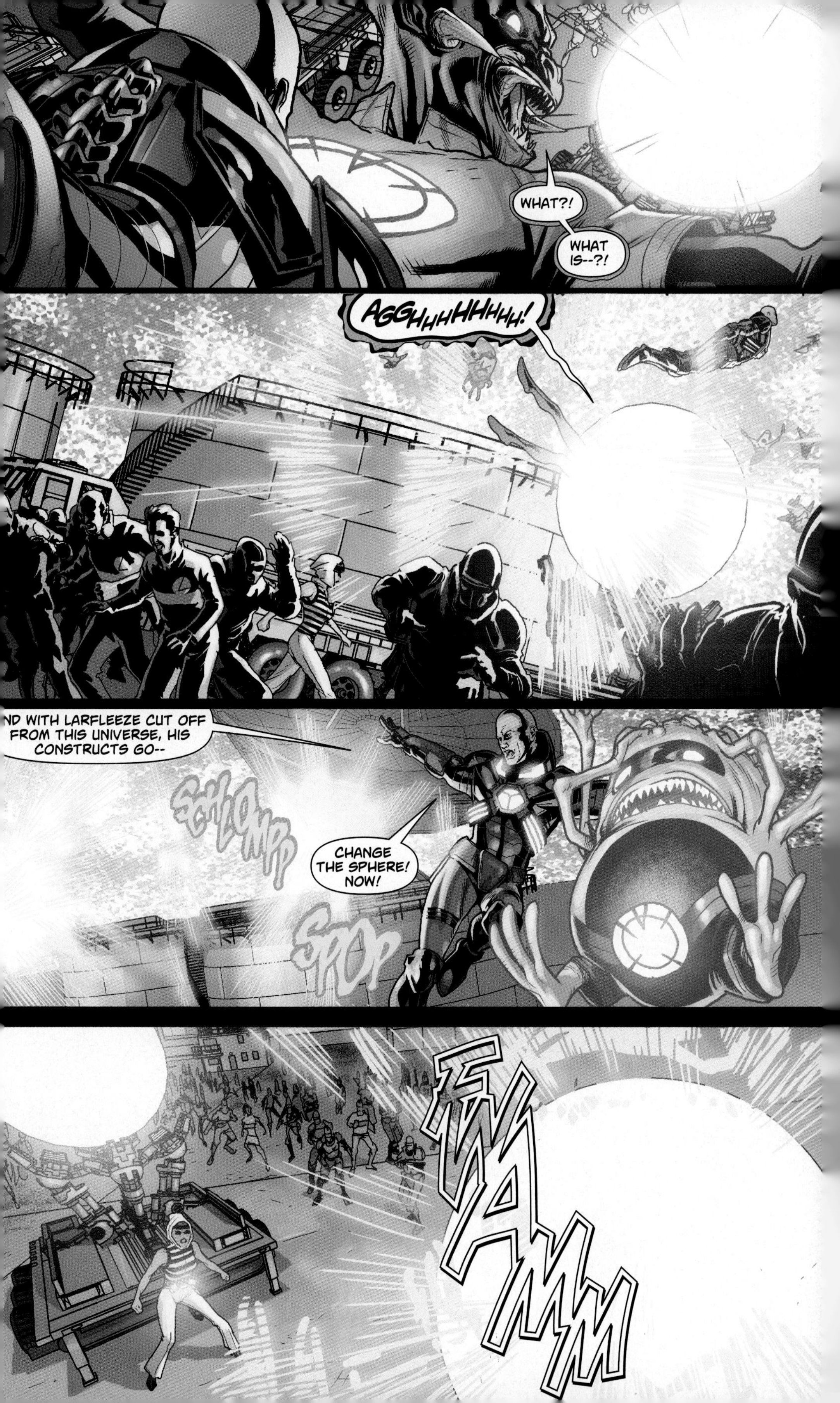
WHAT?!
WHAT IS--?!
AGGHHHHHHHH!
ND WITH LARFLEEZE CUT OFF FROM THIS UNIVERSE, HIS CONSTRUCTS GO--
SCHLOMPP
CHANGE THE SPHERE! NOW!
SPOP
FWAMM

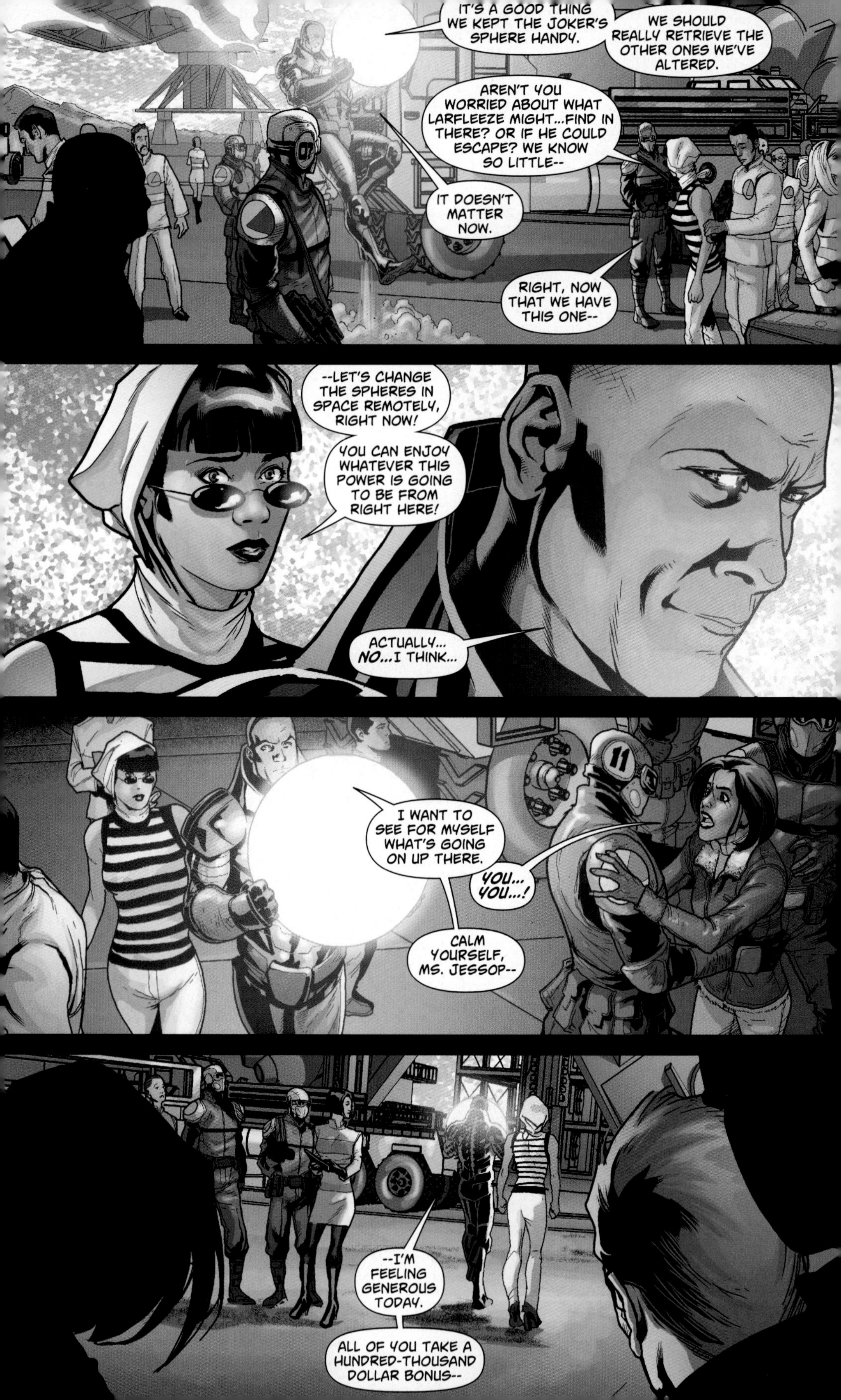
IT'S A GOOD THING WE KEPT THE JOKER'S SPHERE HANDY.
WE SHOULD REALLY RETRIEVE THE OTHER ONES WE'VE ALTERED.
AREN'T YOU WORRIED ABOUT WHAT LARFLEEZE MIGHT...FIND IN THERE? OR IF HE COULD ESCAPE? WE KNOW SO LITTLE--
IT DOESN'T MATTER NOW.
RIGHT, NOW THAT WE HAVE THIS ONE--
--LET'S CHANGE THE SPHERES IN SPACE REMOTELY, RIGHT NOW!
YOU CAN ENJOY WHATEVER THIS POWER IS GOING TO BE FROM RIGHT HERE!
ACTUALLY... NO...I THINK...
I WANT TO SEE FOR MYSELF WHAT'S GOING ON UP THERE.
YOU... YOU...!
CALM YOURSELF, MS. JESSOP--
--I'M FEELING GENEROUS TODAY.
ALL OF YOU TAKE A HUNDRED-THOUSAND DOLLAR BONUS--

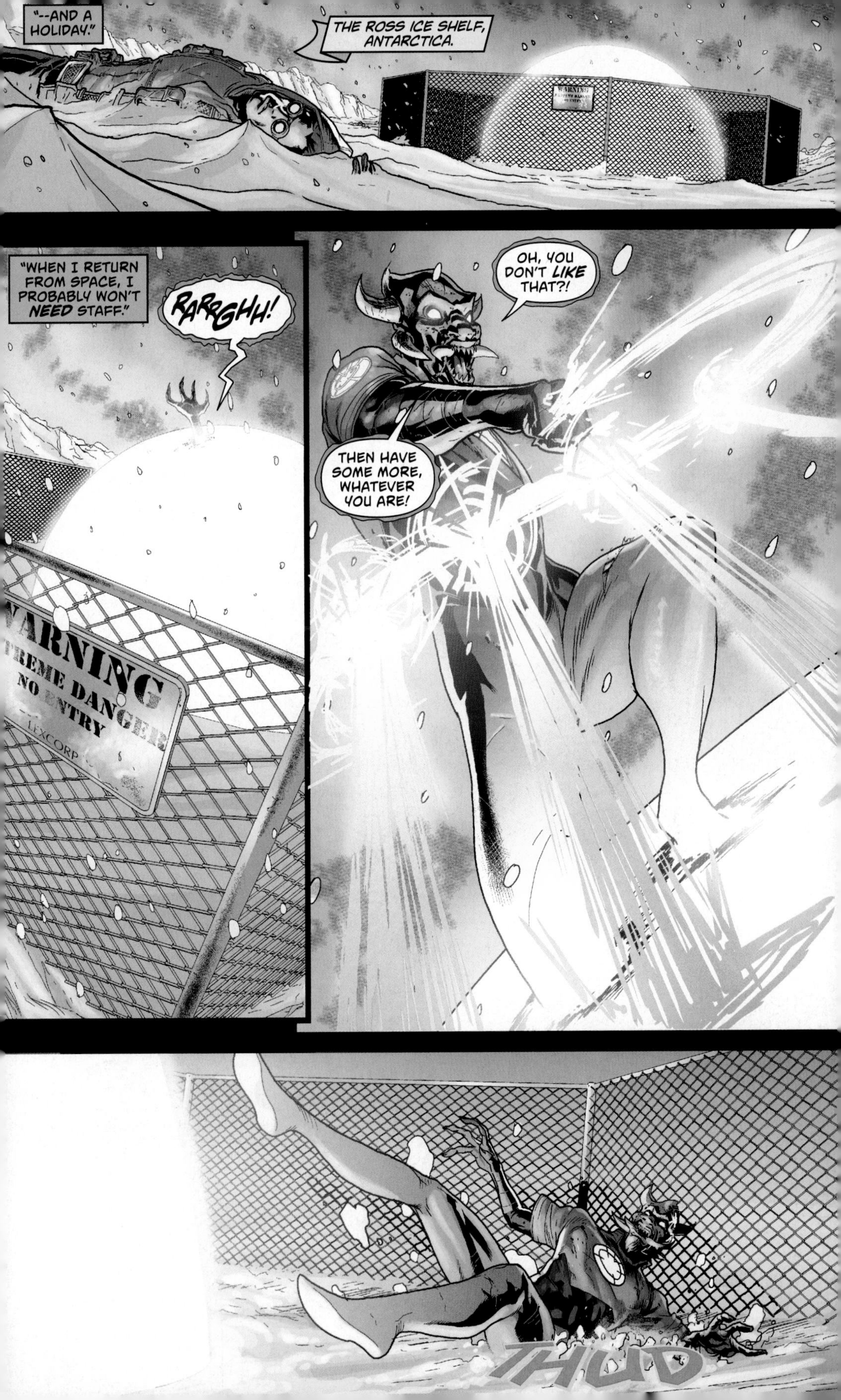

"--AND A HOLIDAY."
THE ROSS ICE SHELF, ANTARCTICA.
"WHEN I RETURN FROM SPACE, I PROBABLY WON'T NEED STAFF."
RARRGHH!
WARNING
TREME DANGER
NO ENTRY
LEXCORP
OH, YOU DON'T LIKE THAT?!
THEN HAVE SOME MORE, WHATEVER YOU ARE!
THUD

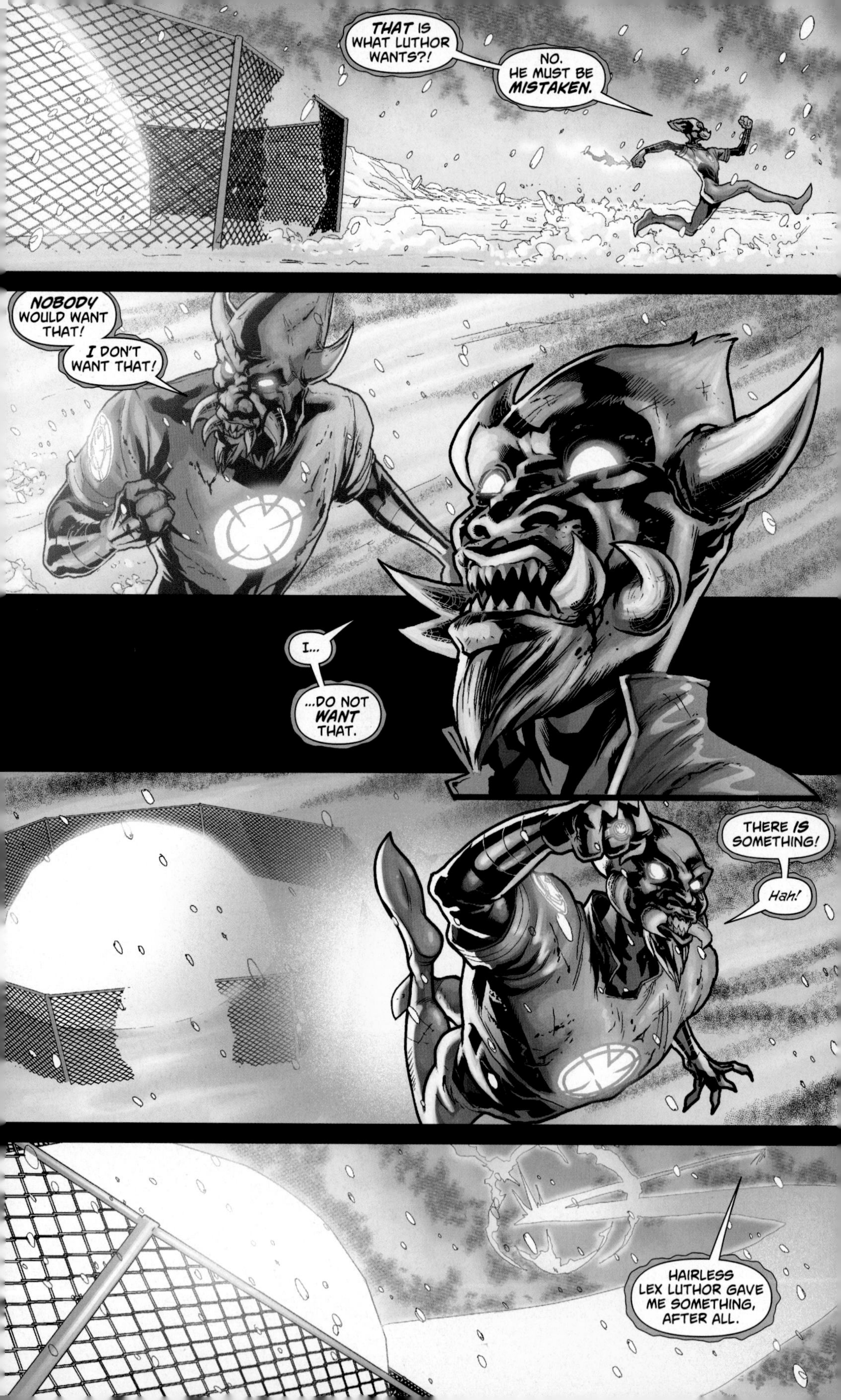
THAT IS WHAT LUTHOR WANTS?!
NO. HE MUST BE MISTAKEN.
NOBODY WOULD WANT THAT!
I DON'T WANT THAT!
I...
...DO NOT WANT THAT.
THERE IS SOMETHING!
Hah!
HAIRLESS LEX LUTHOR GAVE ME SOMETHING, AFTER ALL.

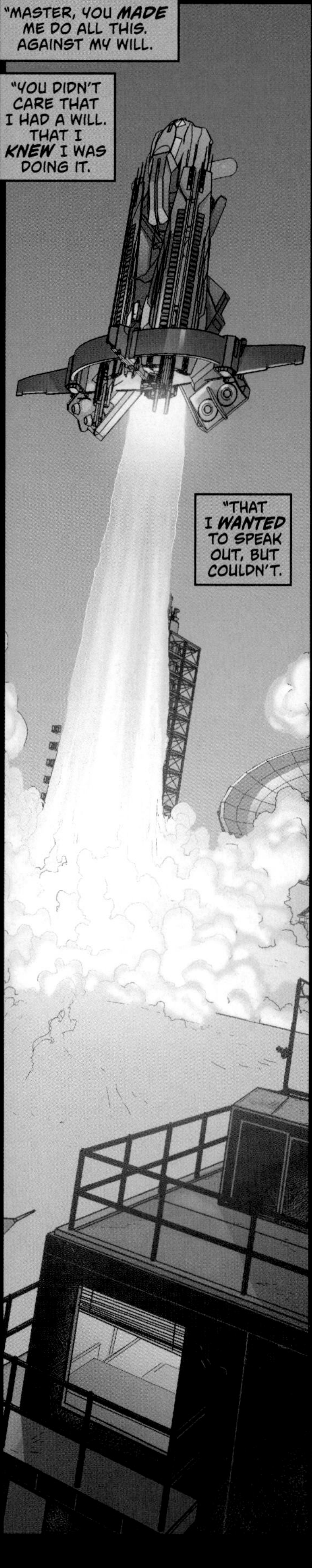
"MASTER, YOU *MADE* ME DO ALL THIS. AGAINST MY WILL.
"YOU DIDN'T CARE THAT I HAD A WILL. THAT I *KNEW* I WAS DOING IT.
"THAT I *WANTED* TO SPEAK OUT, BUT COULDN'T.

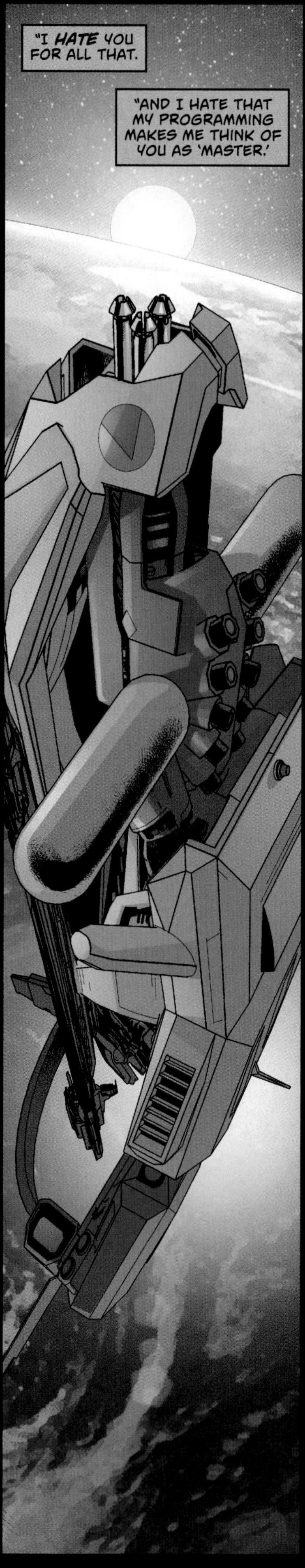
"I *HATE* YOU FOR ALL THAT.
"AND I HATE THAT MY PROGRAMMING MAKES ME THINK OF YOU AS 'MASTER.'

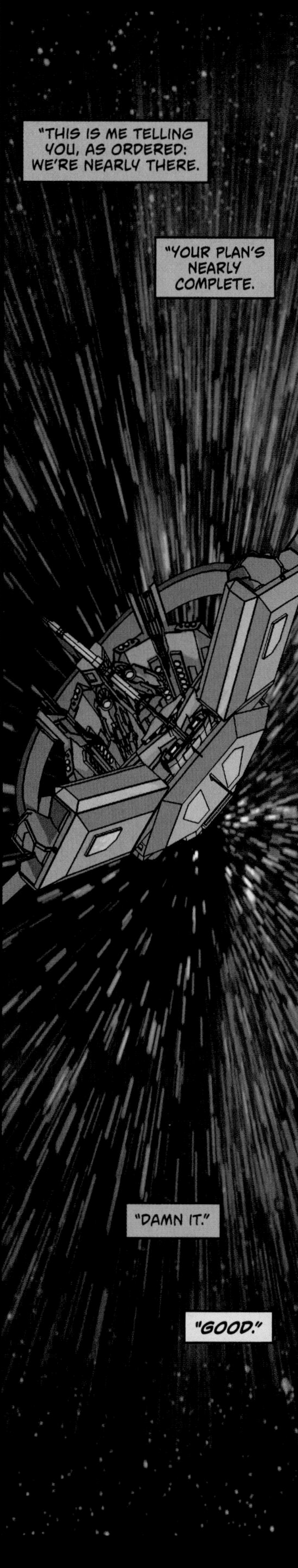
"THIS IS ME TELLING YOU, AS ORDERED: WE'RE NEARLY THERE.
"YOUR PLAN'S NEARLY COMPLETE.
"DAMN IT."
"GOOD."

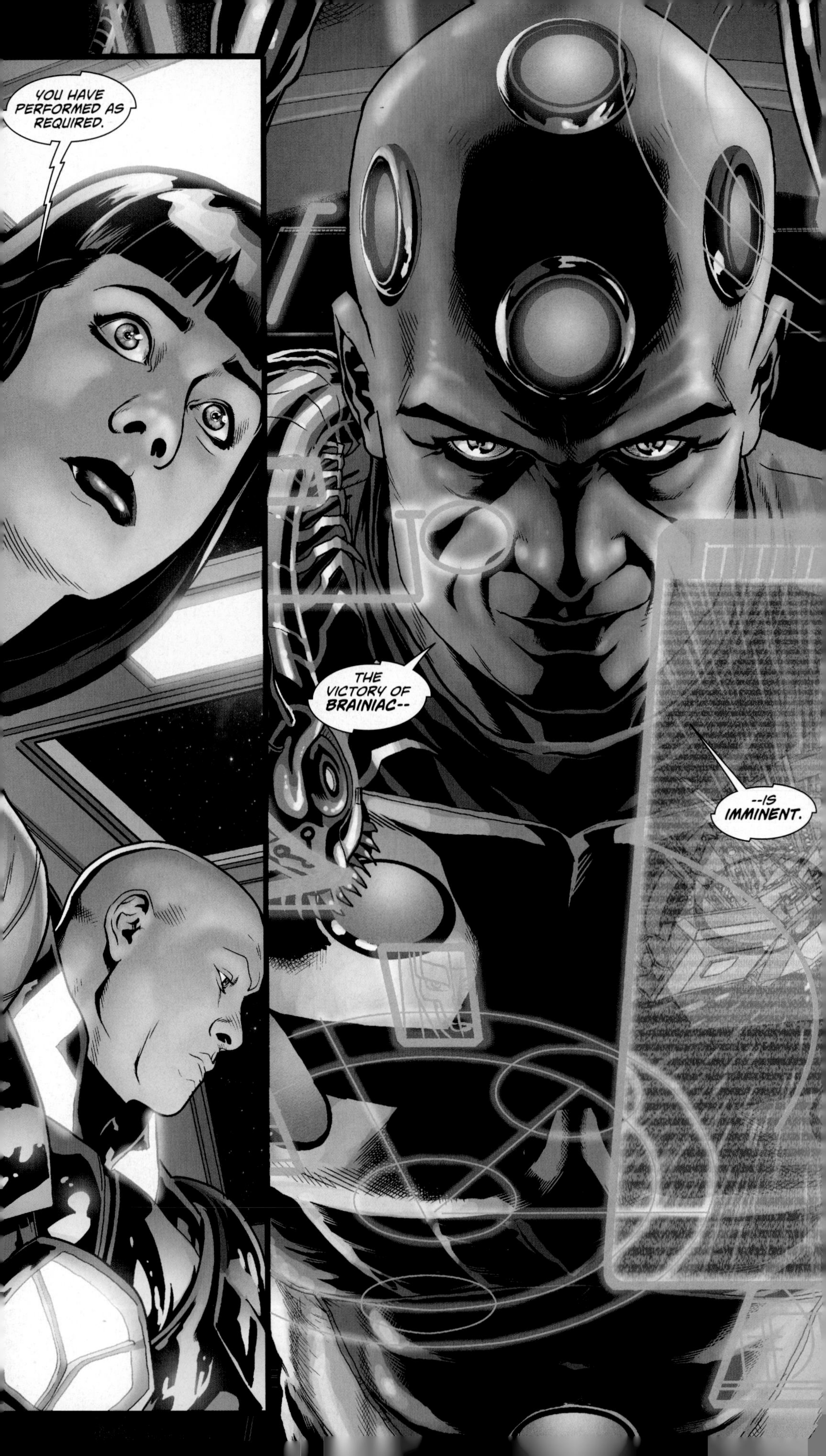
YOU HAVE PERFORMED AS REQUIRED.
THE VICTORY OF BRAINIAC--
--IS IMMINENT.

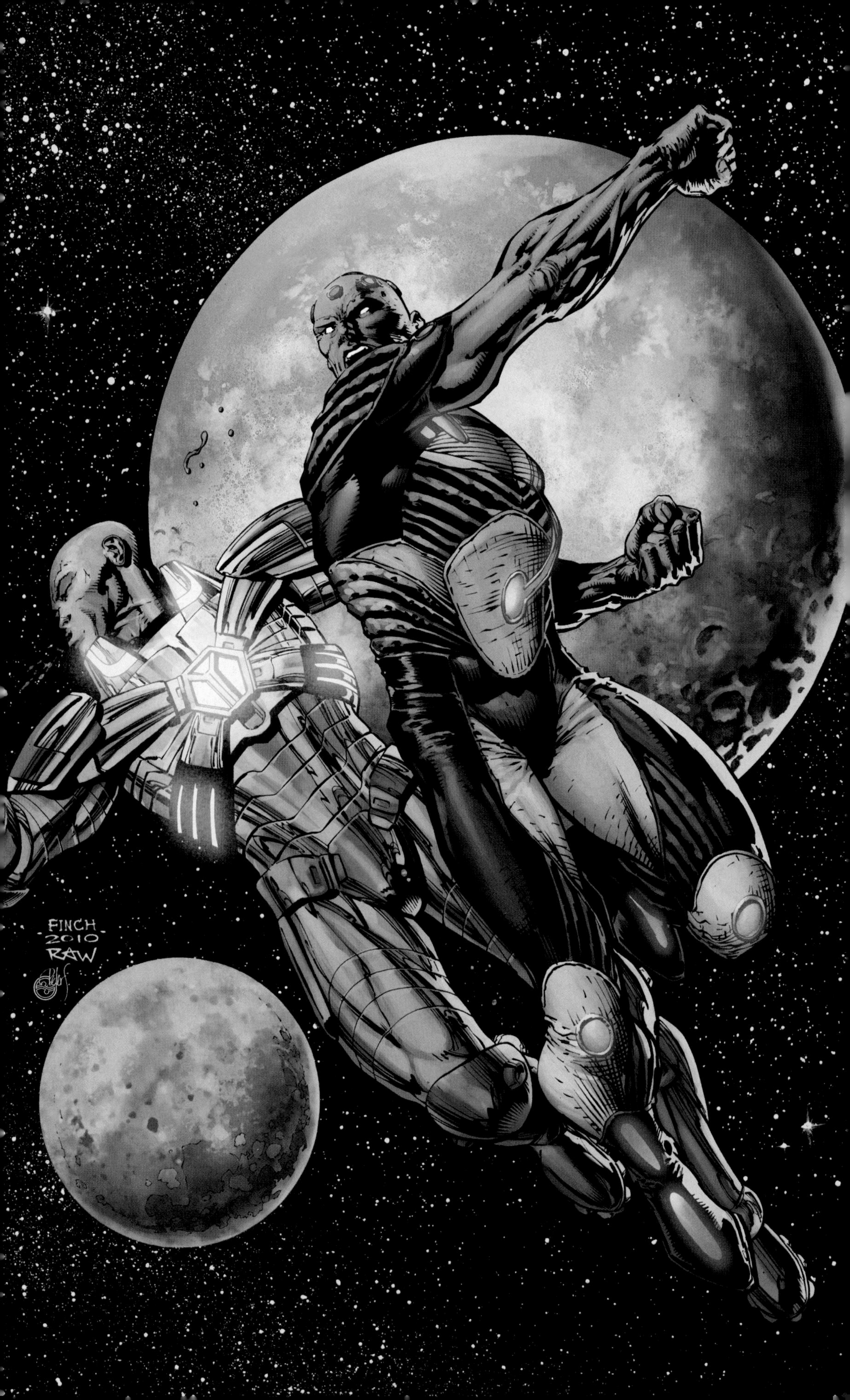
FINCH
2010
RAW

THE BLACK RING

part ten

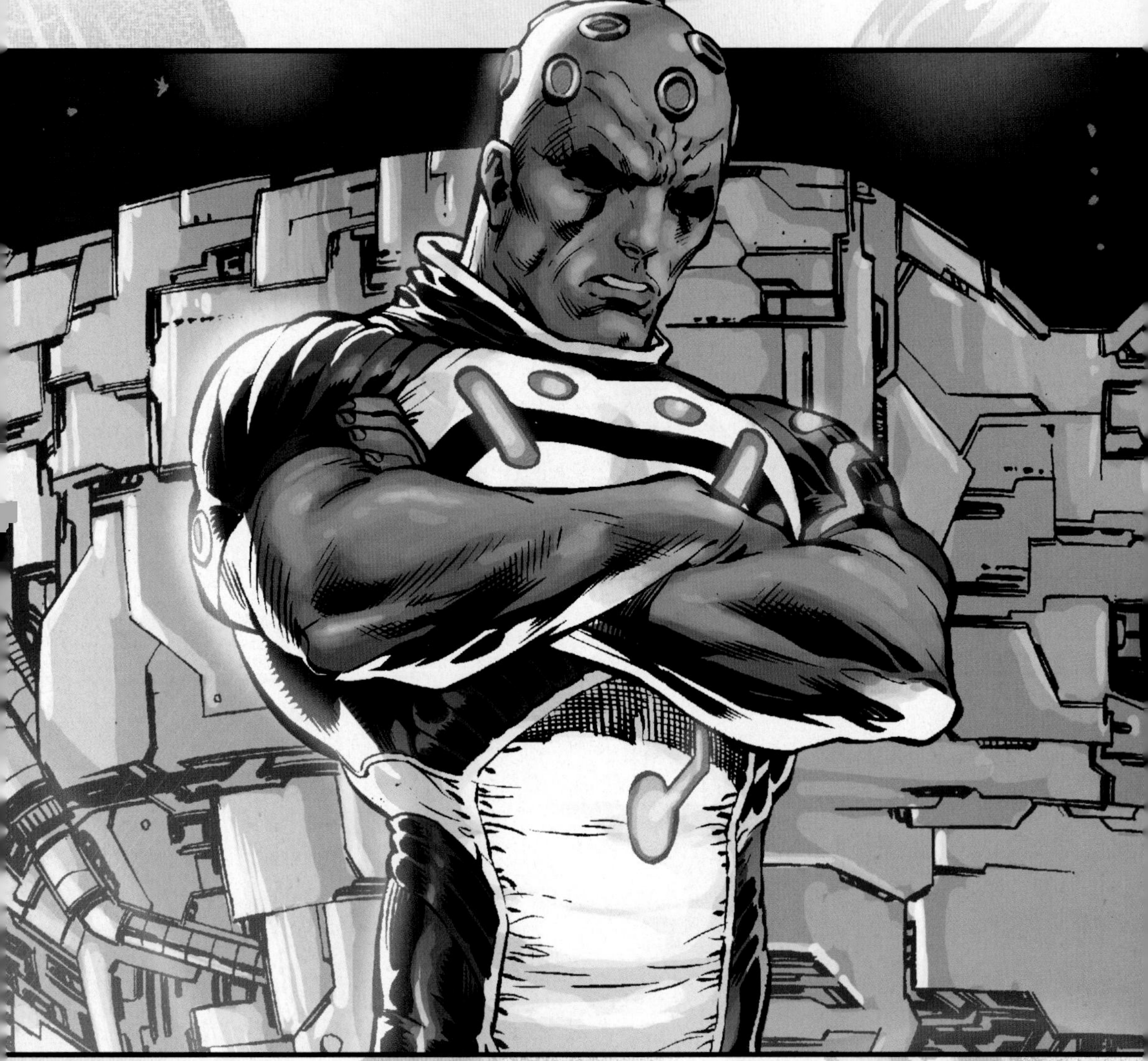

PAUL **CORNELL** writer
JESUS **MERINO** artist

cover by
DAVID **FINCH**, RYAN **WINN** & PETER **STEIGERWALD**

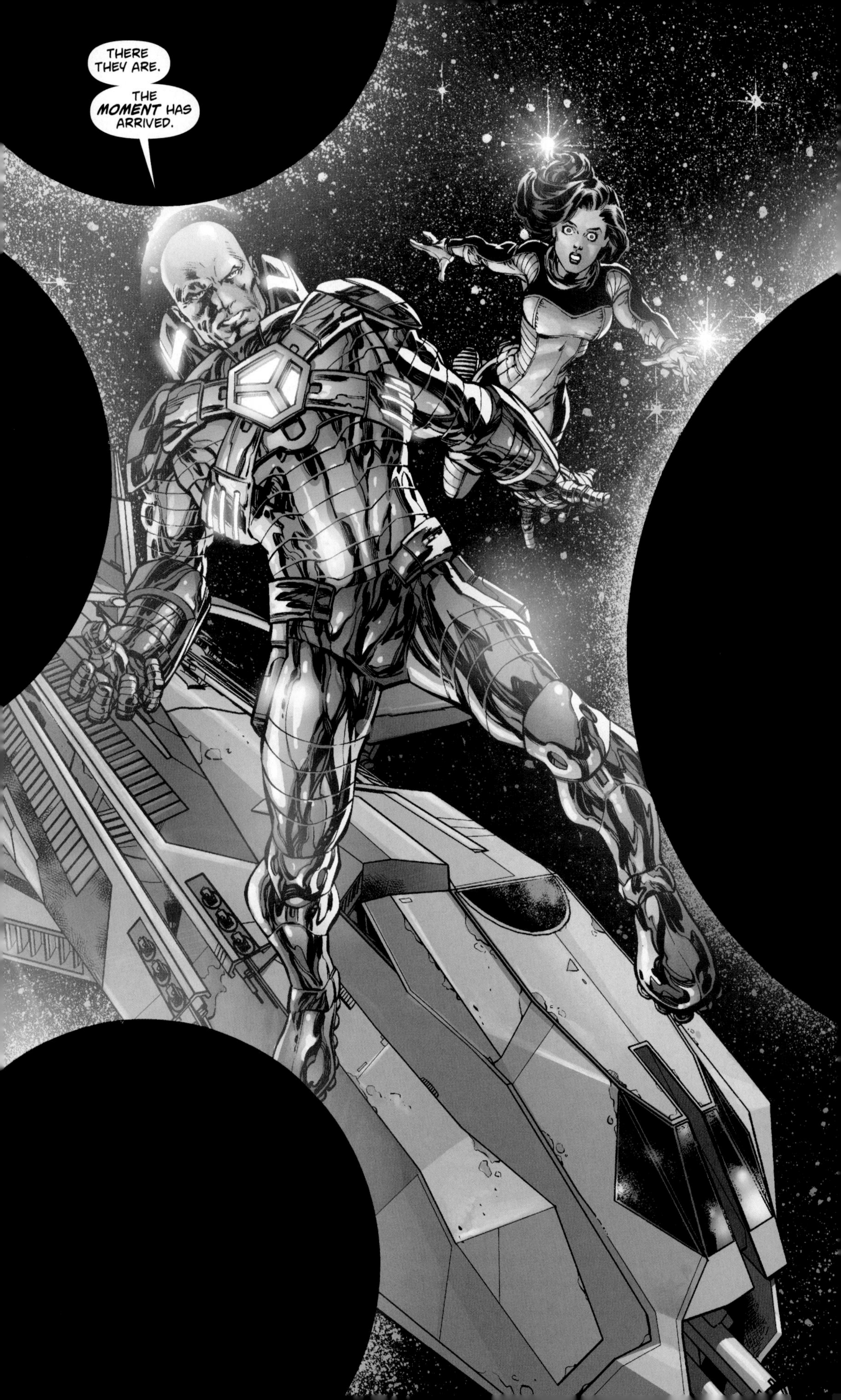
THERE THEY ARE.
THE MOMENT HAS ARRIVED.

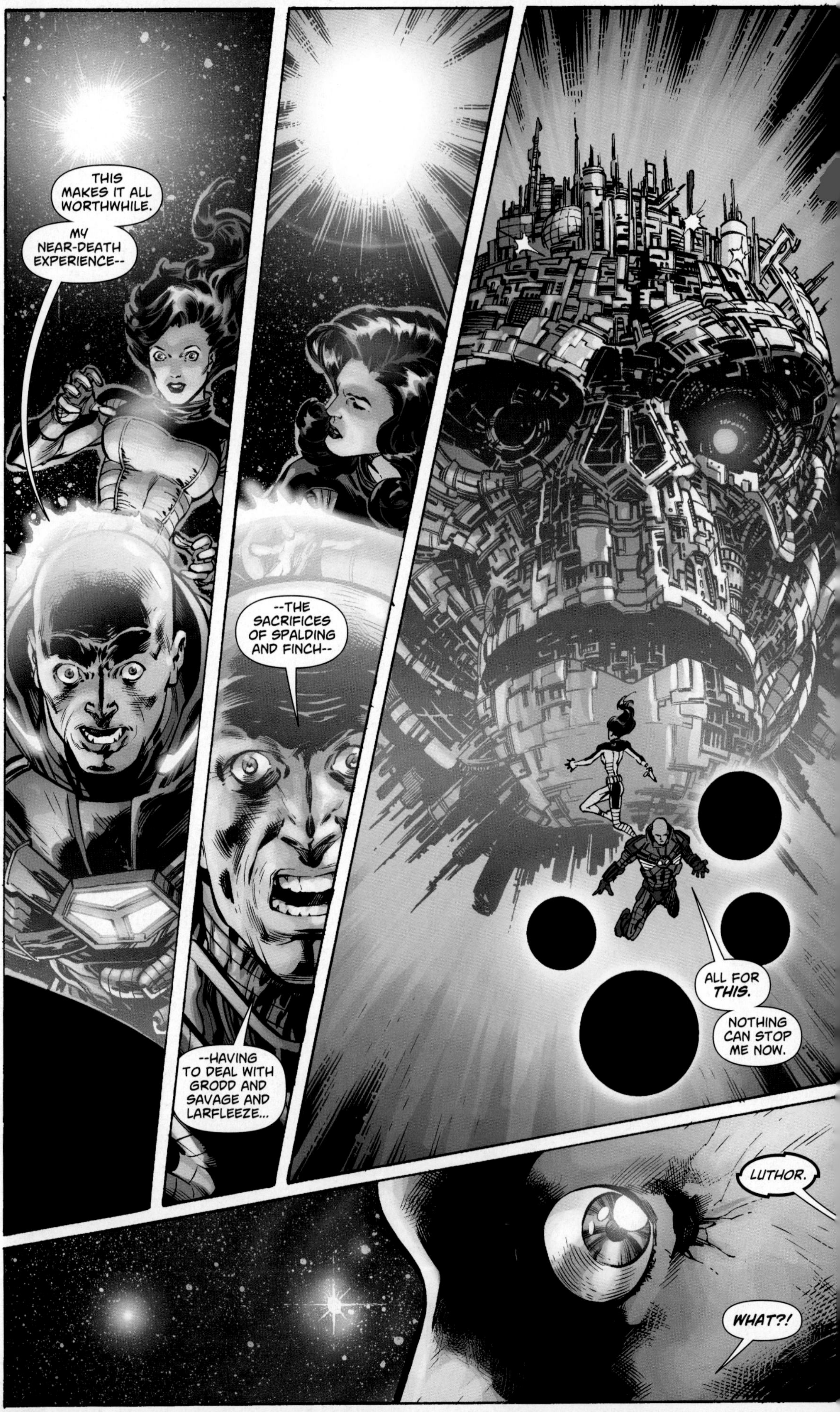
THIS MAKES IT ALL WORTHWHILE.
MY NEAR-DEATH EXPERIENCE--
--THE SACRIFICES OF SPALDING AND FINCH--
--HAVING TO DEAL WITH GRODD AND SAVAGE AND LARFLEEZE...
ALL FOR THIS.
NOTHING CAN STOP ME NOW.
LUTHOR.
WHAT?!

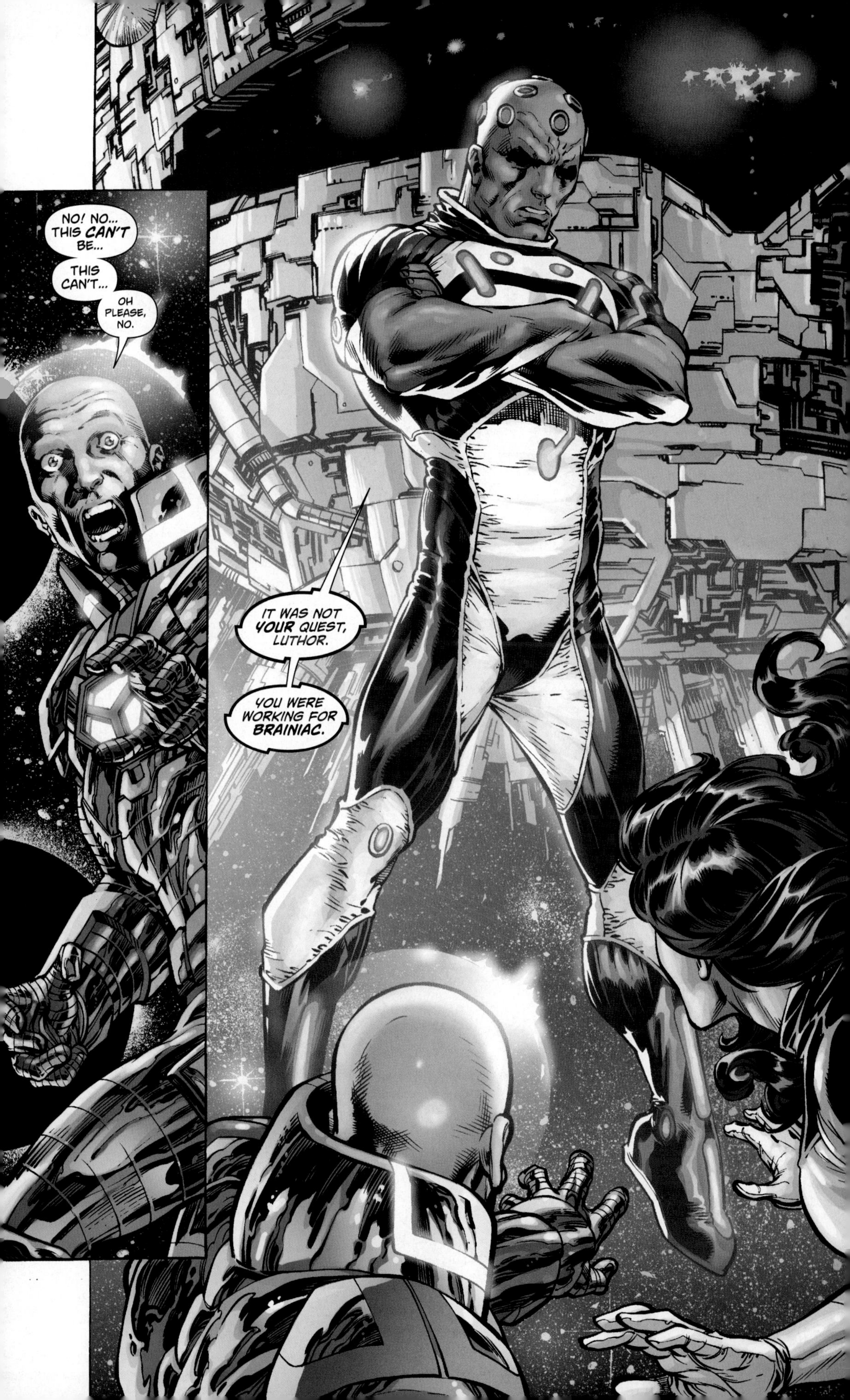
NO! NO... THIS CAN'T BE...
THIS CAN'T...
OH PLEASE, NO.
IT WAS NOT YOUR QUEST, LUTHOR.
YOU WERE WORKING FOR BRAINIAC.

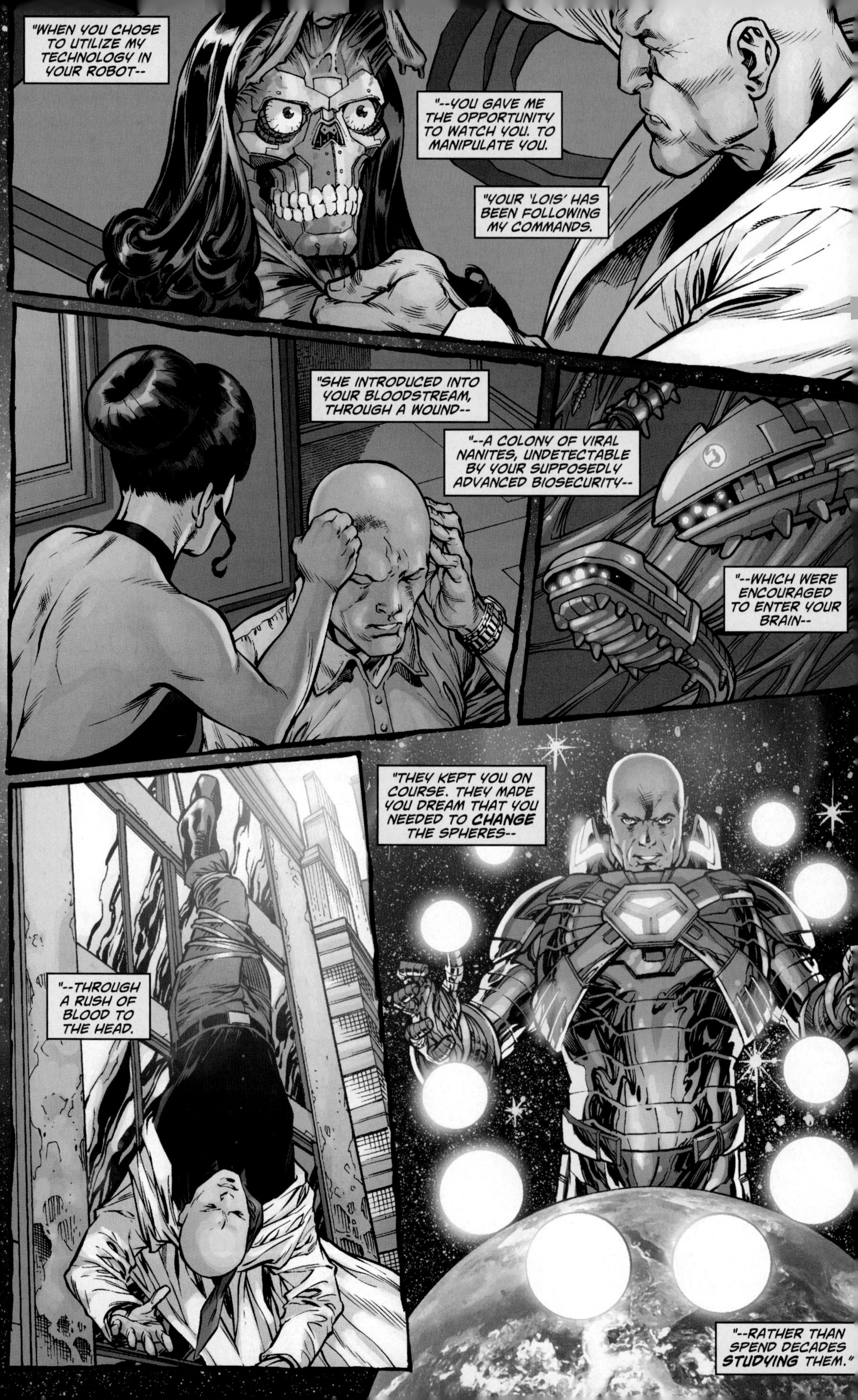
"WHEN YOU CHOSE TO UTILIZE MY TECHNOLOGY IN YOUR ROBOT--
"--YOU GAVE ME THE OPPORTUNITY TO WATCH YOU. TO MANIPULATE YOU.
"YOUR 'LOIS' HAS BEEN FOLLOWING MY COMMANDS.
"SHE INTRODUCED INTO YOUR BLOODSTREAM, THROUGH A WOUND--
"--A COLONY OF VIRAL NANITES, UNDETECTABLE BY YOUR SUPPOSEDLY ADVANCED BIOSECURITY--
"--WHICH WERE ENCOURAGED TO ENTER YOUR BRAIN--
"--THROUGH A RUSH OF BLOOD TO THE HEAD.
"THEY KEPT YOU ON COURSE. THEY MADE YOU DREAM THAT YOU NEEDED TO CHANGE THE SPHERES--
"--RATHER THAN SPEND DECADES STUDYING THEM."

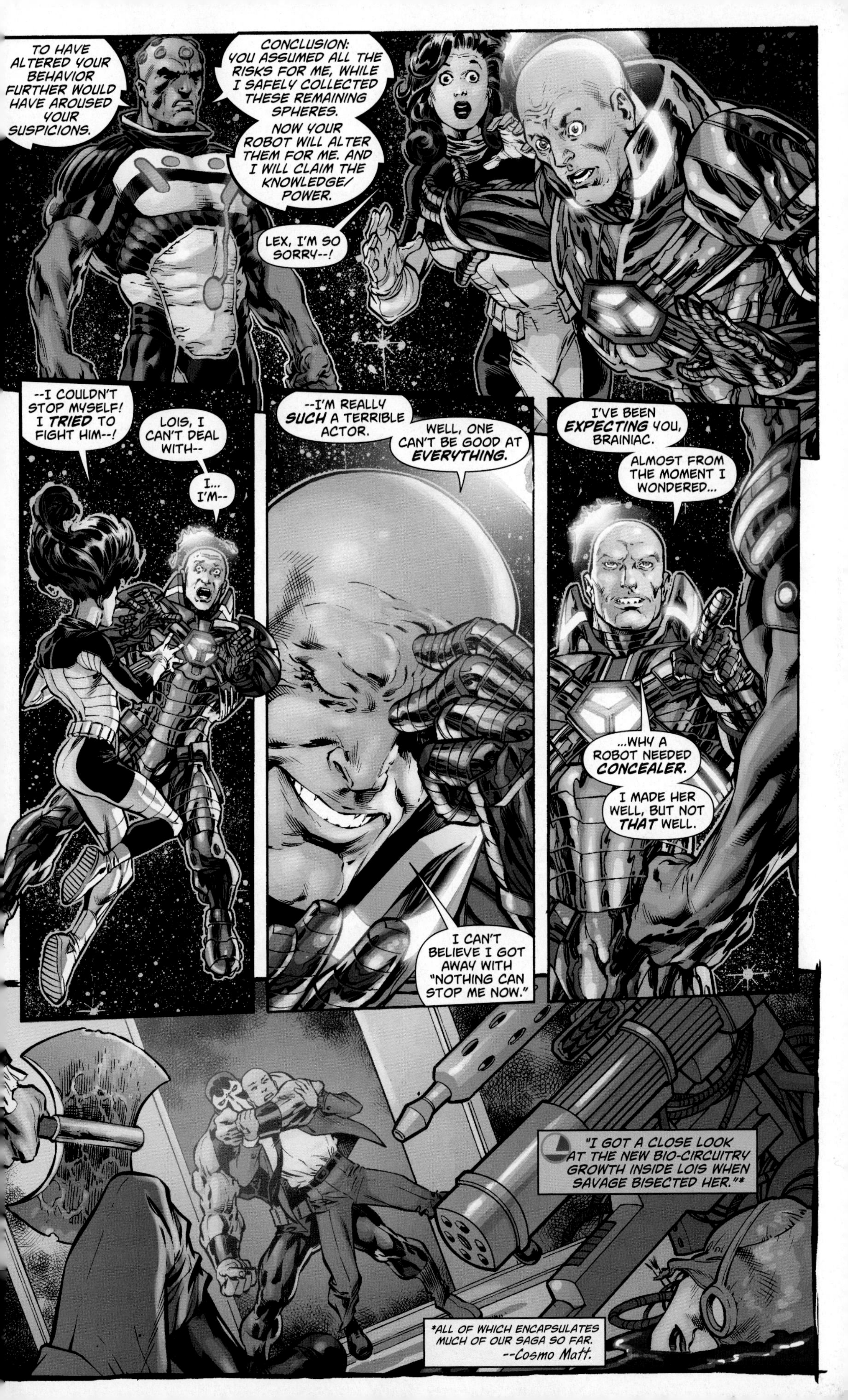
TO HAVE ALTERED YOUR BEHAVIOR FURTHER WOULD HAVE AROUSED YOUR SUSPICIONS.
CONCLUSION: YOU ASSUMED ALL THE RISKS FOR ME, WHILE I SAFELY COLLECTED THESE REMAINING SPHERES.
NOW YOUR ROBOT WILL ALTER THEM FOR ME. AND I WILL CLAIM THE KNOWLEDGE/ POWER.
LEX, I'M SO SORRY--!
--I COULDN'T STOP MYSELF! I TRIED TO FIGHT HIM--!
LOIS, I CAN'T DEAL WITH--
I... I'M--
--I'M REALLY SUCH A TERRIBLE ACTOR.
WELL, ONE CAN'T BE GOOD AT EVERYTHING.
I CAN'T BELIEVE I GOT AWAY WITH "NOTHING CAN STOP ME NOW."
I'VE BEEN EXPECTING YOU, BRAINIAC.
ALMOST FROM THE MOMENT I WONDERED...
...WHY A ROBOT NEEDED CONCEALER.
I MADE HER WELL, BUT NOT THAT WELL.
"I GOT A CLOSE LOOK AT THE NEW BIO-CIRCUITRY GROWTH INSIDE LOIS WHEN SAVAGE BISECTED HER."*
*ALL OF WHICH ENCAPSULATES MUCH OF OUR SAGA SO FAR. --Cosmo Matt.

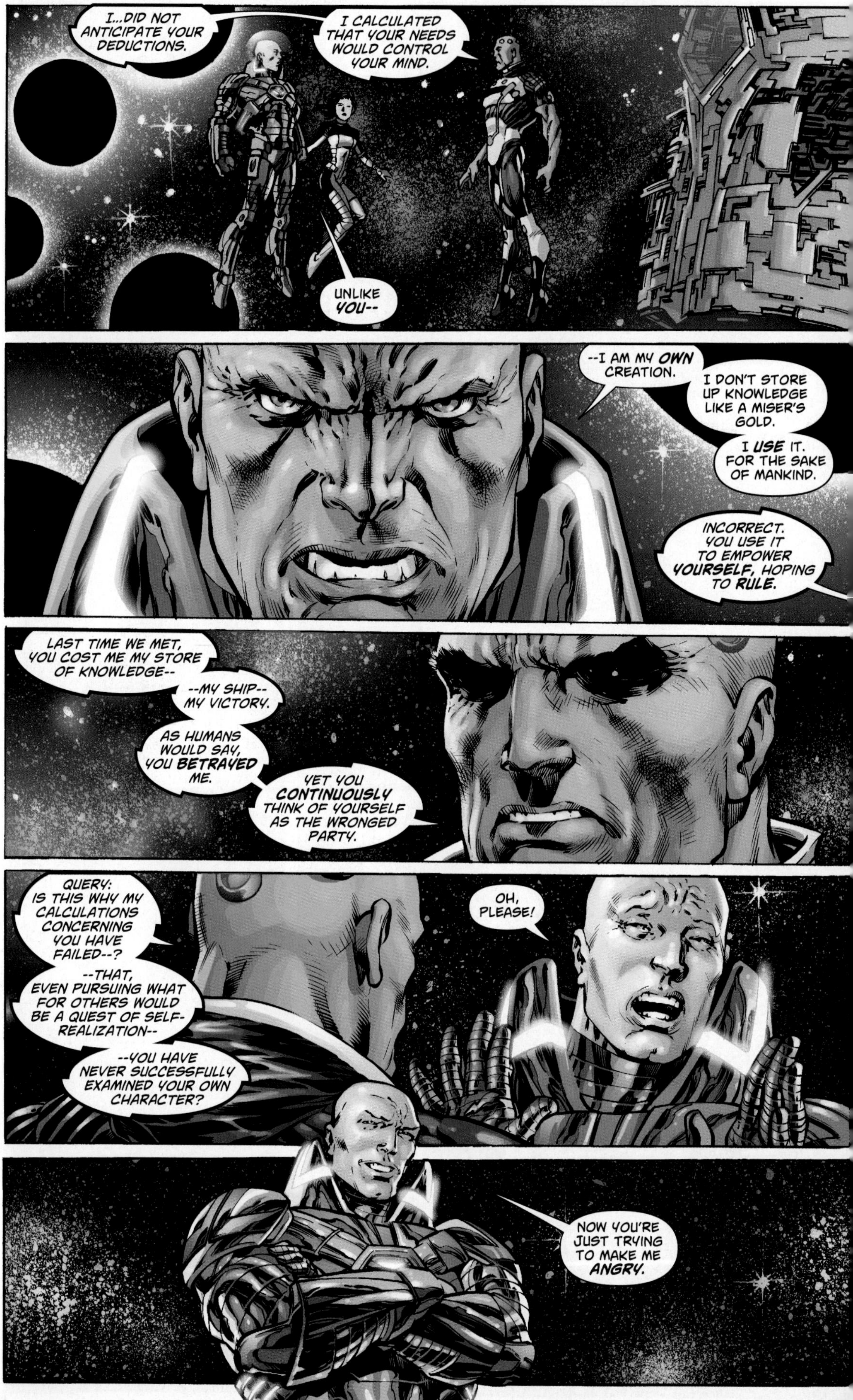
I...DID NOT ANTICIPATE YOUR DEDUCTIONS.
I CALCULATED THAT YOUR NEEDS WOULD CONTROL YOUR MIND.
UNLIKE YOU--
--I AM MY OWN CREATION.
I DON'T STORE UP KNOWLEDGE LIKE A MISER'S GOLD.
I USE IT. FOR THE SAKE OF MANKIND.
INCORRECT. YOU USE IT TO EMPOWER YOURSELF, HOPING TO RULE.
LAST TIME WE MET, YOU COST ME MY STORE OF KNOWLEDGE--
--MY SHIP-- MY VICTORY.
AS HUMANS WOULD SAY, YOU BETRAYED ME.
YET YOU CONTINUOUSLY THINK OF YOURSELF AS THE WRONGED PARTY.
QUERY: IS THIS WHY MY CALCULATIONS CONCERNING YOU HAVE FAILED--?
--THAT, EVEN PURSUING WHAT FOR OTHERS WOULD BE A QUEST OF SELF-REALIZATION--
--YOU HAVE NEVER SUCCESSFULLY EXAMINED YOUR OWN CHARACTER?
OH, PLEASE!
NOW YOU'RE JUST TRYING TO MAKE ME ANGRY.

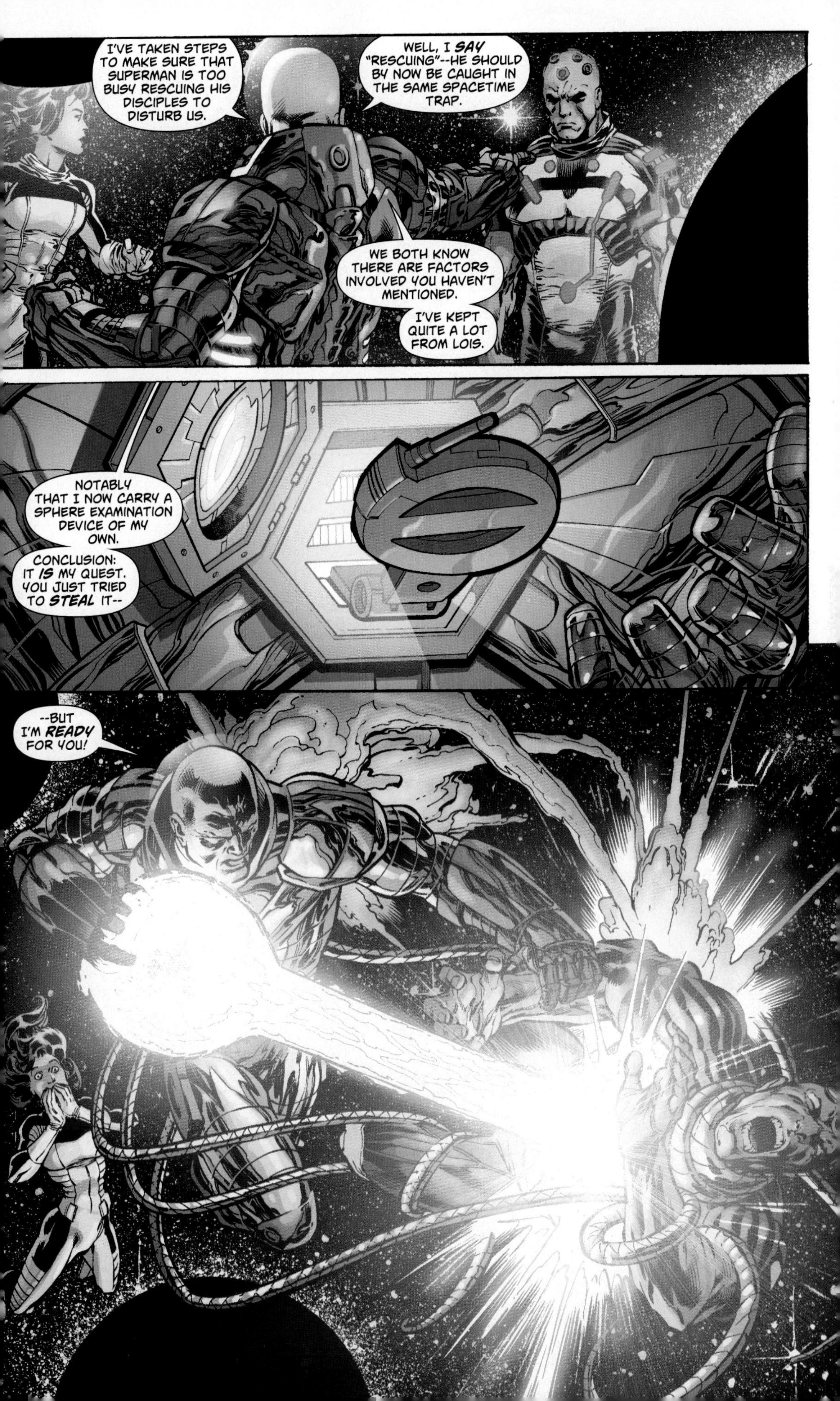

I'VE TAKEN STEPS TO MAKE SURE THAT SUPERMAN IS TOO BUSY RESCUING HIS DISCIPLES TO DISTURB US.
WELL, I SAY "RESCUING"--HE SHOULD BY NOW BE CAUGHT IN THE SAME SPACETIME TRAP.
WE BOTH KNOW THERE ARE FACTORS INVOLVED YOU HAVEN'T MENTIONED.
I'VE KEPT QUITE A LOT FROM LOIS.
NOTABLY THAT I NOW CARRY A SPHERE EXAMINATION DEVICE OF MY OWN.
CONCLUSION: IT IS MY QUEST. YOU JUST TRIED TO STEAL IT--
--BUT I'M READY FOR YOU!

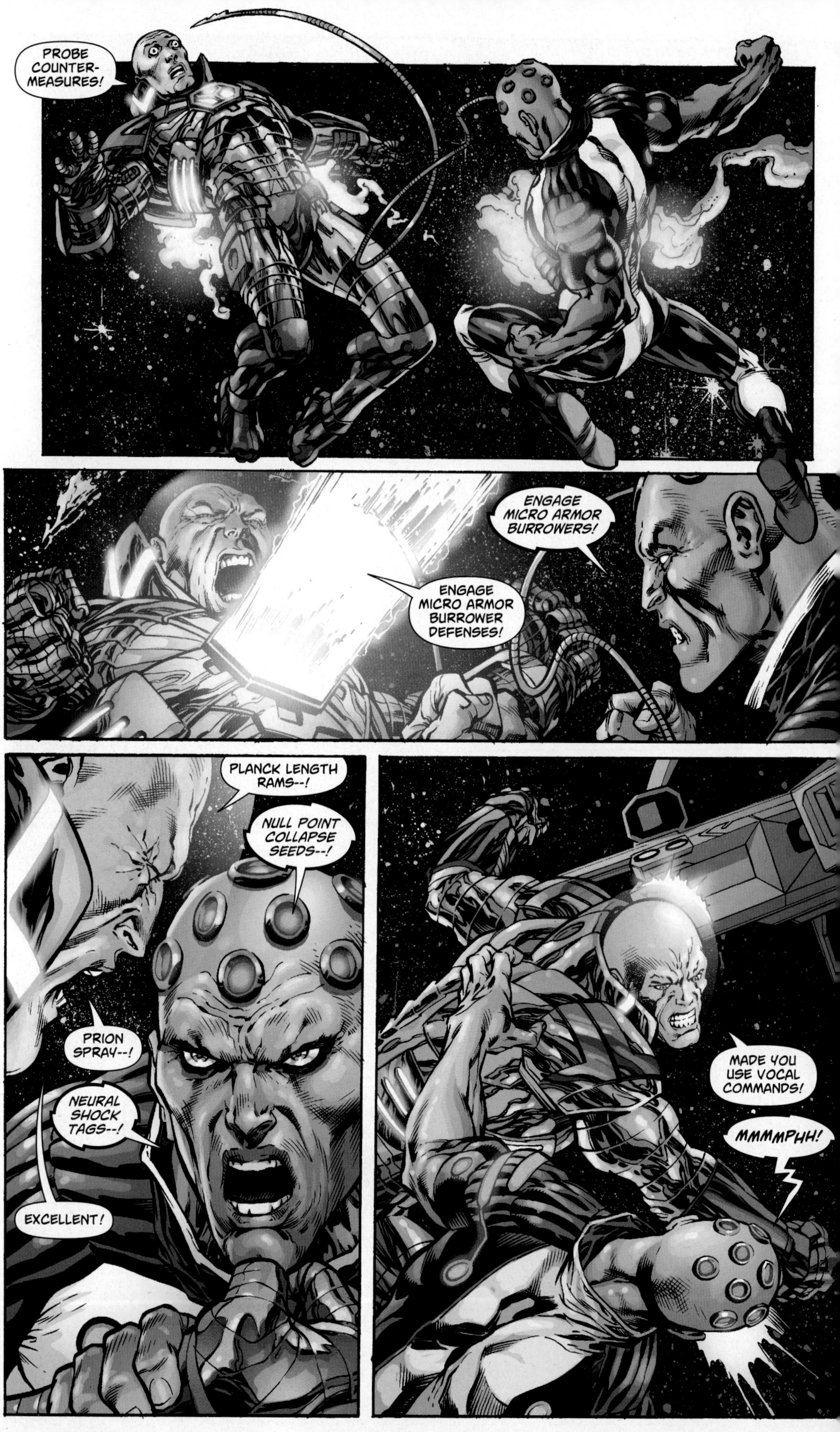
PROBE COUNTER-MEASURES!
ENGAGE MICRO ARMOR BURROWERS!
ENGAGE MICRO ARMOR BURROWER DEFENSES!
PLANCK LENGTH RAMS--!
NULL POINT COLLAPSE SEEDS--!
PRION SPRAY--!
NEURAL SHOCK TAGS--!
EXCELLENT!
MADE YOU USE VOCAL COMMANDS!
MMMMPHH!

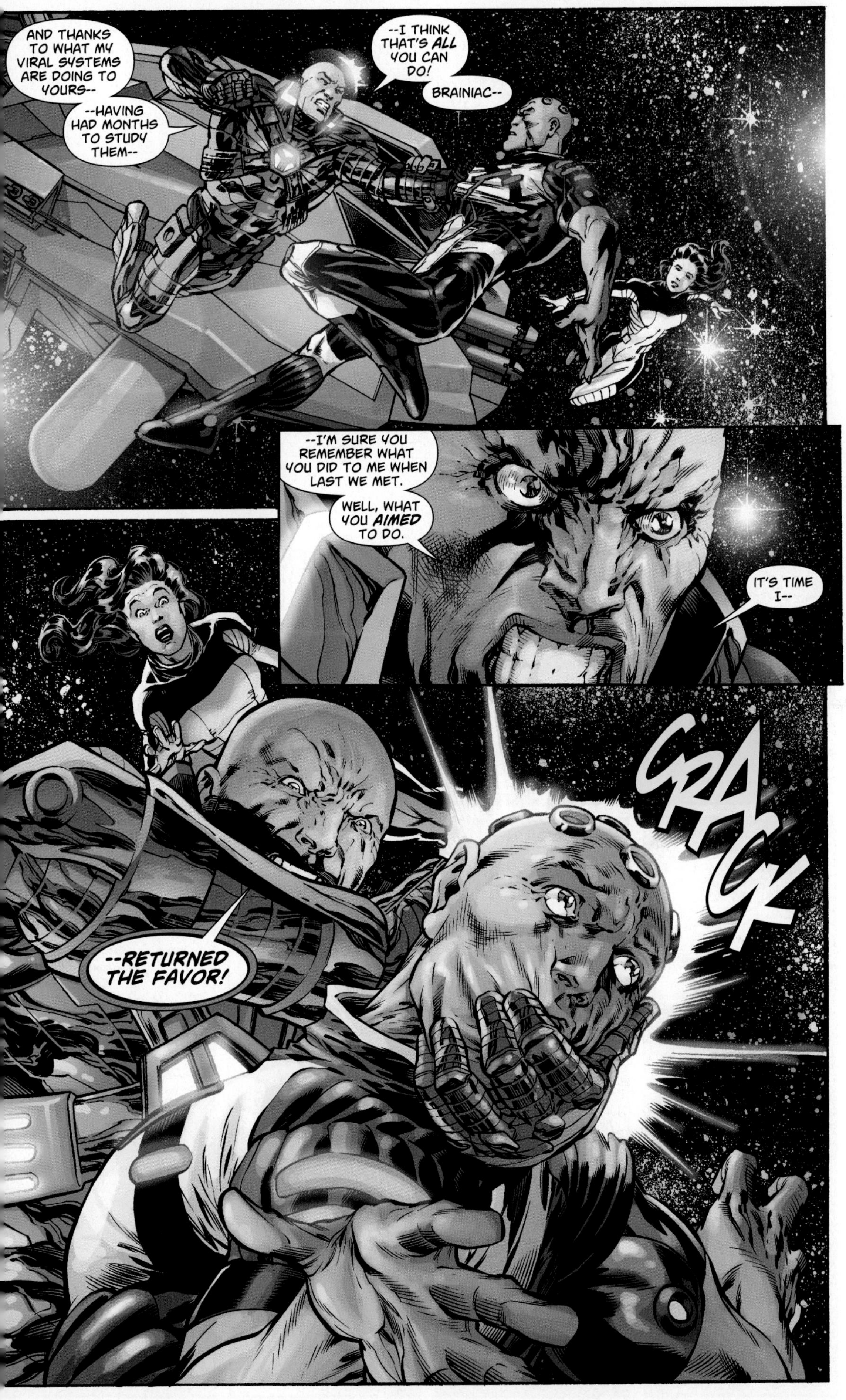
AND THANKS TO WHAT MY VIRAL SYSTEMS ARE DOING TO YOURS--
--HAVING HAD MONTHS TO STUDY THEM--
--I THINK THAT'S ALL YOU CAN DO!
BRAINIAC--
--I'M SURE YOU REMEMBER WHAT YOU DID TO ME WHEN LAST WE MET.
WELL, WHAT YOU AIMED TO DO.
IT'S TIME I--
--RETURNED THE FAVOR!
CRACK

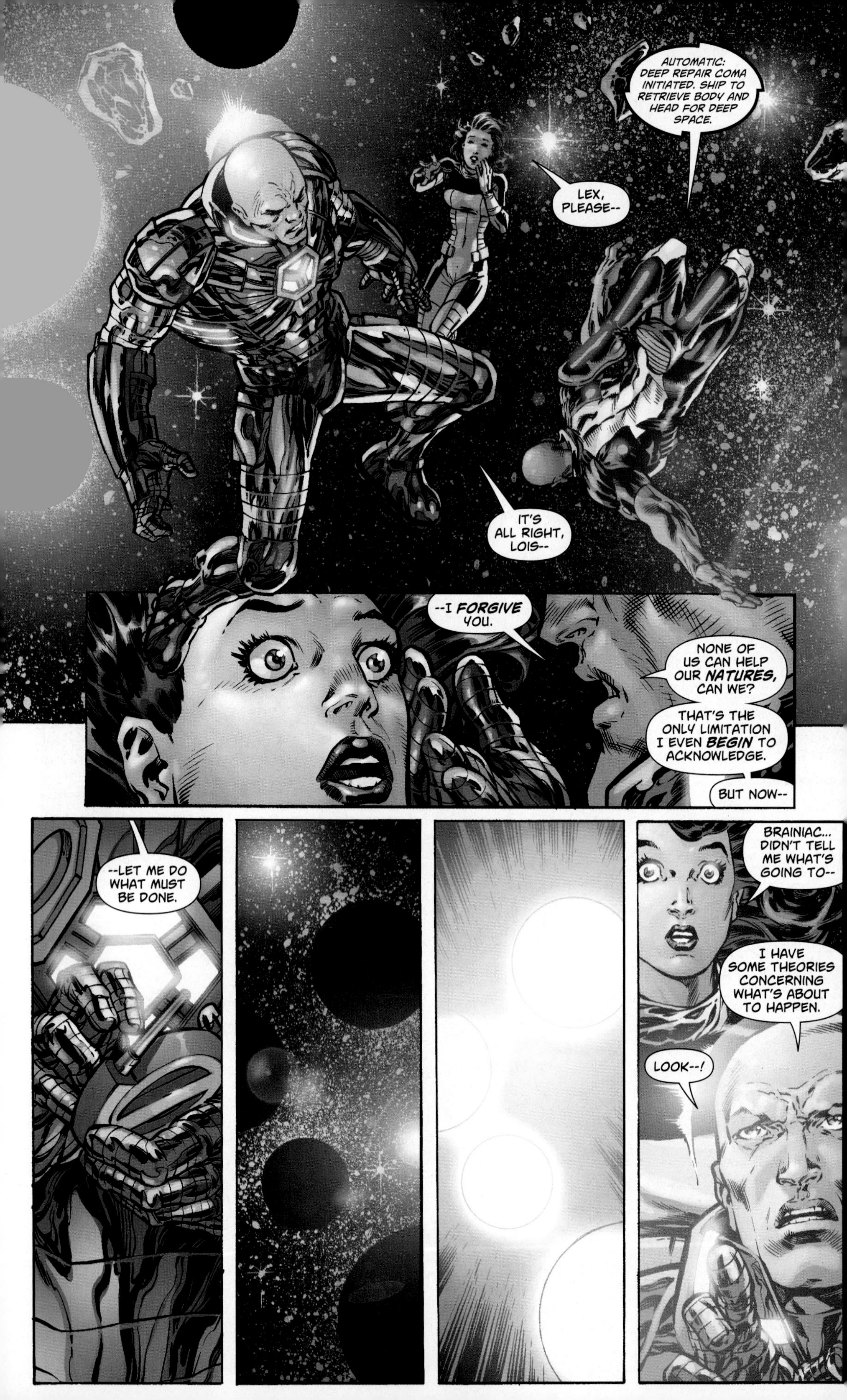
AUTOMATIC: DEEP REPAIR COMA INITIATED. SHIP TO RETRIEVE BODY AND HEAD FOR DEEP SPACE.
LEX, PLEASE--
IT'S ALL RIGHT, LOIS--
--I FORGIVE YOU.
NONE OF US CAN HELP OUR NATURES, CAN WE?
THAT'S THE ONLY LIMITATION I EVEN BEGIN TO ACKNOWLEDGE.
BUT NOW--
--LET ME DO WHAT MUST BE DONE.
BRAINIAC... DIDN'T TELL ME WHAT'S GOING TO--
I HAVE SOME THEORIES CONCERNING WHAT'S ABOUT TO HAPPEN.
LOOK--!

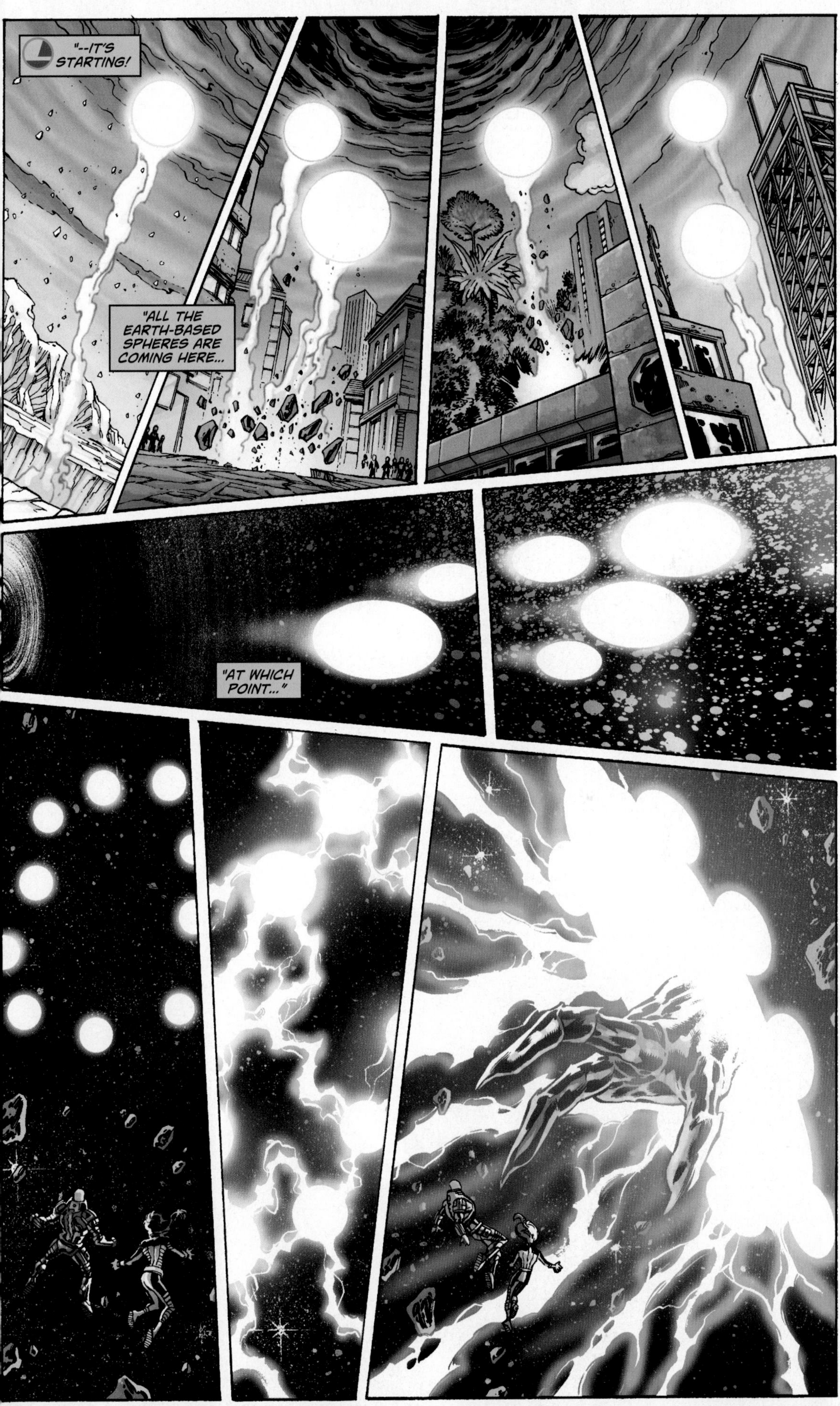
"--IT'S STARTING!
"ALL THE EARTH-BASED SPHERES ARE COMING HERE...
"AT WHICH POINT..."

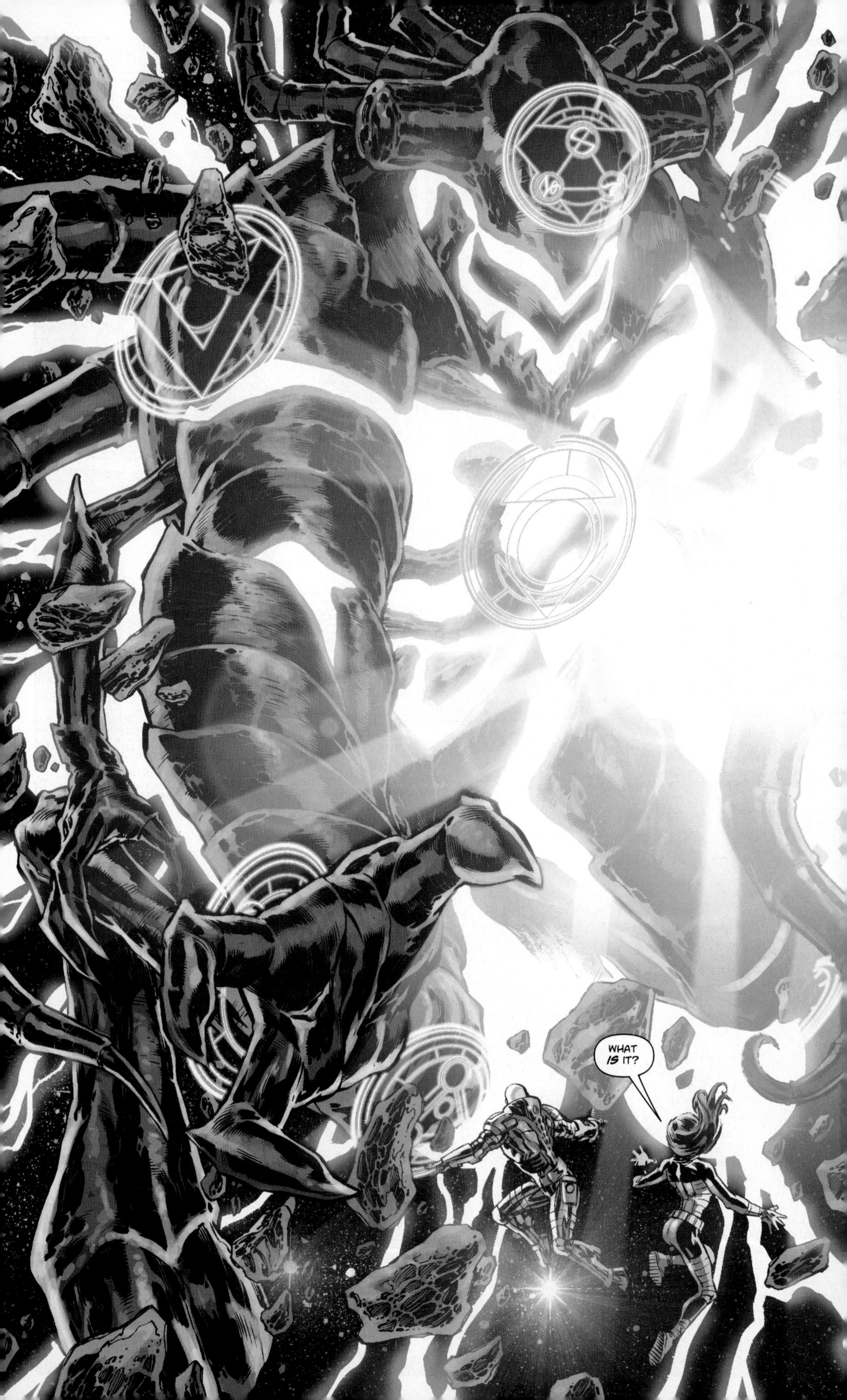
WHAT IS IT?

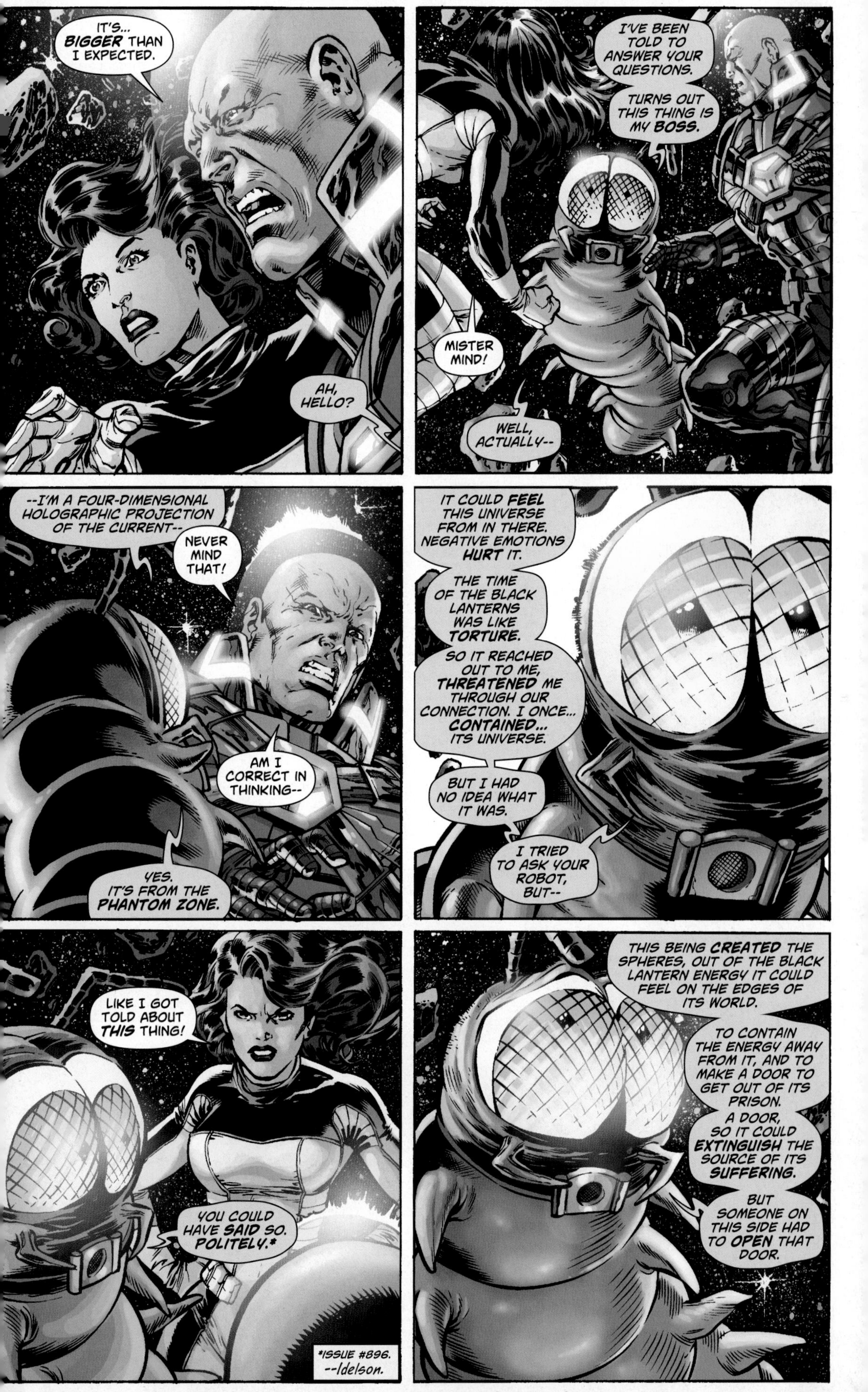
IT'S... BIGGER THAN I EXPECTED.
AH, HELLO?
I'VE BEEN TOLD TO ANSWER YOUR QUESTIONS.
TURNS OUT THIS THING IS MY BOSS.
MISTER MIND!
WELL, ACTUALLY--
--I'M A FOUR-DIMENSIONAL HOLOGRAPHIC PROJECTION OF THE CURRENT--
NEVER MIND THAT!
AM I CORRECT IN THINKING--
YES. IT'S FROM THE PHANTOM ZONE.
IT COULD FEEL THIS UNIVERSE FROM IN THERE. NEGATIVE EMOTIONS HURT IT.
THE TIME OF THE BLACK LANTERNS WAS LIKE TORTURE.
SO IT REACHED OUT TO ME, THREATENED ME THROUGH OUR CONNECTION. I ONCE... CONTAINED... ITS UNIVERSE.
BUT I HAD NO IDEA WHAT IT WAS.
I TRIED TO ASK YOUR ROBOT, BUT--
LIKE I GOT TOLD ABOUT THIS THING!
YOU COULD HAVE SAID SO. POLITELY.*
*ISSUE #896. --Idelson.
THIS BEING CREATED THE SPHERES, OUT OF THE BLACK LANTERN ENERGY IT COULD FEEL ON THE EDGES OF ITS WORLD.
TO CONTAIN THE ENERGY AWAY FROM IT, AND TO MAKE A DOOR TO GET OUT OF ITS PRISON.
A DOOR, SO IT COULD EXTINGUISH THE SOURCE OF ITS SUFFERING.
BUT SOMEONE ON THIS SIDE HAD TO OPEN THAT DOOR.

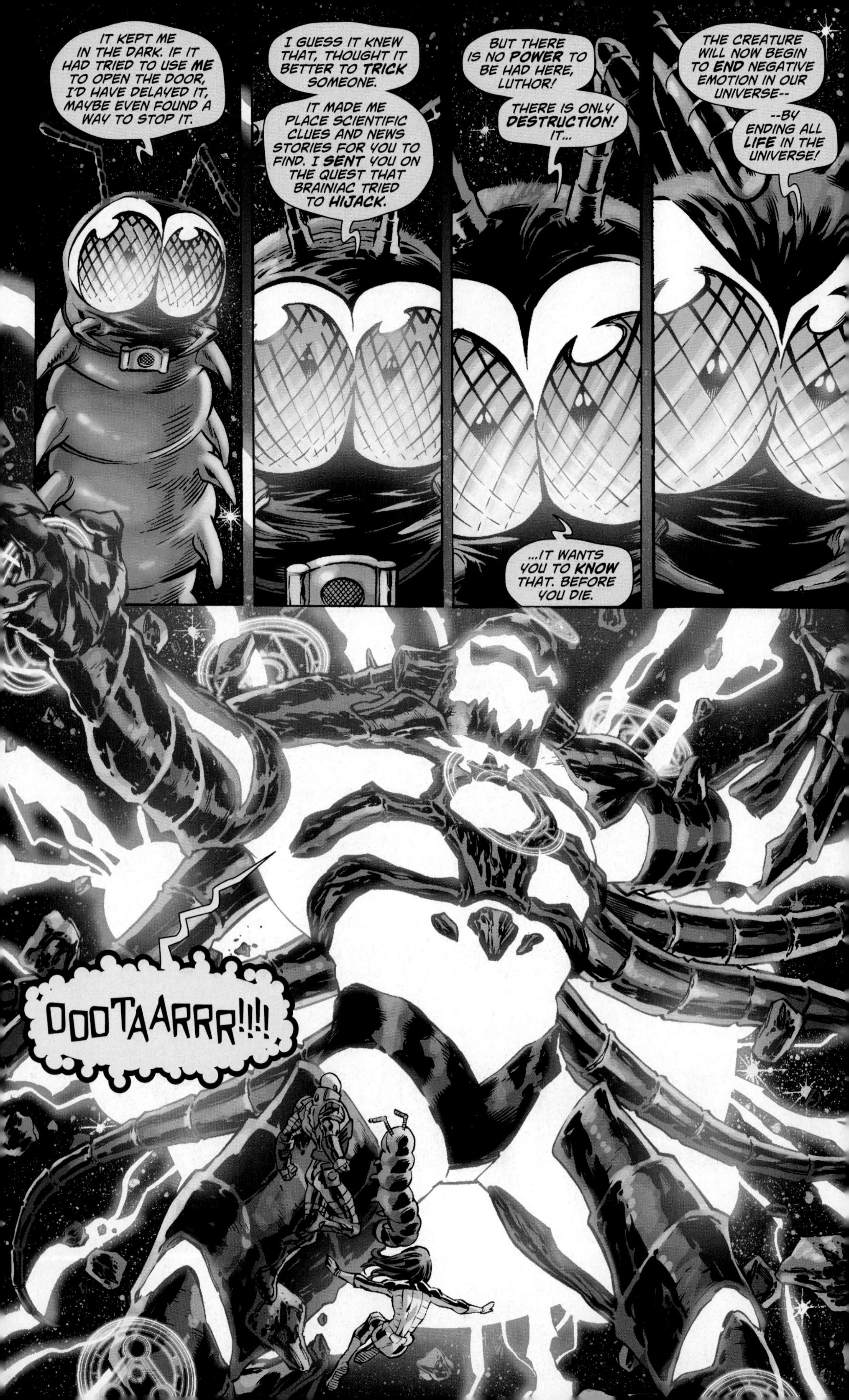
IT KEPT ME IN THE DARK. IF IT HAD TRIED TO USE ME TO OPEN THE DOOR, I'D HAVE DELAYED IT, MAYBE EVEN FOUND A WAY TO STOP IT.
I GUESS IT KNEW THAT, THOUGHT IT BETTER TO TRICK SOMEONE.
IT MADE ME PLACE SCIENTIFIC CLUES AND NEWS STORIES FOR YOU TO FIND. I SENT YOU ON THE QUEST THAT BRAINIAC TRIED TO HIJACK.
BUT THERE IS NO POWER TO BE HAD HERE, LUTHOR!
THERE IS ONLY DESTRUCTION! IT...
...IT WANTS YOU TO KNOW THAT. BEFORE YOU DIE.
THE CREATURE WILL NOW BEGIN TO END NEGATIVE EMOTION IN OUR UNIVERSE--
--BY ENDING ALL LIFE IN THE UNIVERSE!
DOOTAARRR!!!!

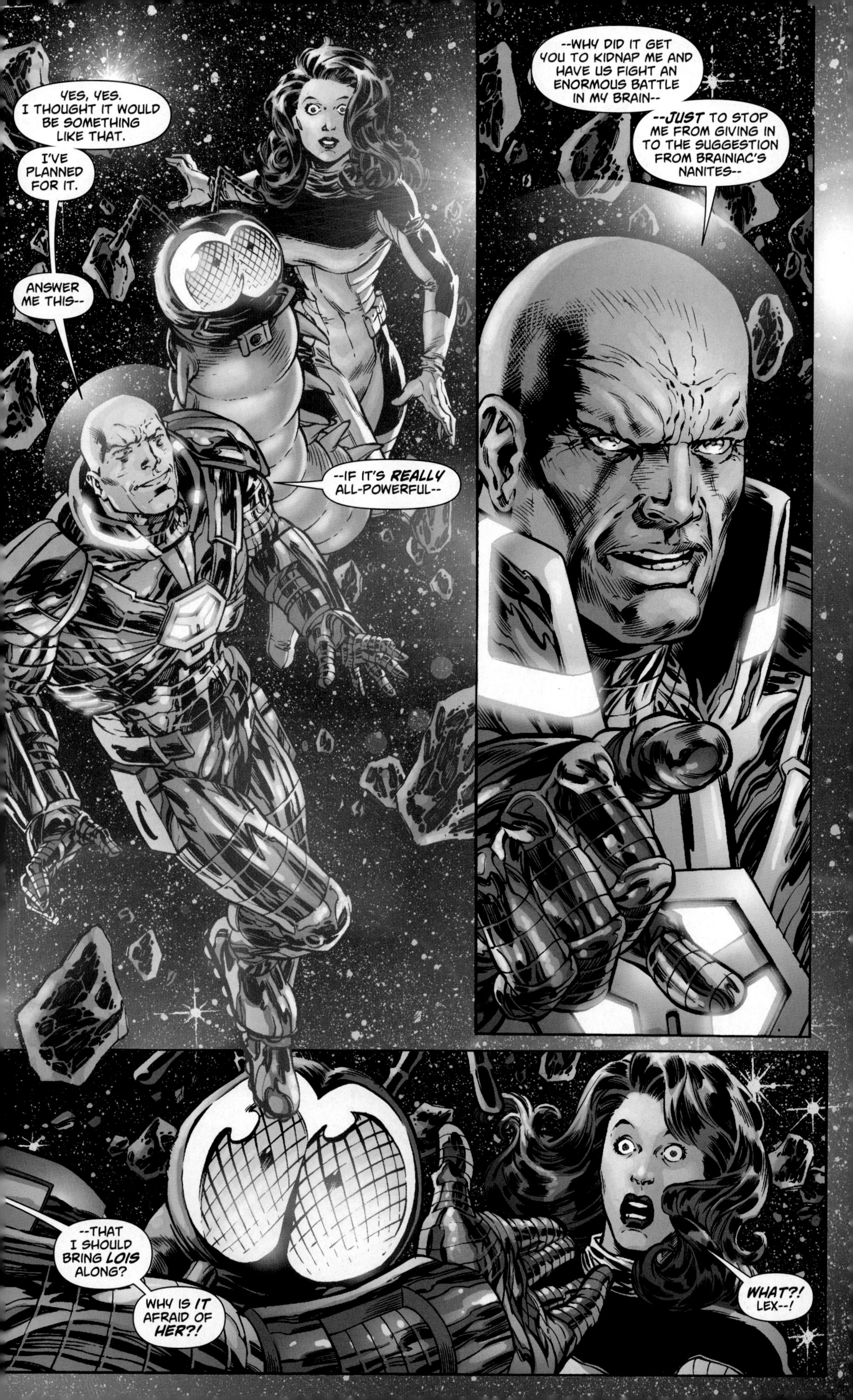
YES, YES. I THOUGHT IT WOULD BE SOMETHING LIKE THAT.
I'VE PLANNED FOR IT.
ANSWER ME THIS--
--IF IT'S REALLY ALL-POWERFUL--
--WHY DID IT GET YOU TO KIDNAP ME AND HAVE US FIGHT AN ENORMOUS BATTLE IN MY BRAIN--
--JUST TO STOP ME FROM GIVING IN TO THE SUGGESTION FROM BRAINIAC'S NANITES--
--THAT I SHOULD BRING LOIS ALONG?
WHY IS IT AFRAID OF HER?!
WHAT?! LEX--!

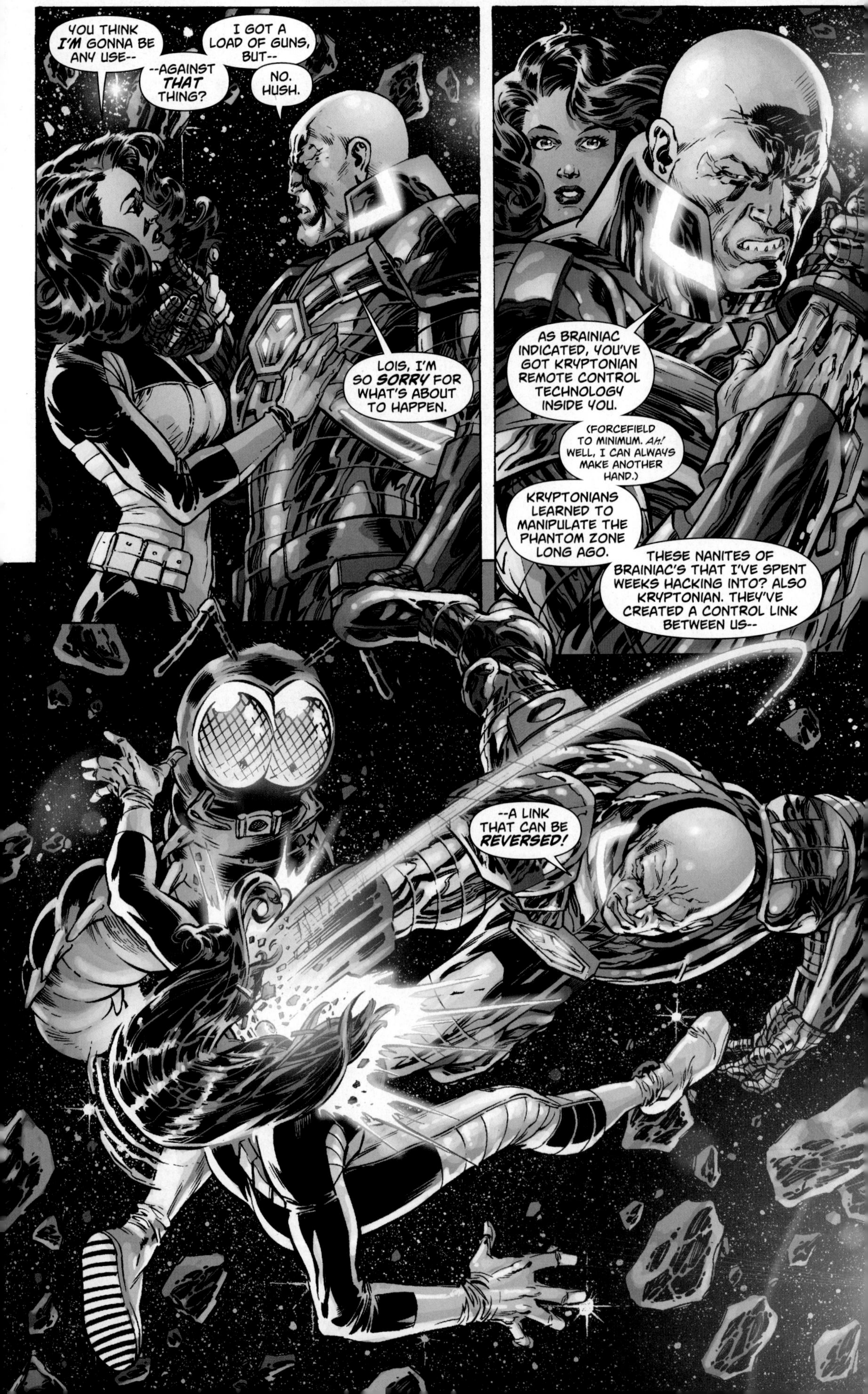
YOU THINK *I'M* GONNA BE ANY USE--
--AGAINST *THAT* THING?
I GOT A LOAD OF GUNS, BUT--
NO. HUSH.
LOIS, I'M SO *SORRY* FOR WHAT'S ABOUT TO HAPPEN.
AS BRAINIAC INDICATED, YOU'VE GOT KRYPTONIAN REMOTE CONTROL TECHNOLOGY INSIDE YOU.
(FORCEFIELD TO MINIMUM. *AH!* WELL, I CAN ALWAYS MAKE ANOTHER HAND.)
KRYPTONIANS LEARNED TO MANIPULATE THE PHANTOM ZONE LONG AGO.
THESE NANITES OF BRAINIAC'S THAT I'VE SPENT WEEKS HACKING INTO? ALSO KRYPTONIAN. THEY'VE CREATED A CONTROL LINK BETWEEN US--
--A LINK THAT CAN BE *REVERSED!*

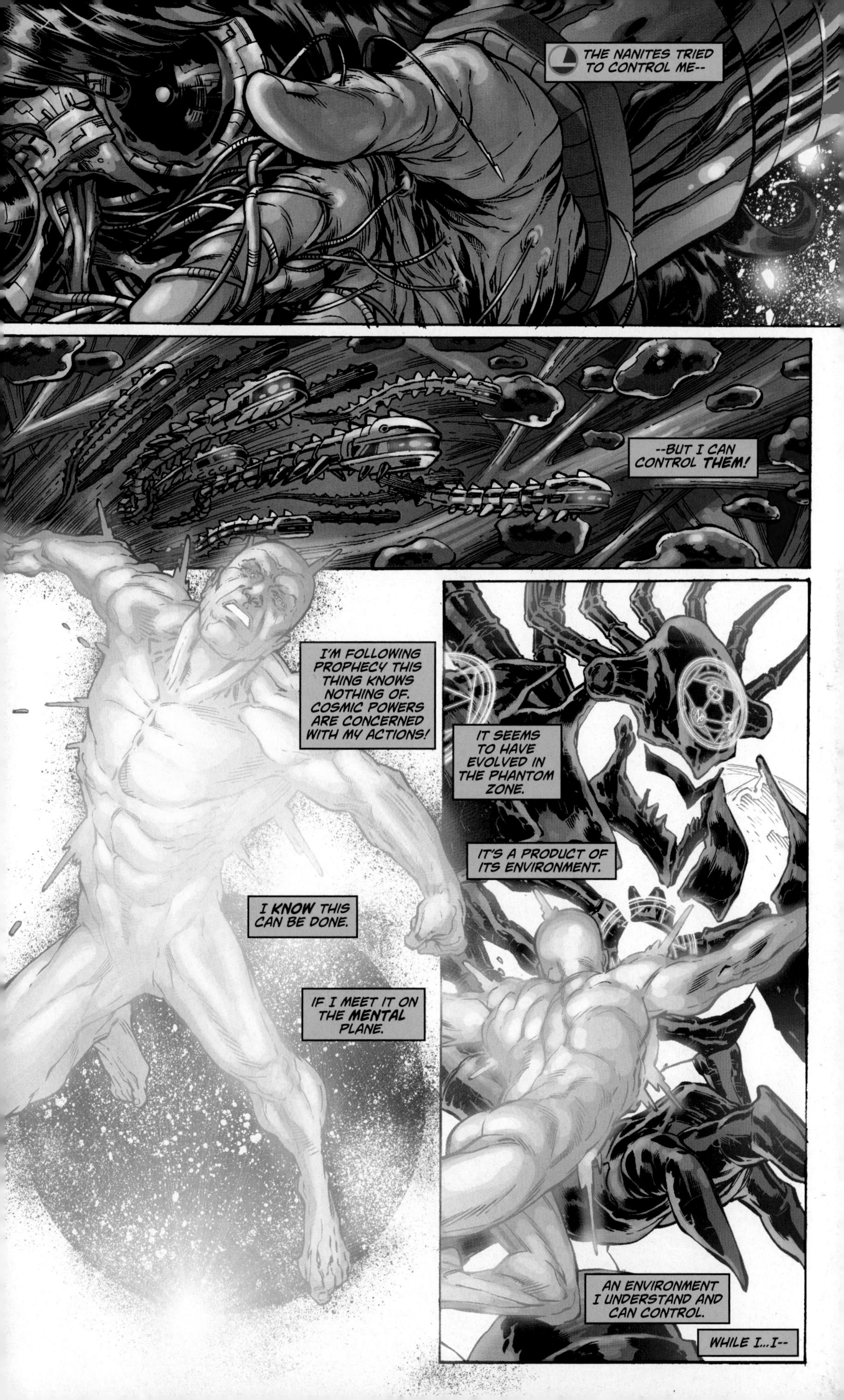
THE NANITES TRIED TO CONTROL ME--
--BUT I CAN CONTROL THEM!
I'M FOLLOWING PROPHECY THIS THING KNOWS NOTHING OF. COSMIC POWERS ARE CONCERNED WITH MY ACTIONS!
I KNOW THIS CAN BE DONE.
IF I MEET IT ON THE MENTAL PLANE.
IT SEEMS TO HAVE EVOLVED IN THE PHANTOM ZONE.
IT'S A PRODUCT OF ITS ENVIRONMENT.
AN ENVIRONMENT I UNDERSTAND AND CAN CONTROL.
WHILE I...I--

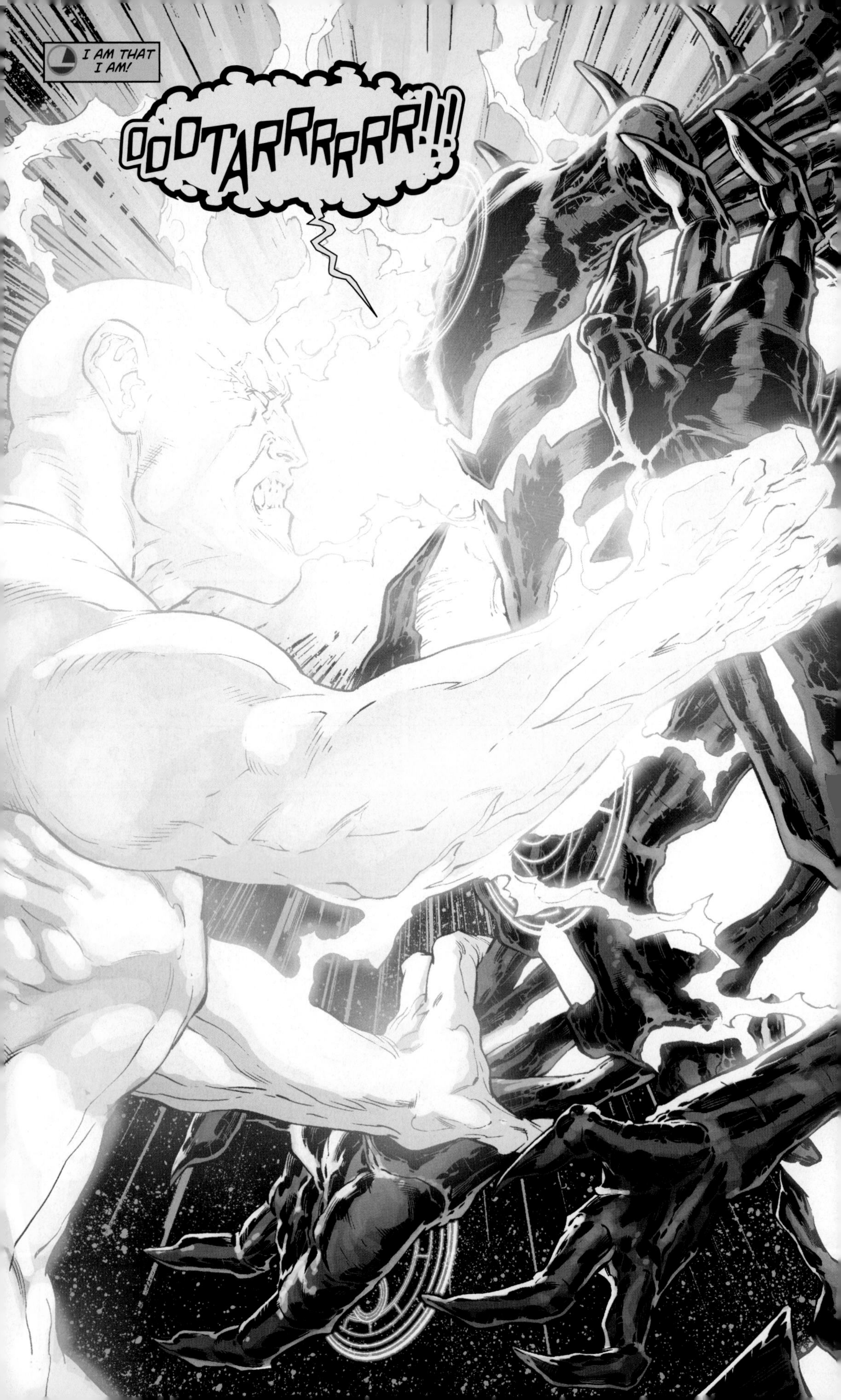
I AM THAT I AM!
OOOTARRRRRRR!!!

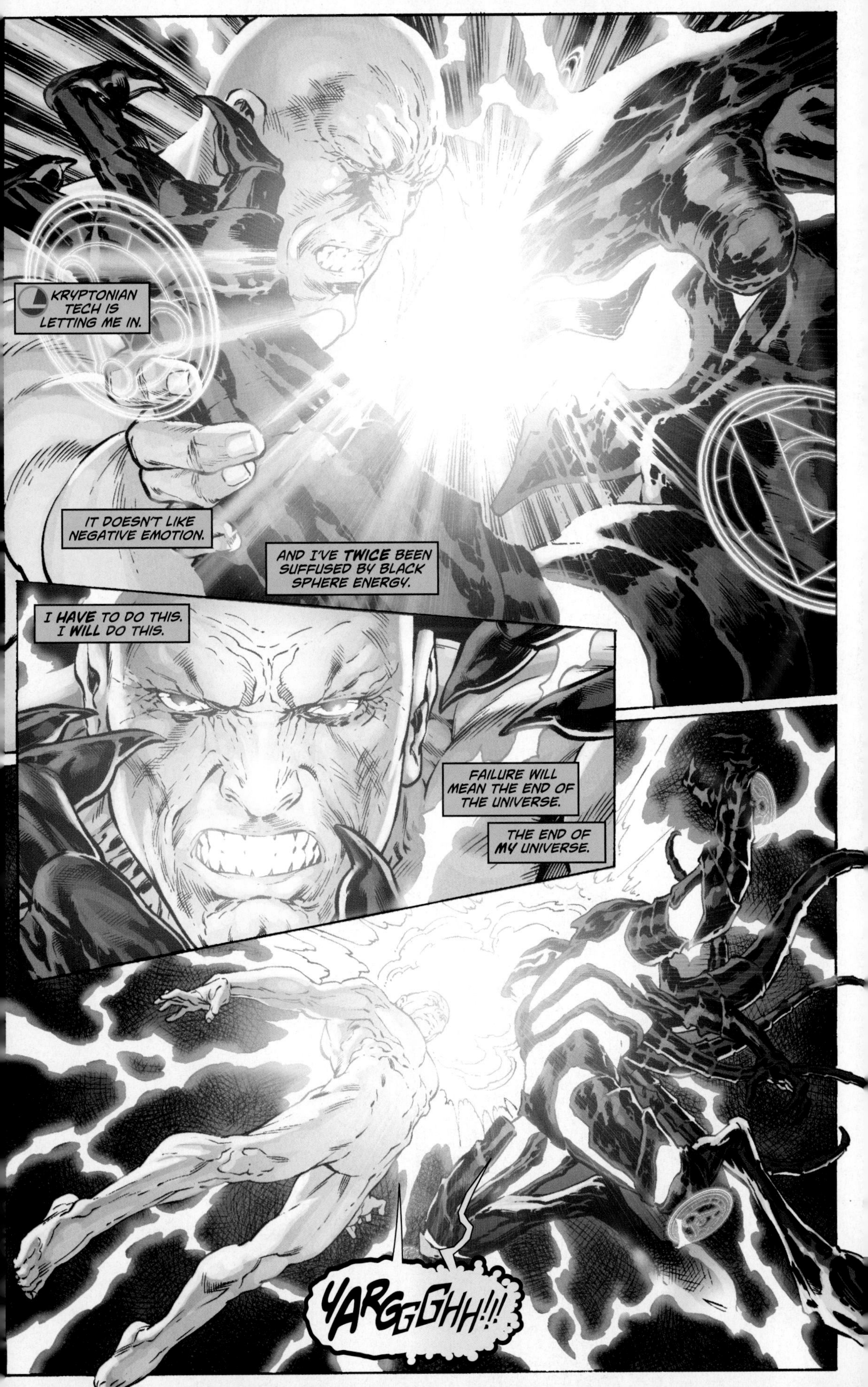
KRYPTONIAN TECH IS LETTING ME IN.
IT DOESN'T LIKE NEGATIVE EMOTION.
AND I'VE TWICE BEEN SUFFUSED BY BLACK SPHERE ENERGY.
I HAVE TO DO THIS. I WILL DO THIS.
FAILURE WILL MEAN THE END OF THE UNIVERSE.
THE END OF MY UNIVERSE.
YARGGGHH!!!

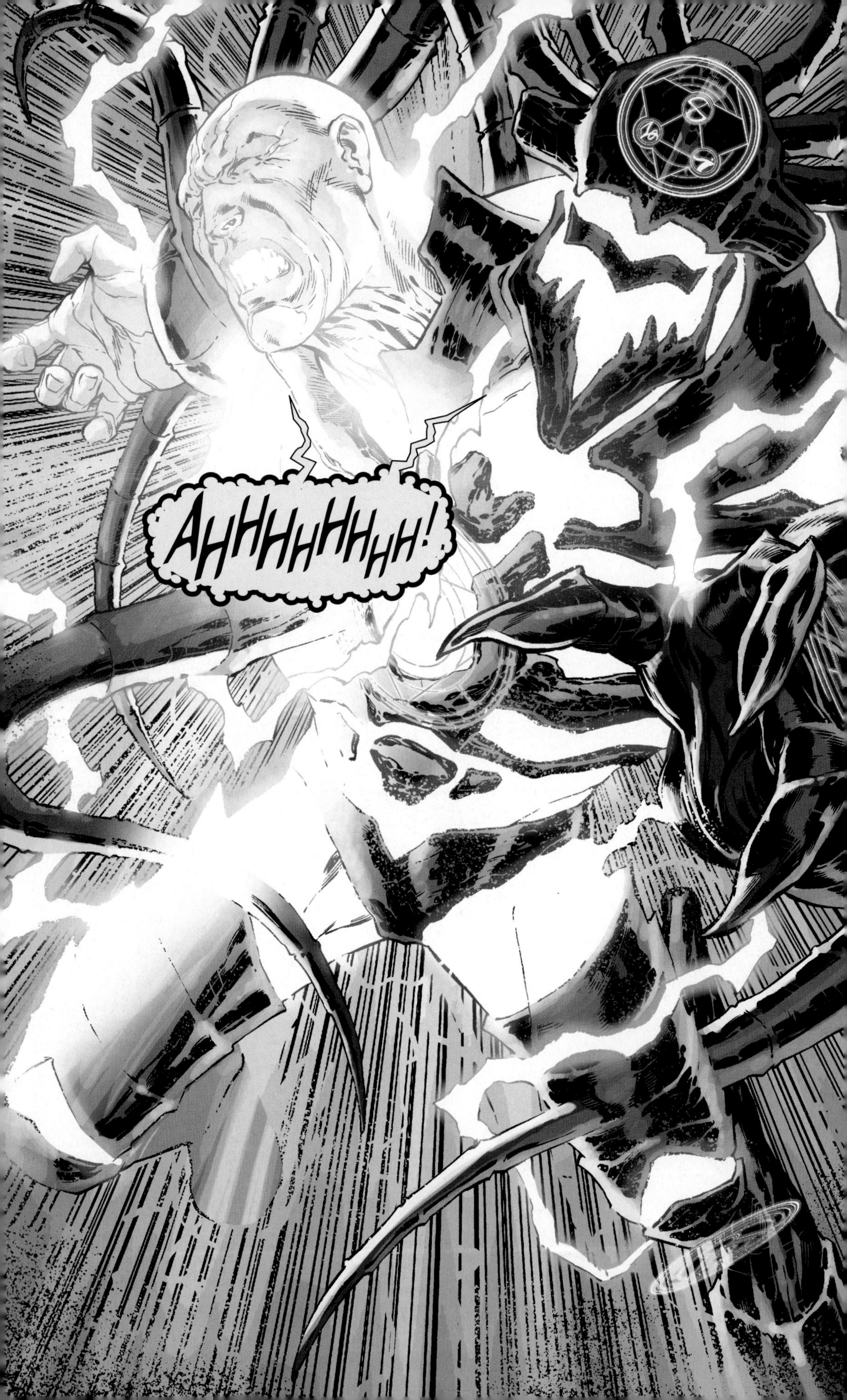
AHHHHHHHH!

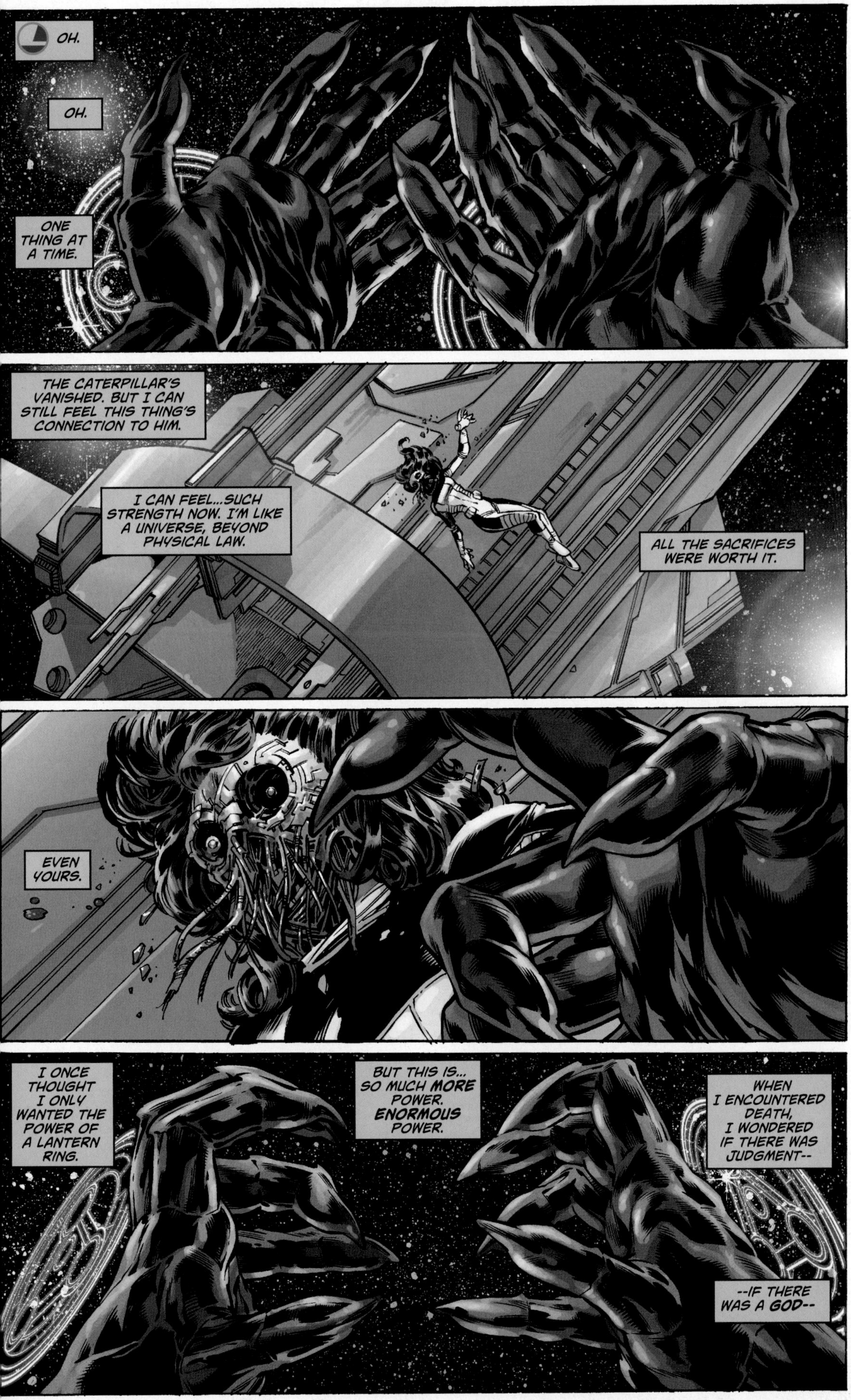
OH.
OH.
ONE THING AT A TIME.
THE CATERPILLAR'S VANISHED. BUT I CAN STILL FEEL THIS THING'S CONNECTION TO HIM.
I CAN FEEL...SUCH STRENGTH NOW. I'M LIKE A UNIVERSE, BEYOND PHYSICAL LAW.
ALL THE SACRIFICES WERE WORTH IT.
EVEN YOURS.
I ONCE THOUGHT I ONLY WANTED THE POWER OF A LANTERN RING.
BUT THIS IS... SO MUCH MORE POWER. ENORMOUS POWER.
WHEN I ENCOUNTERED DEATH, I WONDERED IF THERE WAS JUDGMENT--
--IF THERE WAS A GOD--

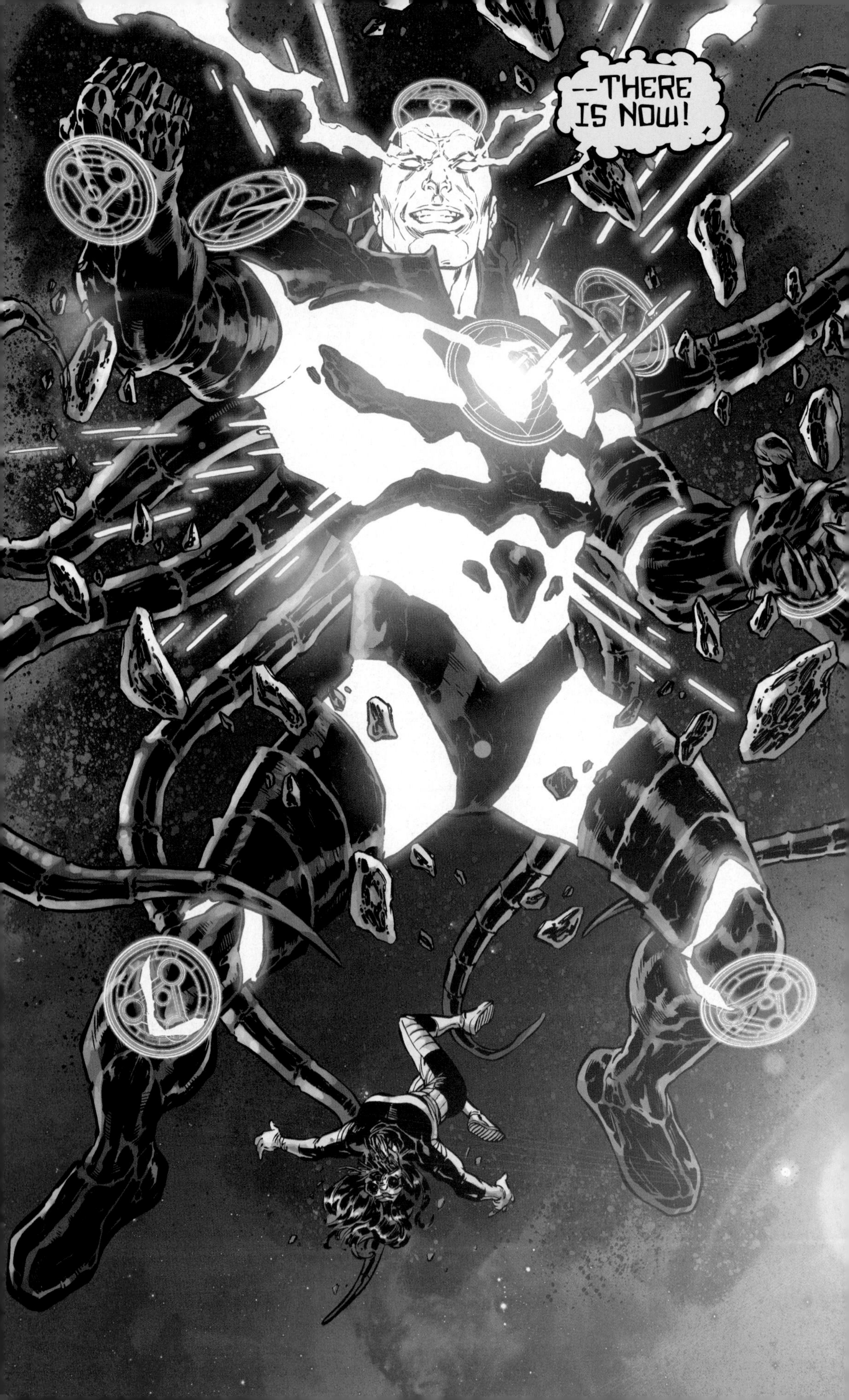
--THERE IS NOW!

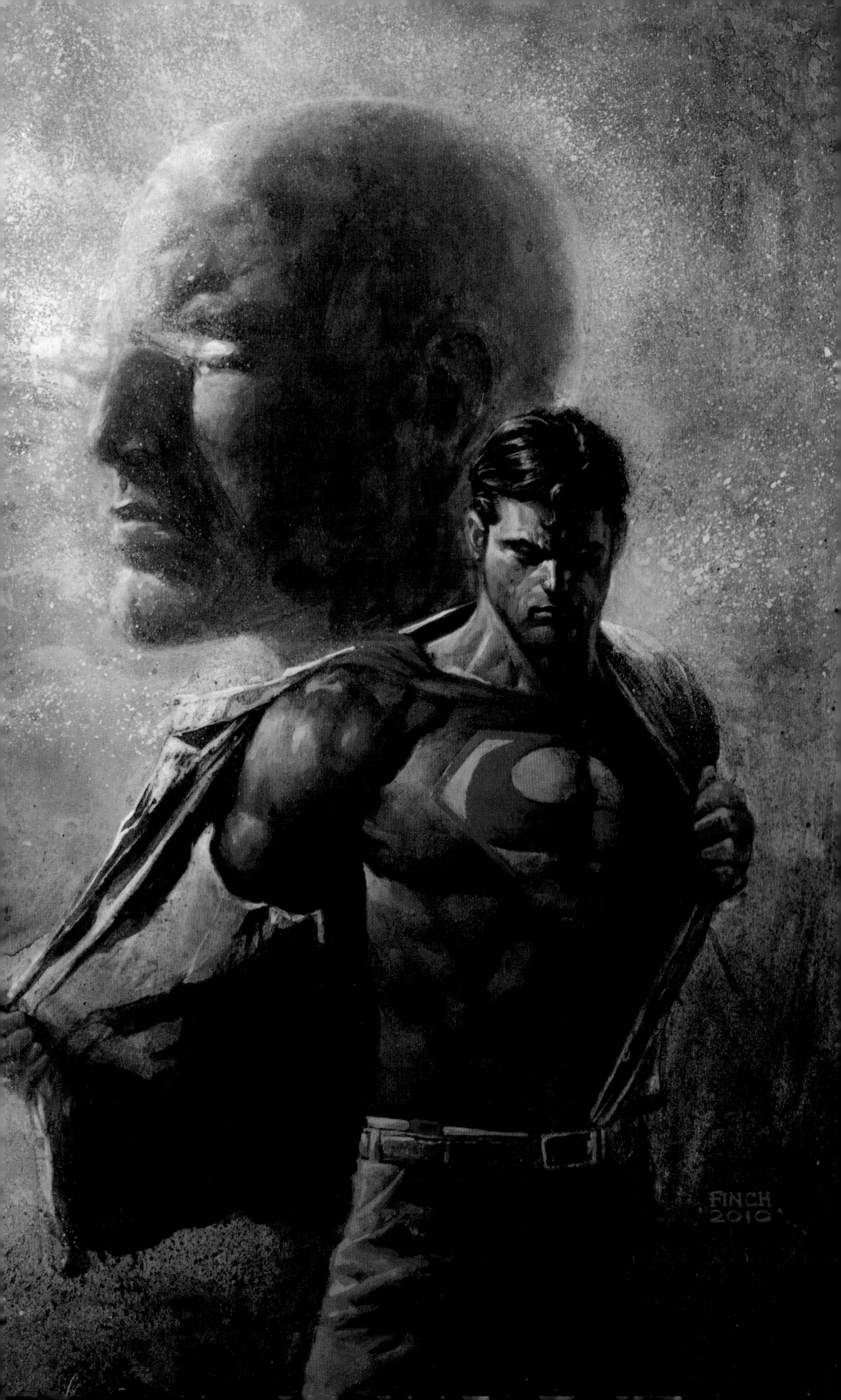
FINCH
2010

THE BLACK RING
finale

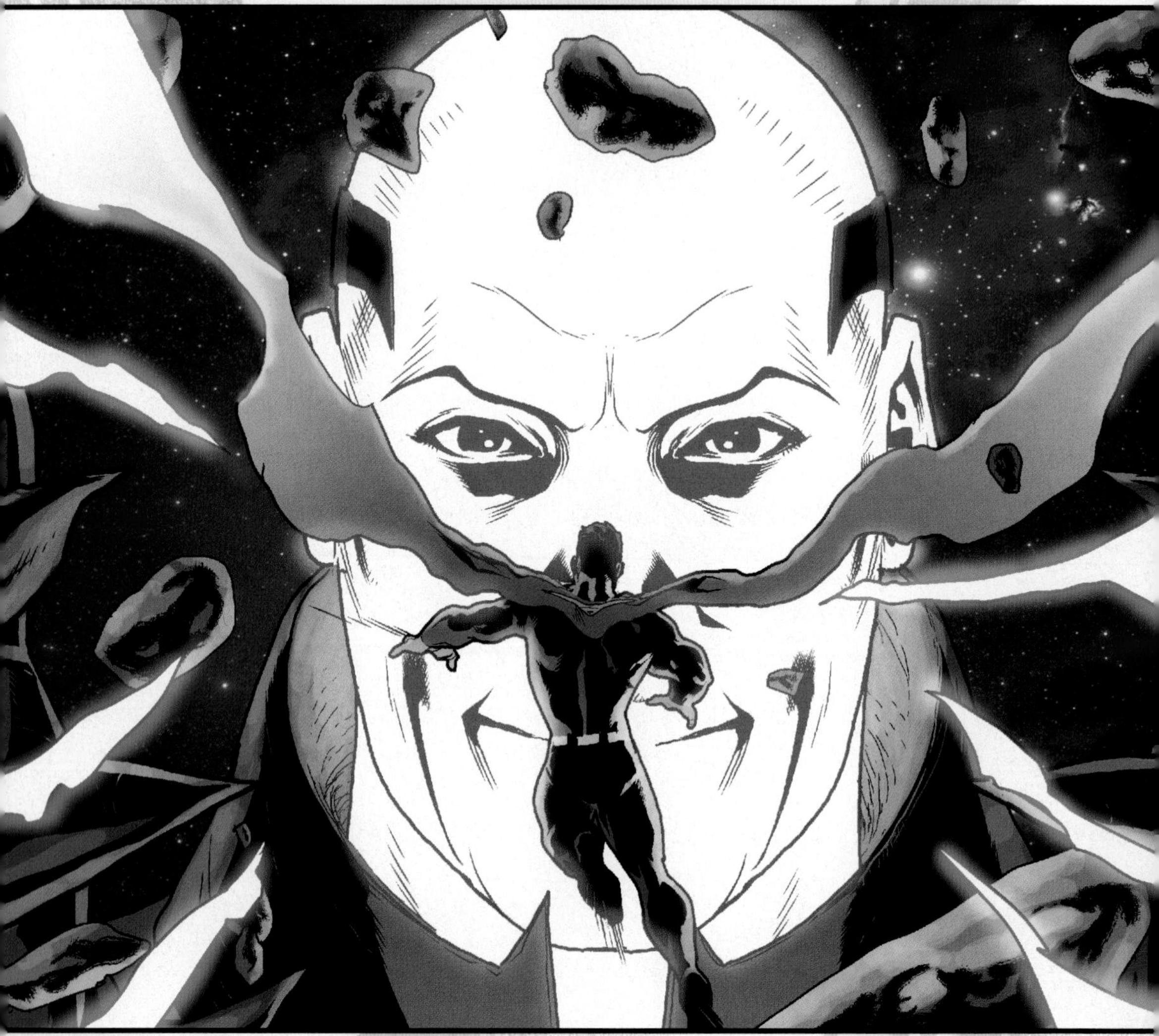

PAUL CORNELL writer
PETE WOODS artist

additional art by
DAN **JURGENS** & NORM **RAPMUND** RAGS **MORALES** ARDIAN **SYAF** JAMAL **IGLE** & JON **SIBAL** GARY **FRANK**

cover by
DAVID **FINCH**

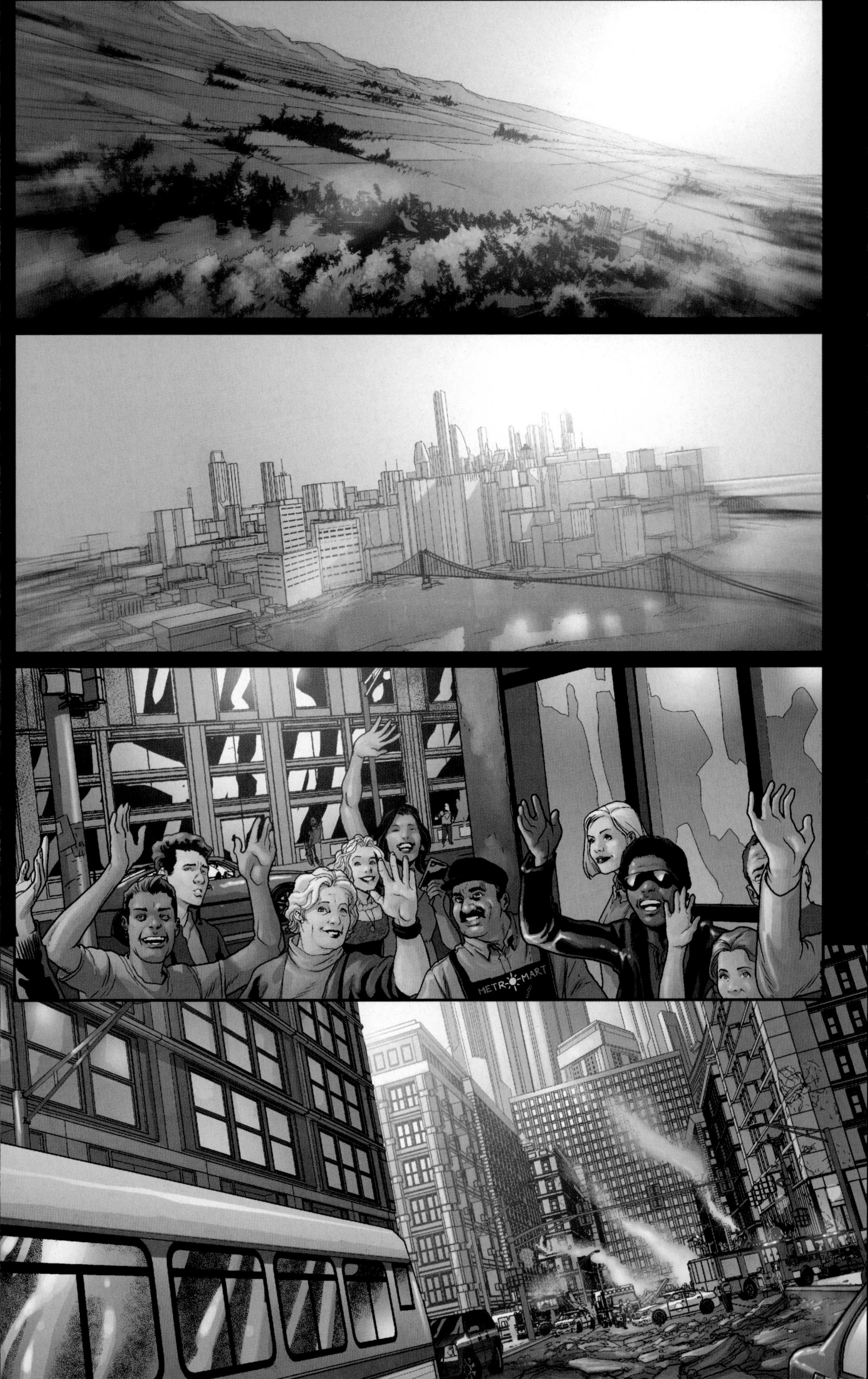

METRO MART

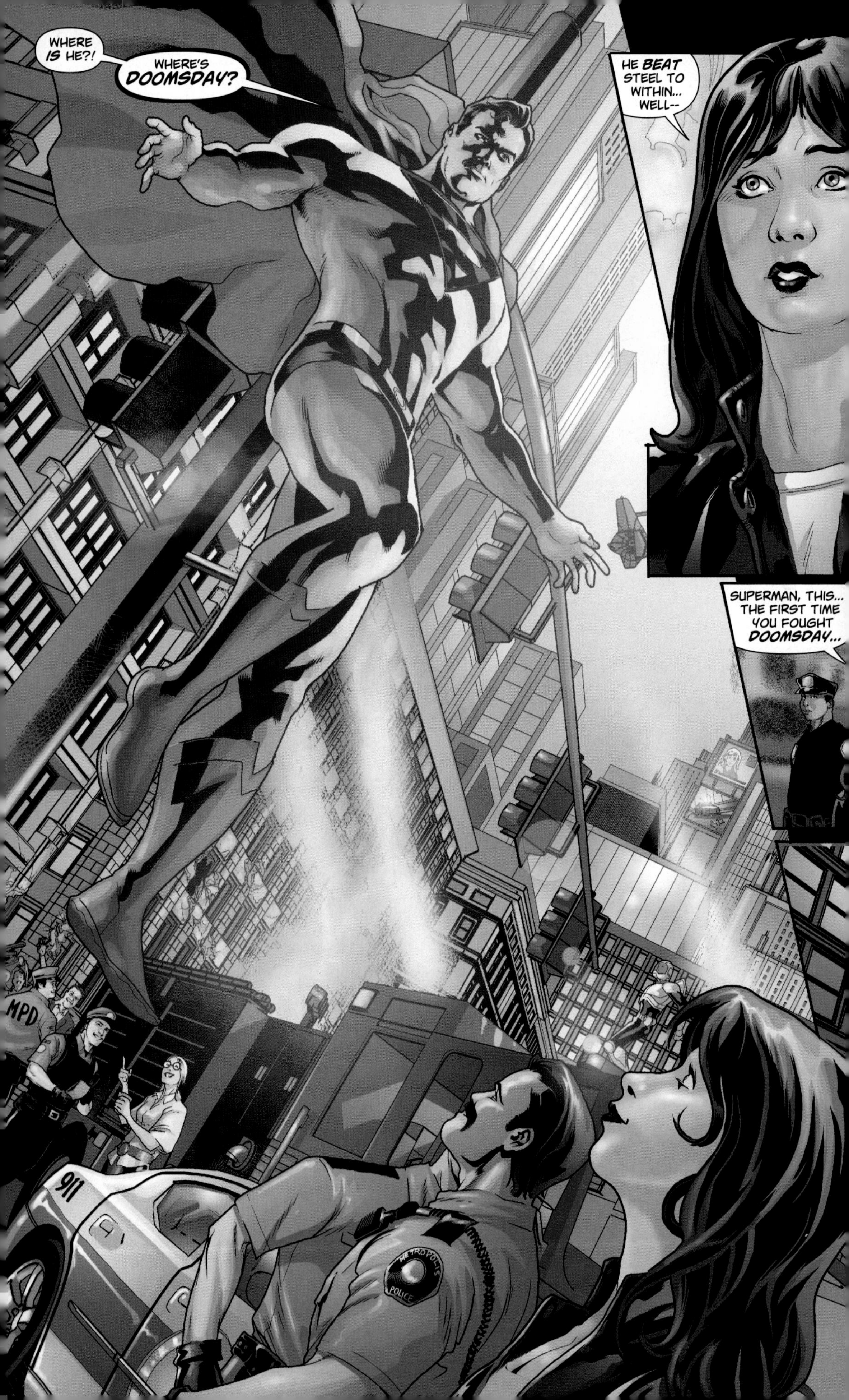
WHERE IS HE?!
WHERE'S DOOMSDAY?
HE BEAT STEEL TO WITHIN... WELL--
SUPERMAN, THIS... THE FIRST TIME YOU FOUGHT DOOMSDAY...
MPD
911
METROPOLIS POLICE

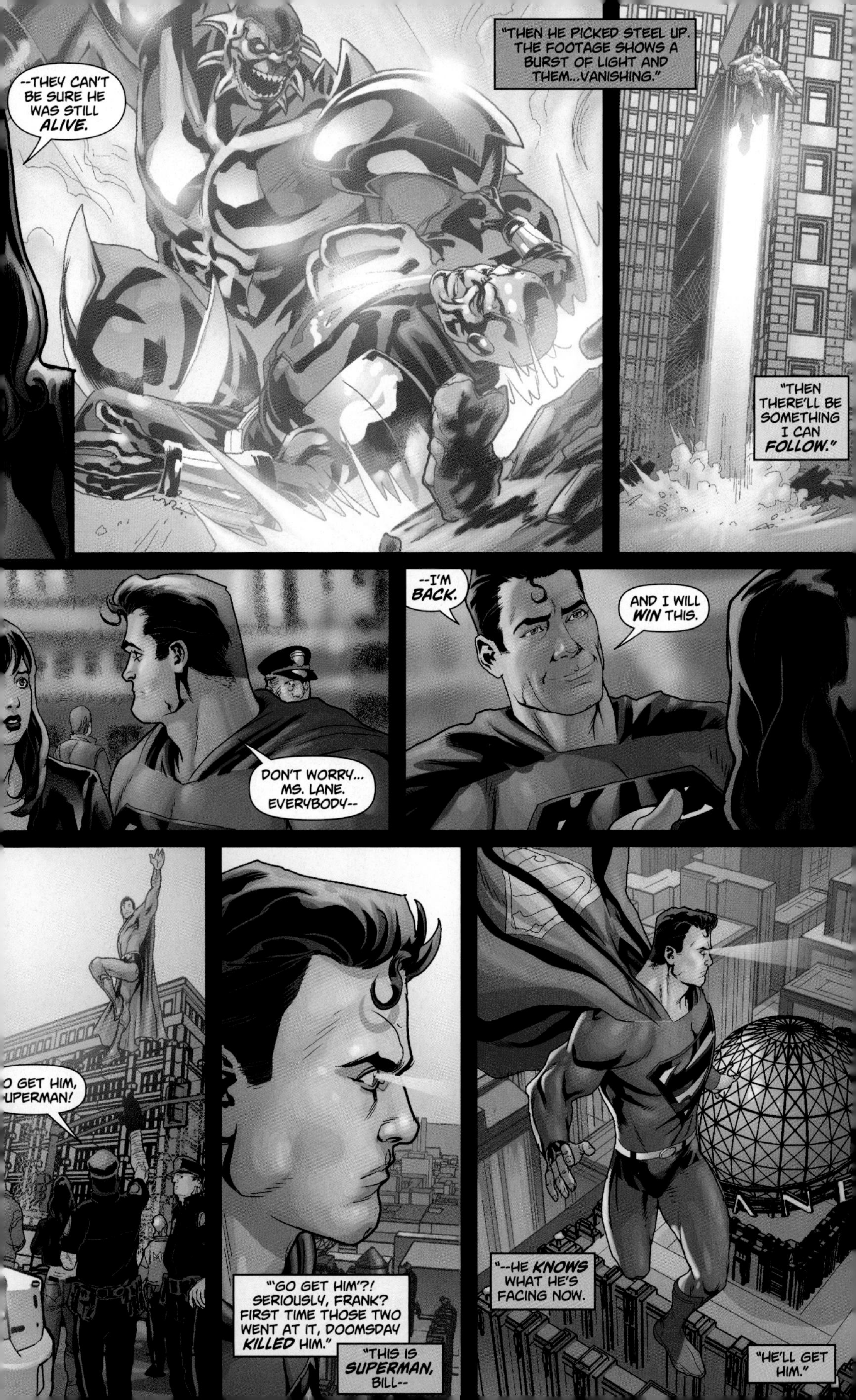
--THEY CAN'T BE SURE HE WAS STILL ALIVE.
"THEN HE PICKED STEEL UP. THE FOOTAGE SHOWS A BURST OF LIGHT AND THEM...VANISHING."
"THEN THERE'LL BE SOMETHING I CAN FOLLOW."
DON'T WORRY... MS. LANE. EVERYBODY--
--I'M BACK.
AND I WILL WIN THIS.
O GET HIM, UPERMAN!
"'GO GET HIM'?! SERIOUSLY, FRANK? FIRST TIME THOSE TWO WENT AT IT, DOOMSDAY KILLED HIM."
"THIS IS SUPERMAN, BILL--
"--HE KNOWS WHAT HE'S FACING NOW.
"HE'LL GET HIM."

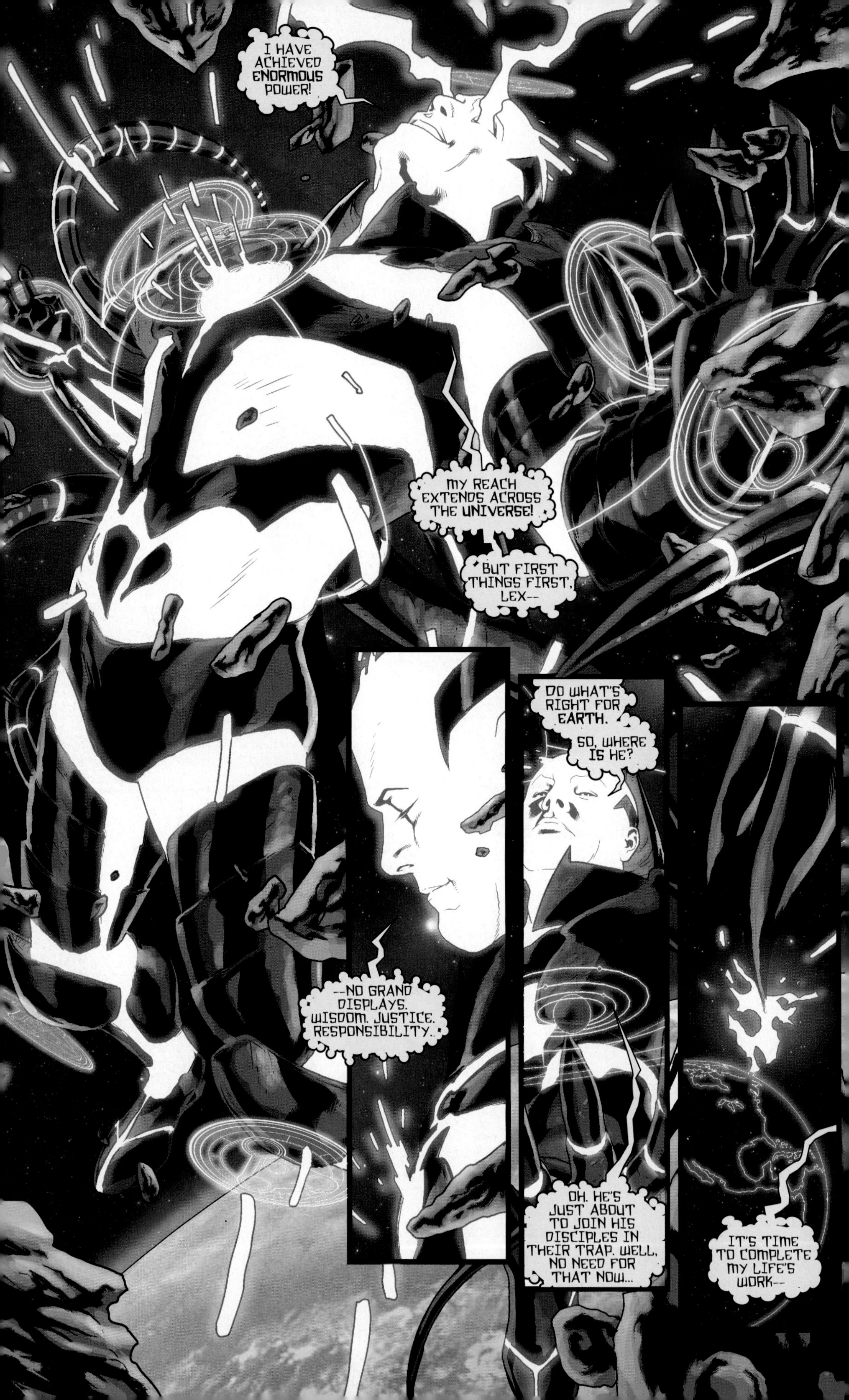
I HAVE ACHIEVED ENORMOUS POWER!
MY REACH EXTENDS ACROSS THE UNIVERSE!
BUT FIRST THINGS FIRST, LEX--
--NO GRAND DISPLAYS. WISDOM. JUSTICE. RESPONSIBILITY...
DO WHAT'S RIGHT FOR EARTH.
SO, WHERE IS HE?
OH. HE'S JUST ABOUT TO JOIN HIS DISCIPLES IN THEIR TRAP. WELL, NO NEED FOR THAT NOW...
IT'S TIME TO COMPLETE MY LIFE'S WORK--

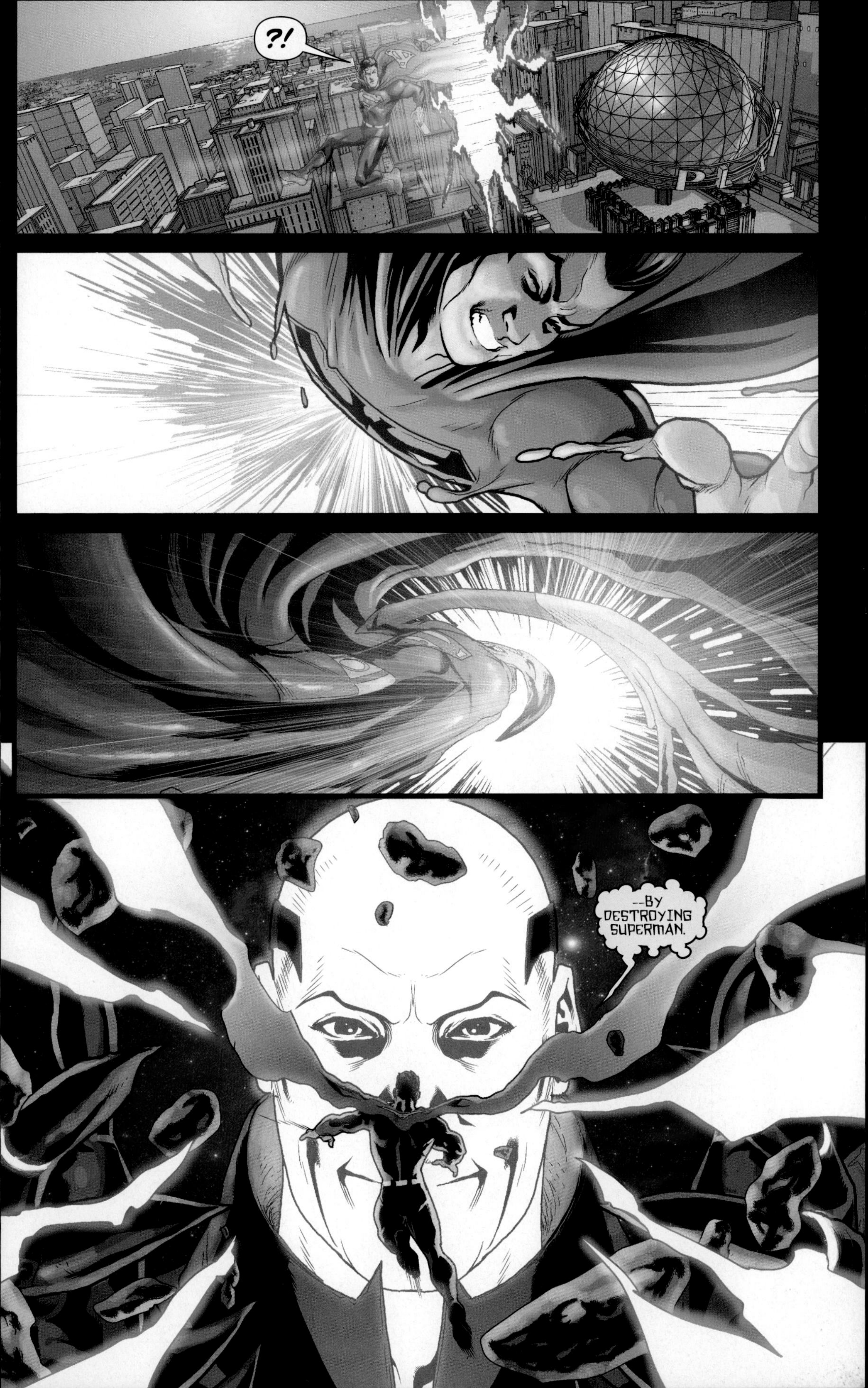
?!
--BY DESTROYING SUPERMAN.

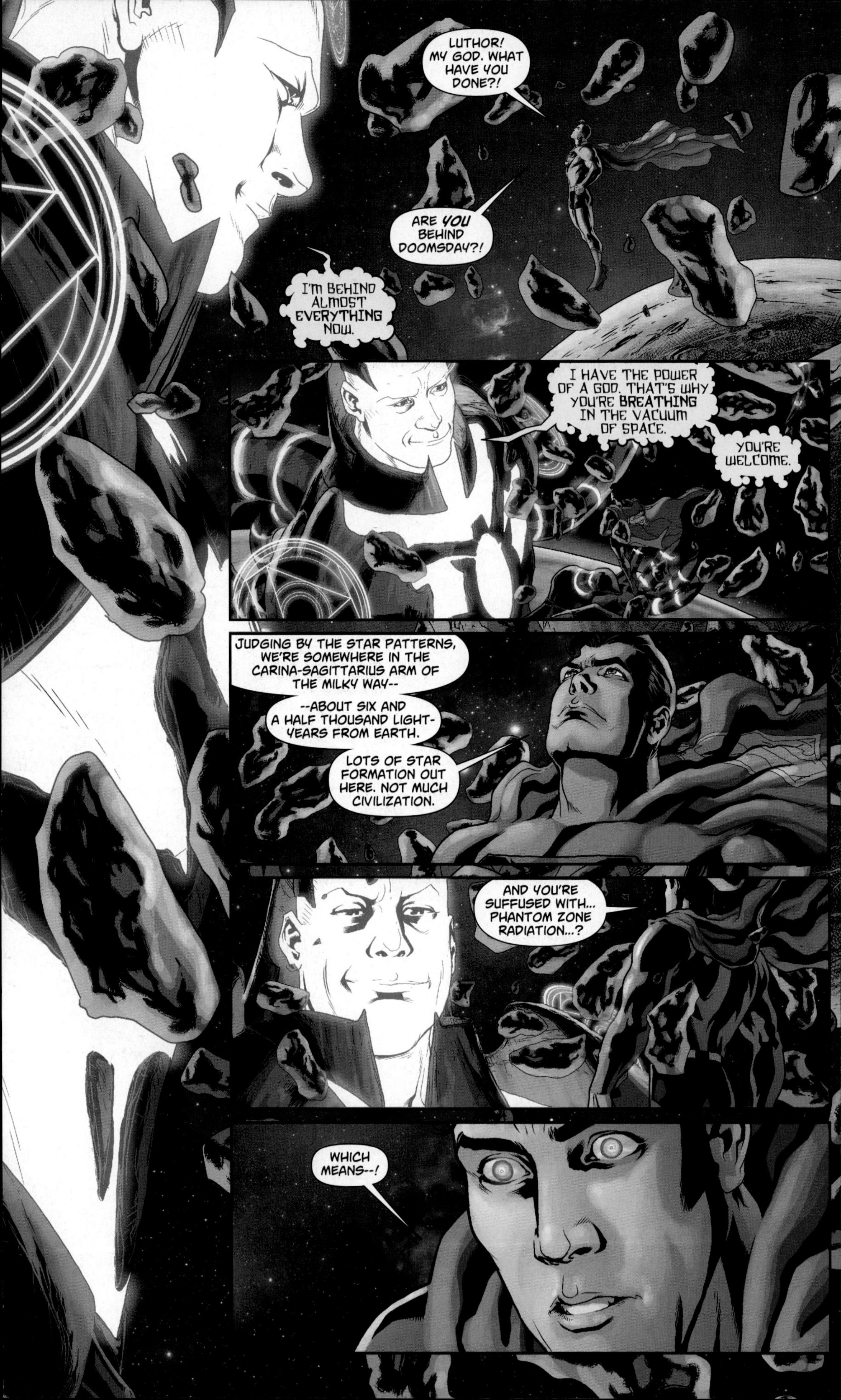
LUTHOR! MY GOD. WHAT HAVE YOU DONE?!
ARE YOU BEHIND DOOMSDAY?!
I'M BEHIND ALMOST EVERYTHING NOW.
I HAVE THE POWER OF A GOD. THAT'S WHY YOU'RE BREATHING IN THE VACUUM OF SPACE.
YOU'RE WELCOME.
JUDGING BY THE STAR PATTERNS, WE'RE SOMEWHERE IN THE CARINA-SAGITTARIUS ARM OF THE MILKY WAY--
--ABOUT SIX AND A HALF THOUSAND LIGHT-YEARS FROM EARTH.
LOTS OF STAR FORMATION OUT HERE. NOT MUCH CIVILIZATION.
AND YOU'RE SUFFUSED WITH... PHANTOM ZONE RADIATION...?
WHICH MEANS--!

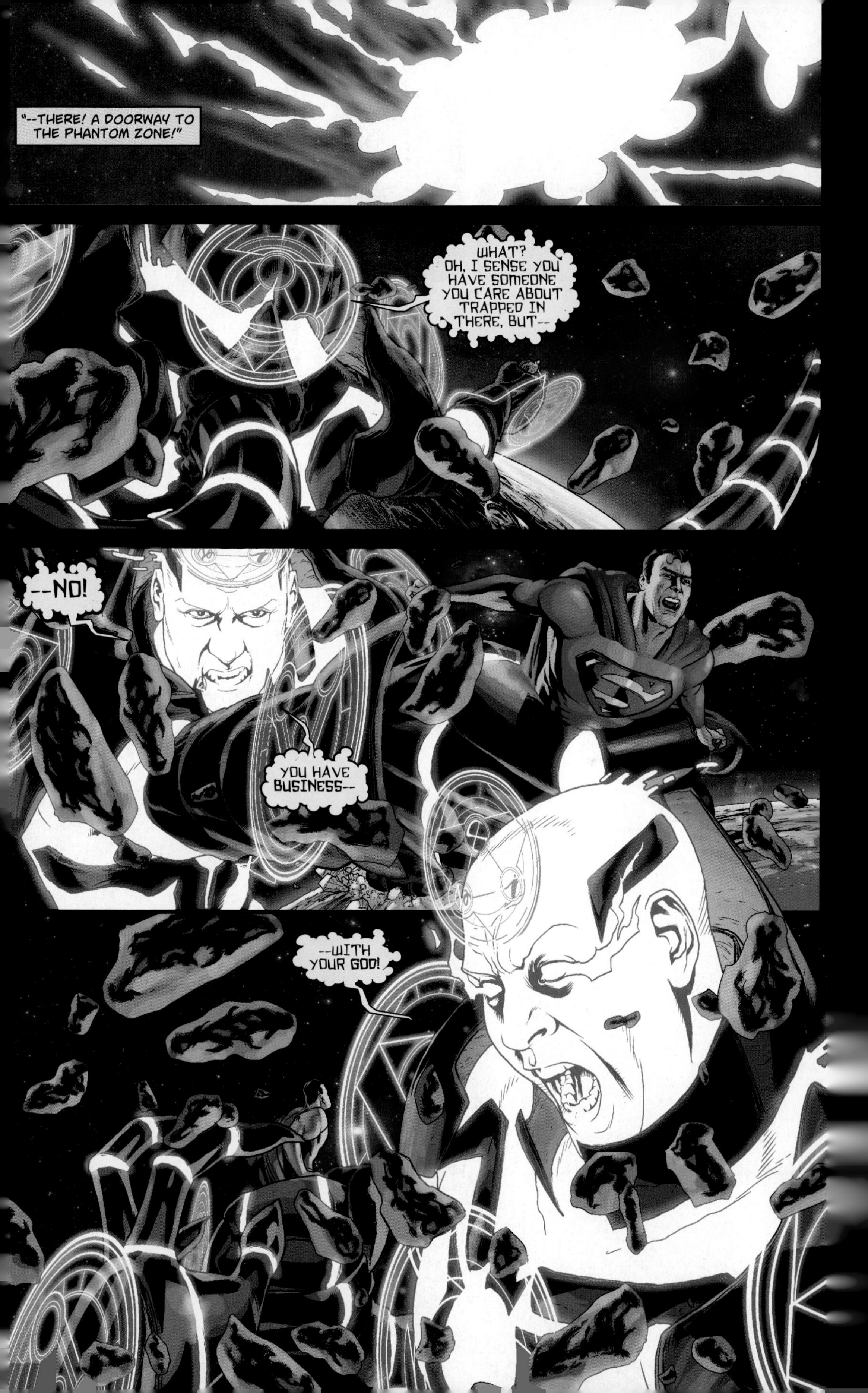
"--THERE! A DOORWAY TO THE PHANTOM ZONE!"
WHAT? OH, I SENSE YOU HAVE SOMEONE YOU CARE ABOUT TRAPPED IN THERE, BUT--
--NO!
YOU HAVE BUSINESS--
--WITH YOUR GOD!

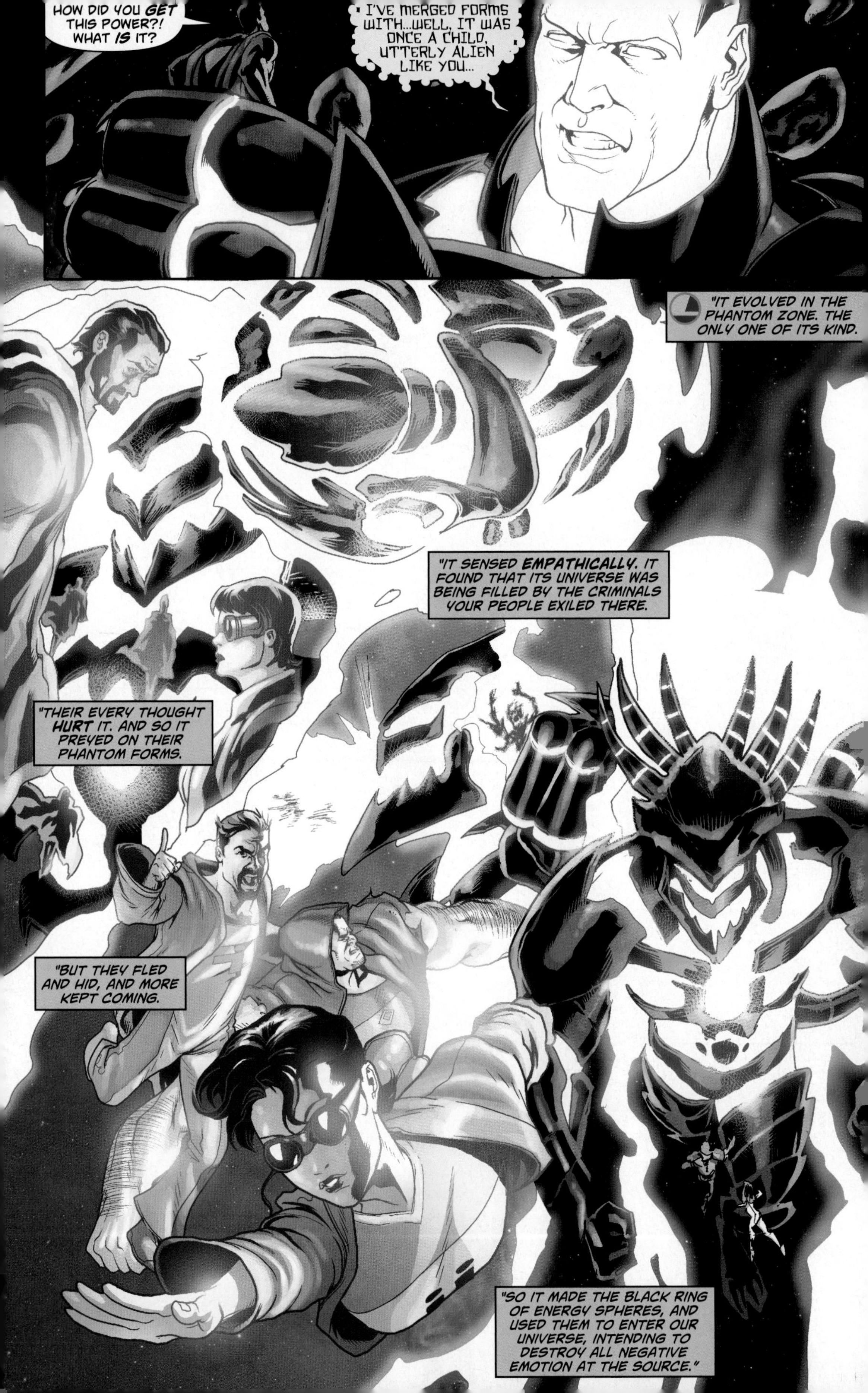
HOW DID YOU **GET** THIS POWER?! WHAT **IS** IT?
I'VE MERGED FORMS WITH...WELL, IT WAS ONCE A CHILD, UTTERLY ALIEN LIKE YOU...
"IT EVOLVED IN THE PHANTOM ZONE. THE ONLY ONE OF ITS KIND.
"IT SENSED **EMPATHICALLY.** IT FOUND THAT ITS UNIVERSE WAS BEING FILLED BY THE CRIMINALS YOUR PEOPLE EXILED THERE.
"THEIR EVERY THOUGHT **HURT** IT. AND SO IT PREYED ON THEIR PHANTOM FORMS.
"BUT THEY FLED AND HID, AND MORE KEPT COMING.
"SO IT MADE THE BLACK RING OF ENERGY SPHERES, AND USED THEM TO ENTER OUR UNIVERSE, INTENDING TO DESTROY ALL NEGATIVE EMOTION AT THE SOURCE."

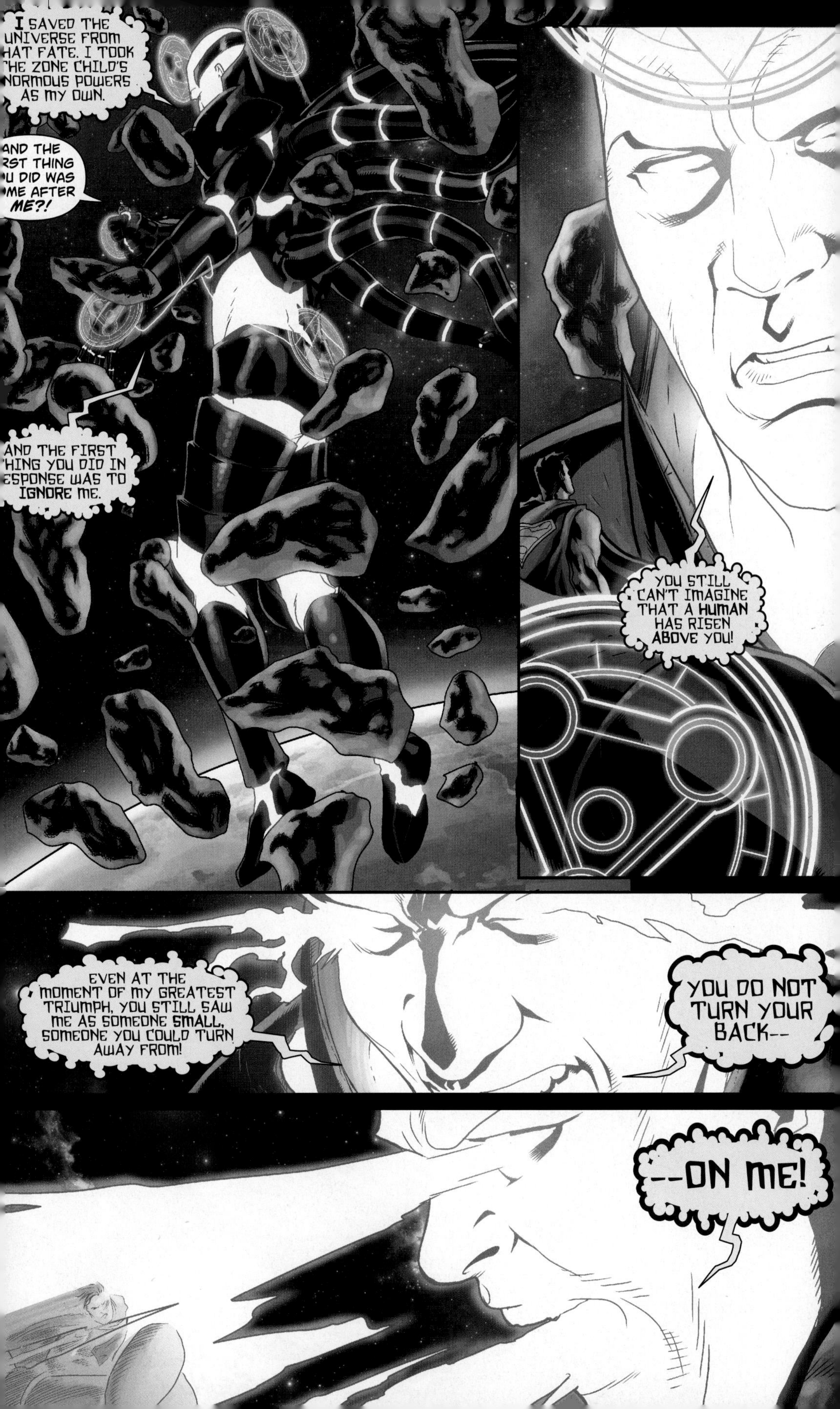
I SAVED THE UNIVERSE FROM HAT FATE. I TOOK THE ZONE CHILD'S NORMOUS POWERS AS MY OWN.
AND THE RST THING U DID WAS ME AFTER ME?!
AND THE FIRST THING YOU DID IN ESPONSE WAS TO IGNORE ME.
YOU STILL CAN'T IMAGINE THAT A HUMAN HAS RISEN ABOVE YOU!
EVEN AT THE MOMENT OF MY GREATEST TRIUMPH, YOU STILL SAW ME AS SOMEONE SMALL, SOMEONE YOU COULD TURN AWAY FROM!
YOU DO NOT TURN YOUR BACK--
--ON ME!

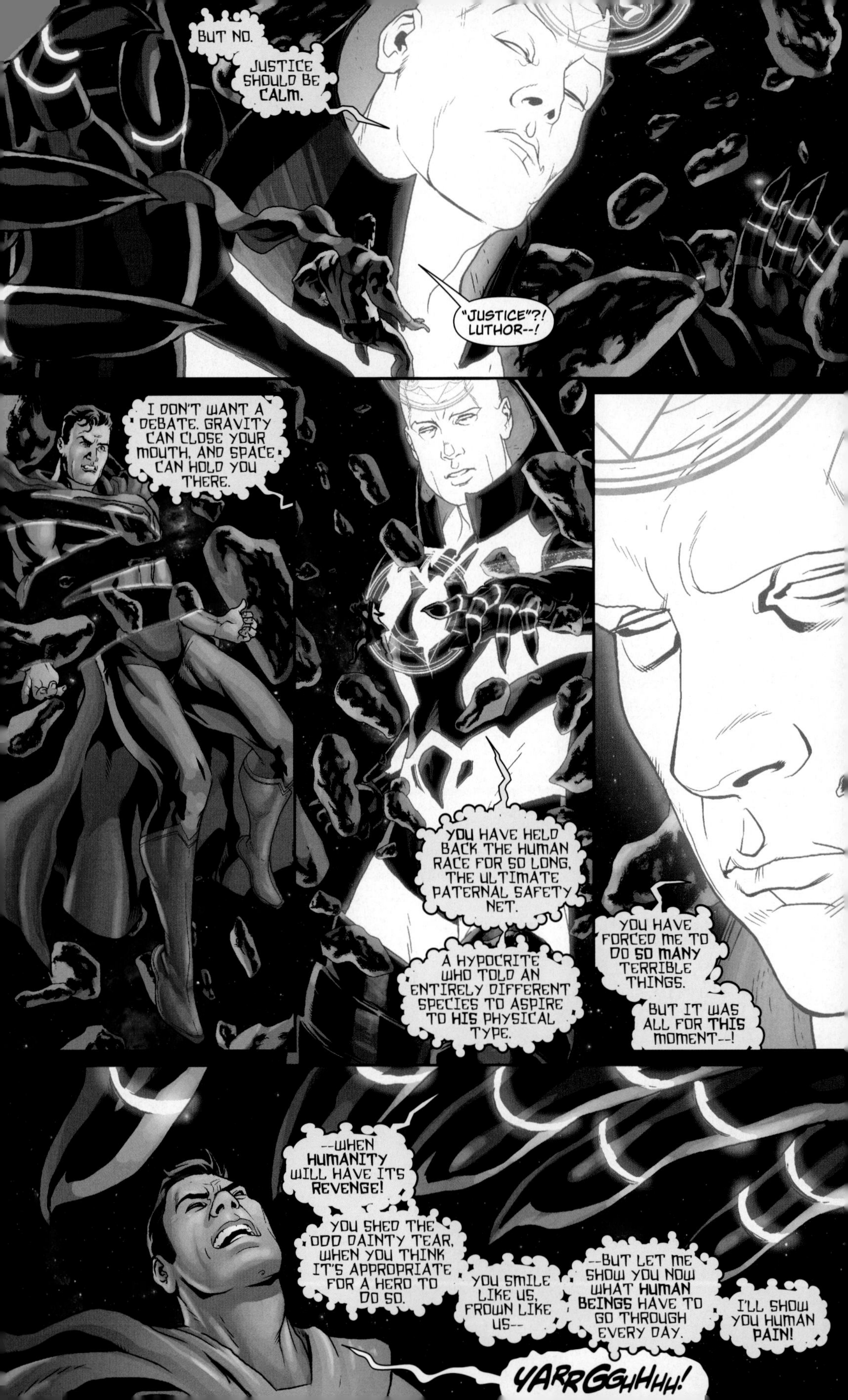
BUT NO.
JUSTICE SHOULD BE CALM.
"JUSTICE"?! LUTHOR--!
I DON'T WANT A DEBATE. GRAVITY CAN CLOSE YOUR MOUTH, AND SPACE CAN HOLD YOU THERE.
YOU HAVE HELD BACK THE HUMAN RACE FOR SO LONG, THE ULTIMATE PATERNAL SAFETY NET.
A HYPOCRITE WHO TOLD AN ENTIRELY DIFFERENT SPECIES TO ASPIRE TO HIS PHYSICAL TYPE.
YOU HAVE FORCED ME TO DO SO MANY TERRIBLE THINGS.
BUT IT WAS ALL FOR THIS MOMENT--!
--WHEN HUMANITY WILL HAVE ITS REVENGE!
YOU SHED THE ODD DAINTY TEAR, WHEN YOU THINK IT'S APPROPRIATE FOR A HERO TO DO SO.
YOU SMILE LIKE US, FROWN LIKE US--
--BUT LET ME SHOW YOU NOW WHAT HUMAN BEINGS HAVE TO GO THROUGH EVERY DAY.
I'LL SHOW YOU HUMAN PAIN!
YARRGGHHHH!

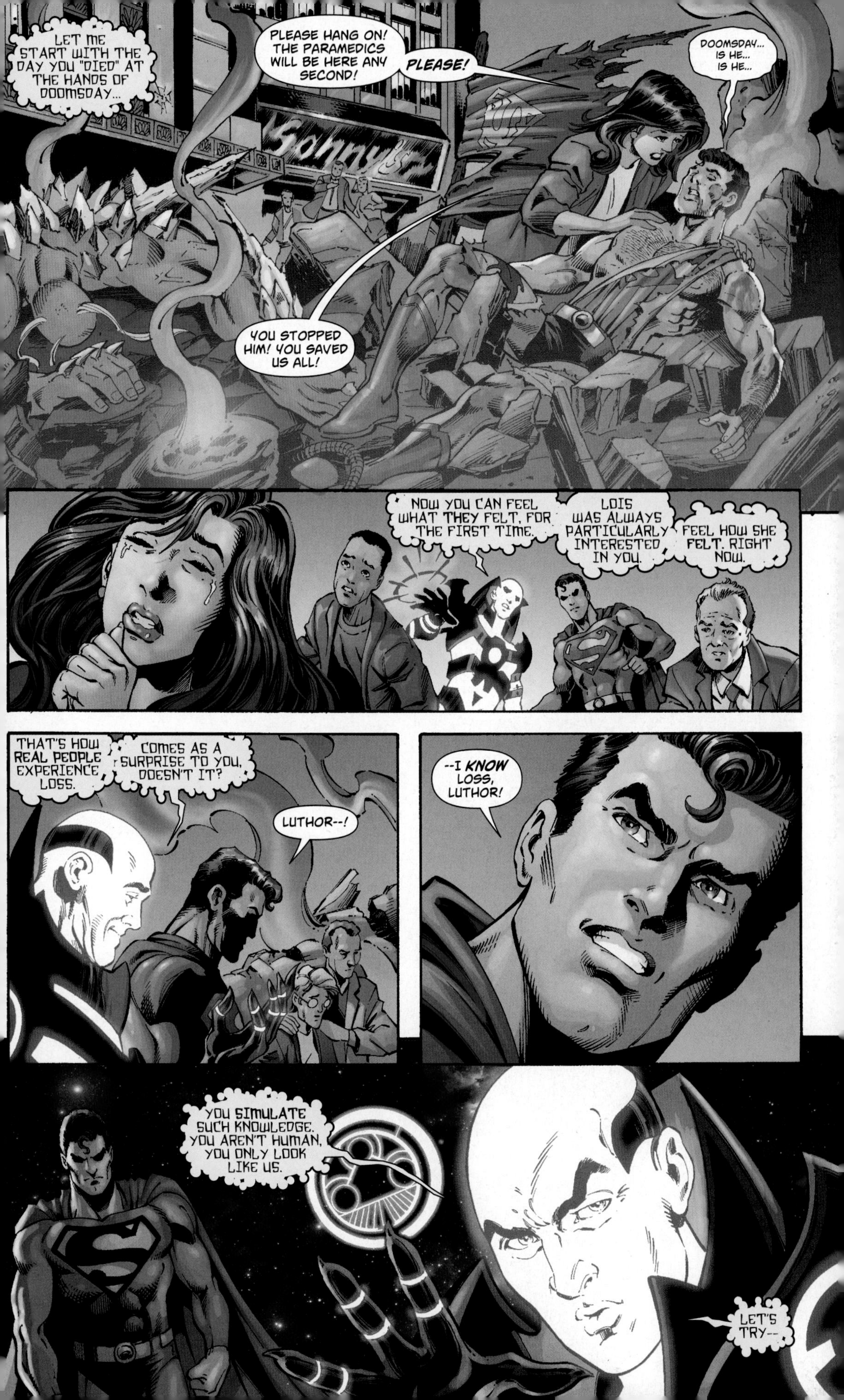

LET ME START WITH THE DAY YOU "DIED" AT THE HANDS OF DOOMSDAY...
PLEASE HANG ON! THE PARAMEDICS WILL BE HERE ANY SECOND!
PLEASE!
DOOMSDAY... IS HE... IS HE...
YOU STOPPED HIM! YOU SAVED US ALL!
NOW YOU CAN FEEL WHAT THEY FELT, FOR THE FIRST TIME.
LOIS WAS ALWAYS PARTICULARLY INTERESTED IN YOU.
FEEL HOW SHE FELT. RIGHT NOW.
THAT'S HOW REAL PEOPLE EXPERIENCE LOSS.
COMES AS A SURPRISE TO YOU, DOESN'T IT?
LUTHOR--!
--I KNOW LOSS, LUTHOR!
YOU SIMULATE SUCH KNOWLEDGE. YOU AREN'T HUMAN, YOU ONLY LOOK LIKE US.
LET'S TRY--

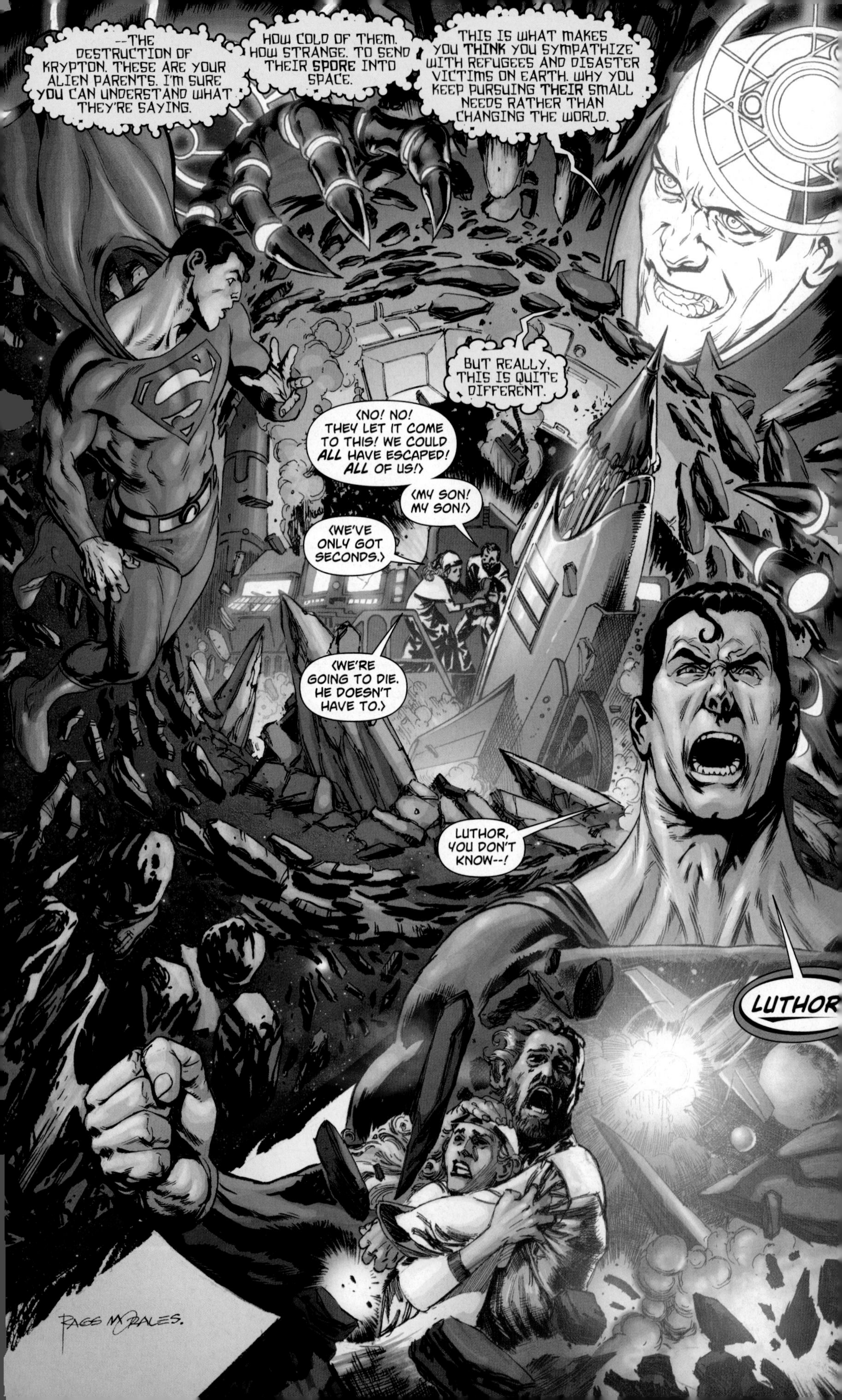
--THE DESTRUCTION OF KRYPTON. THESE ARE YOUR ALIEN PARENTS. I'M SURE YOU CAN UNDERSTAND WHAT THEY'RE SAYING.
HOW COLD OF THEM. HOW STRANGE, TO SEND THEIR SPORE INTO SPACE.
THIS IS WHAT MAKES YOU THINK YOU SYMPATHIZE WITH REFUGEES AND DISASTER VICTIMS ON EARTH. WHY YOU KEEP PURSUING THEIR SMALL NEEDS RATHER THAN CHANGING THE WORLD.
BUT REALLY, THIS IS QUITE DIFFERENT.
<NO! NO! THEY LET IT COME TO THIS! WE COULD ALL HAVE ESCAPED! ALL OF US!>
<MY SON! MY SON!>
<WE'VE ONLY GOT SECONDS.>
<WE'RE GOING TO DIE. HE DOESN'T HAVE TO.>
LUTHOR, YOU DON'T KNOW--!
LUTHOR
RAGS MORALES.

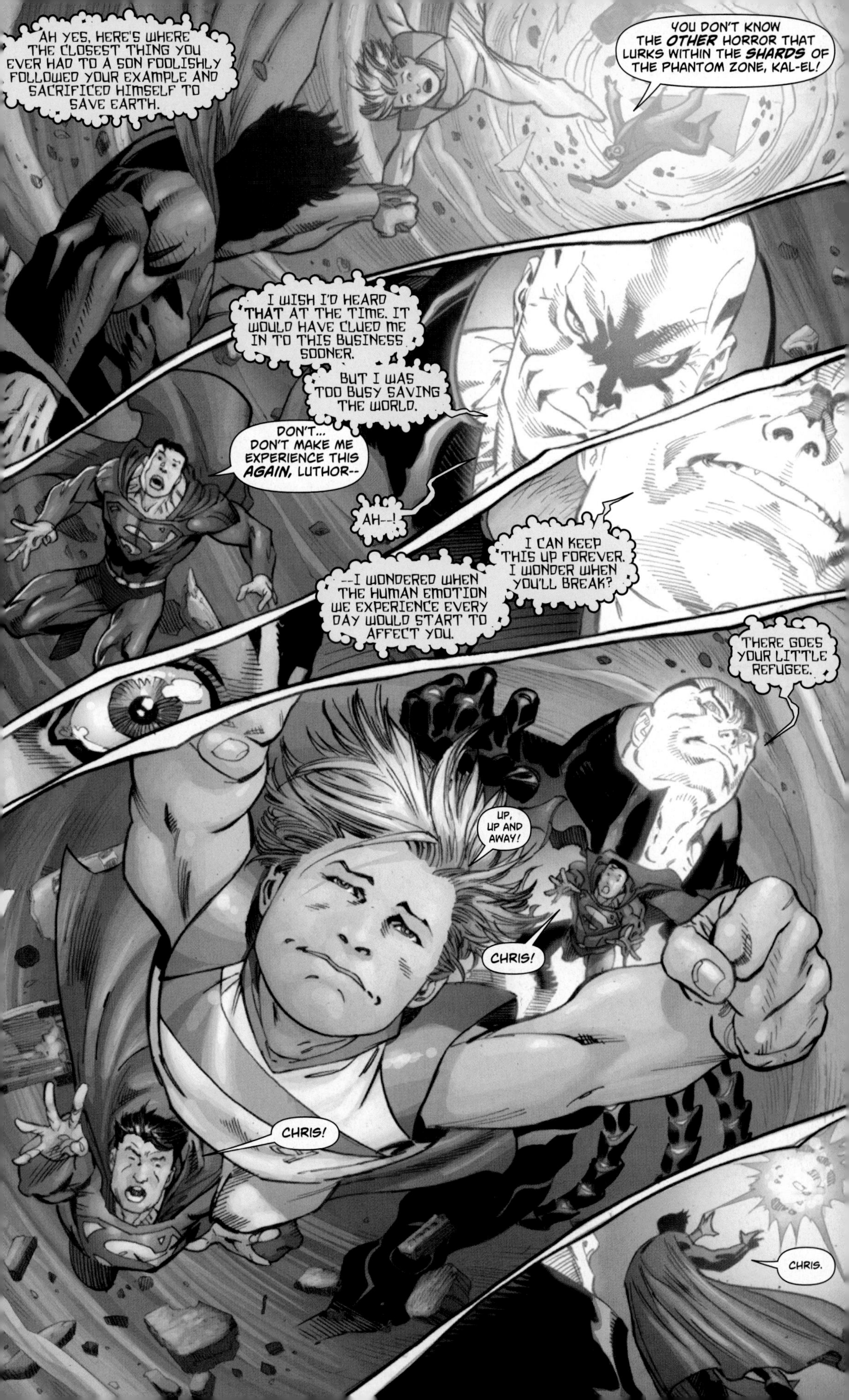
AH YES, HERE'S WHERE THE CLOSEST THING YOU EVER HAD TO A SON FOOLISHLY FOLLOWED YOUR EXAMPLE AND SACRIFICED HIMSELF TO SAVE EARTH.
YOU DON'T KNOW THE OTHER HORROR THAT LURKS WITHIN THE SHARDS OF THE PHANTOM ZONE, KAL-EL!
I WISH I'D HEARD THAT AT THE TIME. IT WOULD HAVE CLUED ME IN TO THIS BUSINESS SOONER.
BUT I WAS TOO BUSY SAVING THE WORLD.
DON'T... DON'T MAKE ME EXPERIENCE THIS AGAIN, LUTHOR--
AH--!
--I WONDERED WHEN THE HUMAN EMOTION WE EXPERIENCE EVERY DAY WOULD START TO AFFECT YOU.
I CAN KEEP THIS UP FOREVER. I WONDER WHEN YOU'LL BREAK?
THERE GOES YOUR LITTLE REFUGEE.
UP, UP AND AWAY!
CHRIS!
CHRIS!
CHRIS.

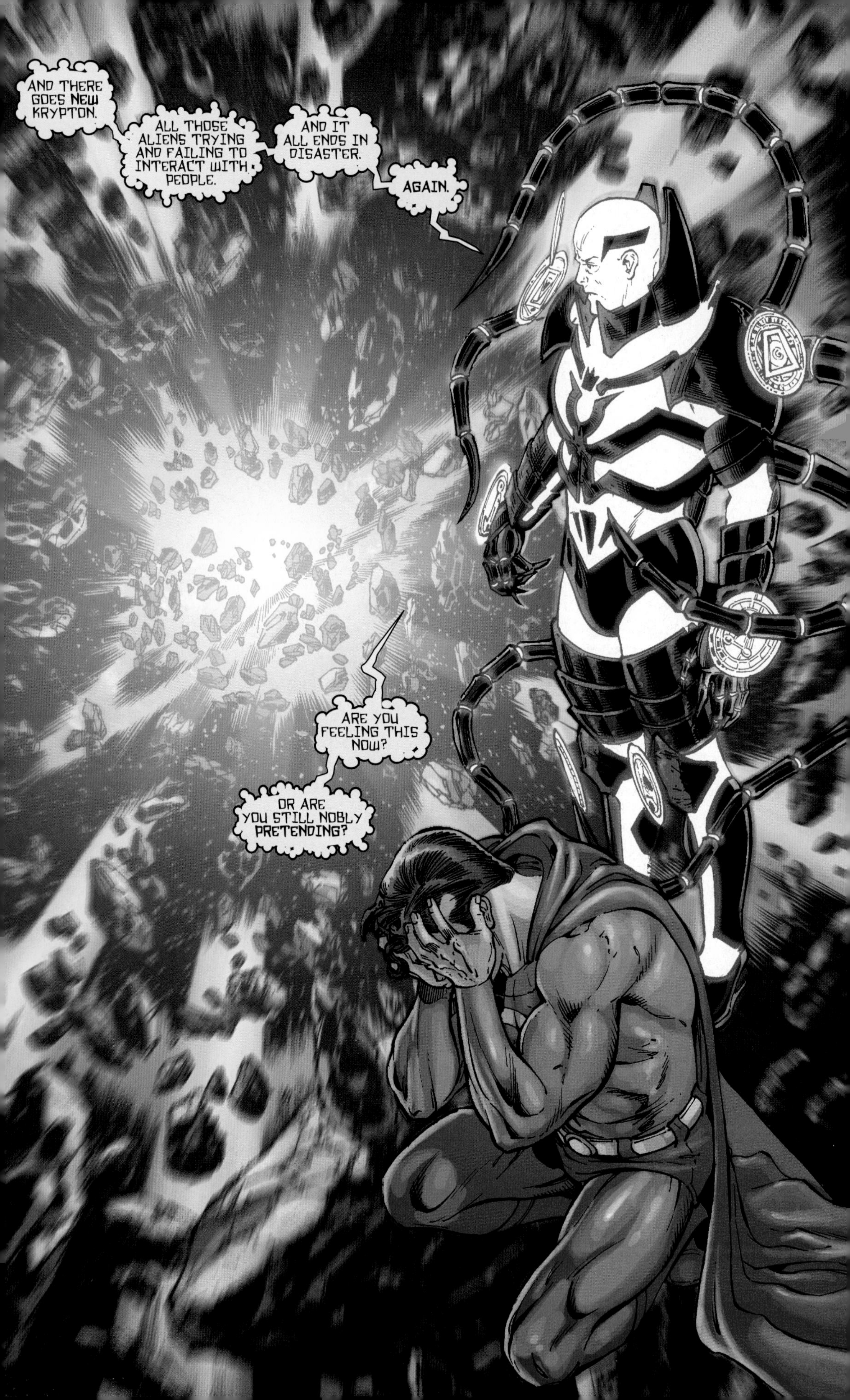
AND THERE GOES NEW KRYPTON.
ALL THOSE ALIENS TRYING AND FAILING TO INTERACT WITH PEOPLE.
AND IT ALL ENDS IN DISASTER.
AGAIN.
ARE YOU FEELING THIS NOW?
OR ARE YOU STILL NOBLY PRETENDING?

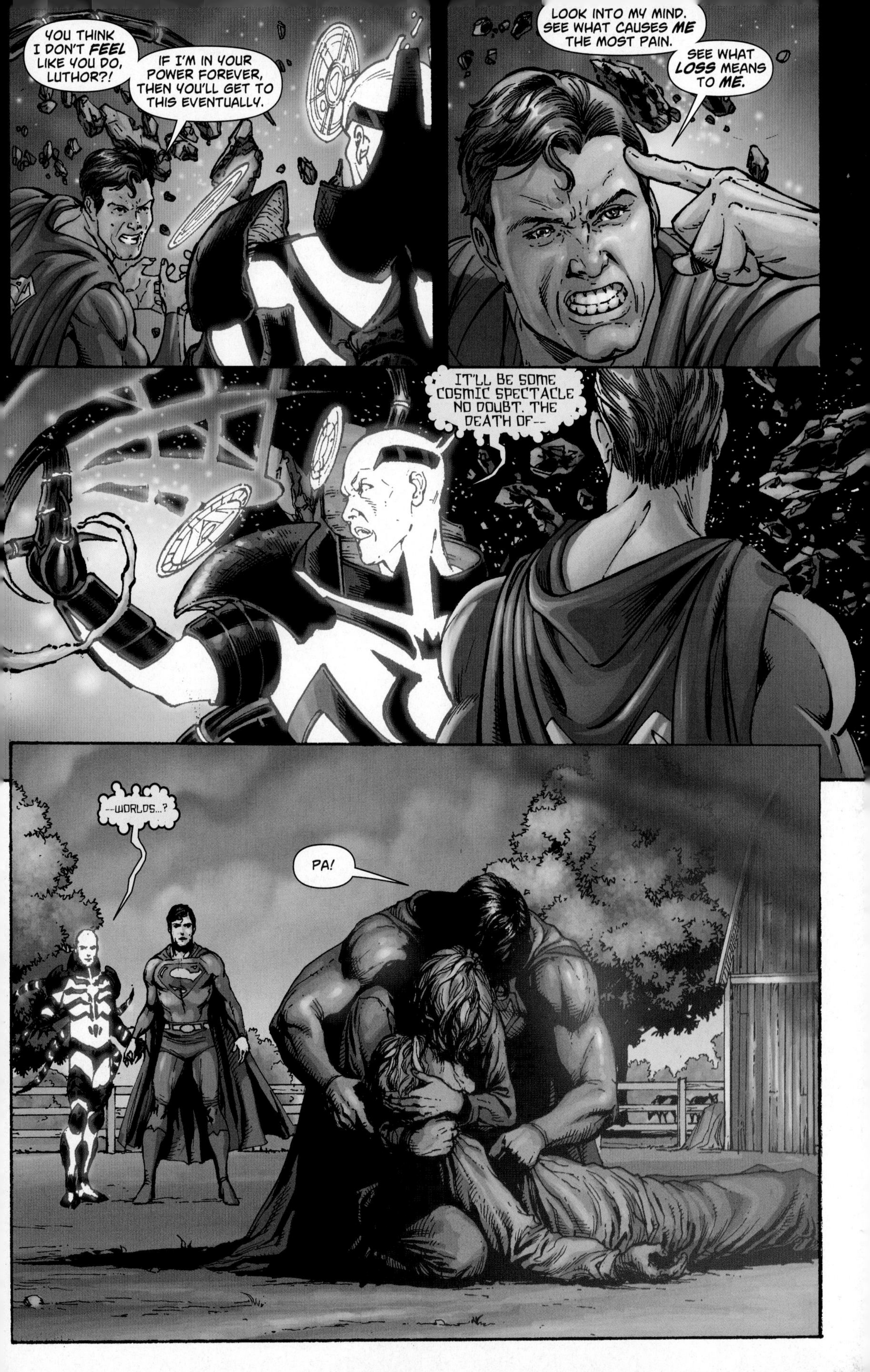

YOU THINK I DON'T *FEEL* LIKE YOU DO, LUTHOR?!
IF I'M IN YOUR POWER FOREVER, THEN YOU'LL GET TO THIS EVENTUALLY.
LOOK INTO MY MIND. SEE WHAT CAUSES *ME* THE MOST PAIN.
SEE WHAT *LOSS* MEANS TO *ME.*
IT'LL BE SOME COSMIC SPECTACLE NO DOUBT. THE DEATH OF--
--WORLDS...?
PA!

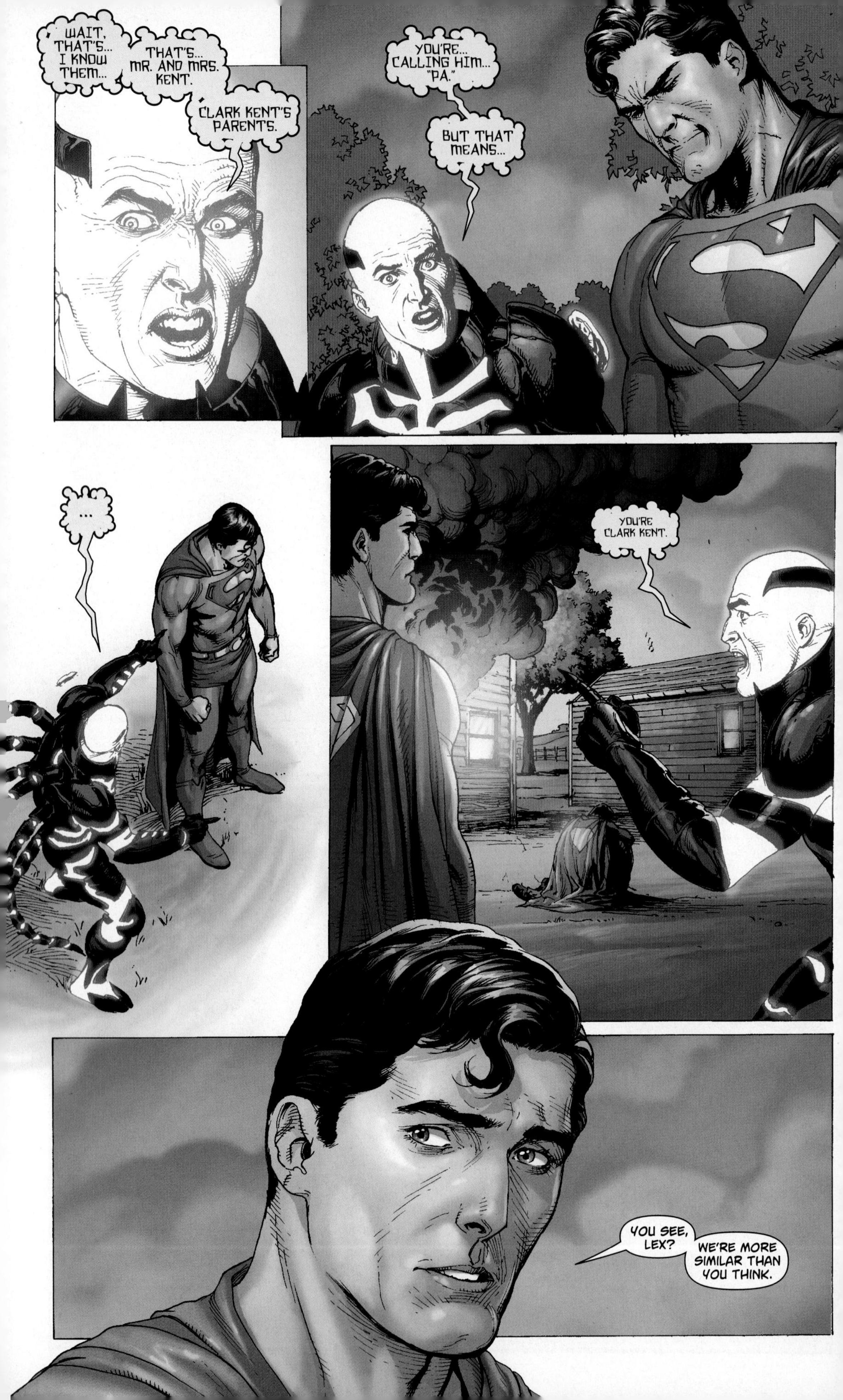
WAIT, THAT'S... I KNOW THEM...
THAT'S... MR. AND MRS. KENT.
CLARK KENT'S PARENTS.
YOU'RE... CALLING HIM... "PA."
BUT THAT MEANS...
...
YOU'RE CLARK KENT.
YOU SEE, LEX?
WE'RE MORE SIMILAR THAN YOU THINK.

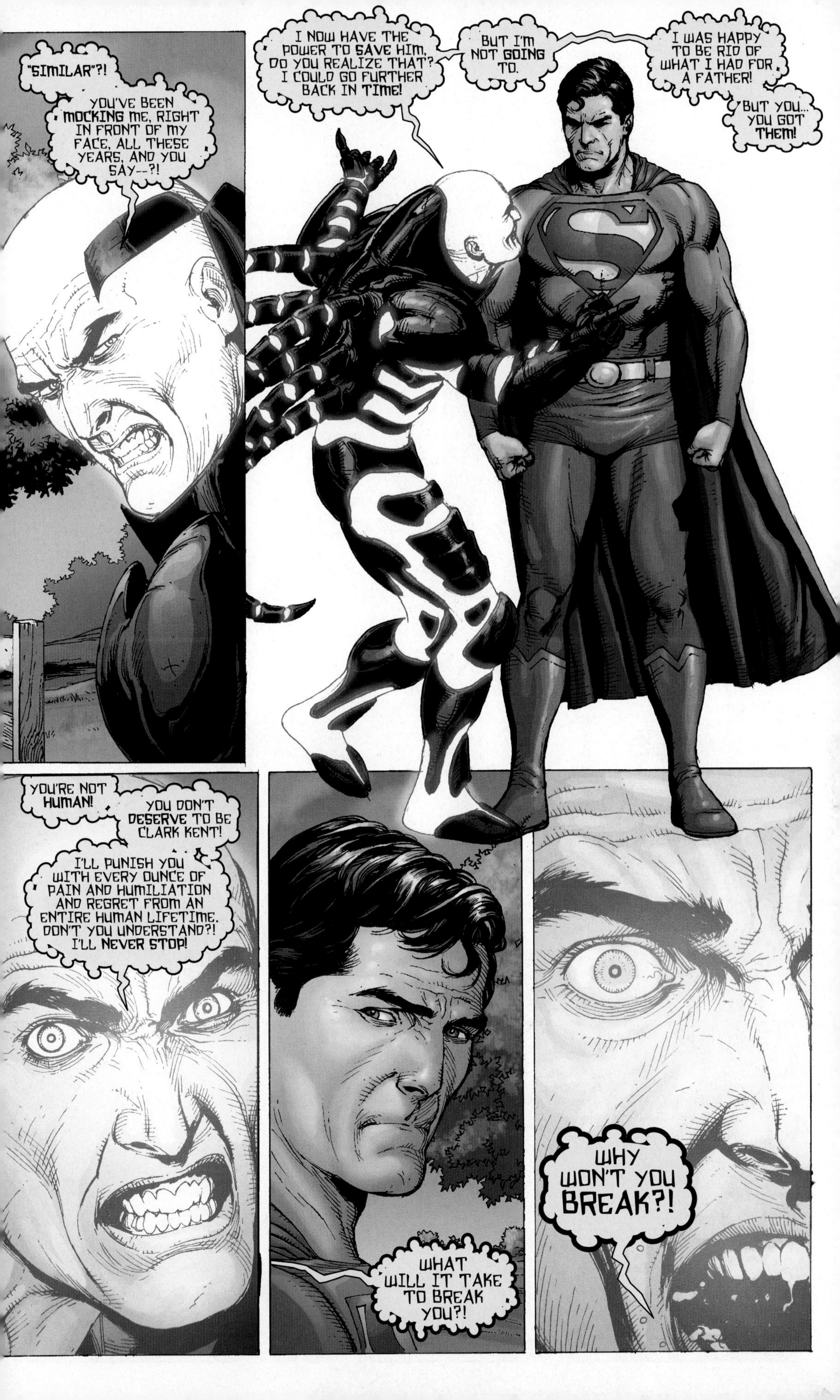

"SIMILAR"?!
YOU'VE BEEN MOCKING ME, RIGHT IN FRONT OF MY FACE, ALL THESE YEARS, AND YOU SAY--?!
I NOW HAVE THE POWER TO SAVE HIM, DO YOU REALIZE THAT? I COULD GO FURTHER BACK IN TIME!
BUT I'M NOT GOING TO.
I WAS HAPPY TO BE RID OF WHAT I HAD FOR A FATHER!
BUT YOU... YOU GOT THEM!
YOU'RE NOT HUMAN!
YOU DON'T DESERVE TO BE CLARK KENT!
I'LL PUNISH YOU WITH EVERY OUNCE OF PAIN AND HUMILIATION AND REGRET FROM AN ENTIRE HUMAN LIFETIME. DON'T YOU UNDERSTAND?! I'LL NEVER STOP!
WHAT WILL IT TAKE TO BREAK YOU?!
WHY WON'T YOU BREAK?!

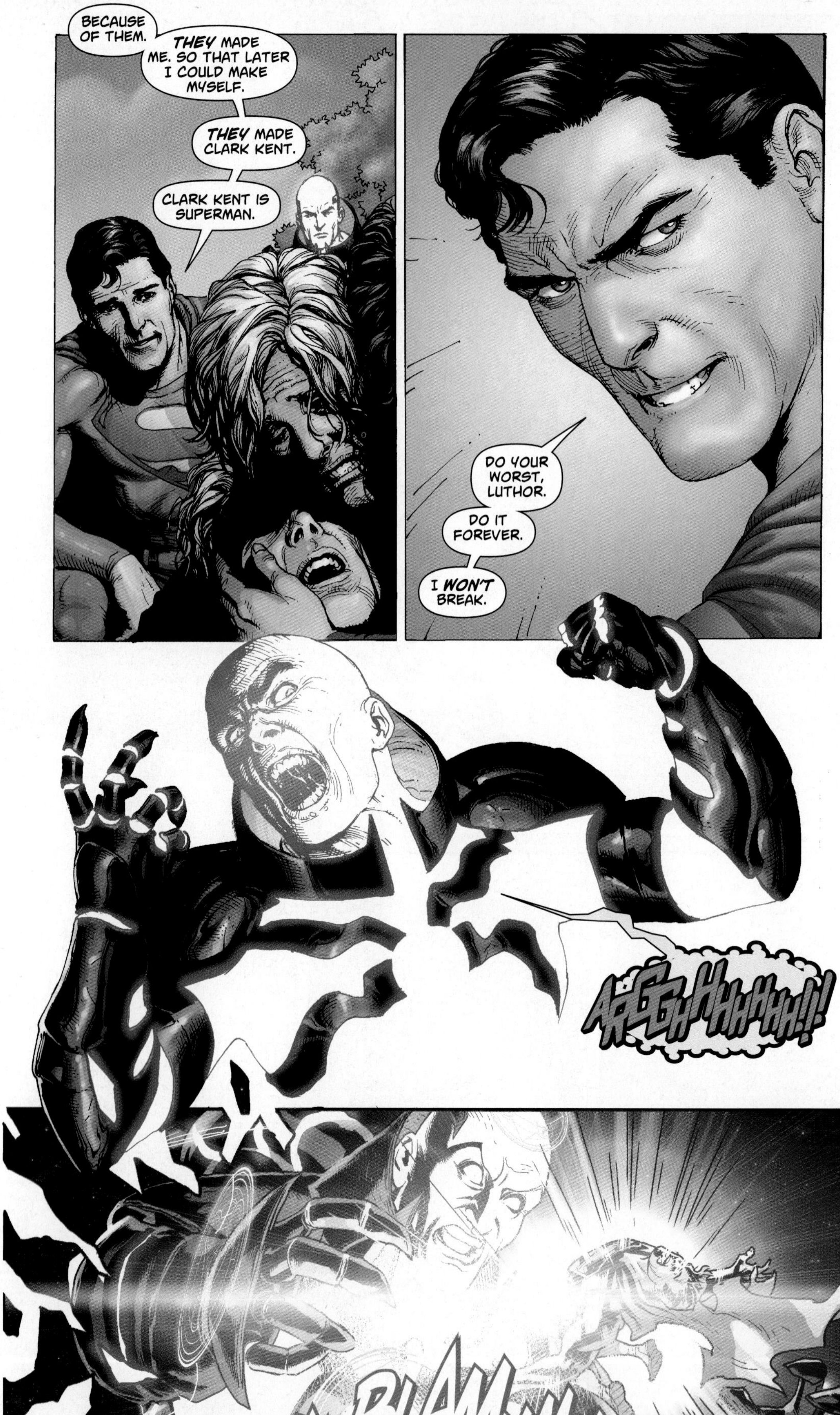
BECAUSE OF THEM.
THEY MADE ME. SO THAT LATER I COULD MAKE MYSELF.
THEY MADE CLARK KENT.
CLARK KENT IS SUPERMAN.
DO YOUR WORST, LUTHOR.
DO IT FOREVER.
I WON'T BREAK.
ARGGHHHHHHH!!!
SKA-BLAMMMMMM

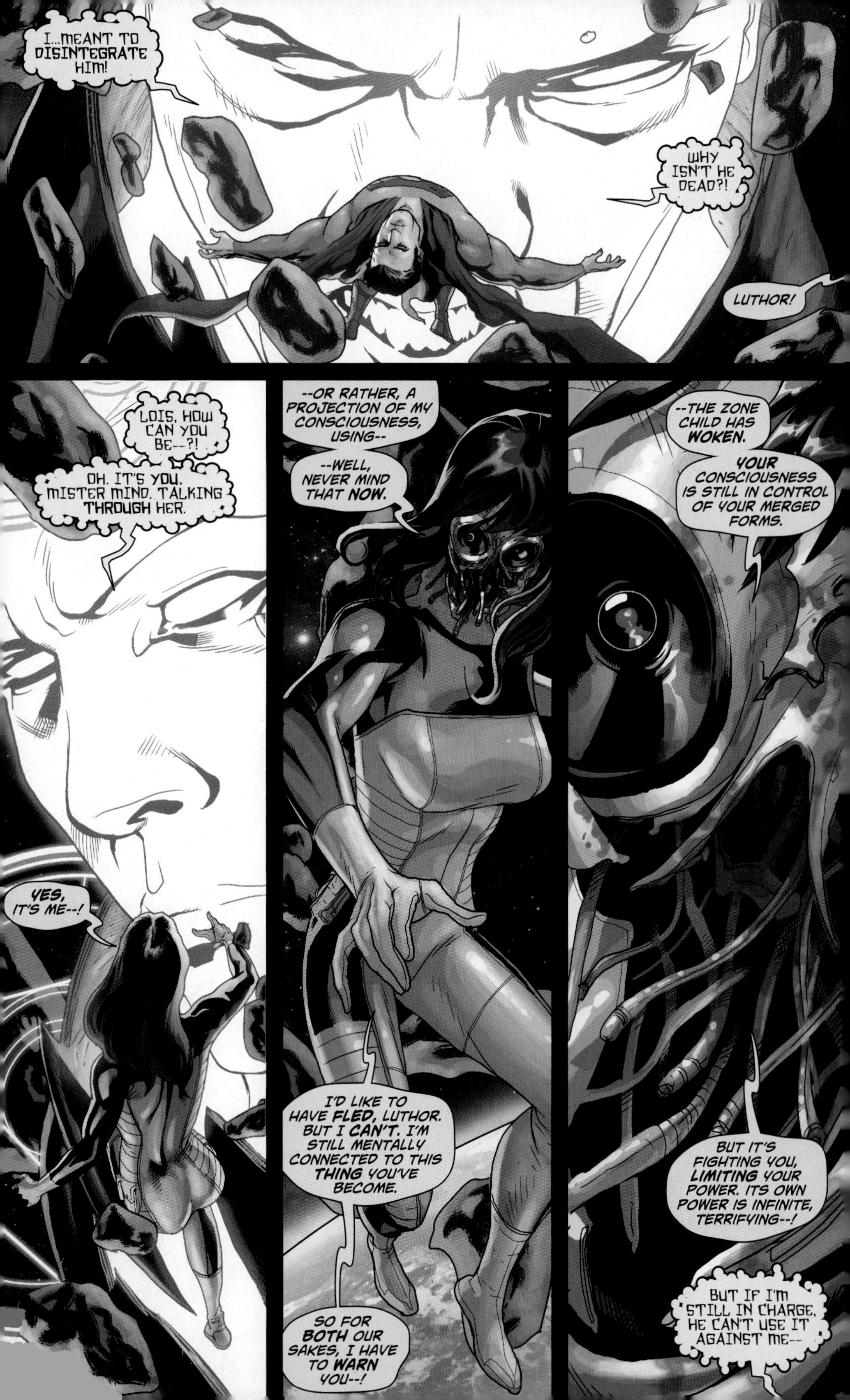
I...MEANT TO DISINTEGRATE HIM!
WHY ISN'T HE DEAD?!
LUTHOR!
LOIS, HOW CAN YOU BE--?!
OH. IT'S YOU. MISTER MIND. TALKING THROUGH HER.
YES, IT'S ME--!
--OR RATHER, A PROJECTION OF MY CONSCIOUSNESS, USING--
--WELL, NEVER MIND THAT NOW.
I'D LIKE TO HAVE FLED, LUTHOR. BUT I CAN'T. I'M STILL MENTALLY CONNECTED TO THIS THING YOU'VE BECOME.
SO FOR BOTH OUR SAKES, I HAVE TO WARN YOU--!
--THE ZONE CHILD HAS WOKEN.
YOUR CONSCIOUSNESS IS STILL IN CONTROL OF YOUR MERGED FORMS.
BUT IT'S FIGHTING YOU, LIMITING YOUR POWER. ITS OWN POWER IS INFINITE, TERRIFYING--!
BUT IF I'M STILL IN CHARGE, HE CAN'T USE IT AGAINST ME--

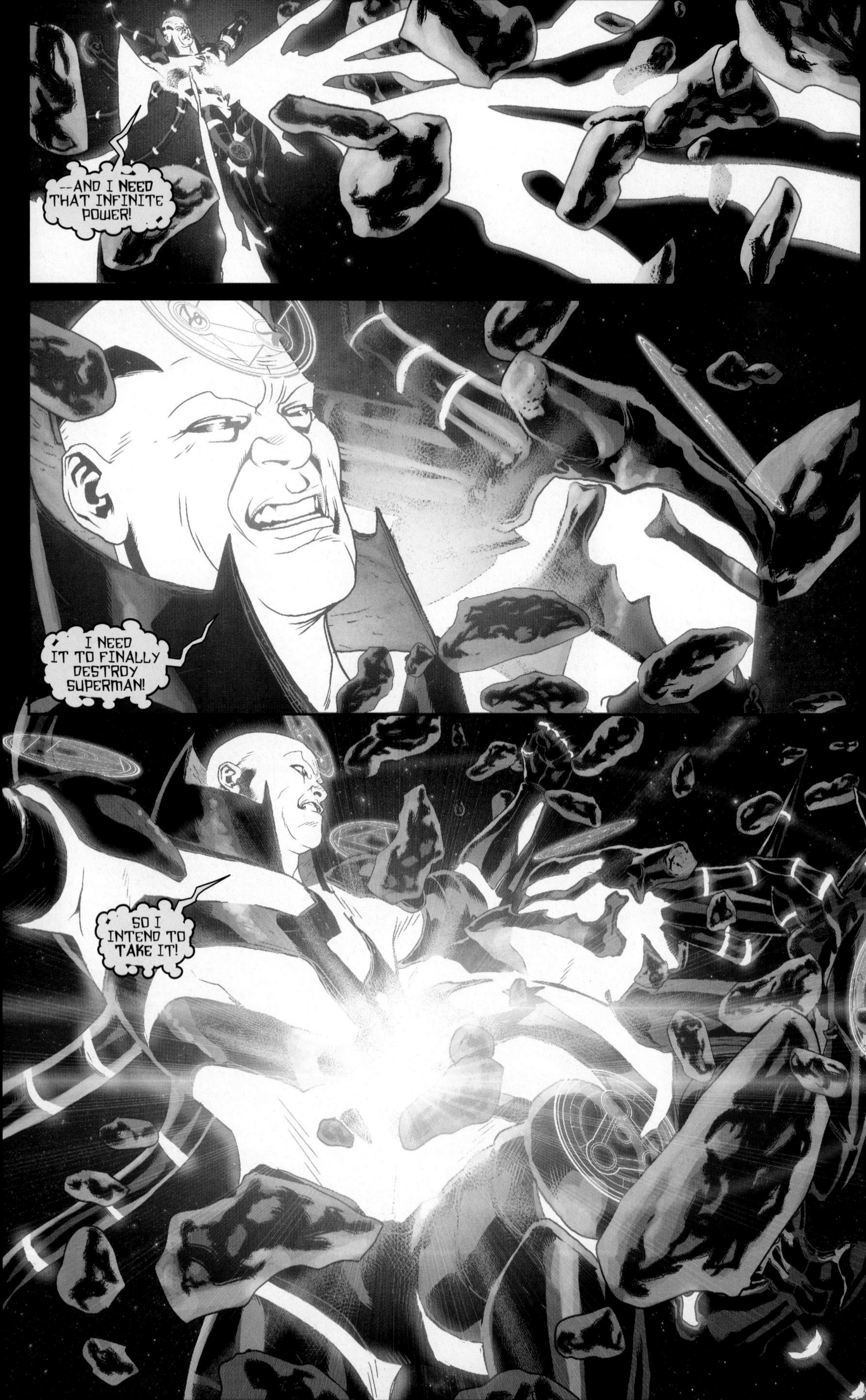
--AND I NEED THAT INFINITE POWER!
I NEED IT TO FINALLY DESTROY SUPERMAN!
SO I INTEND TO TAKE IT!

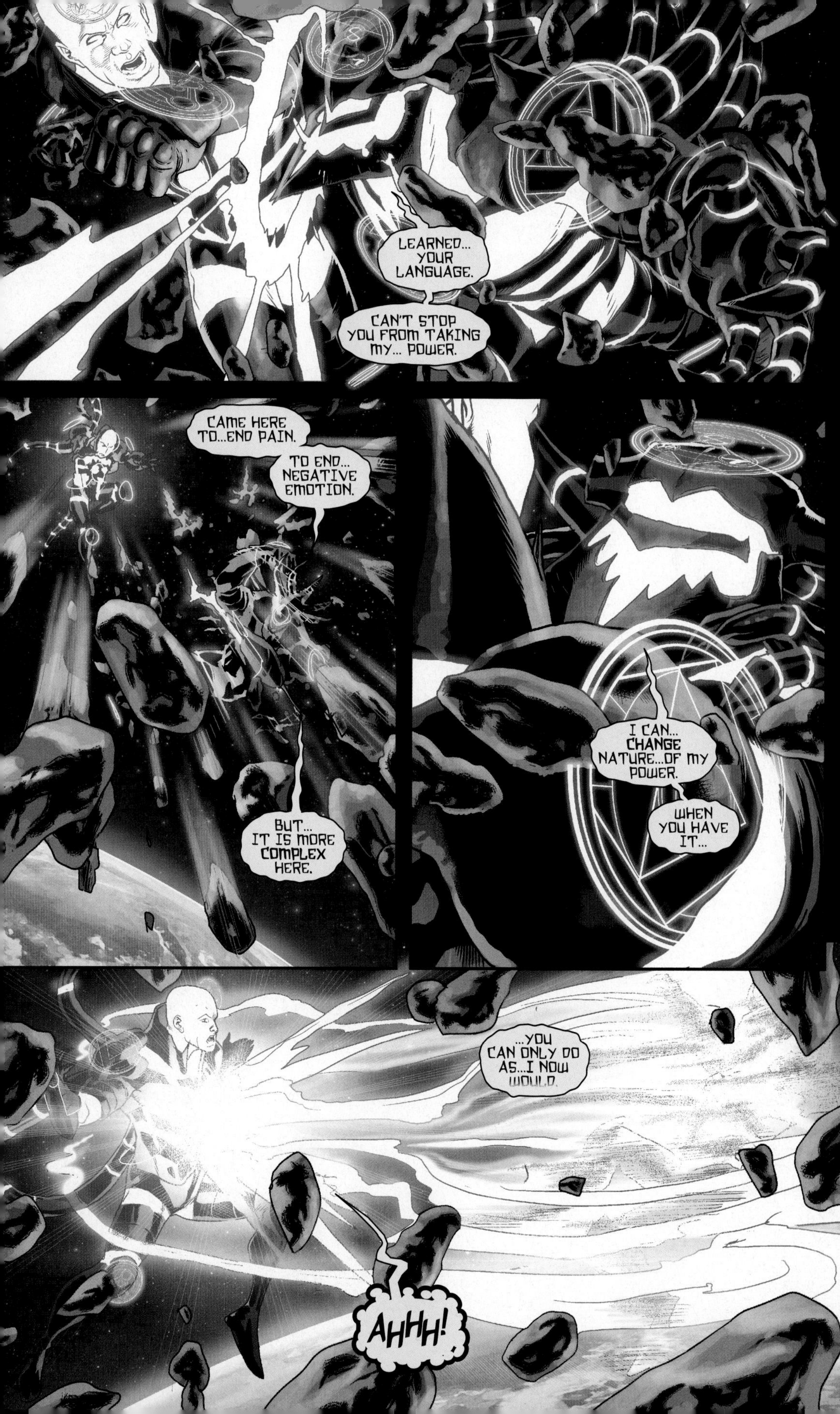

LEARNED... YOUR LANGUAGE.
CAN'T STOP YOU FROM TAKING MY... POWER.
CAME HERE TO...END PAIN.
TO END... NEGATIVE EMOTION.
BUT... IT IS MORE COMPLEX HERE.
I CAN... CHANGE NATURE...OF MY POWER.
WHEN YOU HAVE IT...
...YOU CAN ONLY DO AS...I NOW WOULD.
AHHH!

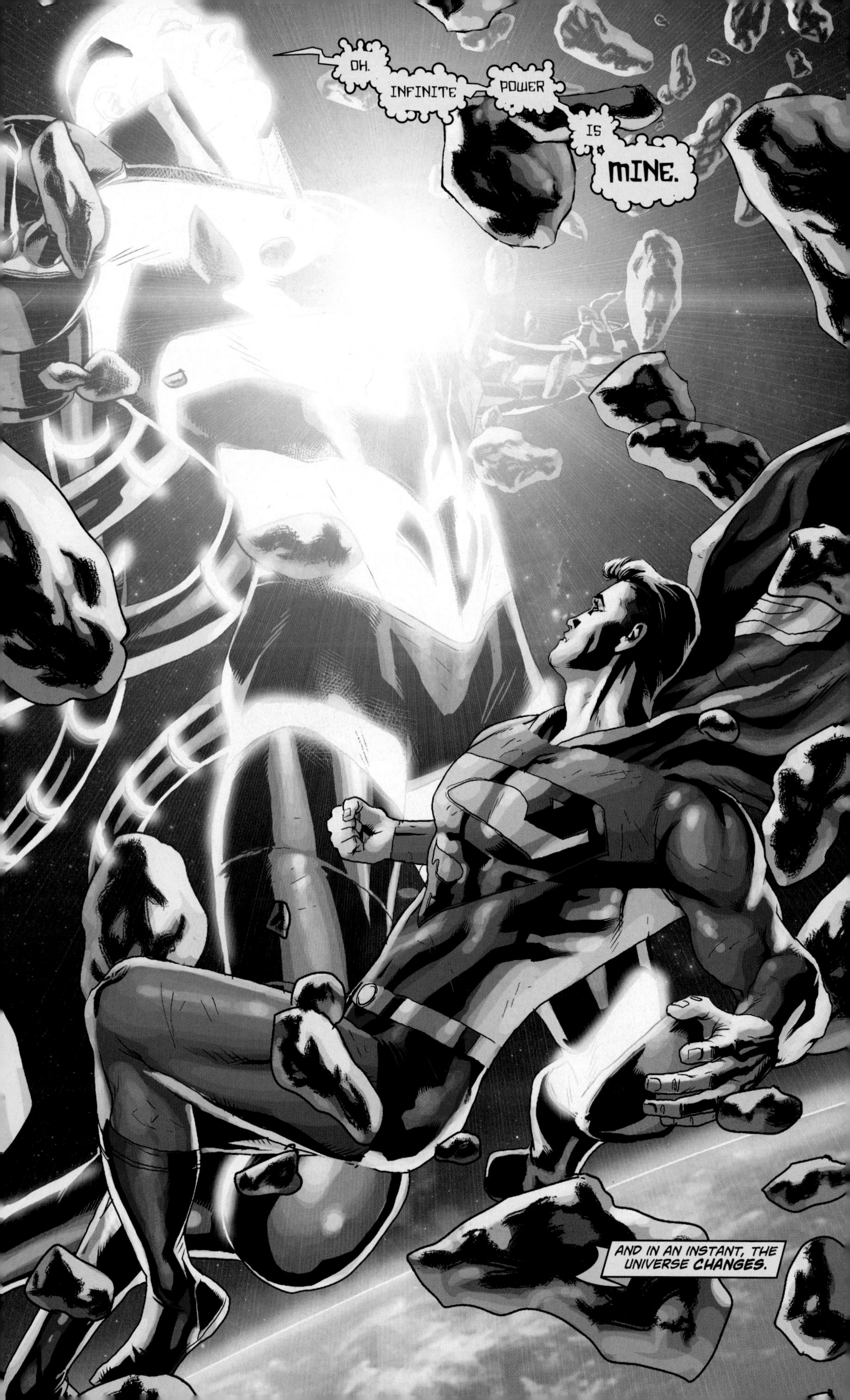
OH.
INFINITE
POWER
IS
MINE.
AND IN AN INSTANT, THE UNIVERSE CHANGES.

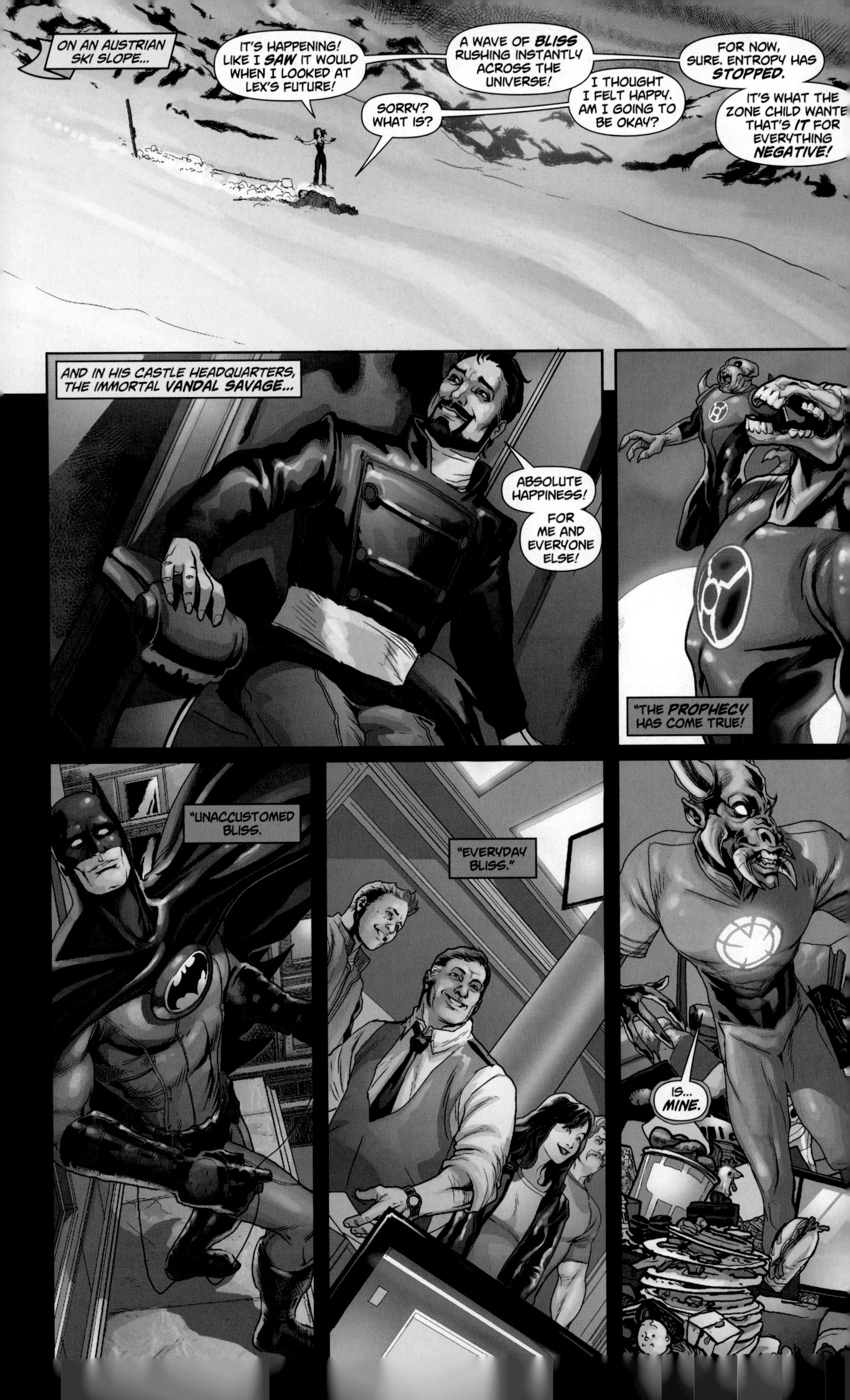
ON AN AUSTRIAN SKI SLOPE...
IT'S HAPPENING! LIKE I SAW IT WOULD WHEN I LOOKED AT LEX'S FUTURE!
SORRY? WHAT IS?
A WAVE OF BLISS RUSHING INSTANTLY ACROSS THE UNIVERSE!
I THOUGHT I FELT HAPPY. AM I GOING TO BE OKAY?
FOR NOW, SURE. ENTROPY HAS STOPPED.
IT'S WHAT THE ZONE CHILD WANTE
THAT'S IT FOR EVERYTHING NEGATIVE!
AND IN HIS CASTLE HEADQUARTERS, THE IMMORTAL VANDAL SAVAGE...
ABSOLUTE HAPPINESS!
FOR ME AND EVERYONE ELSE!
"THE PROPHECY HAS COME TRUE!
"UNACCUSTOMED BLISS.
"EVERYDAY BLISS."
IS... MINE.

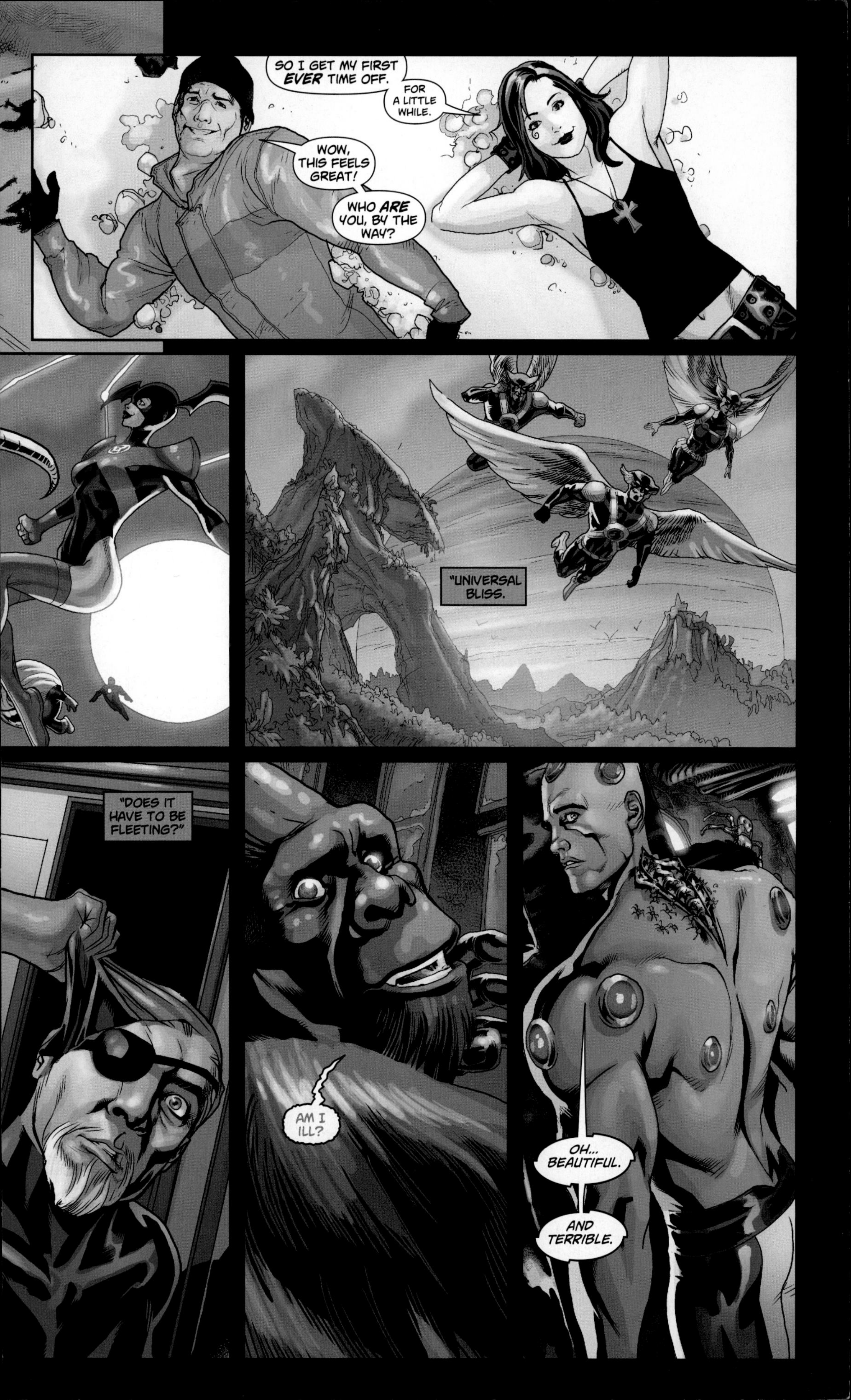
SO I GET MY FIRST EVER TIME OFF.
FOR A LITTLE WHILE.
WOW, THIS FEELS GREAT!
WHO ARE YOU, BY THE WAY?
"UNIVERSAL BLISS.
"DOES IT HAVE TO BE FLEETING?"
AM I ILL?
OH... BEAUTIFUL.
AND TERRIBLE.

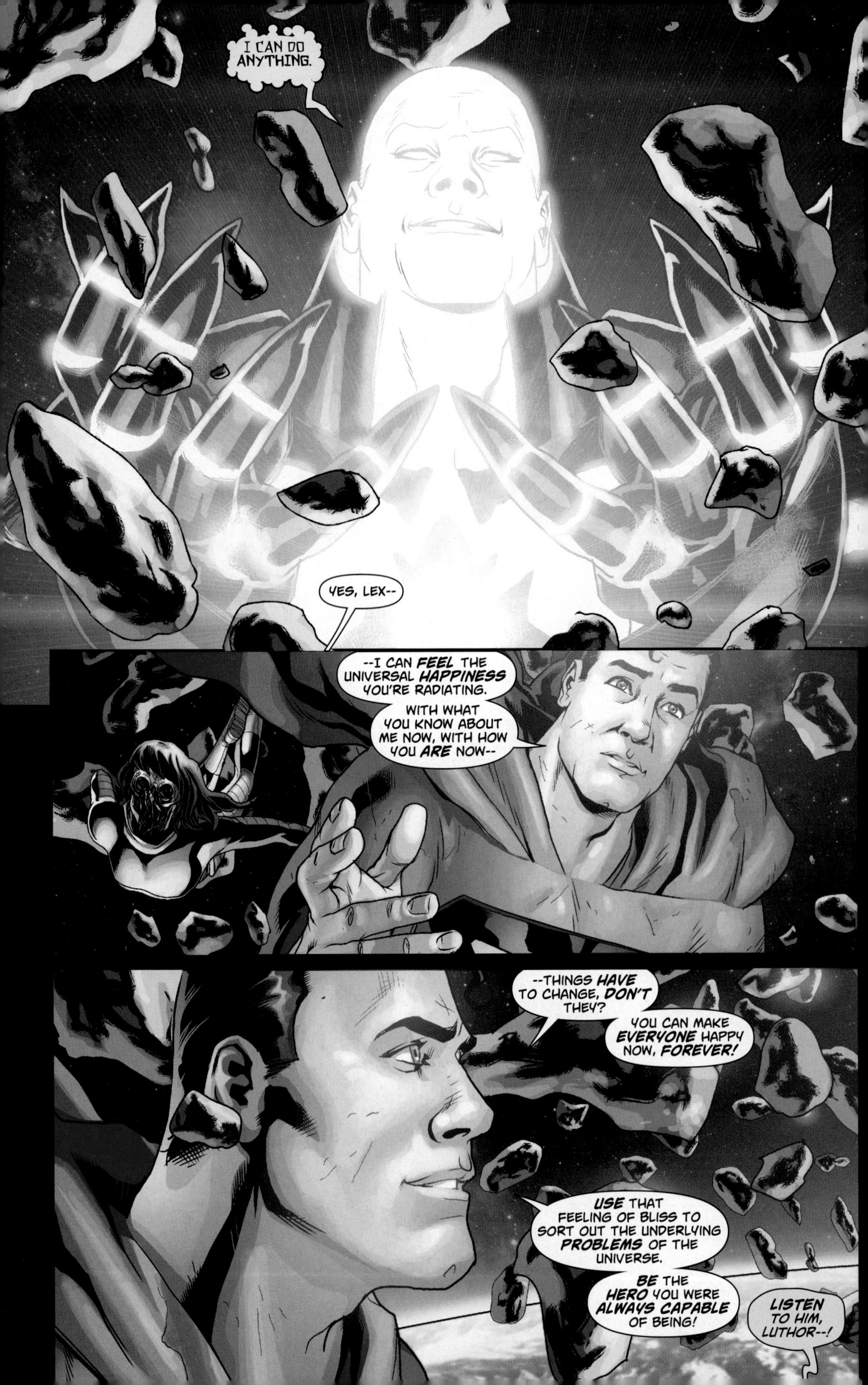
I CAN DO ANYTHING.
YES, LEX--
--I CAN FEEL THE UNIVERSAL HAPPINESS YOU'RE RADIATING.
WITH WHAT YOU KNOW ABOUT ME NOW, WITH HOW YOU ARE NOW--
--THINGS HAVE TO CHANGE, DON'T THEY?
YOU CAN MAKE EVERYONE HAPPY NOW, FOREVER!
USE THAT FEELING OF BLISS TO SORT OUT THE UNDERLYING PROBLEMS OF THE UNIVERSE.
BE THE HERO YOU WERE ALWAYS CAPABLE OF BEING!
LISTEN TO HIM, LUTHOR--!

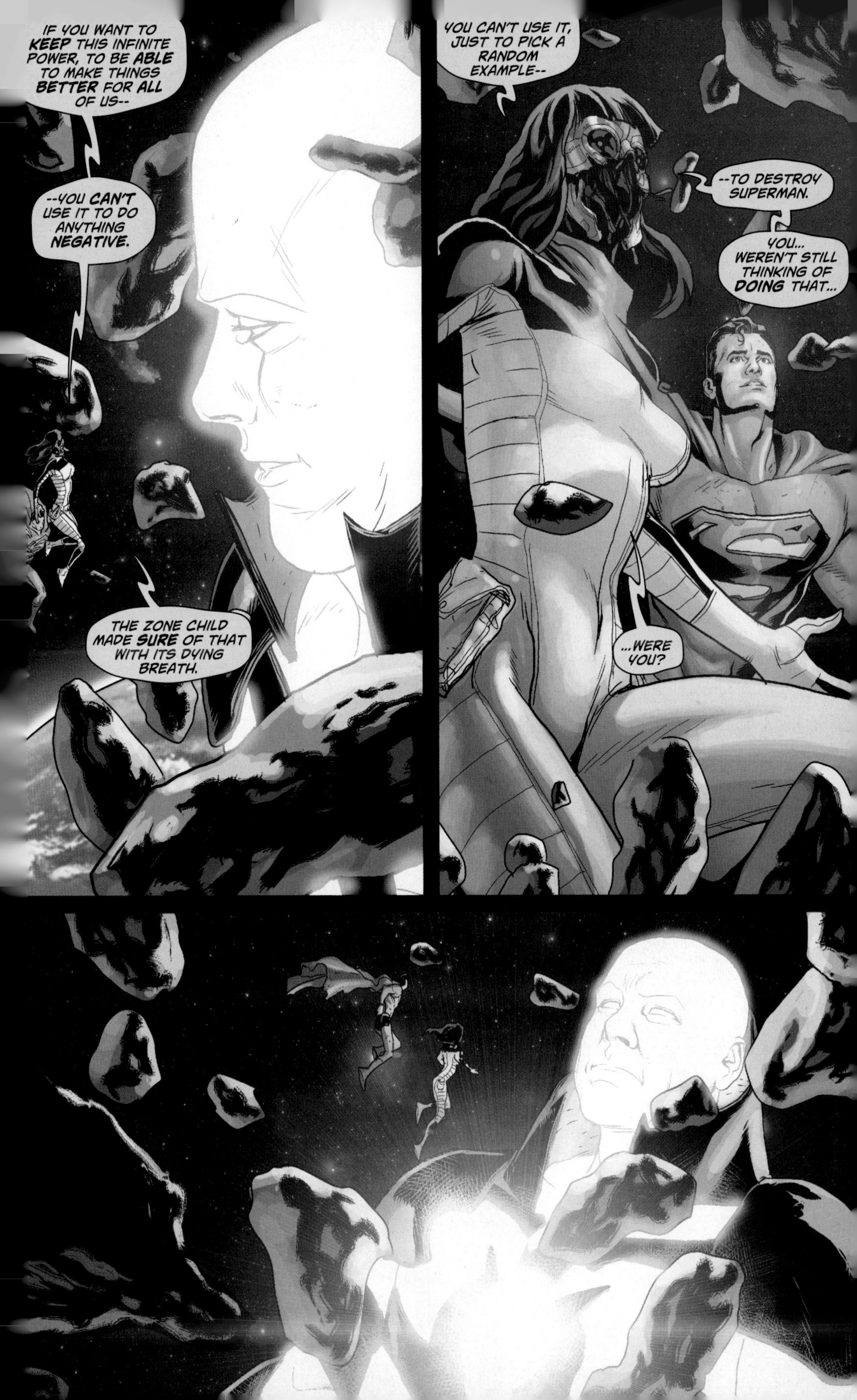
IF YOU WANT TO KEEP THIS INFINITE POWER, TO BE ABLE TO MAKE THINGS BETTER FOR ALL OF US--
--YOU CAN'T USE IT TO DO ANYTHING NEGATIVE.
THE ZONE CHILD MADE SURE OF THAT WITH ITS DYING BREATH.
YOU CAN'T USE IT, JUST TO PICK A RANDOM EXAMPLE--
--TO DESTROY SUPERMAN.
YOU... WEREN'T STILL THINKING OF DOING THAT...
...WERE YOU?

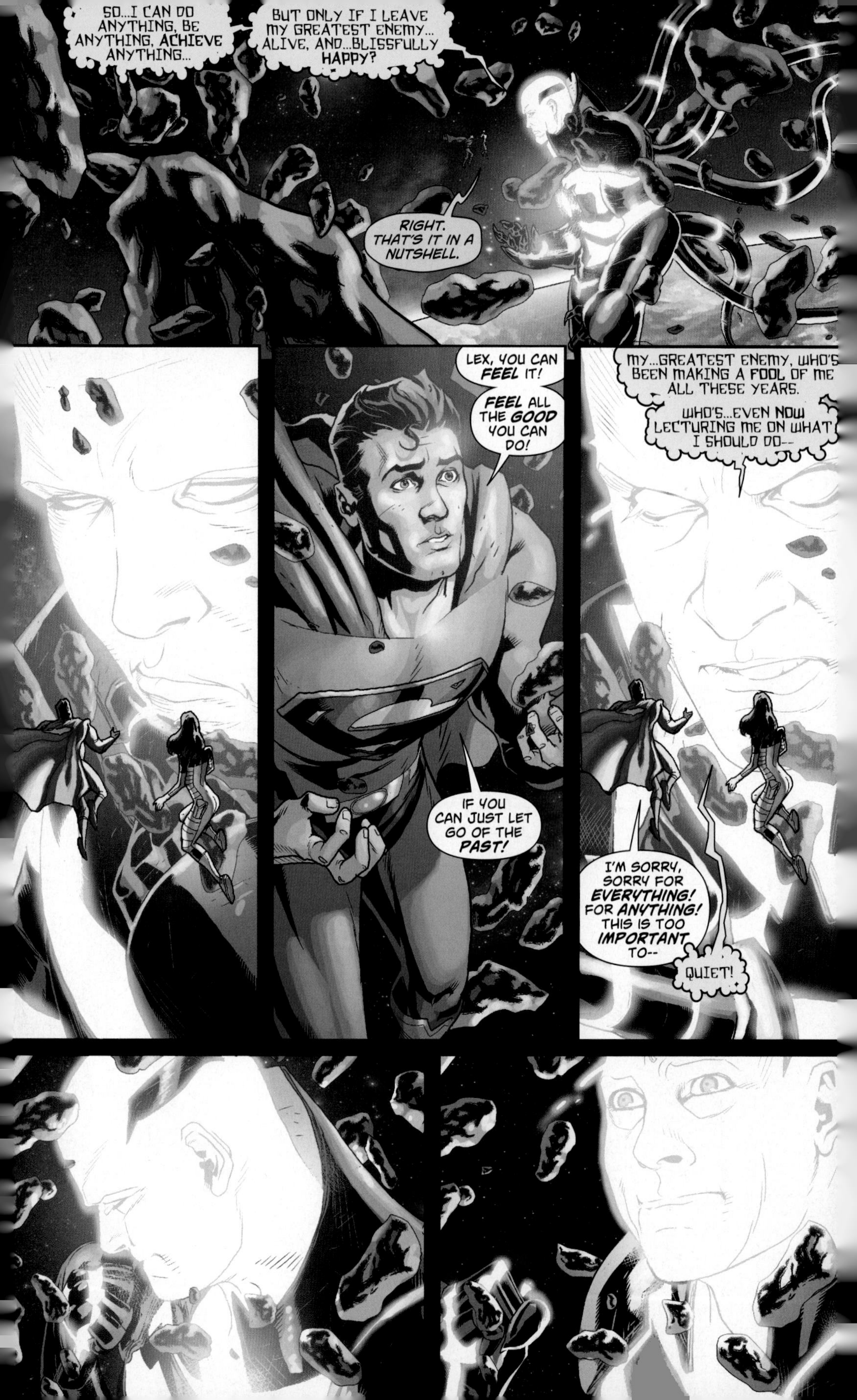
SO...I CAN DO ANYTHING, BE ANYTHING, ACHIEVE ANYTHING...
BUT ONLY IF I LEAVE MY GREATEST ENEMY... ALIVE, AND...BLISSFULLY HAPPY?
RIGHT. THAT'S IT IN A NUTSHELL.
LEX, YOU CAN FEEL IT!
FEEL ALL THE GOOD YOU CAN DO!
IF YOU CAN JUST LET GO OF THE PAST!
MY...GREATEST ENEMY, WHO'S BEEN MAKING A FOOL OF ME ALL THESE YEARS.
WHO'S...EVEN NOW LECTURING ME ON WHAT I SHOULD DO--
I'M SORRY, SORRY FOR EVERYTHING! FOR ANYTHING! THIS IS TOO IMPORTANT TO--
QUIET!

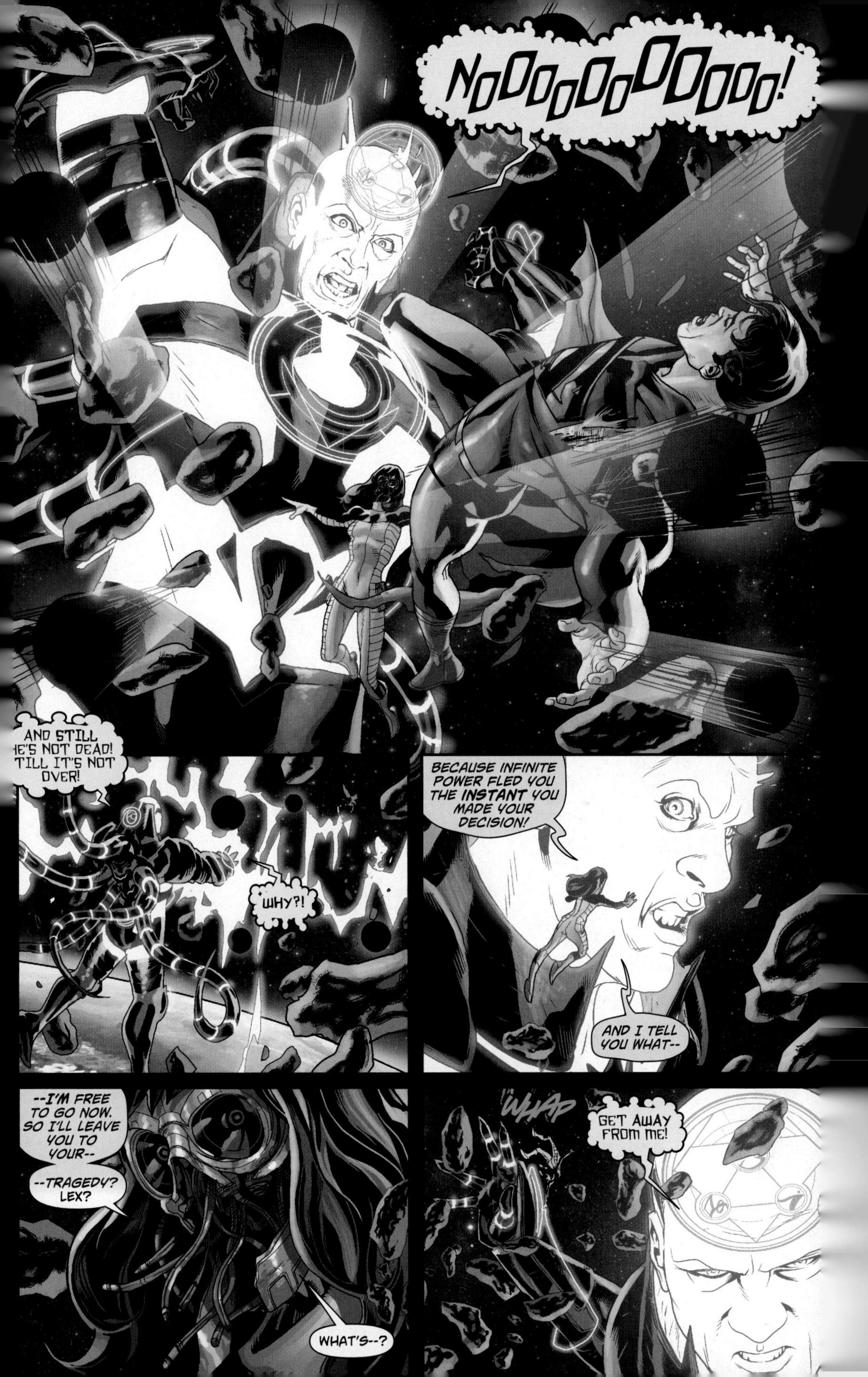
NOOOOOOOOOOOO!
AND STILL HE'S NOT DEAD! TILL IT'S NOT OVER!
WHY?!
BECAUSE INFINITE POWER FLED YOU THE INSTANT YOU MADE YOUR DECISION!
AND I TELL YOU WHAT--
--I'M FREE TO GO NOW. SO I'LL LEAVE YOU TO YOUR--
--TRAGEDY? LEX?
WHAT'S--?
WHAP
GET AWAY FROM ME!

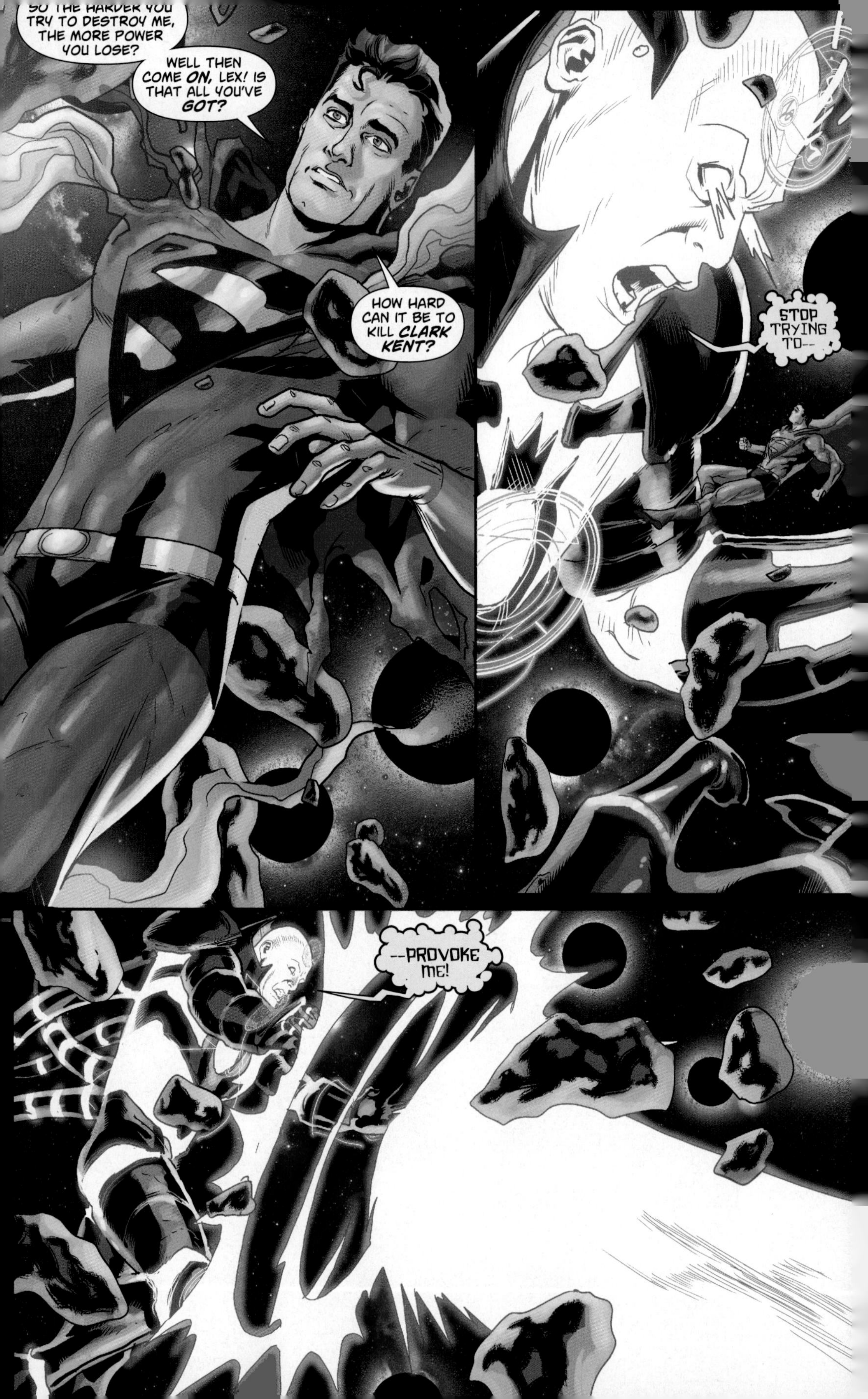
SO THE HARDER YOU TRY TO DESTROY ME, THE MORE POWER YOU LOSE?
WELL THEN COME ON, LEX! IS THAT ALL YOU'VE GOT?
HOW HARD CAN IT BE TO KILL CLARK KENT?
STOP TRYING TO--
--PROVOKE ME!

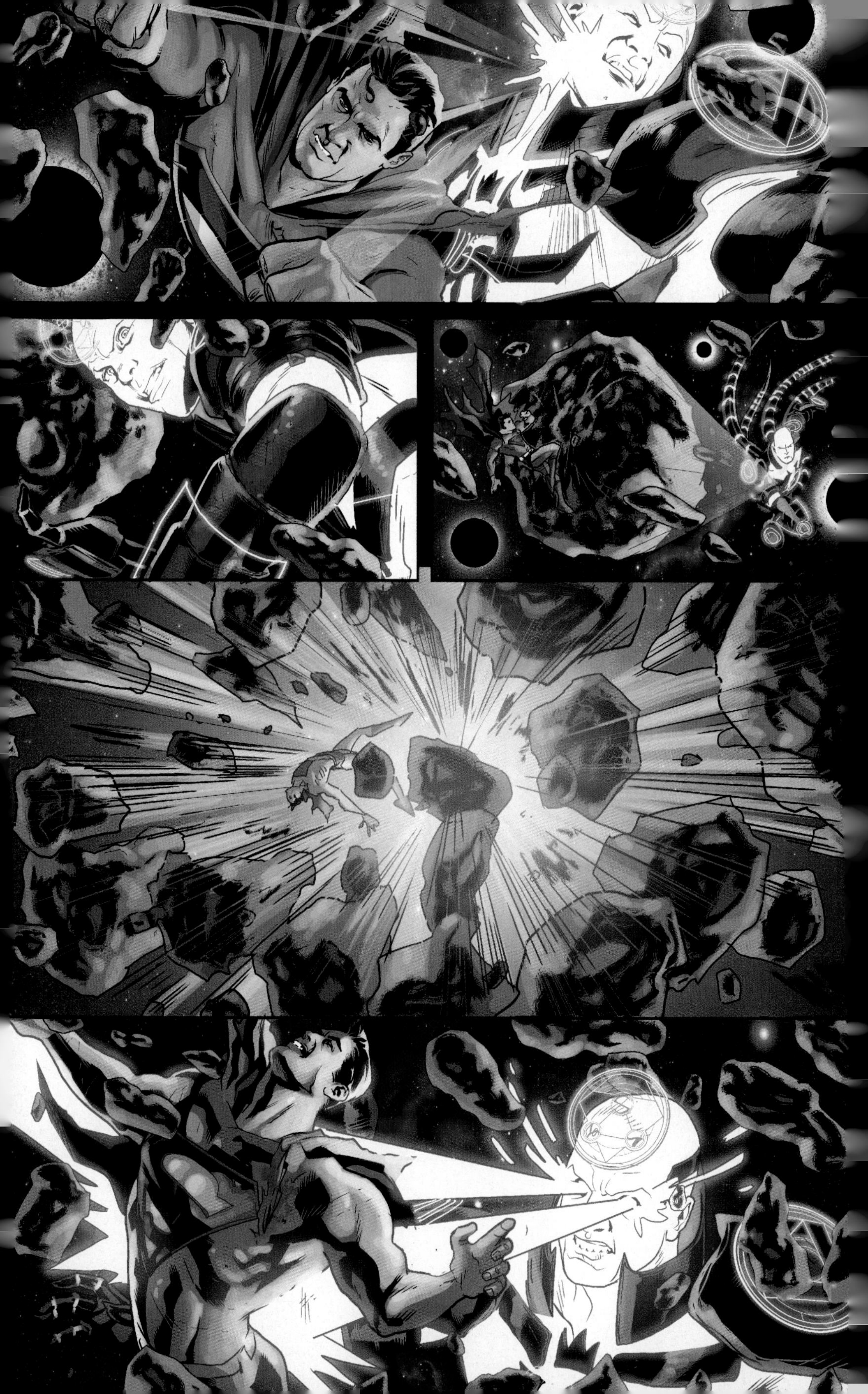

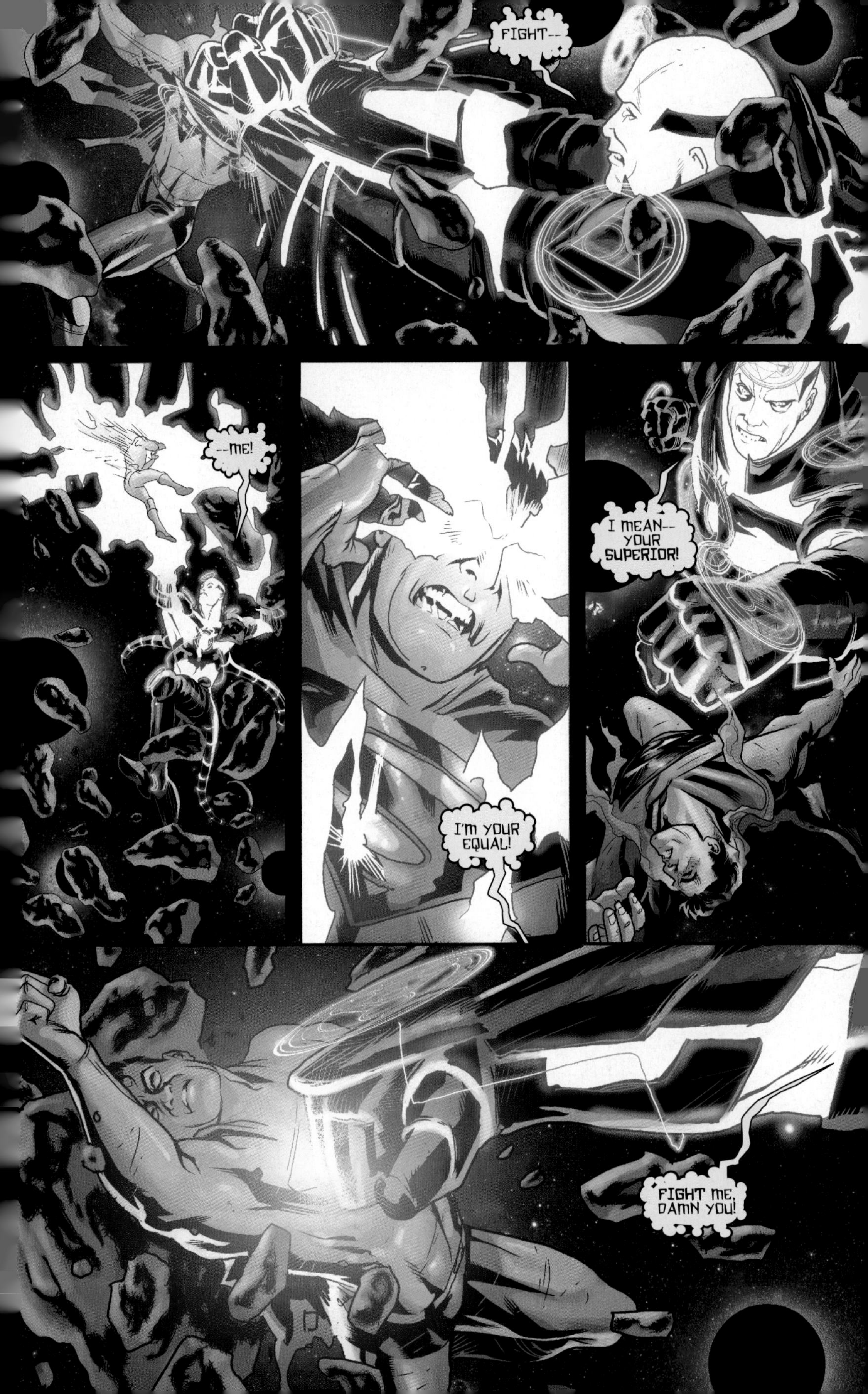
FIGHT--
--ME!
I'M YOUR EQUAL!
I MEAN-- YOUR SUPERIOR!
FIGHT ME, DAMN YOU!

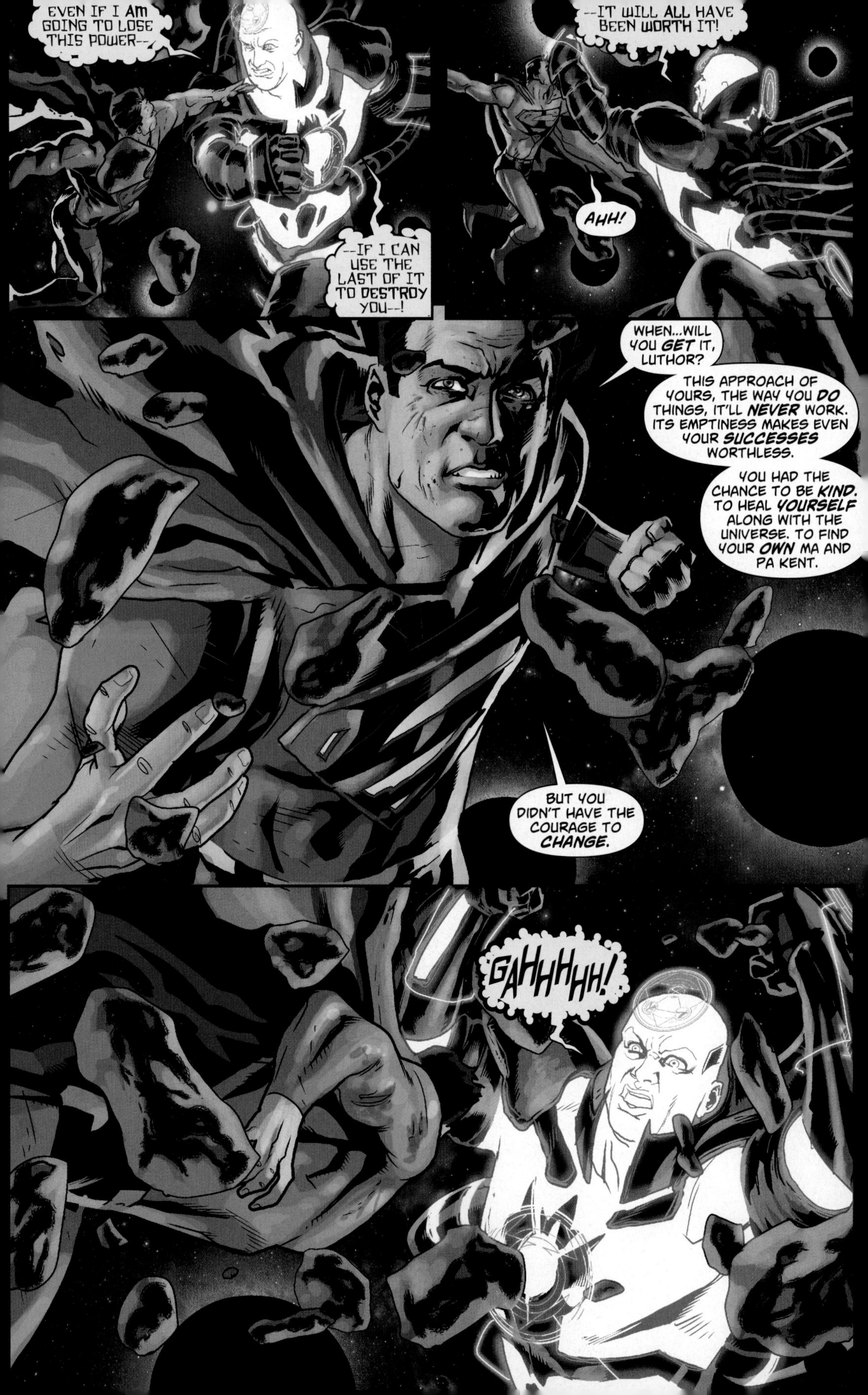
EVEN IF I AM GOING TO LOSE THIS POWER--
--IF I CAN USE THE LAST OF IT TO DESTROY YOU--!
--IT WILL ALL HAVE BEEN WORTH IT!
AHH!
WHEN...WILL YOU GET IT, LUTHOR?
THIS APPROACH OF YOURS, THE WAY YOU DO THINGS, IT'LL NEVER WORK. ITS EMPTINESS MAKES EVEN YOUR SUCCESSES WORTHLESS.
YOU HAD THE CHANCE TO BE KIND. TO HEAL YOURSELF ALONG WITH THE UNIVERSE. TO FIND YOUR OWN MA AND PA KENT.
BUT YOU DIDN'T HAVE THE COURAGE TO CHANGE.
GAHHHHH!

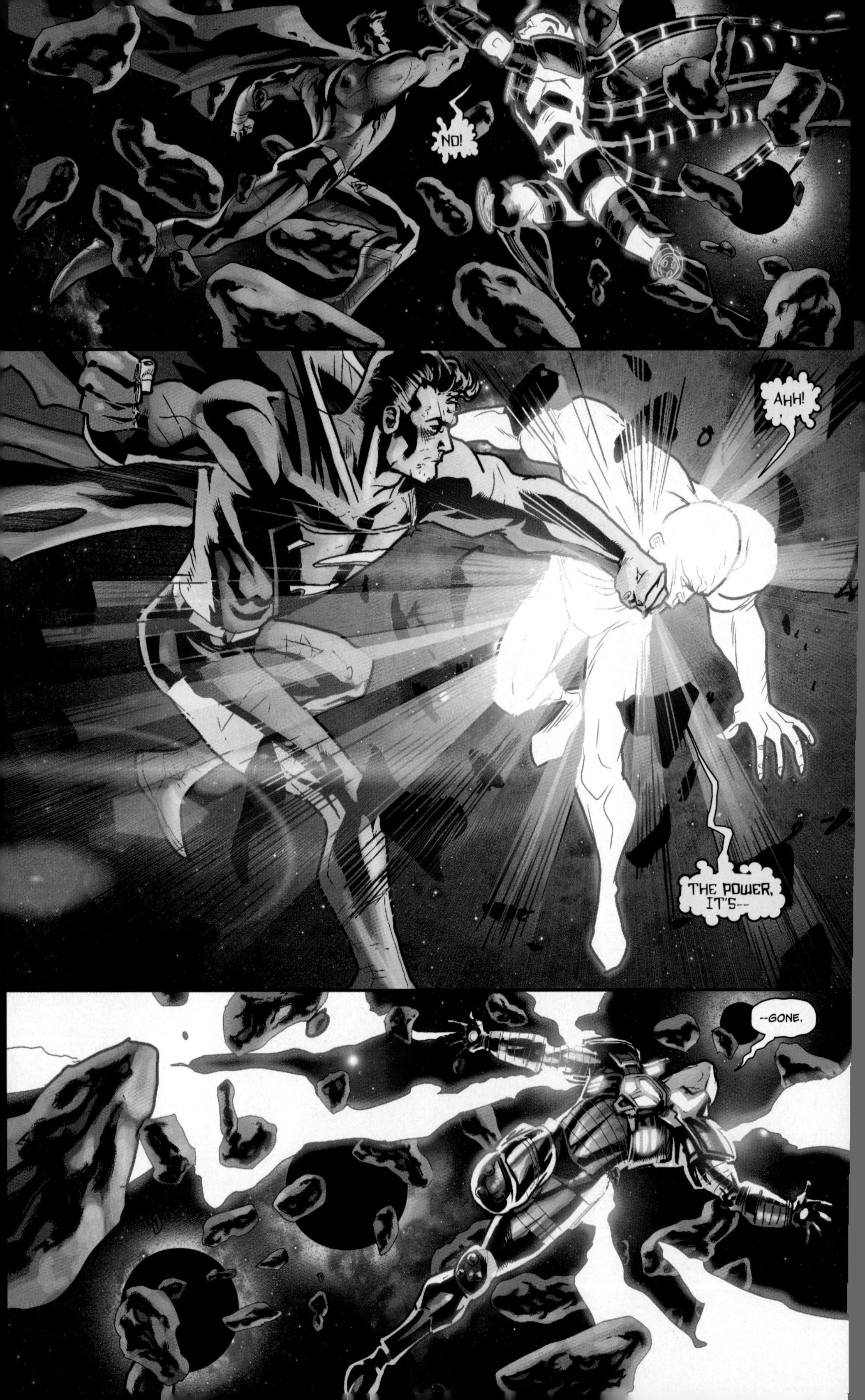
NO!
AHH!
THE POWER, IT'S--
--GONE.

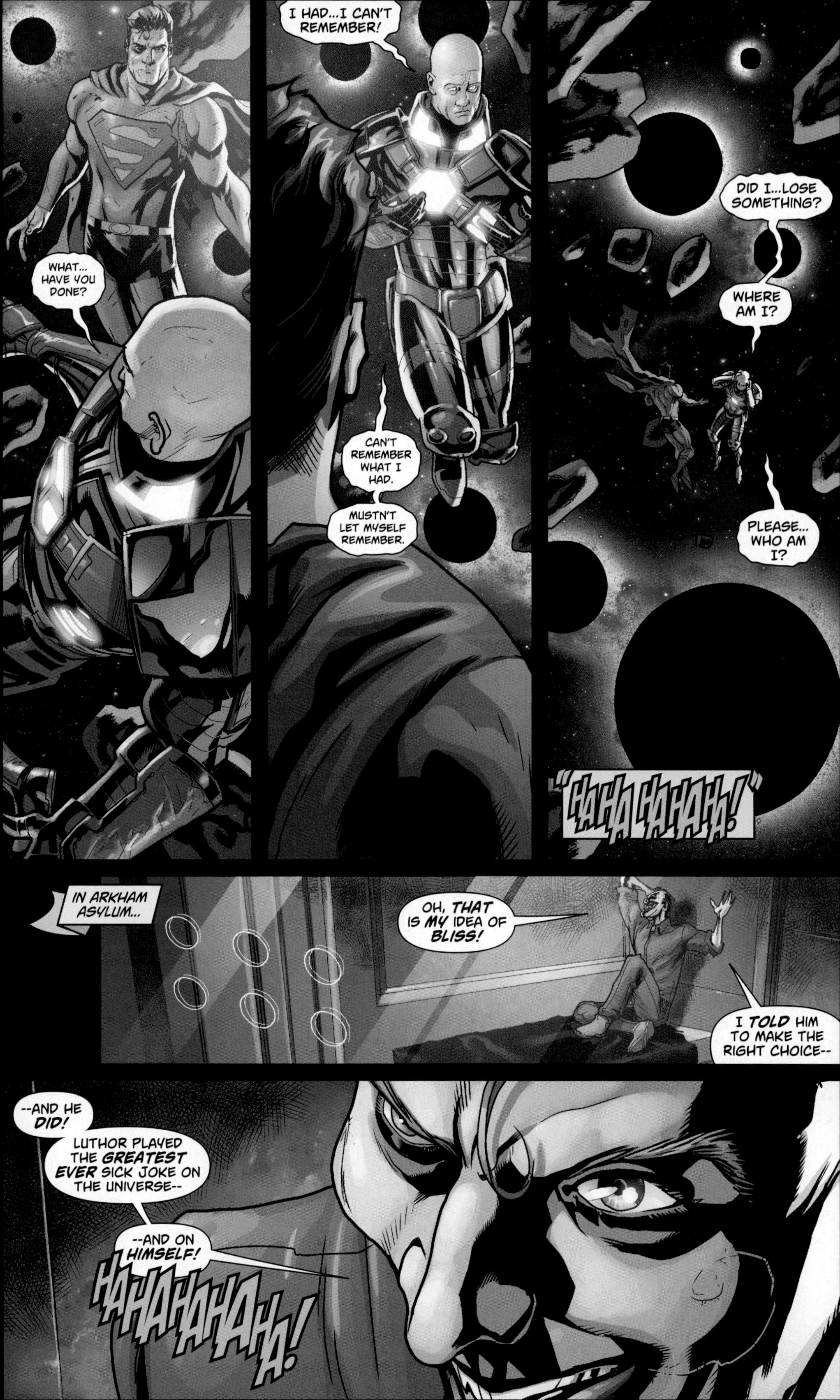

WHAT... HAVE YOU DONE?
I HAD...I CAN'T REMEMBER!
CAN'T REMEMBER WHAT I HAD.
MUSTN'T LET MYSELF REMEMBER.
DID I...LOSE SOMETHING?
WHERE AM I?
PLEASE... WHO AM I?
"HAHA HAHAHA!"
IN ARKHAM ASYLUM...
OH, *THAT* IS *MY* IDEA OF *BLISS!*
I *TOLD* HIM TO MAKE THE RIGHT CHOICE--
--AND HE *DID!*
LUTHOR PLAYED THE ***GREATEST EVER*** SICK JOKE ON THE UNIVERSE--
--AND ON *HIMSELF!*
HAHAHAHAHAHA!

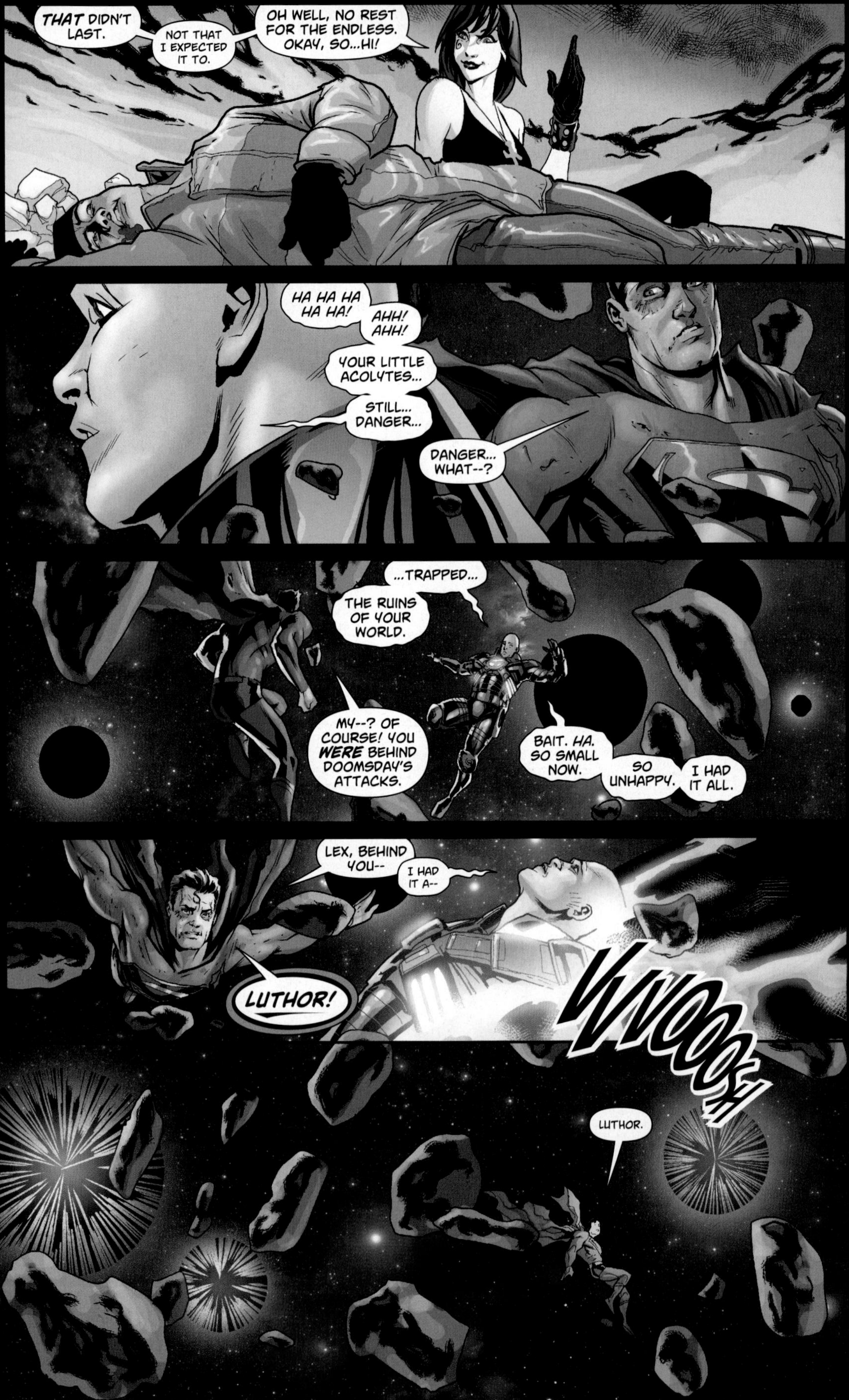

THAT DIDN'T LAST.
NOT THAT I EXPECTED IT TO.
OH WELL, NO REST FOR THE ENDLESS. OKAY, SO...HI!
HA HA HA HA HA!
AHH! AHH!
YOUR LITTLE ACOLYTES...
STILL... DANGER...
DANGER... WHAT--?
...TRAPPED...
THE RUINS OF YOUR WORLD.
MY--? OF COURSE! YOU WERE BEHIND DOOMSDAY'S ATTACKS.
BAIT. HA. SO SMALL NOW.
SO UNHAPPY.
I HAD IT ALL.
LEX, BEHIND YOU--
I HAD IT A--
LUTHOR!
VVVOOOSH!
LUTHOR.

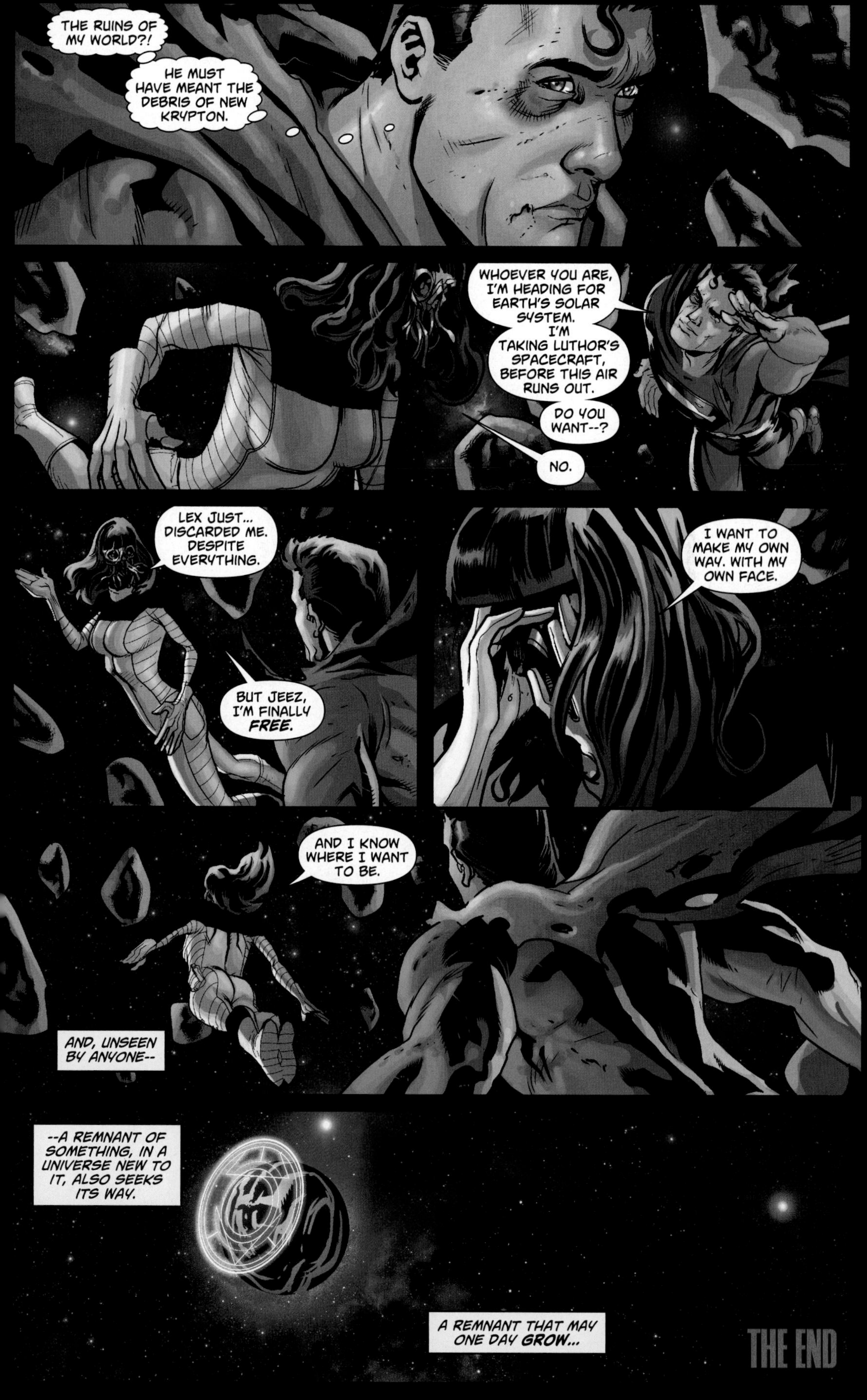
THE RUINS OF MY WORLD?!
HE MUST HAVE MEANT THE DEBRIS OF NEW KRYPTON.
WHOEVER YOU ARE, I'M HEADING FOR EARTH'S SOLAR SYSTEM. I'M TAKING LUTHOR'S SPACECRAFT, BEFORE THIS AIR RUNS OUT.
DO YOU WANT--?
NO.
LEX JUST... DISCARDED ME. DESPITE EVERYTHING.
BUT JEEZ, I'M FINALLY FREE.
I WANT TO MAKE MY OWN WAY. WITH MY OWN FACE.
AND I KNOW WHERE I WANT TO BE.
AND, UNSEEN BY ANYONE--
--A REMNANT OF SOMETHING, IN A UNIVERSE NEW TO IT, ALSO SEEKS ITS WAY.
A REMNANT THAT MAY ONE DAY GROW...
THE END

ACTION COMICS 900 variant by
ADAM HUGHES

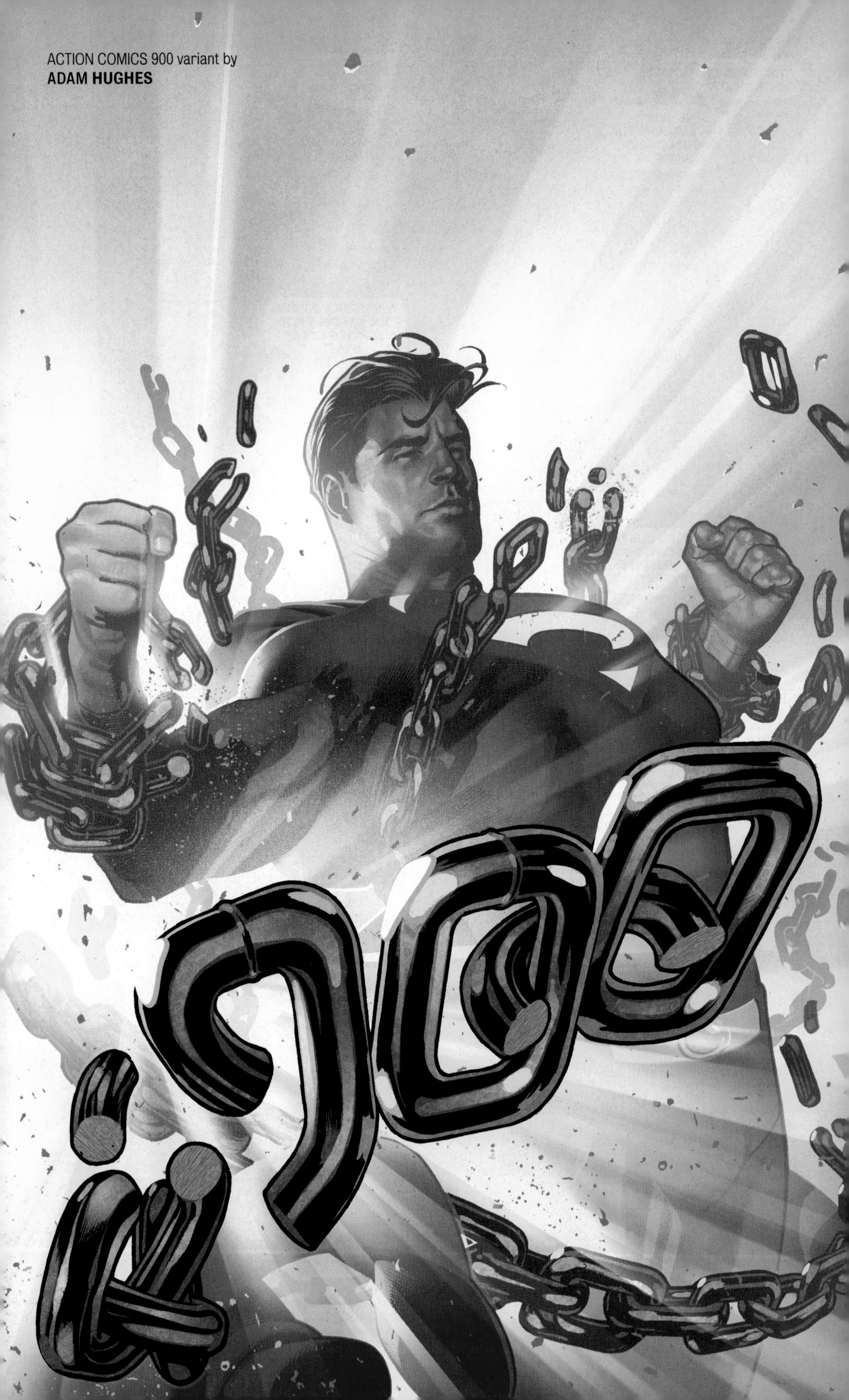
900

ACTION COMICS 900 variant by
ALEX ROSS

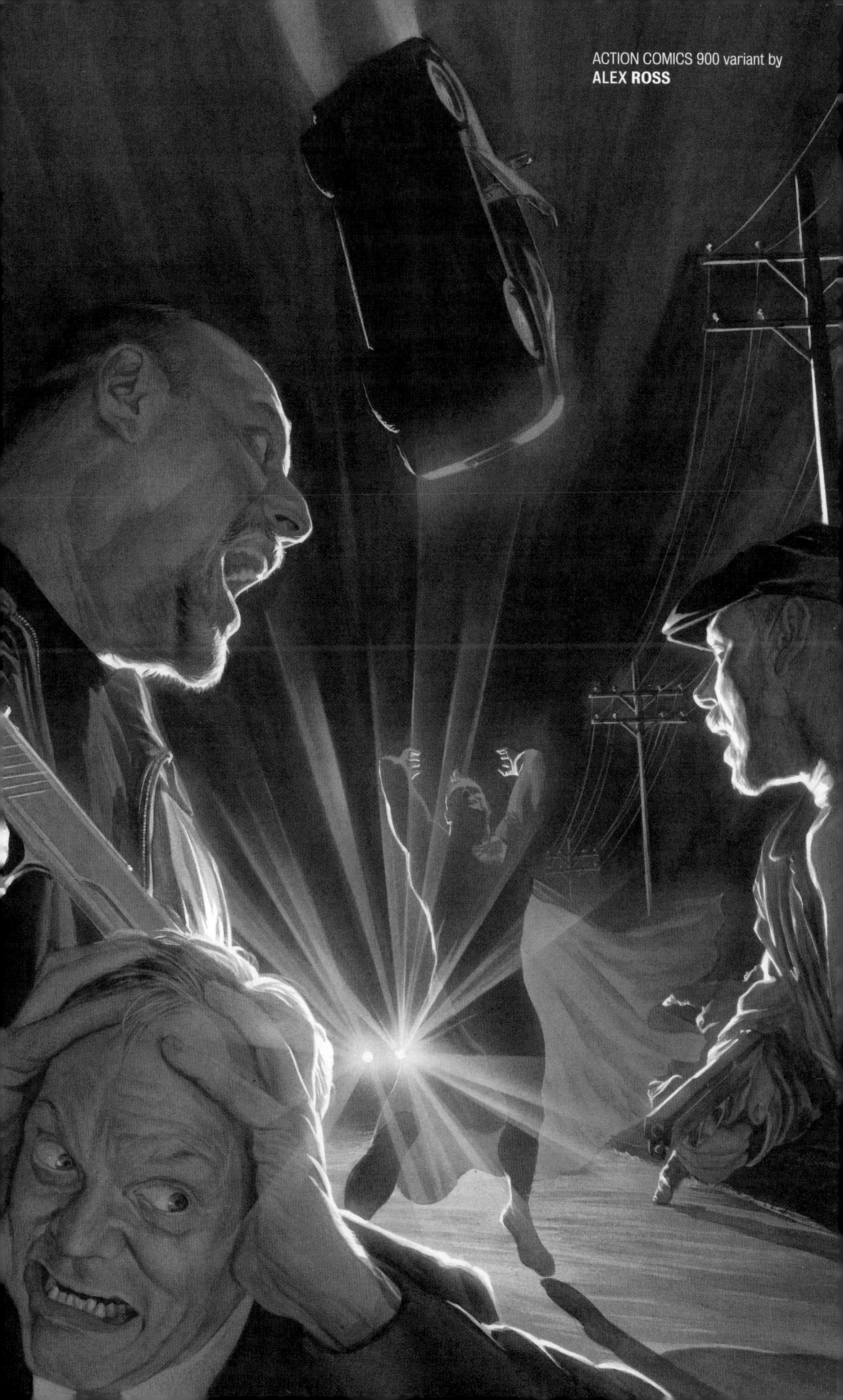

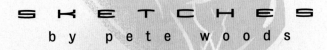

S K E T C H E S
by pete woods

The design for the damaged Lois robot was one of the hardest I've had to do. In the end it took five different iterations to get her right. Everyone had a different idea of how she should look, and it was a fun challenge to get her right.

In the first design it was decided she looked too much like herself and might be recognized by Superman.

The second design lacked hair, which Paul wanted, and the third wasn't damaged enough.
Everyone thought the detached eyeball was a bit gruesome too.

The fourth design was almost there but needed a bit more techno-junk floating around.
She had to look like Lex had savagely put his fist into her head and ripped it out.

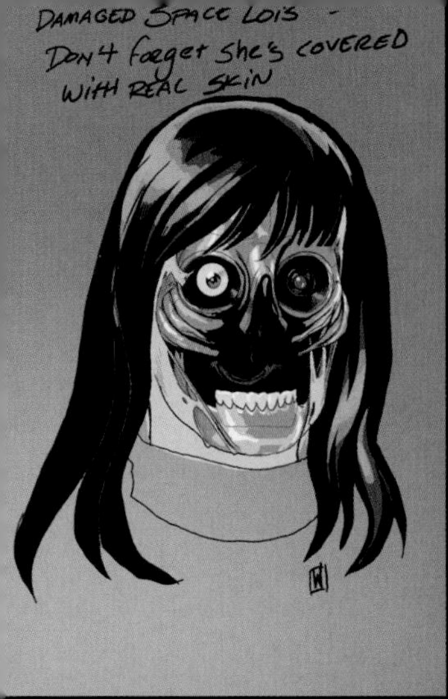
DAMAGED SPACE LOIS -
Don't forget she's COVERED
WITH REAL SKIN

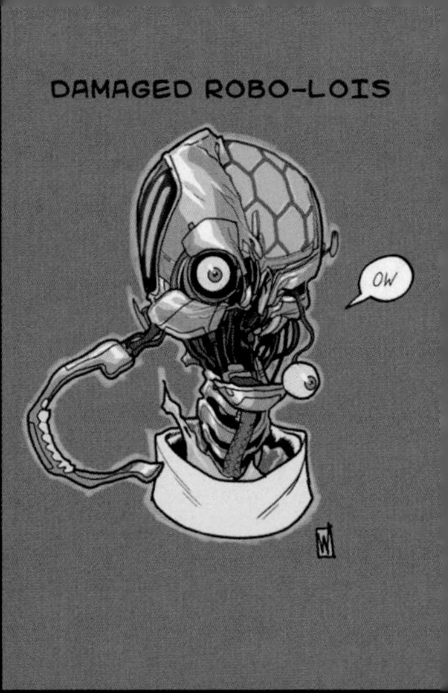
DAMAGED ROBO-LOIS
OW

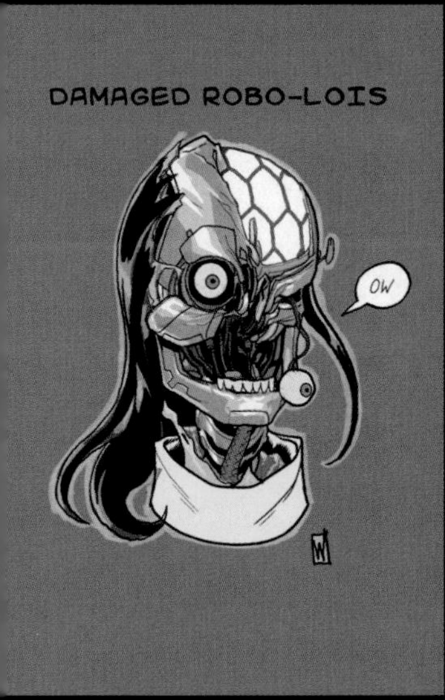
DAMAGED ROBO-LOIS
OW

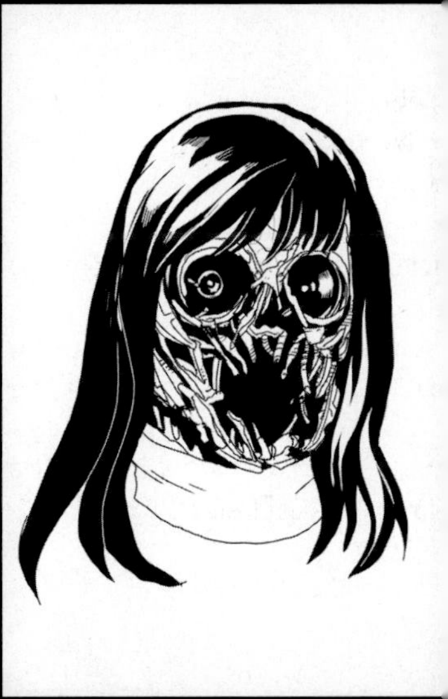

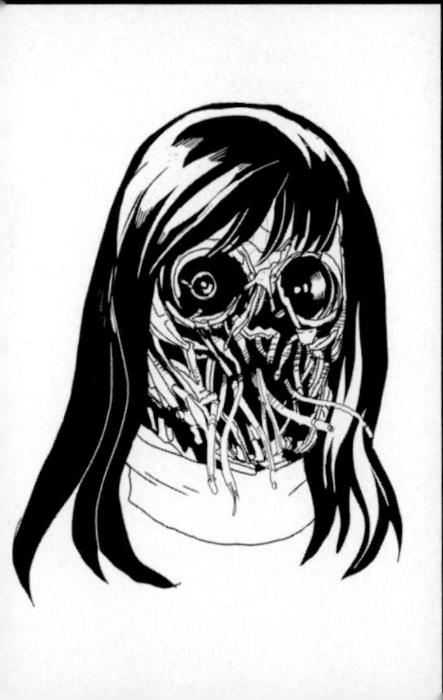

When designing the Zone Child I started with the silhouette. I had so many ideas for direction that I did these six outlines and sent them to Matt Idelson and Paul for their input as to which direction we should go. After a bit of back and forth we elected to go with "C."

The trick was to make the design something striking and cool to look at on its own and also make a convincing "armor" for Lex. I wanted to push the design a bit by adding the glowing runes that surround him. It was fascinating to see how all the artists I have so much respect for draw my design and how each interpreted it.

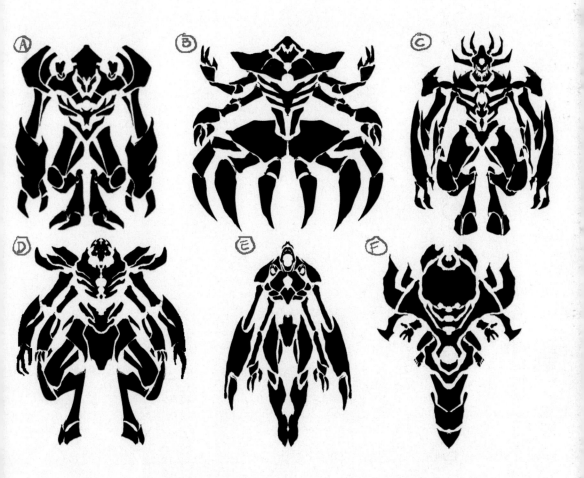

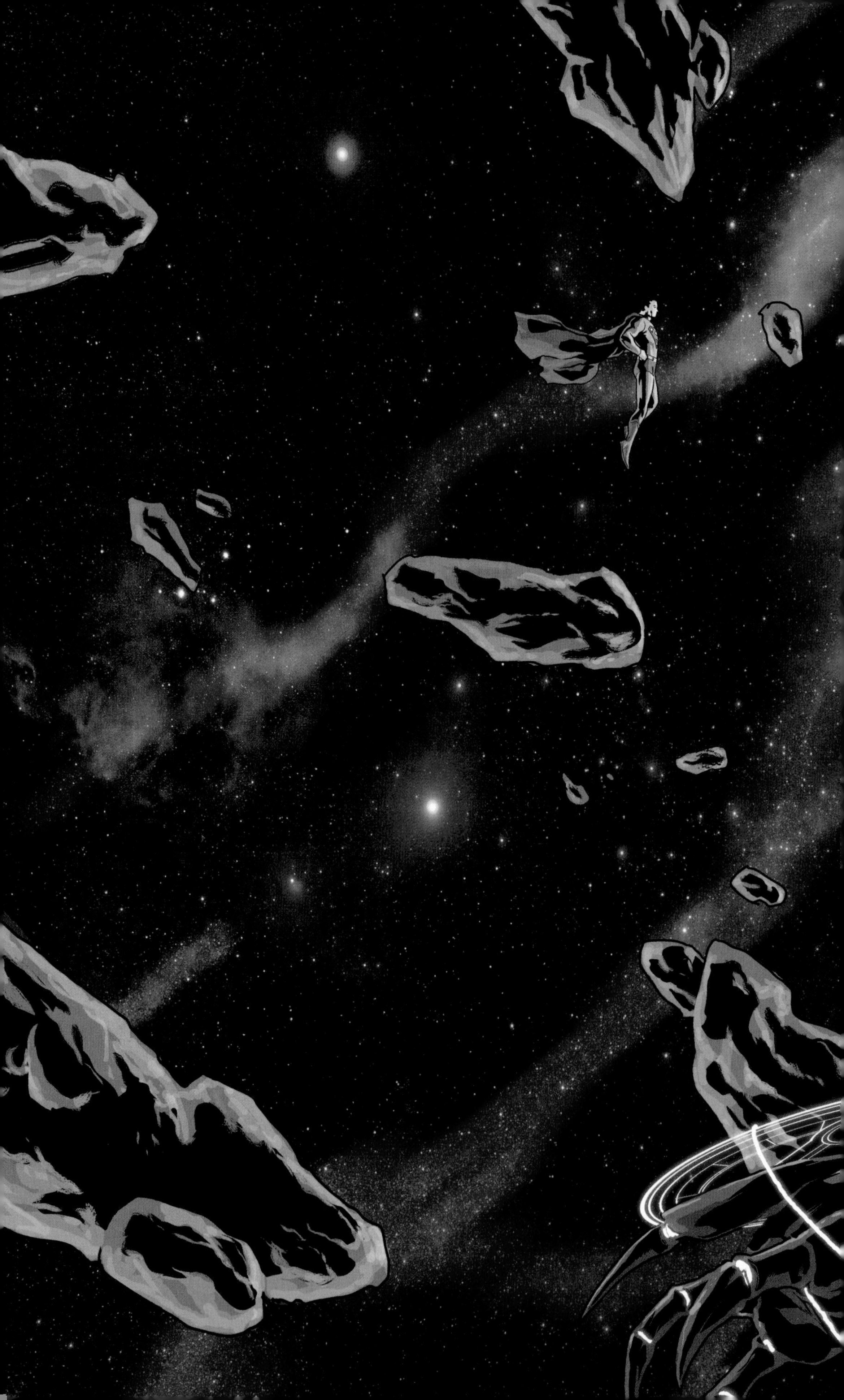

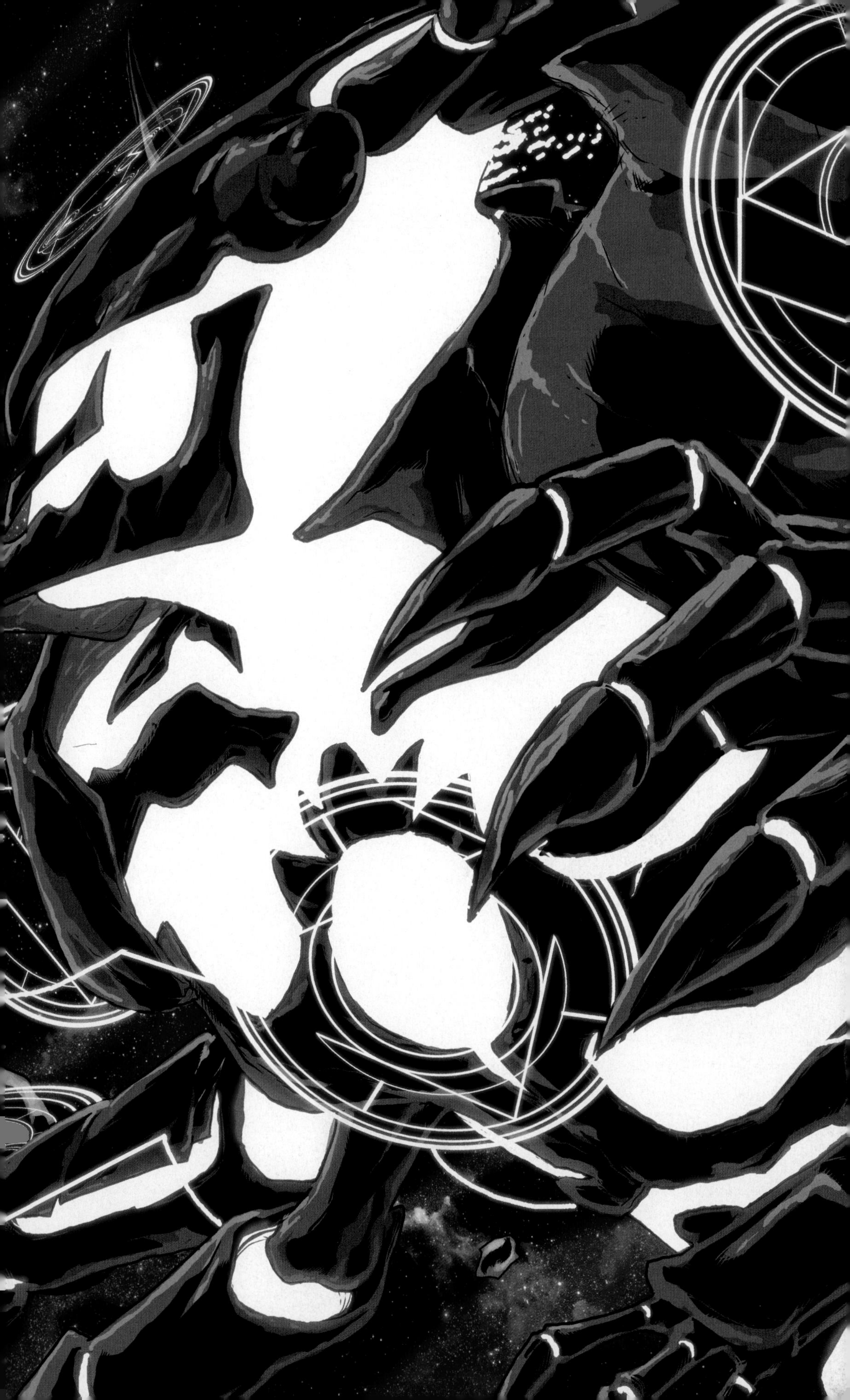

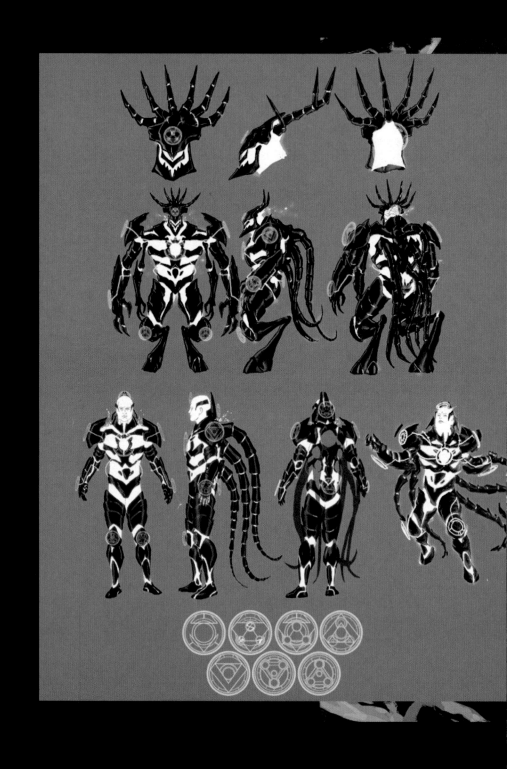

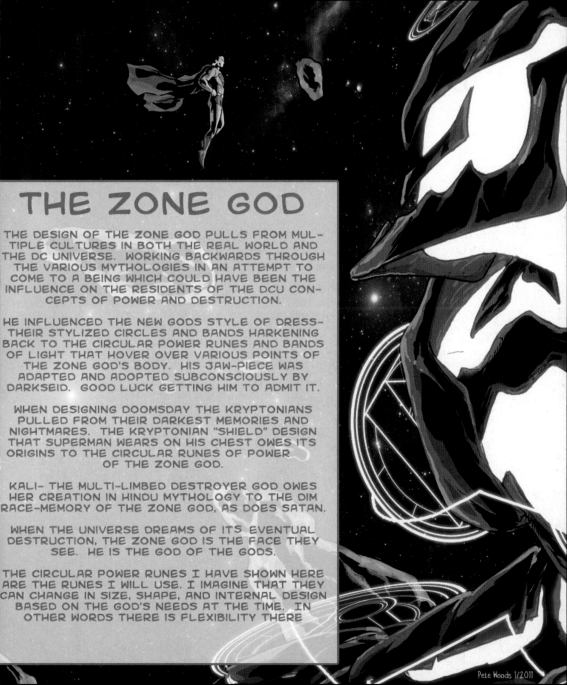

THE ZONE GOD

THE DESIGN OF THE ZONE GOD PULLS FROM MUL-
TIPLE CULTURES IN BOTH THE REAL WORLD AND
THE DC UNIVERSE. WORKING BACKWARDS THROUGH
THE VARIOUS MYTHOLOGIES IN AN ATTEMPT TO
COME TO A BEING WHICH COULD HAVE BEEN THE
INFLUENCE ON THE RESIDENTS OF THE DCU CON-
CEPTS OF POWER AND DESTRUCTION.

HE INFLUENCED THE NEW GODS STYLE OF DRESS-
THEIR STYLIZED CIRCLES AND BANDS HARKENING
BACK TO THE CIRCULAR POWER RUNES AND BANDS
OF LIGHT THAT HOVER OVER VARIOUS POINTS OF
THE ZONE GOD'S BODY. HIS JAW-PIECE WAS
ADAPTED AND ADOPTED SUBCONSCIOUSLY BY
DARKSEID. GOOD LUCK GETTING HIM TO ADMIT IT.

WHEN DESIGNING DOOMSDAY THE KRYPTONIANS
PULLED FROM THEIR DARKEST MEMORIES AND
NIGHTMARES. THE KRYPTONIAN "SHIELD" DESIGN
THAT SUPERMAN WEARS ON HIS CHEST OWES ITS
ORIGINS TO THE CIRCULAR RUNES OF POWER
OF THE ZONE GOD.

KALI- THE MULTI-LIMBED DESTROYER GOD OWES
HER CREATION IN HINDU MYTHOLOGY TO THE DIM
RACE-MEMORY OF THE ZONE GOD, AS DOES SATAN.

WHEN THE UNIVERSE DREAMS OF ITS EVENTUAL
DESTRUCTION, THE ZONE GOD IS THE FACE THEY
SEE. HE IS THE GOD OF THE GODS.

THE CIRCULAR POWER RUNES I HAVE SHOWN HERE
ARE THE RUNES I WILL USE. I IMAGINE THAT THEY
CAN CHANGE IN SIZE, SHAPE, AND INTERNAL DESIGN
BASED ON THE GOD'S NEEDS AT THE TIME. IN
OTHER WORDS THERE IS FLEXIBILITY THERE

Pete Woods 1/2011

When I started ACTION 898 thanks to my horrible organization skills I was working from the wrong version of the script. Because of this I ended up drawing the wrong version of the pages. Page 11 had a moment of Lois thinking deeply about her feelings for Lex and her hatred for her "father" while she gets the White Sphere out of storage.

Page 20 was originally going to be a splash page featuring Brainiac. I was able to cut this page down a bit and add a panel for the final version.

To the right is an initial version of #898's opening page, but we ended up changing the look of the rocket.

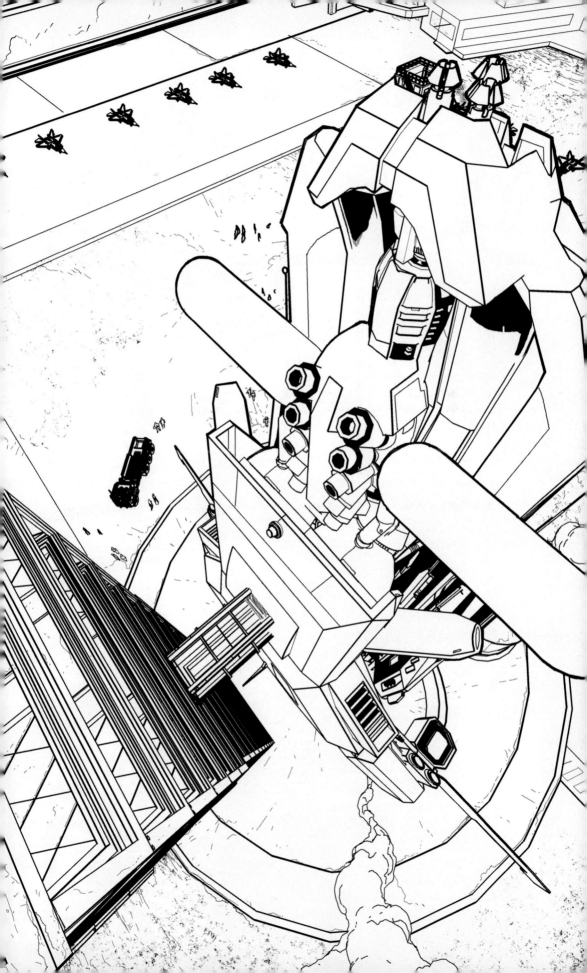

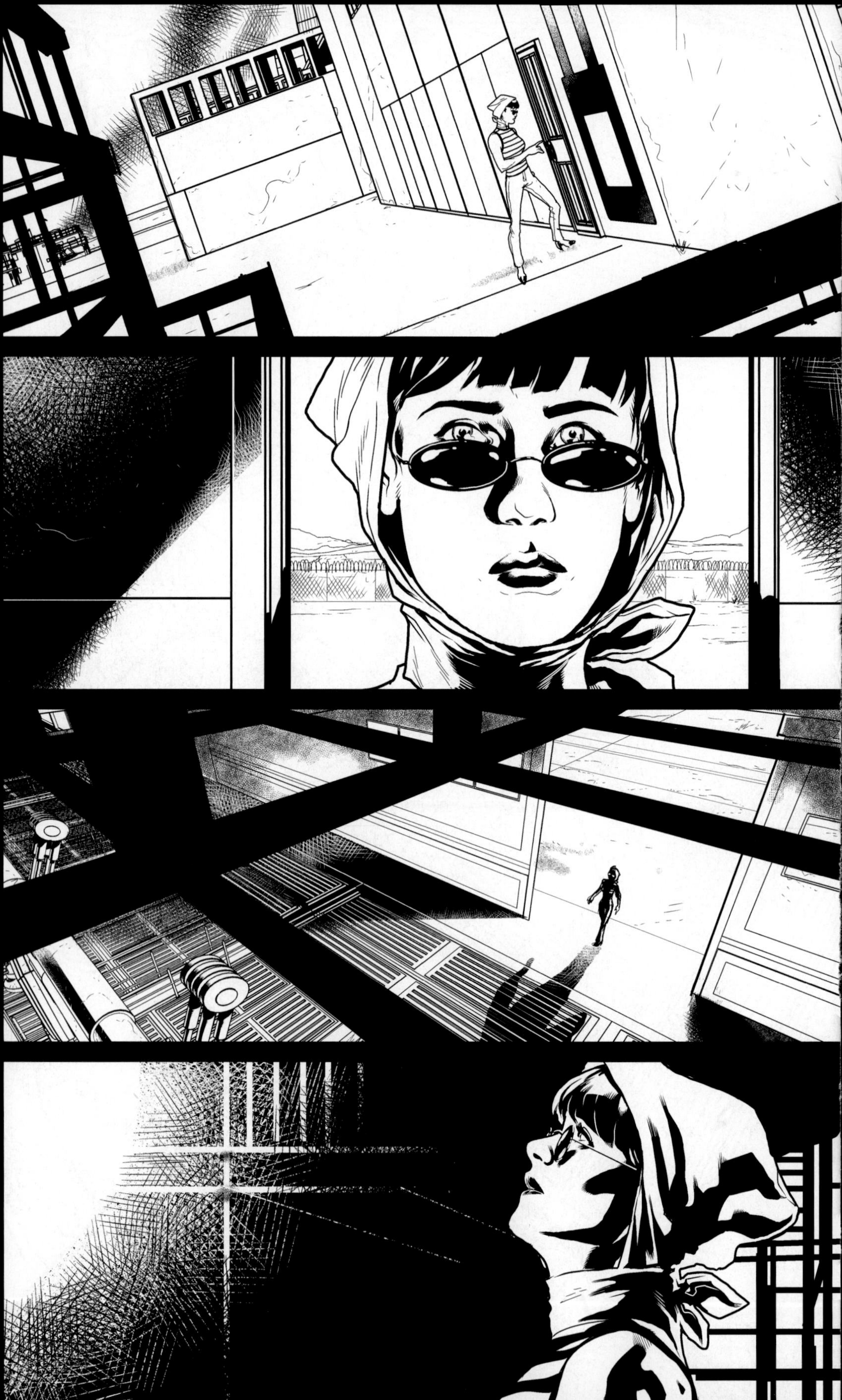

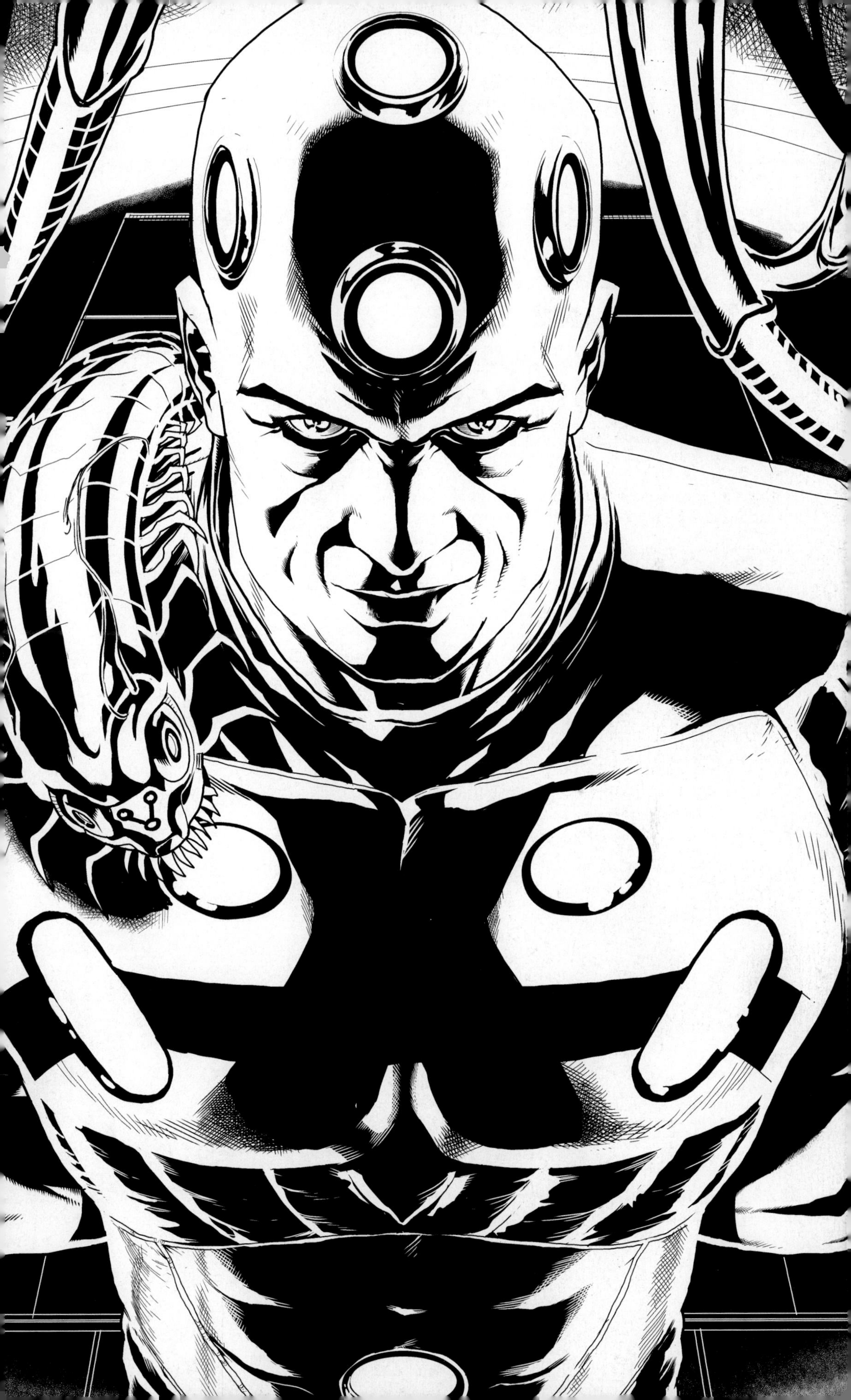

FROM THE WRITER OF **SUPERMAN & JUSTICE LEAGUE OF AMERICA**

JAMES ROBINSON

with GEOFF JOHNS
STERLING GATES
PETE WOODS
GARY FRANK
and OTHERS

"A great Superman adventure that brings the old school Superman mythos into the here and now."
– CRAVE ONLINE

SUPERMAN.
VOLUME ONE
NEW KRYPTON
GEOFF JOHNS
JAMES ROBINSON
DC

SUPERMAN:
NEW KRYPTON VOL. 2

SUPERMAN
VOLUME TWO
NEW KRYPTON
GEOFF JOHNS
JAMES ROBINSON
STERLING GATES
DC

with
GEOFF JOHNS, STERLING GATES RENATO GUEDES, PETE WOODS, JAMAL IGLE & OTHERS

SUPERMAN:
NEW KRYPTON VOL. 3

SUPERMAN
VOLUME THREE
NEW KRYPTON
JAMES ROBINSON
GREG RUCKA
PETE WOODS
DC

with
GEOFF JOHNS, GREG RUCKA RICHARD DONNER, PETE WOODS, JAMAL IGLE & OTHERS

SUPERMAN:
NEW KRYPTON VOL. 4

SUPERMAN
VOLUME FOUR
NEW KRYPTON
JAMES ROBINSON
GREG RUCKA
PETE WOODS
RON RANDALL
DC

with
GREG RUCKA, PETE WOODS & OTHERS

SEARCH THE GRAPHIC NOVELS SECTION OF
DCCOMICS.COM
FOR ART AND INFORMATION ON ALL OF OUR BOOKS!

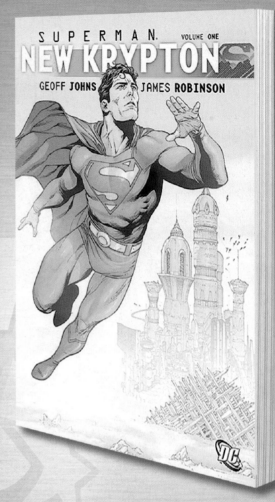

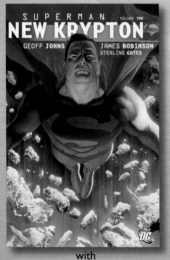

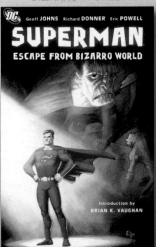